The "Jew" in Cinema

The Helen and Martin Schwartz Lectures in Jewish Studies

Sponsored by the Robert A. and Sandra S. Borns Jewish Studies Program, Indiana University

THE "JEW"

in

CINEMA

From *The Golem* to *Don't Touch My Holocaust*

Omer Bartov

INDIANA UNIVERSITY PRESS   BLOOMINGTON & INDIANAPOLIS

Publication of this book was assisted by the Jewish Studies Fund
and the Schwartz Endowment of Indiana University Press.

This book is a publication of

Indiana University Press
601 North Morton Street
Bloomington, IN 47404-3797 USA

http://www.iupress.indiana.edu

Telephone orders 800-842-6796
Fax orders 812-855-7931
Orders by e-mail iuporder@indiana.edu

The paper used in this publication meets the minimum
requirements of American National Standard for Information Sciences—Permanence of Paper for Printed Library
Materials, ANSI Z39.48-1984.

Manufactured in the United States of America

Library of Congress Cataloging-in-Publication Data

Bartov, Omer.
The "Jew" in cinema : from The golem to Don't touch my
Holocaust / Omer Bartov.
p. cm. — (The Helen and Martin Schwartz lectures in
Jewish studies)
Includes index.
ISBN 0-253-34502-2 (alk. paper) — ISBN 0-253-21745-8 (pbk. :
alk. paper)
1. Jews in motion pictures. I. Title. II. Series.
PN1995.9.J46B37 2005
791.43'6529924—dc22
2004013503

1   2   3   4   5   10   09   08   07   06   05

FOR MY FATHER

Your life as apes, gentlemen, insofar as something of that kind lies behind you, cannot be farther removed from you as mine is from me. Yet everyone on earth feels a tickling at the heels; the small chimpanzee and the great Achilles alike. . . . I soon realized that there were two alternatives before me: the Zoological Gardens or the variety stage. I did not hesitate. I said to myself: do your utmost to get on to the variety stage; the Zoological Gardens means only a new cage; once there, you are done for. . . . With an effort which up to now has never been repeated I managed to reach the cultural level of an average European. In itself that might be nothing to speak of, but it is something insofar as it has helped me out of my cage and opened a special way out for me, the way of humanity. . . . I have fought through the thick of things. There was nothing else for me to do, provided always that freedom was not to be my choice.

—Franz Kafka, "A Report to an Academy"

CONTENTS

INTRODUCTION

This book is an attempt to trace a particular theme in cinematic representations of Jews. What I have in mind is the dialogue between the representation of Jews as perpetrators, victims, heroes, and anti-heroes (which at times verge on being perpetrators). What interests me in this book is the manner in which such representations inform each other and tend to be fed by, or to react to, certain stereotypical depictions of Jews dating back to the early years of cinema, which were themselves influenced by age-old prejudices about Jews. The figure of the "Jew" has appeared in a variety of roles in cinema and literature, ranging from the comic to the tragic, and from nostalgic recreations of traditional life to epic depictions of assimilation or Zionism. The present study, however, focuses on a single, albeit pervasive theme: The manner in which the cinematic "Jew" reflects the popularization, transformation, resistance to, and reintroduction of antisemitic imagery.

This is not a comprehensive history of films about Jews, or of films with Jewish characters. It cannot even claim to discuss all films pertinent to its particular focus. Nor does it propose a new theory on the cinematic depiction or representation of Jews. Film critics may be disappointed: Both by training and by inclination I eschew complex theoretical analyses. Rather, what fascinates me is the manner in which, from its very beginning, the cinematic representation of the "Jew"—that is, a certain type of individual identified by the filmmaker and/or the audience as having some Jewish characteristics—has revolved around the status of the "Jew" as either perpetrator or victim, hero or anti-hero. There is a certain chronological logic to this evolution of stereotypes. Antisemitic cinematic images that portrayed the "Jew" as *perpetrator*—especially those disseminated by the Nazis—were followed by cinematic representations of the "Jew" as *victim* of antisemitism—especially of the Nazi genocide. Conversely, the seemingly excessive focus on Jews as helpless victims, the emphasis in much of post–World War II representation and commemoration on heroic resistance to Nazism, and the violent emergence of the State of Israel, generated a new cinematic representation of the "Jew" as *hero*. But more recently, such factors as the Israeli occupation of the Palestinians, growing criticism of Zionism, a more complex view of Jewish conduct and fate in the Holocaust, and a certain revival of antisemitic rhetoric and imagery, have led to the emergence of the "Jew" as *anti-hero*. This last incarnation of the cinematic Jew has occasionally also borrowed traits from the original image of the "Jew" as perpetrator or from "his" victimizers.

Nevertheless, as I hope to demonstrate, what I am sketching here is not merely a chronological evolution but rather a process whereby certain cinematic types and images are constantly informed by each other, creating a kind of treasure house or arsenal of representations that can be drawn upon irrespective of the ideological or artistic predilections of the filmmaker and the social, political, or cultural context in which the film is made. To be sure, this is not a static condition, for the use of existing images nonetheless reshapes them and rewrites their meanings. At the same time, what I propose is also that we do not simply see progress from stereotyping and dehumanization to complexity and humanity, for the origins of the images used by filmmakers are inscribed on them despite their insertion into radically different narrative situations and plots. It is precisely this relationship between the changing face of the cinematic "Jew" and the hearkening back to a relatively limited store of stereotypes that interests me here.

I trace the evolution of the cinematic "Jew" from his early appearance in post–World War I cinema all the way to some recent films. Because, as I have indicated, this is a lengthy essay rather than a voluminous encyclopedic survey, I chose several films as representative of each of the four main manifestations of the "Jew" in cinema. Obviously, it was difficult to decide what to include and what to leave out, and to strike a balance between discussing a sufficient number of films to make my point without obscuring the cinematic forest I had in mind with a deluge of celluloid trees. I am sure that many readers will wonder why some of their favorite films are missing and why I spend so much time on films they would have omitted altogether. But I hope that they will nevertheless find some use in my discussion of those seventy-odd films I chose to include. It must be emphasized, however, that the goal of this book is not to analyze discrete films, but to isolate and examine a certain theme that, to my mind, is to be found in these and other films. While this theme—the relationship between the four faces of the cinematic "Jew"—may not be the conscious or intentional preoccupation of some of these films, it is, nevertheless, a central motif in an important body of European, Israeli, and American cinema. There are other motifs in films about Jews that I do not discuss here. This concerns especially American films on Jewish assimilation, an important issue that deserves a separate discussion but is outside of my present focus.

This book began as a series of lectures delivered at Indiana University in 1999. I thank Alvin Rosenfeld for inviting me to this series and Janet Rabinowitch for proposing that I turn these lectures into a book. I thank Brown University for allowing me to accept a fellowship from the Radcliffe Institute for Advanced Study at Harvard University, without which I would have been unable to complete this book, and the Radcliffe Institute for providing the ideal conditions for writing. I am also grateful to Roberto Mori of Harvard's Media and Technology Services, whose help with producing the images included in the book was indispensable, and to my research assistant, Yuri Vedenyapin, whose aesthetic and linguistic abilities were of great help to me. Finally, I thank my family for allowing me to spend so much time watching films as well as for reminding me that there is a much more cheerful world just a few steps away from the video monitor.

POSTSCRIPT

As this book goes to print, it is difficult, though tempting, to avoid any mention of Mel Gibson's film, *The Passion of the Christ* (2004). For a film that received so much free publicity before its first screening and made about a quarter-of-a-billion dollars within weeks of its release, one is reluctant to add a single word either of praise or of condemnation. And since it is a blatantly antisemitic film, one would prefer to simply ignore it. But a few words are in order, both because this book is about representations of the "Jew," and also because this film is a symptom of a new antisemitism that, to my mind, needs to be identified and condemned.[1]

One did not expect such a film to come to American screens in the first decade of the third millennium. What is surprising is not the style of the film—after all, its explicit violence is very much part of the Hollywood film industry these days—but its subject matter. It is not surprising that the film is about Jesus; it is hardly the first movie on this theme. Rather, what is unexpected is the fact that the film combines fanatical faith and brute violence, conveying a sadistic pleasure in watching the infliction of pain and a self-righteous satisfaction that it is all for the good of humanity, including the good of the very body against which this torture is being directed. This is the realm of religious zealotry and fascist fantasy. There is no humor or playfulness here. One does not exit the theater saying, "I had a good time," as is expected from audiences after most of Hollywood's exercises in cinematic violence. One is supposed to be inspired and filled with faith. But love, either divine or the more lowly, human kind, does not enter into the experience.

The extent to which the film freely, perhaps unselfconsciously, but pervasively borrows the most explicit stereotypes of antisemitic representation is nothing short of extraordinary. Indeed, there is so much of this representation that it may have escaped the eyes of some reviewers and critics. But they may also simply be ignorant. After all, antisemitic cinema is not the regular fare of film critics these days, certainly not in the United States. Some of them may have not even heard of *Jew Süss* (discussed below). Others, like many of their predecessors in the past, may feel uncomfortable about pointing out that a film allegedly filled with faith for humanity—or simply, a supposedly deeply Christian film—is in fact antisemitic. But it does not take a genius, nor even a historian of cinema or of antisemitism, to recognize that *The Passion of the Christ* is based on two basic models of representing Jews.

The first model is that of medieval Christianity and its interpretation of the story of the Crucifixion. This version, according to which the Jews were directly responsible for the torture and assassination of God, was of course at the root of much of the antisemitic violence that characterized Europe for centuries. The evil influence of this interpretation was finally and belatedly recognized by the Vatican in the aftermath of the Holocaust. Thus the Pope eventually rejected the doctrine of the Jews' guilt in the crucifixion of Jesus. Yet as we know, Gibson does not accept Vatican II, and prefers to stick with medieval perceptions of the Passion.[2]

But Gibson's personal beliefs and interpretations of the Gospels should be of little interest to us. What matters is the manner in which they mold his film. And here it is not so much the story, which is bad enough, but the images used to propel the narrative and influence the audience that are of importance. At this point the second model kicks in. Whether consciously or through a process of unconscious internalization, Gibson's characters are directly lifted from the antisemitic cinematic imagination, one of whose most powerful and influential representatives was *Jew Süss,* brought to German screens in 1940, at the height of Hitler's power and on the eve of the Final Solution. It should be said that *Jew Süss,* a truly pernicious piece of work, was also a well-made and well-acted film—which is why it has remained a prime example of its genre until today. Conversely, Gibson's film is at best mediocre, making up for the director's lack of cinematic subtlety and creativity by the excessive use of pyrotechnics, as is so much the case in Hollywood these days. Gibson's focus on violence is not only a result of his interpretation of the Crucifixion: it is also a consequence of his inability to do anything cinematic that is not about violence and brutality. And, of course, the Crucifixion serves as well as it possibly can for this purpose, since no matter how much gratuitous violence is tacked onto it, the story is nevertheless about the opposite of destruction, about resurrection and eternal love, even if the few manifestations of the latter sentiment are crassly depicted.

The film proposes two types of humanity, each of which is made of a positive and a negative aspect. The Romans—the gentiles—are made up of fundamentally decent, if weak, types, such as Pontius Pilate (Hristo Naumov Shopov), who wishes to save Jesus but, driven by opportunism, bows to the pressure of the Jews and has him flagellated and then crucified. The other Romans are simple men, some of them decent legionnaires and others brutal SS types, who simply like beating people to death. In other words, the Romans are normal people, some basically decent, others brutes. The second type is the Jews. Here physical features and comportment count as much as moral qualities. The Jews, too, are made up of two kinds. The first kind, which is hardly identified in the popular imagination as Jewish but out of concern for historical "authenticity" is no longer portrayed with explicitly Aryan features, includes such fine Italianate specimens as Jim Caviezel (Jesus) and Monica Bellucci (Mary Magdalene). Opposite them stand the "real" Jews, those who are out to kill Jesus, headed by the High Priest Caiphas (Mattia Sbragia) and the other elders, along with the mob that calls out to Pontius to crucify the already-mangled Jesus. Whereas Jesus by definition cannot be normal, and his macho ability to withstand pain on a truly colossal scale is supposed to be divine, the Jews are reduced to inherently inhuman, not to say subhuman creatures, who demand endless suffering from one who has done them no harm and is in fact promising them salvation.

It would be hard to come up with a more stereotypical portrayal of Jews outside the realm of "official" antisemitic films produced in the Third

Reich. The features of the actors playing malevolent Jews are exaggerated through makeup, lighting, and angle of photography. They sway and gesture and whine and argue just as Jews would in the antisemitic imagination; they are, of course, caricatures, physically repulsive and morally corrupt. Even Satan (Rosalinda Celentano) is a much more attractive figure than these spiteful creeps. One would not need to make a single change in their manner of speech, body language, or physical features to paste them into any scene from *Jew Süss*.

What, then, can we conclude from this film? Much of the debate over the film up to now has been about its potential to incite antisemitism. I doubt that it will have this effect in the United States. Those who are inclined in this direction do not need this film to incite them, and those who are not are hardly its natural audience. Indeed, I think that because this is a truly bad film, it will disappear very quickly, though it will remain as the staple of a certain kind of Christian instruction and possibly a cult movie for some audiences. This may well not be the case elsewhere. In Europe, certainly in its more devoutly Christian eastern parts, and in the Muslim world, this film does have the potential to incite antisemitism. In Poland, for instance, about a million viewers watched the film in its first week of screening, and priests were taking classes of children to the cinema as part of religious instruction. Yasir Arafat exclaimed after watching it that the film reminded him of the plight of the Palestinians. And because the subtitles in these foreign screenings presumably include the line "his blood be on us," which was deleted from the American version, one can expect some people to take this literally, as they have already been doing with such abandon in some parts of the Middle East.

But what the film actually teaches us is that, indeed, as I had written before it was screened, the stereotypical representation of Jews with its rather narrow range of possibilities and characterizations has not changed much over the years. It is part of a cinematic tradition dating back to the early days of film and is itself fed on premodern imagery whose own origins go back to the Middle Ages. *The Passion of the Christ* is the ultimate example of this, a mélange of anti-Jewish Christian prejudices and phobias with the racism of *Jew Süss*. Nauseating though it is, this is an instructive exercise in the power of cinematic imagery. In this sense, it serves as a rather fitting opening for the discussion of the cinematic "Jew."

AHR	*American Historical Review*
ASG	*Archiv für Sozialgeschichte*
CEH	*Central European History*
CI	*Critical Inquiry*
FCM	*Film Comment Magazine (filmlinc.com)*
HJFRT	*Historical Journal of Film, Radio and Television*
IJPA	*International Journal of Psycho-Analysis*
JAPA	*Journal of the American Psychoanalytic Association*
JEMH	*Journal of Early Modern History*
JR	*The Jerusalem Report*
LAT	*Los Angeles Times*
NYRB	*New York Review of Books*
NYT	*New York Times*
NZZ	*Neue Zürcher Zeitung*
PP	*Psychoanalytic Psychology*
S&S	*Sight and Sound*
SEEP	*Slavic and Eastern European Performances*
SWCA	*Simon Wiesenthal Center Annual*
TI	*The Independent*
TNR	*The New Republic*
WP	*Washington Post*
YJC	*Yale Journal of Criticism*

The "Jew" in Cinema

[1]

THE "JEW" AS PERPETRATOR

SORCERER AND ALIEN

In the closing moments of Paul Wegener and Carl Boese's classic film *The Golem: How He Came into the World* (1920), the man of clay fabricated by Rabbi Loew (Albert Steinrück) breaks open the gates of the Jewish ghetto in Prague and steps out into the sunshine. Golden-haired boys and girls are playing in the meadow. Initially frightened, they are also curious about the giant creature who emerges from the dark alleys of the walled city. During the film, the Golem (Paul Wegener) has spread terror throughout the ghetto. He sets fire to the rabbi's house; he kills Knight Florian (Lothar Muthel), the gentile lover of the rabbi's daughter, Miriam (Lyda Salmanova); and he kidnaps Miriam. In these last moments of the film, the Golem is suddenly transformed. He lifts up one of the children, looks into his light, joyous eyes, and for the very first time since his creation, a faint smile appears on his forbidding face. Then the child playfully pulls out the star embedded in the Golem's chest, which contains the secret word that gives the giant life, and the Golem collapses to the ground. Soon the blond children gather around the prostrate corpse, their happy giggles and

The Jew's creature (*The Golem*): Having burst out of the ghetto, the Golem lifts up one of the blond children playing in the meadow, and smiles. The child pulls out the Star of David embedded in the Golem's chest and the creature falls lifelessly to the ground.

wreaths of flowers marking their affinity with Knight Florian, who habitually carried a flower in his hand until the Golem brutally hurled him to his death from the tower by order of Famulus (Ernst Deutsch), the jealous rabbi's assistant. Then the Jews with their distinctive pointed hats storm out of the broken gate. The caftan-wearing, black-bearded, gesticulating figures are both frightened and frightening at the same time. The children run off, and the Golem is carried back into the city. His moment of happiness was brief. Now he will become a mountain of clay once more, until he is called again to serve his Jewish masters.

   This is a curious scene. The Golem of Prague, an old Jewish tale with roots that date back to medieval legends and commentaries, is of course about the rescue of the Jews from the gentiles. In one version of the tale, the rabbi gives life to the clay creature by writing the Hebrew word *emeth* (אמת), or truth, on its forehead. When the Golem develops his own will and begins wreaking havoc on the ghetto, the rabbi erases the first letter from the word, making it into *meth* (מת), or dead. A later version dating probably to the eighteenth century has Rabbi Judah Loew ben Bezalel of Prague creating the Golem, and during the nineteenth and early twentieth centuries the Golem featured in numerous works of fiction. Wegener and Boese's film itself was inspired by the Bohemian writer Gustav Meyrink's 1915 novel *Der Golem.*[1] Fabricated by the Jews to protect them from their foes, the Golem is also a tool of power and violence, and thus contains seeds of annihilation for the Jews themselves. It consequently has to be destroyed. In the film *The Golem,* which is among the earliest and most influential extant cinematic depictions of European images of Jews, the clay giant is a symbol of Jewish magical and destructive capacities; it also represents the Jews' ability to control the powers of nature, to subjugate everything that is beautiful and free, and to cast over the world the dark shadow of their morbid rites.[2]

The Golem is not an overtly antisemitic film. On the contrary, in some ways it is sympathetic to the plight of a community threatened by the power and whims of an arbitrary and frivolous ruler. Indeed, the film contains many of the elements that will surface over the rest of the twentieth century in cinematic depictions of Jews both as perpetrators and as victims. In some ways, *The Golem* is reminiscent of the classic film version of Erich Maria Remarque's novel *All Quiet on the Western Front* (dir. Lewis Milestone, 1930), which similarly provided many of the cinematic tropes and icons that would reappear endlessly in war films, no matter whether they glorify or condemn war.[3] Perhaps it is no coincidence that Wegener (who was in fact a giant, just like the Golem he played in the movie) ended up making propaganda films for the Nazi regime, which reciprocated by naming him "Actor of the State."[4] But what is most important to recognize about this early venture into cinematic stereotypes is the extent to which it reflected existing notions about Jews, further popularized them among ever-larger audiences, and provided models for their depiction that generations of filmmakers with very different goals and agendas have employed or have tried to avoid until the present day. Here we can identify three main motifs. First, there is the notion of the "Jew" as a malevolent outsider, embodied most frighteningly in the figure of the Eternal or Wandering Jew.[5] The second motif is the anxiety about Jewish transformation, accompanied by an insistence on the unchanging Jewish essence. The third motif is the obsession with sexual relations between Jews and gentiles and the racial and cultural implications of these interactions. To be sure, Jewish discourse on these motifs provides an almost exact negative image. For Jews, their outsider status was the consequence of repeated persecutions and expulsions; the act of transformation meant assimilation into an often-unwelcoming society and abandonment of any remnant of Jewish identity. Intermarriage, taboo in traditional communities, usually meant raising

3

children as strangers to the Jewish parent's heritage, even long after the Jews came out of the ghetto.[6]

The Golem's depiction of the Jews as living in physical and mental seclusion from their natural environment and the gentile social fabric constitutes a fundamental leitmotif in the film. This is of course reasonable in the case of Prague's medieval ghetto, but it remains a theme, albeit sometimes more subtle, in films about the modern era as well. The "Jew" as the outsider, a stranger or foreigner who is nevertheless living in the midst of society and is an integral part of events, indeed, is the principal focus and prime mover of disaster and misfortune, and who must therefore be contained, transformed, or removed, is a constant trope whose cinematic origins are clearly identifiable in *The Golem* and whose theological, ideological, and political roots date back many centuries.[7] The strangeness of the Jews is depicted through dress, beards, facial expressions, gesticulations, modes of living, sites of habitation, and language, which is understandable yet apparently distorted, and sometimes comical or menacing. In *The Golem* the Jews live in a stage-set whose architecture reflects an Expressionist *imaginaire*, strongly influenced by a fascination with what Wegener called "the fantastic world of the past" found in the medieval Jewish ghetto.[8] People dart in and out of narrow alleys like rats (a favorite antisemitic metaphor), climbing impossibly crooked staircases and leaning out of asymmetrical windows. Hidden passageways open and close, high walls block out the sunlight, and no trees or flowers are to be seen anywhere within the confines of the ghetto.

This external foreignness indicates something deeper about the uncanny aspects of Jewish nature and faith, where religion and the supernatural seem to be inextricably linked. When they go off to pray, the men assume a particularly threatening demeanor. They strike their breasts in recognition of their eternal guilt, or hold out their hands in supplication, or lift their arms in thanks; they bend and bow, tilt and swing, casting menacing shadows on the uneven walls. The synagogue, in other words, reveals itself as the heart of darkness, the very center of all that is weird and ominous about the Jews. But beyond this there is magic. Here we find Rabbi Loew doing what can only be described as witchcraft, black magic, and wizardry. The books he consults, the demons he calls forth, the secret formulas he recites, all evoke the images of evil consorting with the powers of the devil. The Jews may be threatened, but the forces they arouse are greater than any the gentiles can muster.

This is most powerfully expressed in an extraordinary scene in the movie. As the Emperor Rudolf II (Otto Gebühr) invites Rabbi Loew and

his Golem to entertain his guests at the palace, the rabbi reluctantly con-
jures the Eternal Jew, who bears a disturbing physical resemblance to the
figure popularized a few years later in Nazi posters and subsequently in the
most notorious "documentary" produced in the Third Reich. Trudging
through the desert at the head of his people, leaning on a rough cane, the
Eternal Jew is either heading into Exile, or about to invade yet another
civilization; he may be paying for his past crimes or setting out on another
destructive mission. We will meet him again in different guises in other
films. But this image is, in fact, being projected on a screen as if the
emperor and his entourage are being shown a film by Rabbi Loew. Yet the
rabbi warns the audience not to laugh, for this is indeed a figure which is
just as comical as it is vaguely threatening. The emperor, however, cannot
suppress his merriment at the sight of this ridiculous image, and as he
begins laughing the rest of the guests join in. And, as often happened in
the early days of film, when viewers were not yet used to the illusion of
perspective and movement on the screen, once the Eternal Jew begins
walking toward the audience in an apparently angry response to their
mockery, the guests panic and try to flee from the hall. Will the Eternal Jew
step out of the screen and destroy them? Is the film-within-a-film only an
indication that *The Golem* itself is no mere cinematic fantasy but an urgent
warning? As the hall begins to fall apart around the terrified guests, it
seems that the conjured image—whether filmic or magic—has indeed
turned into reality. It is now the turn of another creature of Jewish wizardry
to save the day. On orders of the rabbi, the Golem himself holds up the
ceiling of the palace with inhuman strength, and the audience narrowly
escapes the wrath of the Eternal Jew.[9]

In *The Golem* the "Jew" is not yet transformed into a gentile, a recurring
theme in later cinematic representations. But two other transformations
are already suggested, both of which are destined for a long life in the
movies. The first is the Golem himself. As noted above, this is an ambiguous creature. On the one hand, he is the tool of the Jews, created to rescue
them from their persecutors. On the other hand, he shows some characteristics of belonging to that other world of nature and beauty populated
by the gentiles, or at least he exhibits a desire to escape to it, away from the
demonic hold of the Jews. Thus, while the gate of the ghetto is meant to
protect the Jews from attacking intruders, the Golem breaks it from within
so as to liberate himself from the city and reach the sunlight, joy, and love
awaiting him on the other side. When enraged, the Golem does kill the
blond, flower-bearing knight who has just spent the night with the rabbi's
daughter, but he does this as the tool of a jealous suitor. The rest of his rage

is directed against the rabbi, his maker and jailer, and he appears to be more of a threat within the ghetto walls than outside them. Hence he miraculously transforms into a gentle ogre once he is out in the sunlight and gazing into the bright eyes of a gentile child. In this sense, the Golem may be seen not merely as the Jews' defensive tool but also as symbolizing their transformation, with all the violent but redeeming potential encompassed in such a metamorphosis. The shift is from symbols of physical weakness and satanic rites into the epitome of physical prowess and the most intimate proximity to nature: the clay monster in search of sunlight and beauty.

The second transformation is symbolized by Miriam Loew, the rabbi's daughter, who is already showing signs of rebellion against the established order by her sensuous demeanor and barely contained lust. In one sense, she portrays the lecherous Jewish woman who tempts the heroic knight into her bed and thus spells his doom. In another sense, she is used by the rabbi as the bait that will enable him to receive an audience with the emperor and get him to reverse his edict to expel the Jews, thus echoing the story of Esther and other biblical Jewish heroines. She is therefore both a victim and a perpetrator. Once the knight Florian is dead, she happily accepts Famulus as her lover. But she may also represent the growing urge to escape the confines of the ghetto, if only by consorting with a gentile within the walls of the rabbi's house. Moreover, she is the source of the Golem's second passion. If the gaze of the gentile child melts his heart, the sight of Miriam being fought over by two men awakens his lust and calls forth his violence. The young Jewish woman's attempt to break loose of the ghetto by liberating herself from the hold of convention and authority is bound to bring evil consequences. Sex and the Jews, the threat posed by Jewish women and men to the natural order of things and the transformation that sexual intercourse with gentiles entails, are at the center of the cinematic imagination from its very cradle, just as they haunt other forms of representation concerned with the relationship between Jews and gentiles at least since the Middle Ages.[10]

ANTISEMITIC PERSPECTIVES

Despite the disastrous effects of antisemitism on European Jewry during the twentieth century, blatantly antisemitic films are in fact not as common as one would expect. The most explicit were, of course, produced during the Third Reich. Even there the crop was meager and the results, with one important exception to be discussed below, were often neither artistically impressive nor commercially successful. The combination of entertainment and propaganda calls for a more subtle approach. The Nazi regime did succeed in disseminating antisemitic messages to a population that was hardly immune to anti-Jewish prejudice even before Adolf Hitler's "seizure of power." But this was accomplished either by means of explicit propaganda—couched, to be sure, in the language of scientific objectivity and historical truth—in speeches, newsreels, the print media, educational material and courses, and so forth, or by means of subliminal messages inserted into what appeared to the public as mere entertainment. This is a topic on which much has already been written and I will therefore not discuss it here.[11]

The one openly antisemitic film produced in the Third Reich that was a tremendous commercial success, creating the ideal-type of the cinematic "Jew" as perpetrator, both reflecting existing images and influencing subsequent, less-blatant representations, was Veit Harlan's *Jew Süss* (1940). Seen by over twenty million Germans within two years of its first screening and distributed to many other countries allied with or occupied by Germany during the war, this was arguably the most effective combination of "historical" drama, tale of passion and deception, and lesson in racial prejudice and hatred ever produced in a film studio.[12] Arriving in German theaters the same year as Fritz Hippler's truly repulsive "documentary" (and box-office flop), *The Eternal Jew,* the film prepared the German public for the "disappearance" of the Jews in the "east" by depicting the expulsion of the Jews in eighteenth-century Stuttgart as a defensive measure against the machinations of Süss and the "invasion" of the Swabian capital by the inhabitants of the Jewish ghetto in Frankfurt.

Considering both films together, one can see how the antisemitic potential of *The Golem* was fully realized in *Jew Süss*. To be sure, in the latter all ambiguity between the "Jew" as victim and as perpetrator completely vanishes. The ability of the "Jew" to perpetrate "his" crimes of theft, abuse of power, and sexual exploitation is tremendously enhanced the moment he is released from the confines of the ghetto and allowed to enter the city in the guise of a "normal" human being. Ironically, however, although he removes his caftan and beard, the "Jew" is recognized by everyone for what he is. For even as he sheds his external marks of recognition, his gesticulations, manners of speech, and, most important, his schemes and maneuvers, betray him as an authentic Jew hiding beneath a respectable veneer. Still, the structural similarities between *The Golem* and *Jew Süss* are striking. Both films exploit stories originating in Jewish legend, fiction, or history whose intention was precisely the opposite of their antisemitic retelling.

Lion Feuchtwanger's eponymous best-selling novel of 1925 was based on the career of Joseph Süss Oppenheimer, who served as the personal advisor of Duke Karl Alexander of Wurttemberg and was eventually executed in 1738 following the duke's death, when his court enemies invoked a forgotten law prohibiting Jews from having sexual relations with gentiles.[13] For the German-Jewish author Feuchtwanger, writing during the Weimar Republic, Süss epitomized the failed attempt to assimilate into German society. Indeed, he initially wanted to write a fictional account of the life of Walter Rathenau, the republic's Jewish foreign minister assassinated by right-wing extremists in 1922. The novel was first made into a relatively unsuccessful British film in 1934, starring the exiled German actor Conrad Veidt. While the British version accurately represented Feuchtwanger's view, it quickly attracted the attention of Joseph Goebbels, Hitler's propaganda minister, as containing all the crucial ingredients of modern antisemitic phobias and demonology.[14]

Harlan's *Jew Süss* uses the setting of a lively court drama, full of dance, music, lust, and intrigue, to depict the infiltration into German society of a poisonous and polluting foreign element. This alien penetration reaches its climax when Süss Oppenheimer (Ferdinand Marian) rapes Dorothea (Kristina Söderbaum), the daughter of District Councilor Sturm (Eugen Klöpfer) and the newly wedded wife of the young notary Darius Faber (Malte Jaeger). Having wriggled his way out of the filthy and congested ghetto, and obscured those marks of moral and physical degeneration manifested by its inhabitants, the "Jew" has not only taken over political power in a Christian community but has also despoiled an Aryan maiden. Just as the ghetto's muck hides great treasures of obscure—most probably criminal—origins, so, too, Süss's facade of respectability merely masks the old lecherous demon of medieval lore. And just as Jewish religious rites appear both vulgar and menacing, so the Jew's promises of assistance to the duke (Heinrich George) are merely part of a scheme to flood the city with Jews and eventually to dominate the entire land. If Wegener and Boese's ghetto scenes have a mysterious and surreal atmosphere, and Hippler's—shot in actual ghettos brimming with human suffering—are all too realistic, Harlan's studio-set ghetto avoids being unbearably repulsive for German audiences while clearly indicating the Jews' inability to conform to bourgeois ideals of cleanliness and order.[15] But all three films contain the same fundamental elements: the ghetto as the source of filth, disease, and pollution (depicted most memorably in a close-up of rats in *The Eternal Jew*); the "Jew" as the agent of destruction through metamorphosis, either transforming clay into a monster, or transforming himself into a gentile (depicted in the most gruesome manner by Hippler, who shot faces of Jews before and after their beards were cut); and the synagogue as the heart of Jewish occultism and evil. The fact that *Jew Süss* and *The Eternal Jew* were made two years after Germany's synagogues burned down in *Kristallnacht,* and just as Poland's Jews were being ghettoized, must have played an important role in the consciousness of viewers, even as it adds a further layer of horror to our perception of these films today.

In a certain important sense, *Jew Süss* may have evoked even more anxiety and fear among German viewers than *The Eternal Jew,* not only because it was seen by millions, but also because its central theme is the pollution of German blood through rape by a Jew. Coming in the wake of numerous *Rassenschande* or "race defilement" trials, where Jewish males were indicted for having sex with Aryan women, this old antisemitic trope and phobia must have seemed a clear and present danger to many Germans.[16] Moreover, the rape is accomplished through the torture of Dorothea's husband, Faber, which adds an element of violence to the disturbing but for some probably also arousing sexual scene. In some ways, this is a reversal of the situation in *The Golem,* where the rabbi's daughter tempts the Aryan knight and causes his subsequent destruction. But the lecherous Jewish female is not absent from *Jew Süss* either, figuring as Rebecca, the scantily dressed daughter of yet another Rabbi Loew (Werner Krauss)—a name that seems to have haunted German filmmakers—who looks out of the window in the ghetto with what appears to be only one purpose in mind.

But *Jew Süss* contains even deeper layers of meaning, which may have in fact contributed to its commercial success even though they were probably not put there consciously by the filmmaker. Eric Rentschler has already commented that beyond the mask of the gentile worn by Süss is yet another mask, that of the non-Jewish German actor Ferdinand Marian, who assumes all the mannerisms and looks of the "Jew." As the duke says to him, "he should take off his mask. . . . The last one, the last one! Ha, what does he really look like, what does he really look like?" To which Süss answers with what seems to be somewhat confused sincerity: "How am I supposed to look?"[17] This indeed reflects the Nazi racist anxiety that under the mask of every Aryan may lurk a Jew. The fact that Marian received fan mail from female admirers must have been all the more galling to those who idealized the Aryan, since he was seen as especially attractive in his role as a Jew. Moreover, the other key male Jews in the film are all played by the same actor, Werner Krauss, who according to the original film program thereby "demonstrates his art of transformation," an art that is normally attributed to the "Jew" but that he seems to have acquired merely by acting as one.[18]

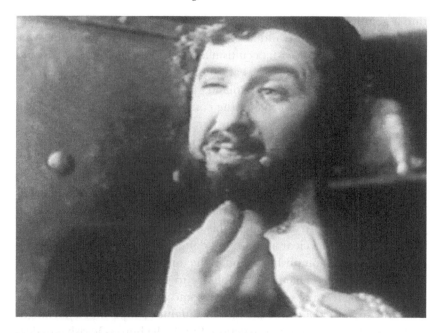

The Nazi as Jew (*Jew Süss*): Ferdinand Marian playing Jew Süss. Marian received fan mail from female admirers especially for playing this role. Veit Harlan, the director, watched films on and by Jews to get his characters "right." Compare with Solomon Mikhoels as Menachem Mendel (see p. 33, below).

The fact that all the Jews are one Jew, and that this one Jew is actually an Aryan, must also mean that just as Aryans could become Jews, the Jews had the uncanny ability to become Aryans and disappear altogether. This quality of both being and not being there at the same time, this assertion of an essential and innate difference that simultaneously could not be uncovered, was obviously a cause of tremendous anxiety.[19] Note, for instance, the conversation between Süss and von Remchingen (Theodor Loos), the duke's chamberlain. As Süss insists on coming himself to Stuttgart, von Remchingen says, "even if I could arrange a pass, everyone would immediately see . . . ," stroking his chin to indicate his meaning. To which Süss replies, "A Jew is recognized by his side-locks, beard, and caftan . . . ? Don't trouble your head over this. . . . I'll take care of my exterior appearance, and you take care of the pass."[20]

However we may interpret the fan mail sent to an Aryan male for his role as a Jew in an antisemitic film enjoyed by millions, *Jew Süss* itself introduces a troubling element into the relationship between the "Jew" and the Aryan woman. Just as in *The Golem* the knight is physically attracted to the rabbi's daughter, so in *Jew Süss*, despite the fact that eventually she is raped, Dorothea seems attracted precisely to that foreignness in Süss that ought to repel her. This obviously threatens to undermine her loyalty to her authoritarian father and stiff, humorless husband, who consequently become Süss's most dedicated foes. But if one tries to read between the lines, it is Dorothea's potential rebellion against form and tradition (or race), as well as the strict injunction not to have any intimate contact with a Jew, that may have excited both her and her German audience in the Third Reich. She is certainly never as lively and attractive as when she is with Süss, who seems to transform her from a "white" to a "red" woman, from the ideal housebound daughter and wife into a young woman seeking erotic adventures and travel to foreign lands.[21] Süss may be a rootless, homeless Jew; but he is also a man of the world and a charmer. Note the very first conversation between the two of them, as she gives him a ride in her carriage and thereby helps him penetrate the gentile city, with all the erotic implications of this situation:

DOROTHEA: How I would love to travel, if I could even around the whole world. I bet you've traveled a lot . . . right? Have you been already to Paris?

SÜSS: Yes.

DOROTHEA: To Versailles?

[Süss nods.]

DOROTHEA: Oh, I'm so jealous of you. Where else have you been?

SÜSS: Oh, London, Vienna, Rome, Madrid.

[Dorothea sighs.]

SÜSS: Lisbon.

DOROTHEA: Dear God, that's practically the whole world. Where was the nicest? I mean, where did you feel most . . . at home?

SÜSS: At home? . . . Everywhere!

DOROTHEA: Everywhere? Don't you have a homeland?

SÜSS: Of course! The world!

DOROTHEA: Nonsense. You must have felt happy somewhere.

SÜSS: Not as happy as I am at the moment, here in Stuttgart next to you, lovely maiden. I have never been so happy in my entire life.

This, we might say, could have been the beginning of a great romance. But since Süss is a Jew, it ends up in a rape and a hanging. Conversely, it is precisely because of Süss's cosmopolitan condition (these days a much-sought-after ingredient by what have been called "virtual Jews"), that Dorothea is so intrigued and excited by him.[22] The Jew has no home, no *Heimat*, and that is a truly horrifying thought; but what could be more romantic than the declaration that she, Dorothea, is a greater source of happiness to this well-traveled man than the entire universe? How different he must seem from the stodgy, narrow-minded burghers of provincial Stuttgart with whom she spent her whole life. The thought of eloping may cross her mind—or occur to her female audience—even if it is followed by anger at herself and a desire to make him go away. Such delusion obviously calls for Faber's penetrating gaze, which unravels Süss's "true" identity at their next meeting. The moment he lays eyes on him, Faber exclaims: "But this is a Jew, this Herr Oppenheimer from Frankfurt!" to which Süss responds by complimenting him on his powers of observation or, literally, his judgment of human beings (*Menschenerkenntnis*). This must indeed put an end to any illicit contact, but it also adds another layer of excitement, transforming this gentleman from Frankfurt into a forbidden fruit whose very infatuation with the young maiden cannot but arouse her own interest. Indeed, Faber suspects as much. When Dorothea complains about the rising prices of food caused by the road tolls imposed by Süss, Faber says to her: "It was you who brought into Stuttgart the person we must thank for all this."

Thus the film creates an ambivalence in Dorothea's relationship with Süss that enhances the dramatic tension and parallels the ambivalence of the entire cinematic situation. For here we have a Jew who openly enters a city forbidden to him, who is masked as a gentile yet is known to be a Jew, who is suspected of innate criminality and palpable mischief yet runs the financial affairs of the state, who provides women and sex to the duke yet is himself seen as the main polluter of family morals. Even the fact that Süss supports the duke in gaining dictatorial powers against the assembly is somewhat curious considering that just a few years earlier this was precisely what Hitler himself had accomplished. From this perspective, while *Jew Süss* does away with any ambivalence regarding the role of the "Jew" as perpetrator, at the same time it introduces even more disturbing elements, which lie just under the surface of a simple court drama about an evil spirit threatening to undermine a righteous society. Süss reveals that no one's identity is certain, even if he, as a Jew, is doubtlessly evil. He demonstrates that no Aryan woman's chastity should be trusted—precisely the subtext of the *Rassenschande* trials, which attempted to define both racial identity and proper gender roles. And he reveals that the rulers of the land may not only become the Jews' stooges, but they may also exploit the Jews to cover up for their own moral corruption, greed, and abuse of power. The "Jew," then, is not only a pollutant that must be cleansed; he is also the element that reveals everyone else's racial, ethical, and political corruption. In that sense he is both necessary and must be disposed of. Once the "Jew" is gone, everything will return to normal; but now we know that things were not normal to begin with, as had been revealed by the "Jew." And what we find is that just like sin, the "Jew" was always there, and can never be cleansed, for he is part of us.

Hence *Jew Süss* successfully introduced the main features of the anti-semitic view of the "Jew" to millions of Germans and other Europeans. Many of these features appear in different guises in the films discussed in the rest of this book. First, the "Jew" is endowed with a protean nature that enables him to transform himself into an unrecognizable gentile and yet to retain the "essence" of his race. Second, he is a homeless cosmopolitan who thrives as a parasite on other nations' wealth. Third, the "Jew" is a lecherous male who pollutes the blood of innocent maidens and thus also their entire race (with all the echoes of anti-Jewish blood-libel myths—related either to the alleged need for Christian blood on Passover or to ritual slaughter—and also phobias about vampires). Fourth, the "Jew" is seen as lining his "filthy pockets," as Faber puts it, with "our good money," rather than being a productive member of society; moreover, he gains what Faber describes as his "blood money" by spilling the blood of gentiles. Fifth, the "Jew" is not shown as being cleverer than the gentiles (which some antisemitic tales dangerously suggest), but "just more cunning," as Sturm explains to his family. Sixth, the "Jew" has been already condemned by religion and tradition, as illustrated by Martin Luther's injunction that "next to the devil, you have no more dangerous foe than the Jew," and by the "ancient criminal code," according to which "where a Jew has carnal knowledge of a Christian woman, he will be hanged by the neck until dead as punishment for his crime and an example for all." Seventh, the "Jew" is shown as calling destruction upon himself by manifesting an annihilating urge against the gentiles, as when Süss tells the duke that the best response to those who oppose him is to "exterminate them by fire and sword." And eighth, the Jews are presented as joined together in a secret cult intent on taking over the world, but simultaneously as a community of abject sinners. Thus Rabbi Loew says to Süss: "The Lord wants his people to walk in sackcloth and ashes, to be scattered throughout the earth, so that they may rule in secret over the peoples of the earth," an obvious reference to

The Wandering Jew (*Jew Süss*): The Jews enter Stuttgart. Harlan visited the Lublin Ghetto and brought back 120 Jews for parts in the film. These must be the people in this scene, who were subsequently presumably murdered.

The Protocols of the Elders of Zion. This notorious forgery, whose role in stoking virulent antisemitism cannot be overestimated, has indeed enjoyed a long and successful career despite being exposed as a fraud some eighty years ago. Its extraordinary longevity and malleability has been recently demonstrated by means of a new Egyptian television soap opera, broadcast to millions of viewers throughout the Arab world, which uses this legend as the "historical" basis of its narrative.[23]

The success of *Jew Süss* as compared to the relative failure of *The Eternal Jew* is telling, because it demonstrates that while viewers will often reject virulent, crass, and pornographic propaganda, even if presented to them as a "documentary," they will more easily be swayed by a well-told tale that contains all the ingredients of a film melodrama yet claims to be based on a true story. Many Germans who supported Hitler's regime rejected Julius Streicher's pornographic and rabidly antisemitic rag *Der Stürmer*, which almost seemed to give antisemitism itself a bad name.[24] The old antisemitic trope, dating back to the Jewish emancipation in the nineteenth century, that assimilated Jews were in fact the most dangerous, because hiding under their mask of civilized conduct lurked the very same mythical Jew of yore, was more welcome to German audiences than the dehumanized

14

figures of starving Jews in rat-infested alleys that made Germans cringe in horror during screenings of *The Eternal Jew*. Wolfgang Liebeneiner's film *I Accuse* (1941), a similar attempt to sell the murder of the handicapped to German audiences—portraying it as a loving euthanasia and deliverance through death—had more mixed results. While the film was popular, Germans ended up protesting against the killing of their kin to an extent never shown vis-à-vis the murder of the Jews.[25] Conversely, *Jew Süss* showed the German public that their next-door neighbors, who seemed very much like themselves, were in fact no different from the terrifying, caftan-wearing, and bearded *Ostjuden* that the SS was in the process of herding into modern ghettos just as the film came out.[26]

PHILOSEMITIC ANTISEMITISM

The Nazis had another and very different manner of representing the "Jew." As the Reich constructed its new "living space" in the east, Jews from all over German-occupied Europe were brought into its necessary counterpart, the "death space" of total annihilation.[27] Cramped into ghettos, pushed into freight trains, chased into gas chambers, piled up in mass graves, and shoved into ovens, their ashes dumped into rivers or used to pave roads, their bones ground to dust, the Jews and their memory were destined to vanish without a trace. And yet, in order to facilitate this very process of total extermination of a people and a culture, the Nazi regime had to undertake elaborate measures of dissimulation, to fool the Jews and deceive international organizations and foes who might hamper the smooth implementation of this most final of all "solutions."

One means of deception was the creation of an ideal ghetto, a place where the Jews were happy and content, running their own lives and protected from the horrors of the war by the Führer's good will and generosity. To be sure, the figure of the "happy Jew" in Nazi Germany only flickered for a few moments before the ignorant gaze of International Red Cross officials as the movie cameras brought by the ministry of propaganda recorded this travesty for posterity. But this elaborate trickery, this transformation of a site of horror and terror into a promised land of milk and honey, this quintessentially Nazi joke of creating a cheerful Jew just before making him disappear altogether, has played its role in the making of the postwar cinematic "Jew" as well. If what Primo Levi called the "ravens" of the Jewish Sonderkommando in Birkenau were one aspect of Nazi humor that strove to implicate the victims in their own extermination, the sinister hoax of the happy Jews of Terezín has left a similarly deep scar on attempts to delineate the figure of the "Jew" in postwar representations.[28] For while the Nazis justified the extermination of the Jews by placing them outside the human species, they covered up the extermination by masquerading their victims as leading an entirely normal existence. If the Sonderkommando did the "dirty work" of the crematoria for the SS, the Jews of Terezín played roles in the theater whose stage-set hid the chimneys of Birkenau.

In some ways, the "happy Jew" shown in the Nazi propaganda film *Theresienstadt* (1944), also ironically titled *The Führer Gives a City to the Jews*, is arguably the most horrifying of all Nazi images of the "Jew." Here we do not see the Eternal Jew on his path of destruction, the *Ostjude* with his beard and caftan, the conniving, westernized Jew plotting and robbing. Rather, we see healthy, blond, muscular teenagers playing soccer; gifted musicians from all over Europe playing concerts; smiling children eating bread in the sunlight; bohemian cafes filled with clients. The "Jew" has been returned to the fold of European society by Nazi propaganda moments before boarding the trains to Auschwitz. We know that the faces we see were thus mostly recorded for the last time: of 140,000 Jews deported to Terezín, close to 35,000 died there and 87,000 were deported to death camps.[29]

Here, then, the Nazis turned the tables on the Jews. It was, after all, the "Jew" who had been the master of transformation, fooling the innocent and naive gentiles by appearing just like them yet never shedding his pernicious essence. In the Potemkin village of Terezín, however, precisely the opposite happened. Of course, the Germans were all supposed to know by then what the "real Jew" looked like. Under his Western facade persisted his "oriental" nature. But now it was the Nazis who forced the Jews to look normal and to conceal the fact that they had already been torn out of their society and were dying of hunger and disease as they waited for the transports to take them to the gas chambers. The Jews had to appear "normal" in order to conceal their extermination, just as previously, according to the Nazi logic, they had assumed a normal facade so as to pollute and eradicate the Aryans. This was the core of the Nazi joke, similar to but more elaborate than the speeches made by SS officers to exhausted and debilitated Jews just out of the horribly congested train cars and about to enter the undressing rooms leading to the "showers," promising them that they would be washed, given clean clothing, and sent to do hard but healthy work. The "Jew" in *The Führer Gives a City to the Jews* is of course still a perpetrator in the eyes of the Nazi watching the film. Indeed, the Jews still seem to be faring better than the Germans: they eat, do sports, play music, while the Germans are being bombed at home and are fighting bitterly at the front. But on another level of consciousness, the German viewer knows that the Jews are being "done away with," and that the image of momentary joy is a mere prelude to extinction, a well-deserved one precisely because the Jews are still happy while the Germans suffer.

It is this image of the "happy Jew," provided courtesy of the Nazi regime, that has haunted several filmmakers in the postwar period, just as the extraordinary works of art, music, and literature produced at Terezín under the shadow of death have haunted the memory of this camp in particular. Consisting of Jews from the so-called Protectorate of Bohemia and Moravia (the Czech part of pre–World War II Czechoslovakia), Germany, Austria, the Netherlands, Hungary, Denmark, and Slovenia, Terezín was a concentration of talent and creativity rarely to be found in such a small space. But it was also a death space. Of 10,000 children sent to extermination camps from Terezín, only 150 came back.[30]

The happy or successful Jew as a somewhat suspect character is, however, hardly the invention of the Nazis. Nor is he the domain of strictly or overtly antisemitic films. Jean Renoir, one of the most prominent filmmakers of interwar France and a man closely associated with the Popular Front headed by the Jewish prime minister Léon Blum, exhibited an ambivalent attitude toward the "Jew" in his highly popular masterpiece made on the eve of World War II, *The Grand Illusion* (1938). The tale of a group of French soldiers captured by the Germans and their repeated and persistent attempts to escape, *The Grand Illusion* is about the relationships between a series of types who represent different aspects of French society. Both an intensely patriotic and a vehemently anti-militaristic film, *The Grand Illusion* demonstrates how the old social and military values of honor and chivalry were ground to dust by the brutality of World War I. While Renoir was committed to the *cinéma engagé* of the French left, he also exhibited a certain nostalgia for the old European aristocracy, be it French or German, which lived and died according to strict codes of conduct and disdained the growing impact of the modern nation-state, the philistine bourgeoisie, and the infiltration of the "best circles" by the canaille, the rabble of mass politics and industrialized urban society.[31]

Part of this somewhat melancholic view of the decline of one kind of social order and the rise of another—which Renoir supported ideologically but whose actual manifestations were less to his liking—includes the stereotypical Jewish arriviste. Tracing his roots to foreign lands (usually being a mongrel of several cultures), this "Jew" had not only taken over the wealth of the nation to which he had attached himself as a parasite but was also trying to appropriate the symbols of its culture and tradition. This, of course, was very much the view of the French right wing, dating back at least to Edouard-Adolphe Drumont, the Dreyfus trial, and the launching of the *Action Française* newspaper and movement in the late nineteenth century. Moreover, in the 1930s, the sense of political anxiety, economic upheaval, and social disarray, accompanied by growing immigration— increasingly of political and economic refugees from Eastern Europe, who included numerous Jews—provided French conservative and fascist circles with a new agenda and greatly enhanced public xenophobia and anti-semitism. The Popular Front, a coalition of the Communist, Socialist, and Radical parties, was formed to stem fascism. Headed by Blum, the Popular Front galvanized the antirepublican, antisemitic, conservative, and fascist elements in France and gave French antiwar sentiment a new twist by presenting those who wanted to stand up to Nazi Germany as foreigners, mostly Jews, who were willing to sacrifice French lives for their own selfish interests: hence the slogan, "Better Hitler than Blum!"[32]

The Grand Illusion reflected many of these sentiments. It was about the disillusionment with war, the decline of French morals, and the unraveling of the social fabric—even more powerfully depicted in Renoir's masterful (though box-office disaster) *The Rules of the Game* (1939)—and the emergence of new types who, for better or for worse, would have to lead France into the future. It is in this context that we must see a crucial conversation, which takes place about thirty minutes into the film, between several French soldiers in a German prisoner-of-war camp discussing their motivation to escape as they prepare costumes for the theater play they are about to put up.[33]

> TEACHER [Jean Dasté]: I wouldn't mind knowing what's happening at home.
>
> ENGINEER [Gaston Modot]: Haven't you received any news?
>
> TEACHER: Nothing!
>
> ACTOR [Julien Carette]: Me, I couldn't care less what my wife is doing. . . . What's driving me crazy is being so bored. Ah! Trocadéro . . . Cadet-Rousselle, and là . . . là . . . là . . .
>
> ROSENTHAL [Marcel Dalio]: In short, you want to escape for the fun of it. . . .
>
> ACTOR: That's right!
>
> ENGINEER: To me it's the spirit of contradiction. Since they won't let me fight, I'm dying to.
>
> MARÉCHAL [Jean Gabin]: Oh! As for me, I just want to do like everybody else. . . . Besides, it irritates me to be here while the others are getting smashed.

The Jew as alien comrade (*The Grand Illusion*): Rosenthal being mocked by his fellow prisoners of war for not being an authentic Frenchman. The actor, Marcel Dalio, was born as Israel Moshe Blauschild in Paris to Romanian-Jewish immigrants. He fled to the United States in 1940 and subsequently played in *Casablanca*.

BOELDIEU [the aristocratic officer played by Pierre Fresnay]: To me there's no question. What is a golf course for? For playing golf. A tennis court? For playing tennis. So! A prisoner-of-war camp is for escaping. . . . What do you think, Rosenthal, being such a sportive sort?

ACTOR: Oh! Him, sportive? . . . Ha! He was born in Jerusalem. [Note that in the original film script, Rosenthal responds first to Boeldieu's question by saying: "Me, I want to escape in order to fight for my homeland." At which point the Actor says: "Your homeland? . . . Ha, tell us already, you were born in Jerusalem!"]

ROSENTHAL: Excuse me! I was born in Vienna, capital of Austria, to a Danish mother and a Polish father, naturalized in France.[34]

MARÉCHAL: Old Breton nobility, what!

ROSENTHAL: That's always possible! But all of you, Frenchmen of ancient stock, you don't own a hundred square meters of your country. So! The Rosenthals have found the means, within thirty-five years, of acquiring three historic châteaux with hunting grounds, ponds, farm land, orchards, rabbits, fishing, pheasants, stud farms . . . and three fully stocked portrait galleries of authentic ancestors! Don't you think that it's worth escaping to defend all this?

BOELDIEU: I have never contemplated the question of patriotism from this truly rather unique angle.

Renoir, of course, is trying to demonstrate that during the war such prejudices and suspicions disappeared. Indeed, unlike the case of Germany, which experienced a rapid growth in antisemitism during World War I, French wartime propaganda insisted on the unity of all the French, no matter their creed or origin.[35] Rosenthal turns out to be a decent fellow after all. Since he comes from a family of great bankers and himself runs a large fashionable-clothing business, he has the wherewithal to procure excellent food to his imprisoned comrades as well as costumes for their theater play, and he eventually proves himself to be as patriotic and brave as the rest of them. Even the bigoted but decidedly straight and honest Maréchal comes around, as when they prepare to cross the Swiss border having at last successfully escaped after endless earlier attempts. By now, indeed, both the enthusiasm of the early days of the war and the prejudices that fueled it have evaporated. Facing the Swiss frontier, the two survivors of the killing fields summarize the message of the film:[36]

MARÉCHAL: You are sure, at least, that that's Switzerland ahead of us.

ROSENTHAL: No doubt whatsoever!

MARÉCHAL: It's just that the Swiss snow and the German snow are ridiculously similar!

ROSENTHAL: Don't worry: the border is there, marked out by men . . . even if nature couldn't care less!

MARÉCHAL: Me too, I couldn't care less. . . . And, when the war is over, I'll come back to look for Elsa [the German peasant woman who gave them shelter].

ROSENTHAL: Do you love her?

MARÉCHAL: Ah! I think I do!

ROSENTHAL: Take care! If we pass the line, you will have to go back to an aircraft squadron, and I'll have to go to an artillery battery.

MARÉCHAL: It's time they put an end to this bloody war . . . let's hope it's the last.

ROSENTHAL: Ah! Don't have such illusions! . . . Let's go! Return to reality: if we encounter a patrol, what do we do?

MARÉCHAL: All right! You go one way, and I'll go the other . . . and each will try his luck.

ROSENTHAL: In case this happens, perhaps it's prudent to say good bye
. . . and see you soon.

[They hug.]

MARÉCHAL: Good bye, you filthy Jew!

ROSENTHAL: Good bye, you old nut!

Nevertheless, it is clear that the new postwar France will have to be constructed by rough and ready types, such as Maréchal, and fundamental outsiders who transformed themselves into Frenchmen, such as Rosenthal: the representatives of the canaille and the métèques. The France represented by Boeldieu, indeed the old Europe represented by the deep link between him and his German-officer equivalent, von Rauffenstein (Erich von Stroheim), ends with the death of the Frenchman and the obviously imminent disappearance of the severely wounded and archaic German. The "Jew" and the man of the people are now the future: but Renoir is hardly optimistic.

Some early reviews of the film found Renoir's lament for the nobility and handing over of the future to honest ruffians and dubious Jews a rather troubling proposition. Jean Barreyre wrote in *Le Jour* in June 1937 that Renoir "seems to believe that the elites are not any longer good for anything, and that they would do best to get killed under fire. Instead, he directs his hopes toward a French democracy whose pure blood would only profit, according to him, from being stirred up by some admixtures of various oriental origins." After World War II, some reacted to the film in precisely the opposite manner, focusing both on the role of the "Jew" in the narrative and on the love affair between Maréchal and Elsa, the German equivalent of the salt of the earth. Georges Altman wrote in the *Franc-Tireur* in 1946:

> What a colossal lack of taste to invite the public to see again *The Grand Illusion*! We loved this film at the time, before the Nazi deluge and hell, when one allowed oneself to be taken in by a mirage, by yet another grand illusion: that of a sentimental pacifism.
> But one does not have the moral right, today, two years after the Wehrmacht, the SS and the ovens of the crematoria, to invoke art in order to demonstrate Franco-German friendship. The blood is too fresh. It is neither hate nor a narrow chauvinism that makes us express our astonishment and our indignation. It is memory.
> Every racism is first introduced in a mild form, as exemplified in the person of a Jewish soldier whose condition is magnanimously pardoned by Gabin. As if Nazism had not already poisoned the world enough![37]

Several years later, however, *The Grand Illusion* found its place in film criticism and in the public mind as a classical creation of interwar French cinema and as a great humanistic cry against the horror of war. And, indeed, Renoir's movie is all of that. But it also reflects—and not only opposes—some of the prejudices of its time, among which the figure of the "Jew," generally ignored in later writings on the film, is quite prominent. Already in 1958, André Bazin could write in *Le Parisien libéré* that Renoir

> offers us the most important social and moral truths without ever falling into [the trap of making] a thesis-driven film. And yet Renoir says precisely what he wants to say: classes divide men in reality much more than borders. But these divisions of class themselves cannot resist the need for comradeship and fraternity, and finally, if man cannot live without friendship, he can live even less without love.[38]

In notes about the film left behind after his death that same year, Bazin writes that the grand illusion "is that of hate, that which divides: war, class, frontiers," but "also, perhaps, the dreams that allow one to live: the desire to escape, women, manias." The genius of Renoir, he believes, is "to stake out a position not only without diminishing those who failed the test, but also by giving them the best opportunity and even a beautiful role (Boeldieu vis-à-vis Maréchal, Stroheim vis-à-vis Boeldieu: their comprehension joins them together)." Most important for Bazin, it seems, is "the theme of the aristocracy, explicit and implicit. The formal aristocracy and the popular aristocracy. The aristocracy of the heart."[39]

Thus, just over a decade after the end of the war, the entire issue of the representation of the "Jew" as one of the central stereotypes in *The Grand Illusion* more or less vanished. The juxtaposition of the "popular aristocracy" (Maréchal/Gabin) with the Jewish upstart who had taken over the châteaux, the hunting fields, even the ancestral paintings of the aristocracy of the blood, who had transformed himself into a Frenchman without ever shedding his obvious (and in this film not necessarily always negative) Jewish essence, is never mentioned. And yet, it hardly disappeared from postwar cinema.

In Harlan's *Jew Süss*, the cunning Oppenheimer tries to persuade Rabbi Loew to help him raise money from the Jews to finance the hiring of foreign soldiers by the duke. This would facilitate the establishment of an authoritarian rule controlled by the Jews. The duke—who eventually goes along with it—calls the plan to unleash mercenaries against his Swabians "a typical Jewish idea." Süss, for his part, clinches his case to the rabbi by reference to the Bible:

> It cannot be the will of the Lord to prevent me from making Wurttemberg into the Promised Land for Israel. It is already spread out before us. I only need to grasp it with my hand. And I already see how milk and honey

flow there—for Israel! So now, because of the Lord's will, I may not stretch my hand beyond the Jordan? Could that be the will of the Lord?[40]

Rabbi Loew observes quite rightly that while princes are pardoned for their mischief, the Jews get hanged. But eventually the mention of the Promised Land, which in this context means of course what he calls rule over the "goyim," wins the day. This concept of Israel's Promised Land was manipulated by the Nazis not only to turn the population against the Jews, but also to mislead both the Jews and outside observers about the actual nature and course of events. This is how the description of Terezín, or Theresienstadt, as a "privileged" ghetto constituting a sort of Promised Land for the Jews under Hitler's rule, came about. Indeed, the entire euphemistic edifice of Nazi terminology for the genocide of the Jews was built around this concept. The Jews were "resettled," first in ghettos, then, by way of endless and often lethal transports, in the death camps. The *Schlauch,* or hose, the narrow pathway that led to the gas chambers, was called the "path to heaven"; the process of cremating the bodies was said to accomplish the final goal of resettling the Jews in the sky. Everywhere across Europe the Jews were pressed into ever-narrower and more con-gested spaces. But the ultimate destination of the Jews was a unique Land of Promise given them graciously by the Führer, a final heavenly abode where, as the poet Paul Celan wrote in his *Death Fugue,* they would no longer be crowded.

Three decades after the end of World War II, however, the Polish direc-tor Andrzej Wajda made an extraordinary yet disturbing film called *Land of Promise* (*Ziemia obiecana*) (1974). By then Wajda was already the best-known postwar filmmaker in Poland, with an international reputation firmly built on his trilogy of films about Nazi-occupied Poland—*A Genera-tion* (1955), *Canal* (1957), and *Ashes and Diamonds* (1958)—to which some would also add *Lotna* (1959). His contribution to the collaborative film *Love at Twenty* (*L'amour a vingt ans*), with François Truffaut, Marcel Ophuls, and Shintaro Ishihara, exposed him to a large European audience. In-deed, Wajda became one of the most popular foreign directors in Western Europe, especially in France and Italy. Conversely, his film *Samson* (1961), which I will discuss in greater detail in chapter 3, showed his ability to focus also on the unique fate of Polish Jewry.

Wajda had worked early on in his career with the veteran Polish-Jewish filmmaker Aleksander Ford. In the immediate aftermath of the war, Ford's documentaries and feature films attempted both to depict the singularity of the Holocaust and to suggest active and heroic collaboration between the best elements of gentile Polish society and the Jews, often through fictionalized accounts of the Polish underground's assistance (in actuality, almost nonexistent) to the Jewish rebels of the Warsaw Ghetto.[41] Such themes indeed surface in Wajda's first film, *A Generation,* obviously influenced not only by Ford but also by the reigning political, ideological, and aesthetic conventions of Stalinism. By the time the film came out, however, Poland was undergoing a post-Stalinist thaw. This made it possible to deal with more sensitive issues, such as the Polish uprising of summer 1944— whose violent suppression was passively watched by the Red Army from the eastern bank of the Vistula until the Wehrmacht had completely destroyed the Polish nationalist and anti-communist underground. Similarly, one could now more openly confront the liberation of Poland by the Soviets, which many Poles experienced as merely a new kind of occupation. These are the main themes of *Canal* and *Ashes and Diamonds,* from which the Jews vanished entirely, as they in fact did also from the new Soviet-imposed conventions of representing the "Great Patriotic War." Here Wajda also introduced his favorite polarity of national heroism versus individual love and compassion, the willingness for sacrifice versus the meaninglessness of loss and death.[42]

Wajda was born as the son of a professional soldier in 1926 in the northeastern Polish town of Suwałki, which incidentally had at the time a significant Jewish population.[43] By the early 1970s he had made a large number of films, many of them based on literary works, some lyrical and personal, others using a large canvas to recreate past events in Polish history. Nevertheless, *Land of Promise* was something of a departure. Based on the epic nineteenth-century novel by Władysław Stanisław Reymont, *The Promised Land,* about the rapid industrialization of Lodz in the 1860s, the film presents three types, or stereotypes, of the major ethnic and religious groups in the region: the Catholic Poles, the Lutheran Germans, and the Jews.[44] Filmed on location in Lodz, where the mostly abandoned palatial factories and their owners' mansions were (and in part are) still standing, the movie has an especially realistic texture. Wajda could have also used the more recent history of this location to expand on the original novel and provide it with more contemporary meanings or allusions. Lodz was, of course, the birthplace of postwar Polish cinema, thanks to the relatively minor damage it suffered in the war as compared to Warsaw. But most poignantly, especially considering the narrative of *Land of Promise,* it was the site of the extinction of much of Poland's Jewish population, first in one of the most terrible ghettos under Nazi rule and then by murder in the extermination camps to which the ghetto's survivors were transported. Yet Wajda chose to stay close to the original novel. Moreover, he seems either to have been infected by or to have shared some of Reymont's nationalist and somewhat antisemitic inclinations which, while they reflected the sentiments of many Europeans in the late nineteenth century, were hardly absent from postwar Poland as well.

The main plot of *Land of Promise* revolves around the partnership between Karel Borowiecki (Daniel Olbrychski), an impoverished Polish nobleman, Maks Baum (Andrzej Seweryn), the ethnic-German son of a declining manufacturer, and Moryc Welt (Wojciech Pszoniak), a small-time Jewish entrepreneur. Pulling together their resources and talents, these three young men are hoping to build their own modern factory and thus profit from the industrialization boom that has taken a hold of Lodz. That this process also has to do with a great deal of misery among poor Polish workers, and entails tremendous corruption, speculation, and fraud, is vividly portrayed in the film. Historically, the Jews and the Germans indeed played a major role in the modernization of the city. Wajda, however, opens his film by sharply contrasting the wretched Polish industrial workers with the wealthy and greedy Jews, who begin handling money in their lavish rooms even as they are taking off their prayer shawls. Thus the basic relationship of the film is established. Borowiecki's father warns him: "You've sold your soul to the golden calf!" But the son, who embodies the handsome, elegant, charming but flippant nobleman, responds: "Breeding is claptrap." Breaking the bond of Polish tradition and blood, Borowiecki is drawn to Jewish speculation, greed, and quick riches. An inveterate womanizer, Karel is engaged to Anka (Anna Nehrebecka), a pious, gentle, sacrificing "white" woman, but is powerfully attracted to Lucy Zukerova (Kalina Jedrusik), the sensuous Jewish wife of a successful businessman. This fatal attraction ends up ruining the partnership and destroying their factory.

If Borowiecki is a typical Polish nobleman, Baum is a typical German. Heavy-set, serious, melancholy, and violent, he too is warned by his father to stick to the traditional ways of caring for one's workers and praying to God. Conversely, Welt is as worldly as his name (*"Welt"* means "world" in German, just as *"Baum"* means "tree," which is also a symbol of "the German" as rooted, strong, and ancient). The only *Weltmensch* or man with international connections among the three, Welt travels far to gain money for their enterprise, and helps them also borrow funds from other local Jewish entrepreneurs. He is the only one who does not seem to have any moral qualms about their undertaking. Generally harmless and likable, if somewhat sly and cowardly, Welt is stereotypically Jewish without appearing particularly insidious.

The lecherous Jewess (*Land of Promise*): The Jewish Lucy Zukerova having a feast before seducing the impoverished nobleman Karel Borowiecki. Meanwhile, her jealous husband burns down the factory built by Karel and his Jewish and German partners.

What gives this film its most disturbing twist is rather the relationship between Borowiecki and Zukerova. Reversing the roles assigned to sexual temptation in *Jew Süss,* here it is the Jewish temptress who brings ruin to everyone. In an extended scene on a train, Lucy feasts both on a lavish dinner and on her handsome lover, Karel. As she devours both with almost animal relish, her ample body heaves over the Pole's wiry, muscular torso. He has been corrupted by her, and has betrayed his fiancée, his blood, and his partners, even as his business venture was similarly a capitulation to Jewish greed. Meanwhile, Lucy's husband takes revenge on her lover by torching the newly built factory. Thus what was built with Jewish greed is destroyed by Jewish vengeance, and the soul that was sold to the Jewish golden calf is finally corrupted by Jewish lust.

This is not to say that Wajda had an antisemitic intention in making *Land of Promise*. Rather, he bought into certain stereotypical notions of race and culture, tradition and modernity, piety and corruption, authenticity and transformation. Clearly the film makes a contrast between the Jew as a rootless *Weltmensch* and upstart (seen also in the gaudy jewelry and dresses of the philistine Jewish wives of newly enriched industrialist husbands, who still behave like typical shtetl "Yids") and the dignified but decaying and

26

eventually corruptible Polish nobility. The Pole must enter the world of business in order to survive, yet doing so leads to his degeneration. He must leave the country estate, which is his "natural" abode, and go to the city, the site of poverty and exploitation, of rootlessness and foreignness, of everything that is essentially un-Polish. Here the Jew is central. Reminiscent of the rabbi's daughter and the knight in *The Golem*, here the Jewish woman sucks the lifeblood of the Polish aristocrat and distracts him from tradition and loyalty—to his father, his estate, his fiancée, his faith. Food, sex, and money replace the deeper and vital ties to the land, to the family, to blood, and to God. That this must end in disaster is a foregone conclusion.

Wajda's final scene, probably more a gesture to the communist authorities than an inherent part of the narrative, in which Borowiecki, now completely in the clutches of capitalism, orders the soldiers to open fire on striking workers, only strengthens the notion that Jewish corruption has broken the deep tie between the Polish aristocracy and the people. Here is, finally, antisemitism as social realism. In a certain sense, this kind of cinematic "Jew" is more disturbing than its more intentional and overt versions. As is common in such films, it is based both on a work of fiction and on a historical past, distorting the past and forgetting some of its most crucial episodes. If *Jew Süss* was made while the Jews were driven into ghettos, *Land of Promise* was made a few decades after Poland's "Jewish question" had been "solved" by the Nazis, with a fair amount of cooperation from the locals. What remained of the Jews were the stereotypes. A few decades later still, at the end of the twentieth and the beginning of the twenty-first century, Poland has been swept by a revived fascination with its Jewish past. Yet the stereotype of the "Jew," whether as a black-and-white figure with caftan and beard or as a capitalist rolling in money, has hardly disappeared from the scene, even if now it is hoped that nostalgia for the former will generate much-needed investments from the latter.[45]

[2]

ALIEN PRESENCE

In Michał Waszynski's *The Dybbuk* (1937), the wedding celebration of Sender's daughter Leah (Lili Liliana) culminates in a terrifying *Totentanz*, featuring a figure wearing a death mask. As is the custom in Leah's shtetl, this dance is performed in the town square, next to a tombstone that commemorates the death of another wedding couple: two centuries earlier, a bride and groom were killed by the Cossacks of Bohdan Khmel'nyts'kyi, just as they were being led to the canopy.[1] As the dance progresses, the skull face of death is transformed into that of Khonon (Leon Liebgold), the young man whose intense love for Leah had robbed him of his life and transformed him into a dybbuk that will cling to her soul. These events take place in Galicia of the 1860s, a period in which the gradual decline of the traditional Jewish way of life in the Pale of Settlement paralleled the rise of a new Jewish entrepreneurial sector further west, as in the Polish city of Lodz of that time (recreated in Andrzej Wajda's *Land of Promise*). This was also the beginning of the era of classic Yiddish literature most closely identified with Mendele Mocher Sforim (1835–1917), Sholem Aleichem (1859–1916), and I. L. Peretz (1852–1915). These years of upheaval, creativity, and destruction, were mirrored in the lives and works of Jewish writers of the time. S. Ansky, the author of *The Dybbuk,* the extraordinary play on which the film is based, was born in 1863 in Vitebsk, the largely Jewish town that also produced Marc Chagall (1887–1985) and served as the model for his nostalgic, dreamlike paintings that subsequently came to represent the "typical" shtetl in the popular imagination.[2]

On the face of it, Ansky's play and Waszynski's film present the Jewish maiden as possessed by an evil spirit that must be exorcized by a "wonder" rabbi. Moreover, the Jews in this tale seem to be victims of superstition and communal social injustice, just as they are also haunted by memories of persecution and massacre. Told entirely from a Jewish perspective, in *The Dybbuk* the "Jew" seems to be the victim of an alien presence, just as in *The Golem* the "Jew" is the maker of a destructive, alien being. In *Jew Süss*—whose perspective is that of gentile society—it is the "Jew" himself who is the alien presence that must be exorcized. In fact, however, both Ansky and Waszynski were trying to resurrect the customs, legends, dances, and melodies of a rapidly vanishing culture, during a time when the shtetl was reeling under the combined impact of modernization, nationalism, war, and discrimination.[3]

Ansky began his life as Shloyme-Zanvl ben Aaron Hacohen Rappoport in Vitebsk, the heartland of Habad Hasidism and a stronghold of Orthodox Judaism. As a young author, Rappoport turned against that world with a vengeance. Describing the "typical" Jewish family as an economically and morally defunct institution in his early Yiddish writings and then discarding *yiddishkayt* altogether, Rappoport spent several years working in a Ukrainian mine, where he changed his name to the Russian-sounding Semyon Akimovich. Not long thereafter he resurfaced as a Russian-language writer for a leading populist journal in St. Petersburg, signing his contributions now as S. A. An-ski, later converted to S. Ansky. But after reading Peretz's collected works in 1901, Ansky decided to abandon his adopted Russian language, in which he felt by now much more comfortable, and to return to Yiddish. Indeed, during 1912–1914 he led the Jewish Ethnographic Expedition, which aimed to collect and preserve Jewish culture. What had initially seemed to him as a decaying and moribund world was now perceived as the wellspring of all future Jewish creativity. World War I, however, not only put an end to the expedition, but also struck a lethal blow at Jewish life in the vast swath of land straddling the old empires where much of Europe's Jewry was concentrated.

It was with these events in mind that Ansky conceived and wrote *The Dybbuk.* This work is not simply an exercise in nostalgia in the midst of endless conflict and ruin. Ansky's play, and Waszynski's cinematic rendition of it, turns the conventions of tradition and religion on their head. For the dybbuk here is not an evil spirit but the finest spiritual expression of love: Khonon dies for Leah and lives within her, and Leah prefers to die with him inside her rather than live without him. The zaddik, or Hasidic sage, of Miropolye loses the battle against youthful, innocent, and pure love, and the rich father's refusal to marry his daughter to a poor lad—despite the vow he had made to Khonon's father even before their children were born—ends in disaster.

This then, is a tale of multiple metamorphoses over which the shadow of catastrophe increasingly looms. Ansky, who abandoned his Jewish identity to seek the freer air of cosmopolitan secular life, returns to find and rescue the very roots of that culture as it is being torn asunder. He is a "wandering Jew," a man of many names and faces, who lives, as the subtitle of *The Dybbuk* suggests, "between two worlds"; at the same time, he is the preserver of that very same *yiddishkayt* he had so ruefully savaged in his youth. Ansky created the Jewish Ethnographic Museum in Petrograd, from which he eventually fled when it was impounded by the Bolsheviks. Just like their author, so too the protagonists of *The Dybbuk* travel "between two worlds" through acts of physical and spiritual metamorphosis. Khonon turns himself into a dybbuk so that he can enter Leah; Leah becomes his lover by dying with him in her; the traditional evil spirit becomes the distillation of pure devotion; and the crumbling world of the shtetl is transformed into a universe still capable of great spirituality. The zaddik, the holy man who ought to be worshipped as a high priest (or feared as the evil sorcerer of antisemitic lore), is transformed into a mystical figure in the tradition of Nahman of Bratslav (1772–1810), who propounded faith in an absent God and declared that "every word which a person speaks from his heart is God's name."

This dramatic, complex, and poetic self-representation of Jewish life and culture, which initially appears to depict a distant, almost mythical past, is closely related to the historical reality in which it was conceived. Completed shortly before Ansky's death in 1920 and performed soon thereafter by the Vilna Troupe at a time of great turmoil and devastation, *The Dybbuk* is arguably the most popular and controversial Jewish play ever written. Waszynski's Yiddish classic was filmed on location in Poland and relied heavily on the Vilna Troupe's production. Habimah, the repertory company founded in Moscow in 1917, performed the play in a Hebrew translation no less than 869 times in the first twenty-eight years of its existence.[4] Its staging in Palestine was the occasion of an intellectual "trial" as early as 1926.[5] With its fine combination of diverse elements—myth and psychology, social criticism and ethnographic reconstruction, rejection of stereotypes and insistence on the overwhelming power of love, and, perhaps most importantly, its focus on the transformation of identity and the blurring of the boundaries between life and death—*The Dybbuk* is at the very center of Jewish self-presentation in an era of transition on a vast scale. It is also, of course, a major point of reference in any discussion concerning representations of the "Jew," represented variously as a timeless spiritual entity, a nostalgic memory, and an ill-understood but keenly felt absence, or as an eternal demonic power, a reminder of horror, and an insidious, destructive presence.[6]

The same years that produced modern Yiddish and Hebrew literature, a great flowering of Jewish culture, an enormous wave of emigration and assimilation, and the beginnings of Zionism also saw the birth and rapid spread of modern antisemitism. The flourishing of Jewish culture and rise of antisemitism are of course closely linked. Jewish self-representations were often critical as well as loving, perhaps filled with self-hate but no less with longing for a more certain past. They were also closely related to antisemitic representations of the "Jew," serving as a model for the latter and borrowing from its logic and modes of expression.[7] This connection between the "Jew" as perpetrator in antisemitic representations and the "Jew" as victim, in both Jewish and non-Jewish representations, is as intriguing as it is complex. Zionism drew on the antisemitic portrayal of the Jewish "condition" in the Diaspora as "unnatural" in order to justify its claim for a "normalization" of Jewish existence in an independent state.[8] Jewish socialists believed that only the dictatorship of the proletariat would liberate the Jews from their social and cultural malaise and eliminate their status as religious and socioeconomic outsiders.[9] Isaac Babel (1894–1940), who came from Odessa, that other great center of Jewish life in pre–World War I Russia, joined the Revolution's Red Cavalry and rode with its Cossacks into the devastated Pale of Settlement only to realize that for such "typical" shtetl Jews as his protagonist Gedali, the Revolution made very little difference. Whether Red Bolsheviks or White monarchists, Russians or Poles, the armies slaughtered, raped, burned, and razed thousands of Jewish communities in Galicia. Babel's dream of a brave new world was drowned in an ocean of blood. In 1939 Babel himself was arrested, and the following year he was executed the day after he was convicted in a twenty-minute trial of "active participation in an anti-Soviet Trotskyite organization" and of "being a member of a terrorist conspiracy, as well as spying for the French and Austrian governments."[10]

Babel's Gedali was resurrected in the figure of Vasily Grossman's Yefim, the protagonist of Grossman's early short story, "In the Town of Berdichev" (1934), on which Alexandr Askoldov's film *The Commissar* is based.[11] This extraordinary Soviet film, shot in 1967 but completed and screened only in the wake of Glasnost in 1988, could hardly have been to the liking of the authorities, not merely because it casts a critical gaze on the Revolution's heroic period, but more specifically because it focuses on the humanization of a ruthless female commissar, who is taken in by a wretchedly poor Jewish family to secretly deliver her illegitimate baby during a brief pause in the fighting of the Civil War. Grossman, who was born in 1905 to a Yiddish-speaking Jewish family in Berdichev, visited Ukraine immediately after its devastation by the Germans in World War II and the almost total destruction of its Jewish population. The film links the horrors witnessed by Grossman in 1944 to the desolation of the Civil War in 1917–1919 by way of a hallucinatory scene suggesting the future extermination of the Holocaust on the eve of an approaching pogrom by the Whites.[12] In this world turned upside down, the only haven of human emotion, compassion, and love is the home of Yefim Magazanik (Rolan Bykov), his wife Mariya (Raisa Nedaskovskaya), his mother (Ludmila Volynskaya), and their six children, into which Klavdia Vavilova (Nonna Morduvka) steps in as a uniformed commissar and where she is transformed into a loving and vulnerable mother, only to leave her newborn baby behind and march back to the front.[13]

Yefim embodies the "typical" shtetl Jew, melancholy yet always ready to dance and sing, fearful yet stubborn, resentful but hospitable, hardworking yet playful, devoted to his family but alienated from national and international politics. These traits of the shtetl Jew appear in countless films—the gestures, expressions, physical appearance, manners of speech, moods, and humor. They appear already, for instance, in the figure of Menachem Mendel, the protagonist of the classic film *Jewish Luck* (1925). Shot in Moscow with the actors of the Moscow Yiddish State Art Theater, headed by Solomon Mikhoels (who plays Menachem Mendel, and whose murder in 1948 initiated Stalin's antisemitic campaign), it is based on Sholem Aleichem's eponymous story. Menachem Mendel is the archetype of the poor Jew of Yiddish lore, striving to eke out a living under the most trying conditions, pursued by the authorities, spurned by his own folk, using every trick and stratagem to find his fortune, and always rising up again after a hard fall, brushing off the dust and starting afresh. The very same figure, however, both loved and ridiculed by Jewish writers and readers, became a staple of antisemitic representations. And, in yet another curious transformation, this type resurfaced in postwar philosemitic rep-

The Jewish Jew (*Jewish Luck*): Solomon Mikhoels as Menachem Mendel, in this silent film shot in 1925 with a cast from the Moscow Yiddish State Art Theater. Mikhoels, who directed the troupe, was murdered by orders of Stalin in 1948 as part of the Soviet dictator's antisemitic campaign.

resentations of the "Jew," intended both to empathize with his fate and to show how different and unique this now long-vanished species used to be.

In Grossman's film, Yefim is also a philosopher, whose views on the world are strikingly similar to those of Babel's Gedali. Witness the conversation between Yefim and Klavdia as they hide in the cellar to escape the bombardment of the town by the Whites:

> YEFIM: I'm for the International of kindness. There are so few kind people in the world. Maybe someday Jews will be able to live in peace, and the Pale of Settlement won't run through the middle of their basement.[14]

> MARIYA: Be quiet. You'll frighten the children.

> YEFIM: Let me finish. All your life it's like this: You are either hiding or burying someone or being buried yourself—never any time to talk to people. You tell me, Comrade Commissar, why is it like this: You remember what an outcry there was when the English attacked the Boers? And the grieving when the Turks massacred the Armenians? But who will say a word if a Jew, Yefim, is dead tomorrow?[15]

33

KLAVDIA: Who told you that fairy tale about the International of kindness? The foundation of the International Community consists of workers' and peasants' blood. This struggle makes people very grim and hard. Fighting, marching, lice! Lice, marching, fighting! Makes your head swim.

YEFIM: Leave people without fairy tales and what will they live for?

KLAVDIA: It's not fairy tales they need, it's truth and justice. Which is worth dying for if need be!

YEFIM: Dying? And when is one to live?

KLAVDIA: You are a good man, Yefim, but you are not class conscious. We'll live, all right! And we will build a world of working fellowship!

YEFIM: You are tired, Klavdia.

KLAVDIA: Yes, I'm tired.[16]

Yefim, then, combines the traditional Yiddish figure of the shtetl Jew with the Jewish philosopher of socialist Jewish writers. These philosopher characters were disenchanted with the Soviet experiment and pleaded for kindness in the whirlpool of the battle for justice. To them, the Yefims and Gedalis of the world provided a certain kind of insight, a humanizing effect, on the harsh and merciless reality of the Revolution. Instead, of course, the shtetl Jews were ground to dust in the titanic struggle between Stalinism and Nazism. Yefim is a persuasive figure because he contains within himself the experience and wisdom of Babel and Grossman. At the same time, for Askoldov, who is not Jewish, Yefim serves to criticize Soviet society. By giving a face and a soul to one of the Revolution's innumerable accidental victims, Askoldov criticizes the society's drab and humorless reality and its distorted heroic narratives of the past that block any effort at humanizing the present.[17]

ONE OF US

On the other extreme of the ideological divide, Hollywood's early attempts to come to grips with the "Jew" as victim were both cautious and innovative. American filmmakers in the 1940s had to be aware of a lingering antisemitism in their society, which increased substantially during World War II. Despite the fact that the United States was fighting a racist and antisemitic regime—and in a certain sense precisely because of it—American politicians, Jewish community leaders, and filmmakers needed to avoid the impression that "our boys" were fighting and dying "just" for

The communist as Jewish mother (*The Commissar*): Commissar Klavdia Vavilova, having given birth to an illegitimate child at a Jewish home in war-torn Ukraine during the Russian Civil War, wanders into a destroyed synagogue. She then leaves the baby with the Jewish family to rejoin the Red Army, as the advancing White Armies prepare another pogrom.

the Jews. Hence, there was a perceived need to shun an excessive emphasis on the ongoing genocide of European Jewry.[18] Furthermore, the notion that the Jews controlled Hollywood was hardly new and certainly played a role in determining cinematic representations of the "Jew."[19]

Nevertheless, especially in the early postwar years, and before the onset of McCarthyism, Hollywood made some remarkable films on this topic. In this unique historical moment, some filmmakers were keenly aware both of the persistence of prejudice and of the awful toll of such sentiments in Europe. Thus, they sought ways of overcoming the stereotype of the "Jew" without ignoring the phenomenon of discrimination and segregation altogether. Rather than presenting antisemitism as a foreign disease, which could easily be seen as another despicable aspect of German culture and "nature," Hollywood focused instead on prejudice within American society. To be sure, the association of the genocide of the Jews with Nazism made criticism of antisemitism more palatable to American viewers, without necessarily influencing attitudes toward women, African Americans, or homosexuals. Still, these early cinematic ventures may have prepared the way for a more extensive preoccupation with other minorities and disadvantaged groups. With a few outstanding exceptions, however, soon thereafter Hollywood slipped back into its conventional presentation of stereotypes, even if the ascribed moral and physical qualities of these types were undergoing profound changes. Thus, the condemnation of prejudice could go hand-in-hand with the assumption of essential racial, cultural, and gender differences.

Vincent Sherman's *Mr. Skeffington* (1944) is among Hollywood's very first attempts to deal with antisemitism. Considering that it was made just as the genocide of the Jews in Europe had reached its climax, this is hardly a powerful portrayal of the deadly effects of prejudice and racism. Rather, the film is the tale of "Fanny" Beatrice Trellis (Bette Davis), a much sought-after woman, who decides to marry Job Skeffington (Claude Rains), a successful Jewish businessman, so as to save the reputation of Trippy (Richard Waring), her bankrupt and corrupt brother. Trippy, however, feels so humiliated by his sister's marriage to a Jew that he volunteers to fight in World War I and is killed. Job adores his wife and their daughter, but Fanny resumes a life of endless affairs until Job decides to try his luck in Germany. Not long thereafter, Job finds himself incarcerated in a Nazi concentration camp (we hear about this only indirectly), and Fanny is terribly ravaged by a grave illness. When Job returns to the United States, impoverished and blind (and thus unable to see her lost beauty), Fanny finally takes him back and they apparently live happily ever after.

Apart from Trippy's overt antisemitism—which is shown in a bad light by the very fact that Trippy had stolen money from Skeffington—there are no other obvious indications of American prejudice against Jews in the film. That Job is a Jew can be surmised, however, from his foreignness: he wears a thin black moustache and speaks with a vaguely un-American accent. On the one hand, his patriotism is as explicit as the huge stuffed eagle in his office; on the other hand, when his marriage breaks down he heads back to his presumed homeland, Germany. Yet even there he is treated abysmally for reasons never made clear in the movie. He is a perfectly correct businessman, but obviously he does not belong to Fanny's social circle. Upright and generous, he seems to lack any sense of humor or a capacity to enjoy life, and exudes a certain air of quiet arrogance based on his financial success. Claude Rains's melancholy, dark, handsome face in this film somehow echoes the villainous roles for which he was well known.

The film, of course, is not about Job Skeffington but about the rise and fall of the socialite Fanny. But it is interesting that, while the film attempts to portray the "Jew" as the most positive character in the cast, Job remains an outsider, despite the fact that by his own account he was actually born in the United States. And while he supposedly exemplifies the American ideal of rags to riches, he also seems as socially awkward as any typical arriviste. Hardly a Süss Oppenheimer, he nevertheless manages to penetrate the elite circles of American society and to win over the woman that everyone is after by his sheer persistence and wealth. In other words, *Mr. Skeffington,* as the foreign-sounding name of its male protagonist indicates, is an early attempt to show the "Jew" in a good light, but it is also suffused with traditional anti-Jewish prejudices that assume an essential difference between Jews and non-Jews, even when the former are portrayed as perfectly decent individuals.

This simplistic portrayal of the "Jew" is completely transformed in the first of the two best American films made on the issue of antisemitism in the late 1940s. Whereas Mr. Skeffington is a distinctly "Jewish" character played by a British-born actor,[20] in Elia Kazan's *Gentleman's Agreement* (1947), strikingly handsome and all-American Gregory Peck plays Phil Schuyler Green, a successful journalist newly arrived in New York, who effortlessly passes as a Jew simply by asserting his identity and dropping his middle name (he also adds the name Greenberg on his mailbox, despite his janitor's complaints). Brilliantly written and played, the movie confronts two central issues concerning the social role of antisemitism and its cinematic representation. First, it vividly portrays the effects of stereotypes. Asked to write about antisemitism, Phil concludes that his best angle on the subject would be to pose as a Jew himself. Once he does so, everyone's behavior toward him changes. Second, it demonstrates the subtle effects of discrimination. Only as a "Jew" can Phil perceive the ways in which prejudice affects his and his family's lives and his interactions with friends, with his lover, and with his colleagues, be they Jewish or gentile. And yet he assumes no "Jewish" characteristics. The simple declaration of his Jewishness suffices, and everyone begins to perceive his imaginary Jewish traits.

To be sure, the film itself is not entirely free of stereotypes. Phil's best friend, Dave Golden, who is "really" Jewish (played by the Jewish actor John Garfield, who was born Julius Garfinkle to poor immigrants in New York's Lower East Side), exhibits the traits of a bitter outsider that moviegoers would have associated with his origins.[21] Phil's secretary, who reveals her "true" Jewish identity to him only after she discovers that he is a Jew, turns out to be prejudiced herself, especially about Jews who behave too much according to type. Moreover, it is again striking that a film made only two years after the fall of Nazism makes so little reference to the genocide of European Jewry, compared to which the phenomenon of "restricted" hotels common in certain part of the United States at the time seems hardly worth mentioning. Nevertheless, the great achievement of *Gentleman's Agreement* is that it exposes the supposedly hidden, and yet—for those willing to look or directly affected—entirely transparent face of

exclusion, marginalization, and humiliation that makes up social prejudice. What perpetuates this phenomenon is not the actively bigoted minority but the predilection of the majority to look the other way. The film
also hints, although rather weakly, that such social mechanisms can turn
into ugly and perhaps murderous policies.

Making the heroically handsome Peck into a Jew both strengthens and
weakens the film. In some ways, it indicates the persistent problem of
representing a character type without resorting to stereotypes. For if Peck
can be a Jew, then there is no telling who is and who is not—a conclusion
that can be either comforting or disturbing depending on one's perspective. But since we know that Peck is actually not a Jew (in the film and in
real life), and the only other important figure who is a Jew (in the film and
in real life) is also transparently Jewish, then we must ask whether the
movie ultimately resolves the problem it set out to confront or ultimately
evades it. Indeed, if we accept Jean-Paul Sartre's view that the Jew is only
the product of the antisemite's gaze, then Green/Peck is the perfect example of this phenomenon: he exists as a Jew only as long as he asserts that
he is one and is consequently treated as such by his environment.[22] But
then we still have to resolve the role of Golden/Garfield/Garfinkle, who is
a Jew without ever asserting it, "simply" because he is, always was, and has
always been treated as one. We also have to remember that at the end of the
movie, indeed, facilitating its happy end, Phil switches out of his role as a
Jew and reverts to what he "really" is, which is "simply" a non-Jew. His
"normalization" is a relief both to the audience and to his lover. While she
reluctantly accepted the game he played—posing as a Jew to unearth the
"invisible" antisemitism that surrounded him—it is only when he transforms himself back into his former, "natural" identity, that everything is
resolved: the tall, handsome Peck will marry the perfect WASP, Kathy
Lacey (Dorothy McGuire), but they will also now turn against the kinds of
manifestations of prejudice they had previously ignored.

This inner conflict in the film, between representing the "Jew" as a
figment of the bigot's imagination and arguing that the experience of
being a Jew can only be understood and felt from within, is built into some
of the lecture-like dialogues. While these lines provide the film with rhetorical strength, they also constitute an elaborate evasion of the fundamental contradiction between these two perspectives. This evasion begins
early on in the film, with Phil's explanation of prejudice to his son, Tom:

TOM: What's antisemitism?

PHIL: Oh, it's where some people don't like other people because they're
Jews.

TOM: Why, are they bad?

PHIL: Some are, sure, some aren't. It's just like everybody else.

TOM: What are Jews, anyway? I mean exactly.

PHIL: Remember last week when you asked me about that big church, I told you there were a lot of different churches? Well, the people who go to that particular church are called Catholics, you see. Then there are those who go to different churches and they are called Protestants. And there are people who go to still different ones and they are called Jews, only they call their churches synagogues or temples.

TOM: So why don't some people like those?

PHIL: That's kind of a tough one to explain. Some people don't like Catholics and sure hate Jews.

TOM: And no one hates us because we are Americans.

PHIL: No, no, that's another thing again. See, you can be an American and a Catholic, an American and a Protestant, or an American and a Jew. Look, Tommy, it's like this. One thing's your country, like America, or France, or Germany, or Russia, all of the countries. The flag is different, the uniform is different, the language is different. . . . But the other thing is religion, like the Jewish, or the Catholic, or the Protestant religion. . . . Don't ever get mixed up on it.[23]

Of course, one might forgive Tom if he did get mixed up. Explaining in 1947 that the only difference between Jews and Christians was their religion not only flew in the face of recent events in Europe but also contradicted the deep anti-Jewish prejudices in the United States, which were based on stereotypes of physical appearance and conduct. After all, when Phil "becomes" a Jew, he does not pretend to have any religious affiliation whatsoever. We never see him in a synagogue. He simply says he is a Jew and everyone ascribes to him the requisite moral and physical qualities, although he may look and behave "better" than other Jews, as his secretary believes. Indeed, when Phil is racking his brain how to write an original analysis of what many already consider the worn-out topic of antisemitism, it occurs to him that he might ask his childhood friend Dave Golden what he feels "about this thing." As he tells his mother:

Over and above how we feel about it, what must a Jew feel about the thing? Dave! Can I think my way into Dave's mind? He's the kind of fellow I'd be if I were a Jew, isn't he? We grew up together, we lived in the same kind of homes, we were the gang, we did everything together. Whatever Dave feels now, indifference, outrage, contempt, would be the feelings of Dave not only as a Jew but the way I feel, as a man, as an American, as a citizen, isn't that right, Mom?[24]

39

To be sure, in order to provide this "view from within," one might have produced a film about Dave, not Phil. But Kazan was probably right in assuming that the only way to reach the audience was to create a faux-Jew, that is, someone like themselves, "a man, an American, a citizen," who nevertheless experiences antisemitism. Thus Phil quickly realizes that he cannot simply ask Dave to report about his experiences:

> Now what do I say? What do I say? Dear Dave, give me the rundown on your guts when you hear about . . . calling people Kikes. How do you feel when you hear about Jewish kids getting their teeth kicked out by Jew-haters in New York City? Could you write that kind of letter, Ma? No, it's no good, all of it. Wouldn't be any good if I could write it. There isn't any way you can tear open the heart of another human being, Ma, you know that.[25]

Again, it is extraordinary that in 1947, when speaking of what it feels like being a Jew, no one bothers to mention that several million Jews had just been exterminated and that this genocide came to an end at least in part because the United States defeated Germany. But not only is the historical context entirely ignored, or rather intentionally suppressed, but also the solution that Phil finds for his own author's dilemma, seemingly so obvious, entirely ignores his own statement that one cannot simply assume another identity. When he says: "I'll become Jewish!" he knows that he will gain a certain insight into prejudice as it is experienced by those subjected to it. But he also simplifies the issue for himself and for the viewers. As he says to his mother:

> Well, all I've got to do is say it. Nobody knows me around here. I can just say it. I can live it myself for six weeks, eight weeks, nine months, no matter how long it takes.[26]

Phil even comes up with the title right away: "I Was Jewish for Six Months," although the final article he produces is titled, "I Was Jewish for Eight Weeks." Anything longer than that, it seems, would have caused irreparable damage to his stormy relationship with Kathy, who is torn between the lingering antisemitism of her New England circle and her love for Phil.[27] Examining his image in the mirror, Phil comments:

> Dark hair, dark eyes, sure, so is Dave, so are a lot of guys who aren't Jewish. No accent, no mannerisms, neither has Dave. . . . Name Phil Green. Skip the Schuyler. Might be anything.[28]

If a gentile can switch into a Jewish identity and then switch right out of it again, can a Jew also switch out of *his* identity? And if he or she can switch, should they? What are the implications of such transformations—do they expose a reality of persecution or conceal a reality of identity? If all Jews

The non-Jew as voluntary Jew (*Gentleman's Agreement*): "Face me now, Miss
Wales, look at me! Same face, same eyes, same nose, same suit, same
everything." This is Phil Green's Shylock-like soliloquy to his outraged Jewish
secretary after he reveals to her that he had merely posed as a Jew to get an
insider's view for an article on antisemitism.

were like Phil, would there still be antisemitism? Is there also room for a
Jew who *does* look "like a Jew"?

In a final conversation between Phil and his secretary, Miss Elaine Wales
(formerly Esthel Wilkowski, as she reveals to him when he "comes out" as
a Jew), she is outraged to find out his "real" identity:

> WALES: Why, Mr. Green, you're a Christian! But, I never . . . But I'd been
> around you more than anybody else, one saw . . .

> PHIL: What's so upsetting about that, Miss Wales? You mean there is some
> difference between Jews and Christians? Look at me, look at me hard.
> I'm the same man I was yesterday. That's true, isn't it? Why should you be
> so astonished, Miss Wales? You still can't believe that anybody would give
> up the glory of being Christian for even eight weeks, can you? If I tell you
> that that's antisemitism, your feeling that being Christian is better than
> being Jewish, you're going to tell me that I'm heckling you again, that I'm
> twisting your words around, or that it's just facing the facts. As someone
> else said to me yesterday. Face me now, Miss Wales, look at me! Same face,
> same eyes, same nose, same suit, same everything. Here, take my hand,
> feel it, same flesh as yours, isn't it? No different today than it was yester-
> day, Miss Wales. The only thing that's different is the word "Christian."[29]

41

This is the rub. For the film actually demonstrates that it *was* better to be a Christian than a Jew in late 1940s America. It shows that the predilection of Jews at that time to change their names and their ways and to look as American as everybody else was indeed a matter of "facing the facts." This was not about accepting the argument of antisemites that being a Christian was superior to being a Jew, but conceding the social reality that dictated such superiority. Indeed, the film won't even come close to a more traditional Jewish defense mechanism, the claim of innate Jewish superiority (sanctioned in the biblical notion of the Chosen People), which compensates for the reality of social and political inferiority. The difference between Miss Wales and Kathy (who also blames Phil for refusing to face the facts) is that Miss Wales had to change her name and conceal her identity so as to get a job (at the "great liberal magazine that fights injustice on all sides" for which Phil is writing), while Kathy wants to hold on to her social superiority and is troubled by undermining it through association with Jews. This is why Phil's variation on the theme of Shylock, claiming that as a Christian he looks no less Jewish than he does as a Jew, rings a little hollow to us, as it probably did to Miss Wales. While for him this identity transformation is the tool to write a powerful article about the persecution of Jews, for Jews such a transformation is the only way to escape prejudice and move up the social ladder.

If the "Jew" in *Gentleman's Agreement* is in fact a non-Jew, the "Jew" in Edward Dmytryk's *Crossfire*, another powerful film made in 1947, is merely an object of violence who has only a passing "real" existence. Indeed, while Joseph Samuels (Sam Levene) is the victim of bigotry in this movie, the book that inspired the film, *The Brick Foxhole*, which was itself based on an actual event, concerns the murder of a homosexual.[30] *Crossfire* is a well-directed, taut film noir that combines excellent acting with an exceptionally good script. Samuels is murdered in a hotel suite after having drinks in a bar with several marines. Finding no direct motive for the killing, police captain Finley (Robert Young), helped by marine sergeant Keeley (Robert Mitchum), tracks down Monty (Robert Ryan), another marine whose violent antisemitism is shown to have been the only motivation for the murder of a man he did not even know.

In some ways, *Crossfire* has affinities with *Gentleman's Agreement*. The main characters are all non-Jews, and the issue of antisemitism is seen very much from the outside rather than through the prism of those subjected to it. In *Gentleman's Agreement*, the effects of antisemitism are mainly social, and the promoters of this sentiment are the bigoted few supported by the indifferent majority. In *Crossfire*, the consequences of antisemitism are more serious, leading to murder, but the sentiment is held in an extreme form only by apparent psychopaths such as Monty, who are allowed to exist because of their ignorant or indifferent environment. Here too not a word is said about the recent genocide of the Jews, nor about America's role in defeating Nazism, whose leader, after all, was the greatest antisemitic psychopath in history. And, once more, antisemitism is made understandable to the audience by translating it into terms of other types of bigotry and prejudice, such as the earlier hatred of Catholic Irish immigrants. Nevertheless, *Crossfire* is superior to *Gentleman's Agreement,* both because it is never distracted from its major theme of a hate crime and also because its combination of suspense and psychological drama helps viewers penetrate the world of violence and hate that is at the core of racism and antisemitism, rather than relegating it to mere social exclusion and offensive humor.

Finley's insight is based on a single conversation with Monty early on in the film about meeting Samuels in the bar:

> MONTY: I've seen a lot of guys like him.
>
> FINLEY: Like what?
>
> MONTY: Oh, you know. Guys that played it safe during the war. Scrounged around. Keeping themselves in civvies. Got swell apartments. Swell dames. You know the kind.
>
> FINLEY: I'm not sure that I do. Just what kind?
>
> MONTY: Oh, you know, some of them are named Samuels, some of them got funnier names.[31]

To be sure, when Finley checks Samuels's record (mainly for the benefit of the film's viewers), he discovers that the man was discharged on August 28, 1945, for wounds received in Okinawa. But the "Jew" in this film is not a war hero. Instead, he is an anonymous victim who is killed merely for his identity. This is how Finley explains his insight to Keeley:

> I look for motives. . . . But I couldn't find it. . . . None of these men had known Samuels long enough to have one. . . . So it had to be inside the killer himself. Something he brought with him. Something he's been nursing for a long time. Something that had been waiting. The killer had to be someone who could hate Samuels without knowing him. Who could hate enough to kill him, under the right circumstances, not for any real reason but mistakenly and ignorantly? The rest wasn't too hard. . . . I knew who killed Samuels. I should have known right away, I guess, but the motive was so simple, so general, that it slipped through the machinery.

The Jew as anonymous victim (*Crossfire*): Joseph Samuels, a war veteran, shortly before being murdered by two marines he has just met in a bar, who kill him solely for the reason of being a Jew (or, in the original story, for being gay).

There is a danger that viewers would believe that such deadly hatred was reserved only for Jews (some filmgoers in 1947 may have still remembered the Nazi death camps), and that they might even think that nobody who is hated so fiercely can be entirely innocent (which is of course the old anti-semitic logic). This assumption is neatly addressed when Finley speaks of his own grandfather's murder to a skeptical young marine from Tennessee:

> Thomas Finley was murdered in 1848 just because he was an Irishman and a Catholic. It happened many times. . . . And last night Joseph Samuels was killed just because he was a Jew. . . . Hating is always the same. Always senseless. One day it kills Irish Catholics, the next day it kills Jews, the next day Protestants, the next day Quakers, it's got to stop, it can end up killing men who wear striped neckties, or people from Tennessee.

Thus *Crossfire* exposes an explosive charge that was at the heart of American society in the aftermath of World War II. Having fought against a racist and genocidal regime, the United States was polluted by the racism, bigotry, and violence of war brought home by the veterans, men who could still not find a place for themselves in society. It was also a land in which much of the black population was segregated, anti-Asian feelings ran high, and antisemitism had actually increased even as the Nazis were being bombed to oblivion. How does the film defuse the explosive charge it has just revealed and provide relief to an anxious public? First, by giving the Jewish victim a hero's record, and second, by comparing antisemitism with anti-Catholicism and anti-Irish prejudice. The first means that, in fact, Jews sacrificed just as much as everyone else, despite rumors to the contrary. The second implies that Jews are not unique in being persecuted (which makes them suspect), since the same happened even to long-accepted groups such as the Irish.

That all this could be related to homosexuals, and eventually even to African Americans, is within the potential of the film. This is the film's strength and its weakness, and in this sense it is also a very American film, since it is clearly linked to the entire discourse on prejudice and discrimination in the United States. Those subjected to bigotry first must show themselves to have some heroic qualities, and second they must be seen as essentially just like everyone else. Resolving this contradiction is the essence of the archetypical, reluctant American hero à la John Wayne, the very embodiment of the ideal American self-image. But this requirement also tends to deprive the *Crossfire* scene of the complexity of identity and personality that should be at its core: the demeaning effects of prejudice on those subjected to it, the self-glorification of the persecutors, the cultural constructs and political structures that facilitate and sanction prejudice, and the media fabrications that conceal the consequences of prejudice even as they claim to expose its reality.

Some of these problems were confronted in Arthur Miller's only novel and first published work, recently made into a film.[32] Neal Slavin's *Focus* (2001) is the story of newlyweds Lawrence Newman (William H. Macy) and his wife Gert (Laura Dern), who are mistakenly identified and gradually ostracized as Jews in a New York suburb during World War II. Initially the couple tries to deny their alleged Jewish identity and to distance themselves from their only Jewish neighbor, the shopkeeper Finkelstein (David Paymer). Lawrence even tries to attend a sermon by Father Crighton (Kenneth Walsh), based on the radio evangelist Father Coughlin, at a gathering of the fascist "Union Crusaders," but he is thrown out after being "recognized" as a Jew. Eventually, however, Lawrence and Gert take up Finkelstein's side and confront the bigots in their neighborhood. While *Gentleman's Agreement*, then, depicts a gentile taking up the role of a Jew in order to report on his experience of antisemitism (before swiftly slipping back into the safe haven of his "true" identity), *Focus* features a gentile who is misidentified as a Jew against his will but eventually decides to appropriate that identity in order to fight discrimination from within. In both films, as well as in *Crossfire*, the "Jew" is both a symbol and an incidental character:

The non-Jew as involuntary Jew (*Focus*): Lawrence Newman, mistakenly identified by his bigoted neighbors as a Jew after he begins to wear glasses, observing his unchanged reflection in the mirror before ultimately deciding to join forces with the single, "real" Jew on the street attacked by antisemites.

he is either "really" a gentile or a mere excuse for the antisemite's violence. While *Focus* includes one "Jewish-looking" victim, whose visiting relatives also exhibit the trademarks of Jewish dress and mannerisms, the main protagonist and victim is a non-Jew.

Although all three films are about antisemitism, in *Gentleman's Agreement* and *Focus* we find a non-Jew victimized as a Jew, while in *Crossfire* the Jewish victim is merely the bigot's bait: he could easily be replaced by a homosexual or an African American. As Lawrence in *Focus* is transformed into a Jew because of a new pair of glasses (which make him appear "intellectual" but also metaphorically focus his gaze on the realities of prejudice), and searches his face in the mirror to find any traces of Jewish features, we realize that here too the "Jew" is merely the creature of the antisemite's fantasy. For Lawrence, Jewish identity boils down to a single element: victimization. His neighbor Finkelstein, the "real" Jew, may have other attributes of identity, but the film provides no clues. Hence being Jewish and being persecuted are synonymous, which may suggest that any person persecuted for their identity is essentially a "Jew," just as any "true" American will fight against discrimination, if necessary with baseball bats (as

Lawrence and Finkelstein actually do). Fundamentally, these films all re-
volve around the same trick of the imagination: the "Jew" exists only in the
minds of others, yet at the same time the best way to have audiences
identify and sympathize with his plight is to transform him into a non-Jew,
or to remove him from the scene altogether, leaving the mere fact of his
discrimination at center stage. In this manner, subjective Jewish identity
disappears, and the solution for discrimination is to become like everyone
else (while also remaining a hero—preferably a reluctant one).

ULTIMATE VICTIMS

Both the representation of non-Jewish victims as Jews, and that of Jewish
victims as non-Jews, has constituted an important aspect of cinematic discourse on the "Jew." One of the first manifestations of this phenomenon in
the aftermath of the Holocaust was the documentary *The Nazi Death Camps*
(1945), the official film record of the camps as photographed by the Western Allied forces that liberated them. The film was screened as evidence
both at the Nuremberg Tribunal in 1945 and at the Eichmann trial in
Jerusalem in 1961. But as Lawrence Douglas has recently argued, this
influential documentary has been seen as conclusive evidence of entirely
different understandings of the very same event.[33] Whereas the Nuremberg Tribunal sought to show that the Nazis had committed crimes against
humanity, and thus portrayed the victims filmed in the camps as representing a cross section of humanity (the word "Jew" appears in the film only
once in the compound term "German Jews"), the Eichmann trial was
explicitly about the Holocaust. Hence the underlying assumption of the
1961 screening was that the victims in the film were Jews.

How many of the skeletal figures and what proportion of the mountains
of corpses photographed by the Allies were in fact Jews is impossible to
determine. The camps shown in the film were, strictly speaking, not the
death or extermination camps, although of course they served as sites of
mass killing and dying nonetheless. The extermination camps were in the
east, and were mostly liberated (and in part filmed) by the Soviets. Until
late in the war, the population of the camps liberated in Germany proper
consisted mostly of political prisoners and those defined by the Nazis as
criminals or "asocial." Toward the end of the war, however, these concentration camps were flooded with the survivors of death marches from the
extermination and labor camps in the east, most of whom were indeed
Jews. Among these inmates the death rate was especially high. Hence both

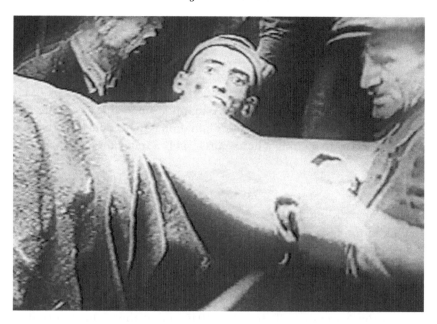

The Jew as musselman (*The Nazi Death Camps*): A (not necessarily Jewish) survivor of a concentration camp, liberated by the Western Allies, stares at the camera as he is being carried out for treatment. Such emaciated figures and haunting eyes have come to be associated with the figure of the musselman, the half-dead or "walking skeleton" most common in Auschwitz.

interpretations of the film were possible, which indicates, of course, that documentary footage is much more ambiguous and susceptible to misinterpretation and manipulation than is conventionally believed.[34]

Especially in the early postwar period, then, the "Jew" as victim could be represented most powerfully precisely when he revealed no traces of Jewish identity. Alain Resnais's celebrated documentary *Night and Fog* (1955), for instance, emptied the sites of victimhood entirely of Jews (here too the word "Jew" appears only once). The horror of the concentration camps seemed to have been perpetrated against Hitler's enemies, active resisters rather than innocent people who happened to have belonged to the wrong race. This assumed link between action and victimhood can diminish the effect of such films as *The Nazi Death Camps,* where the survivors appear just as the Nazis would have liked them to be seen, not only deprived of any heroic qualities but portrayed as quasi human beings, hardly distinguishable from the piles of emaciated corpses bulldozed into mass graves. Rather than evoking sympathy, the survivors are thus transformed into objects of revulsion and disgust. Still, as long as these figures were identified as active opponents of Hitler's regime, even their disfigurement could somehow be construed as heroic—given the right cinematic treatment by such masters as Resnais.

More recent audiences, however, tend to see the victims as Jews who were persecuted simply for what they were rather than for what they did, and consequently the glorifying rhetoric of the early postwar period is replaced by one of pity and sorrow. Moreover, even this sense of pity and sorrow has a somewhat detached quality, not only because we cannot recognize the individual humanity of the victims in this footage but also because it is much more difficult to identify with the alleged passivity of the Jews than with the martyrdom of the resisters. And, since the victims of Nazism tend now to be generalized under the heading of (passively persecuted) Jews, the "Jew" assumes the attributes of the dehumanized body and featureless corpse, which was precisely the goal of the Nazis. In other words, by becoming the victim par excellence, the "Jew" ceases to be a human being.

This elusive quality of the cinematic "Jew" as victim, his ability to appear as a stereotypical character in one depiction and as a non-Jew in another, as the preeminent victim in one screening and as nonexistent in another, was one of the reasons that prompted Claude Lanzmann to make his film *Shoah* (1985), another outstanding and radically different product of French documentary cinema. For Lanzmann, the survivors play another traditional Jewish role, that of vessels of memory. These memories must be recorded and displayed so as to preserve the reality of the genocide from the growing choir of those who will deny it ever happened. There is something disconcerting about this exercise of creating or recreating the conditions most conducive to a spilling out of memories whose nature is so horrific that, if allowed to resurface, they threaten to crack the very vessel that contained them for so many years. Here, then, memory supersedes existence, and the preservation of the past is more important than the hardly possible life of the present. From this perspective, the victim is both saved from oblivion and revictimized by the filmmaker. This victim is made to reexperience the horror; his telling of that experience is duly recorded; and then he is released, allowed to continue a life that has become even more unbearable by this temporary plunge into the abyss.

Nevertheless, by entirely eschewing contemporary documentary footage, Lanzmann allows the victims to become human again by interviewing them several decades after the event. Lanzmann allows the victims to speak about their unique, individual fates, and thereby he rescues them from being mere representatives of the "Jew," whether as victims or as perpetrators.

Mordechai Podchlebnik was one of only two survivors of the Chełmno death camp, in which some four hundred thousand Jews were murdered. His task was to unload corpses from the gas vans. In the words of the interpreter he says:

> The third day he saw his wife and children. He placed his wife in the grave and asked to be killed. The Germans said he was strong enough to work, that he wouldn't be killed yet.[35]

Yitzhak Dugin was in a group of workers ordered to exhume and burn ninety thousand bodies of the murdered Jews of Vilna:

> When the last mass grave was opened, I recognized my whole family. Mom and my sisters. Three sisters with their kids. They were all in there. They'd been in the earth four months, and it was winter. They were very well preserved. I recognized their faces, their clothes, too.[36]

Yet the Jews were not allowed to speak of the dead as human beings. According to Dugin,

> The Germans even forbade us to use the words "corpse" or "victim." The dead were blocks of wood, shit, with absolutely no importance. Anyone who said "corpse" or "victim" was beaten. The Germans made us refer to the bodies as *Figuren,* that is, as puppets, as dolls, or as *Schmattes,* which means "rags."[37]

The Germans did their best to distance themselves too from the humanity of the victims. Franz Suchomel, SS Unterscharführer at Treblinka, told Lanzmann that when he arrived there in the summer of 1942 the camp was "operating at full capacity" (*hochbetrieb*), but the gas chambers could not cope with the vast numbers of Jews arriving in daily transports. Hence

> the trainloads of Jews were left on a station siding. . . . So that while five thousand Jews arrived in Treblinka, three thousand were dead in the cars. . . . The ones we unloaded were half dead and half mad. . . . We stacked them here, here, and here [pointing at a map of the camp]. Thousands of people piled one on top of another on the ramp. Stacked like wood. . . . Just as we went by they were opening the gas-chamber doors, and people fell out like potatoes. . . . The smell was infernal because gas was constantly escaping [from the mass graves]. It stank horribly for miles around. . . . More people kept coming, always more, whom we hadn't the facilities to kill [*wir hatten nicht die Kapazität*].[38]

Suchomel says that because of the smell "we puked and wept." This was obviously unpleasant, even disgusting work, and they wished they were elsewhere. But challenged by Lanzmann that Auschwitz had a greater killing capacity than Treblinka, Suchomel responds that while the former "was a factory," the latter was "a primitive but efficient production line of death" (*ein zwar primitives aber gut funktionierendes Fließband des Todes*).[39]

Lanzmann insists on the difference between the manner in which the Jews experienced their victimhood, as individual human beings, and the manner in which they were seen not only by the killers but also by a variety of bystanders. For these observers they indeed became the "Jew" as victim, even if this observation carried with it little sympathy and at times a fair amount of schadenfreude. Frau Michelson, the wife of a former Nazi schoolteacher at Chełmno, initially confuses between the Poles and the Jews. Asked by Lanzmann whether there is a difference between them, she immediately comes up with a clear distinction: "The Poles weren't exterminated, and the Jews were. That's the difference. An external difference." Asked whether there was also an inner difference, she responds: "I can't assess that. I don't know enough about psychology and anthropology. The difference between the Poles and the Jews? Anyway, they couldn't stand each other."[40]

Indeed, the Polish population in the village of Grabów, just twelve miles from Chełmno, seems to confirm this last statement. One man remembers that the Jews stank because they worked as tanners. Asked whether he is glad or sad that there are no more Jews there, he says that it doesn't bother him since "Jews and Germans ran all Polish industry before the war." They didn't much like the Jews, he goes on, because "they were dishonest. . . . They exploited the Poles. That's what they lived off." Still, asked what he thinks about the Jews being gassed in trucks, he responds through the translator that "he doesn't like that at all. If they'd gone to Israel of their own free will, he might have been glad, but their being killed was unpleasant." A local woman remembers that Jewish women were beautiful and attractive to Polish men "because they did nothing. Polish women worked. Jewish women only thought of their beauty and clothes. . . . All Poland was in the hands of the Jews," she concludes. Asked how they feel about the Jews being gone, another woman says that "before the war she picked potatoes. Now she sells eggs and she's much better off."[41]

If in this conversation the Jewish victims are remembered primarily as exploiters and their "disappearance" is associated with the improvement in housing and working conditions for the Poles, another conversation in the village of Chełmno focuses directly on the "Jew" as victim. Lanzmann asks a group of local inhabitants gathered in front of the church, "Why do [you] think all this happened to the Jews?" Some repeat the old argument, fortified by having lived for forty years under communist rule, that it happened "because they were the richest!" But they add that "many Poles were

"Let his blood fall on our heads..."

The Jew as Christ-killer (*Shoah*): The inhabitants of Chełmno explaining why all this happened to the Jews. The elderly woman at the front says: "So Pilate washed his hands and said: 'Christ is innocent.' . . . But the Jews cried out: 'Let his blood fall on our heads!'" Turning to Simon Srebnik (behind her, arms folded), survivor of the nearby death camp, she says: "That's all, now you know!" and turns away from him.

also exterminated. Even priests." However, in this case a deeper and far more traditional rationale is given. In order to illustrate that the Jews actually brought their victimhood on themselves and were perfectly well aware of their guilt and need for atonement, a Pole named Kantarowski tells the following story:

> The Jews were gathered in a square. The rabbi asked an SS man: "Can I talk to them?" The SS man said yes. So the rabbi said that around two thousand years ago the Jews condemned the innocent Christ to death. And when they did that, they cried out: "Let his blood fall on our heads." Then the rabbi told them: "Perhaps the time has come for that, so let us do nothing, let us go, let us do as we're asked."[42]

Lanzmann asks Kantarowski if he thinks that "the Jews expiated the death of Christ." Kantarowski responds through the interpreter: "He doesn't think so, or even that Christ sought revenge. He didn't say that. The rabbi said it. It was God's will, that's all!" At which point an elderly lady adds:

> So Pilate washed his hands and said: "Christ is innocent," and he sent Barrabas. But the Jews cried out: "Let his blood fall on our heads!"[43]

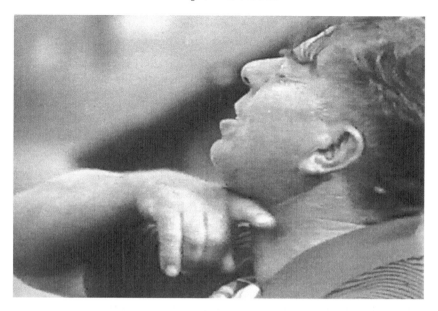

The Jew as object of slaughter (*Shoah*): Czesław Borowi, villager living near the Treblinka death camp, demonstrates the gesture he used to make to the Jews arriving by train.

She then fixes her gaze on Simon Srebnik, one of two survivors of the Chełmno death camp who is standing together with this group of Poles, and says: "That's all; now you know!"[44]

The numerous instances in Lanzmann's film where Poles pass their fingers on their throats to indicate that the Jews were slaughtered, or to show the director that they had tried to tell the Jews at the time what was about to happen to them with this universal gesture, constitute the single most powerful symbol of the manner in which the bystanders perceived the Jews as victims even before they were killed.[45] The rationale may have shifted over time—from jealousy about the prospective victims' assumed or known wealth (even if they were often only marginally better off than their gentile neighbors), to divine judgment, to a sense of helplessness and inevitability in the face of German power and organization. But clearly *Shoah* is primarily focused on different aspects of Jewish victimhood: for the Germans the "Jew" was an entirely abstract target of killing; for the Poles, the German eradication of the "Jew" was itself an indication that he was paying for past and present sins, even if in some cases the "Jew" was one of their neighbors; and solely for the Jews themselves, this abstract victim was made up of specific experiences, faces, names, and dates. The anonymous production line of death (*Fließband des Todes*) is personalized. Abraham Bomba, survivor of Treblinka, tells Lanzmann:

> A friend of mine worked as a barber—he was a good barber in my hometown—when his wife and his sister came into the gas chamber. . . . I can't. It's too horrible. Please.

After a long pause and under pressure from Lanzmann, Bomba, who until this point in his testimony has shown almost no emotion, goes on, his hands mechanically cutting a client's hair and his face a mask of indescribable pain:

> They tried to talk to him and the husband of his sister. They could not tell them this was the last time they stay [*sic*] alive, because behind them [were] the German Nazis, SS men, and they knew that if they said a word, not only the wife and the woman, who were dead already, but also they would share the same thing with them. In a way, they tried to do the best for them, with a second longer, a minute longer, just to hug them and kiss them, because they knew they would never see them again.[46]

Filip Müller, a Czech Jew and survivor of five liquidations of the Auschwitz Sonderkommando, remembers that when the doors of the gas chamber in Birkenau were opened, the victims "fell out like blocks of stone, like rocks falling out of a truck." This is the way SS man Suchomel also described the gassing. But Müller tells how individual victims tried to react to the *Fließband des Todes,* and why the victim was, as Bomba says, already dead even before the gas was thrown in:

> It was pointless to tell the truth to anyone who crossed the threshold of the crematorium. You couldn't save anyone there. . . . One day in 1943 when I was already in Crematorium 5, a train from Bialystok arrived. A prisoner of the Sonderkommando saw a woman in the "undressing room" who was the wife of a friend of his. He came right out and told her: "You are going to be exterminated. In three hours you'll be ashes." The woman believed him because she knew him. She ran all over and warned the other women. "We're going to be killed. We're going to be gassed." Mothers carrying their children on their shoulders didn't want to hear that. They decided the woman was crazy. They chased her away. So she went to the men. To no avail. Not that they didn't believe her; they'd heard rumors in the Bialystok ghetto, or in Grodno, and elsewhere. But who wanted to hear that! When she saw that no one would listen, she scratched her whole face. Out of despair. In shock. And started to scream.
>
> So what happened? Everyone was gassed. The woman was held back. We had to line up in front of the ovens. First, they tortured her horribly because she wouldn't betray him. In the end she pointed to him. He was taken out of the line and thrown alive into the oven. We were told: "Whoever tells anything will end like that."[47]

54

The Jew as object of empathy (*Shoah*): Jan Karski, former courier of the Polish government in exile, recalls visiting the Warsaw Ghetto in 1942: "It was not a world. It was not part of humanity. I was not part of it. I did not belong there. I never saw such things . . . nobody wrote about this kind of reality. . . . I was told these were human beings—they didn't look like human beings" (Claude Lanzmann, *Shoah,* 174).

Nevertheless, Müller remembers the moment at which the helpless victims, realizing what was about to happen, reasserted their humanity. It was when the SS decided to liquidate the Czech family camp, which consisted of former inmates of Theresienstadt, in late February 1944. It is at this point that he too breaks down:

> That night I was at Crematorium 2. As soon as the people got out of the vans, they were blinded by floodlights and forced through a corridor to the stairs leading to the "undressing room." They were blinded, made to run. Blows were rained on them. Those who didn't run fast enough were beaten to death by the SS. The violence used against them was extraordinary. And sudden . . . The violence climaxed when they tried to force the people to undress. A few obeyed, only a handful. Most of them refused to follow the order. Suddenly, like a chorus, they all began to sing. The whole "undressing room" rang with the Czech national anthem, and the *Hatikvah* [the Zionist anthem]. That moved me terribly, that. . . .

That was happening to my countrymen, and I realized that my life had become meaningless. Why go on living? For what? So I went into the gas chamber with them, resolved to die. With them. . . . A small group of women approached. They looked at me and said, right there in the gas chamber . . . One of them said: "So you want to die. But that's senseless. Your death won't give us back our lives. That's no way. You must get out of here alive, you must bear witness to our suffering, and to the injustice done to us."[48]

And this is how Müller, and all the others who survived, were transformed from victims into witnesses.

In *Shoah* the individual Jewish victim is pitted against the view of the "Jew" as a target for killing or victim of his own misdeeds and guilt, and testimony is given in the context of an intimate conversation with Lanzmann, who insists on bringing the individual witness to the breaking point, the moment in which the specific event he or she recalls or the weight of the entire narrative overwhelm the witness and threaten to block any further speech. Conversely, in the documentary *The Eighty-First Blow* (1974), made by Haim Gouri, Jacquot Ehrlich, and David Bergman, the witnesses have been placed within the setting of a courtroom. All the oral testimonies given in this film are recordings taken from the Eichmann trial. This is not a setting intended to bare the heart and soul of the witness, but instead the goal is to determine the guilt of the defendant. It is also not the site for emotional and physical disintegration. When this happens in the trial (as was the case, for instance, during the testimony of Yehiel Dinur, known by his pen name, Ka-Tzetnik), the testimony is stopped, the witness is led away, and the court either adjourns or moves on to the next witness.

Moreover, the makers of this film chose to use documentary footage, mostly taken by the Germans, as a kind of confirmation of the witnesses' words. Indeed, the film never shows the witnesses, or even names them, but rather provides an endless stream of footage accompanied by the words of the witnesses. This makes for a strange and alienating effect. Eventually, the film produces precisely that "Jew" as victim, who, in his collective identity, loses all individual features—just as the antisemitic depiction of the "Jew" provides a single face, a set of "typical" gestures, and a representative name, and denies any personality, difference, and uniqueness to the individual Jew. Indeed, in this sense *The Eighty-First Blow* is representative of many other documentaries which, with the very best intentions, have perpetuated an image of the "Jew" as victim whose links to the image of the "Jew" as perpetrator are all too obvious. For if the voices we hear in the film have no face and no name, so the figures of mutilated, tortured, and butchered Jews in the German footage amply provided in the film have no voice, no name, and only one recurring physical appearance, that of the victim.

The Eighty-First Blow, then, presents the witness as an accuser. The words of the witnesses reveal their pain, suffering, and sorrow, but these revelations are constantly accompanied by the dehumanizing images recorded by the perpetrators, whose intention was to deprive the victims of precisely those human attributes they strive to reassert in the courtroom. Yet the courtroom cannot easily serve as an occasion for understanding the complexity of human emotion, sorrow, guilt (moral rather than legal), complicity, fear, and anxiety that are at the heart of genocide. The trial wishes to carry out legal justice, but its task is complicated—indeed, there is a threat it could be undermined—by narratives that expose both the ambiguity of the defendant's responsibility and the extent of self-recrimination and sense of guilt among the victims. The film might have employed the tension between testimony and documentary footage to demonstrate the vast distance between perceptions of the same event by victims and perpetrators. The filmmakers also might have suggested that by attempting to dehumanize the "Jew," the killers ended up by creating a record for all time of their own inhumanity. But since the film lacks all ironic distance, it in fact uses the Nazi footage to assert the "truth" of faceless narratives by witnesses who are allowed no other identity than that of their victimhood. In this sense, *The Eighty-First Blow* once more dehumanizes the victims, making them into a unified choir rather than allowing for individual renditions of experience.

To be sure, Lanzmann too tells us little about his witnesses beyond their experiences in the Holocaust. We know nothing about their prewar lives and practically nothing about their lives after the war. Their role is to speak only about what happened to them under the Germans. But in Lanzmann's film each witness is given a face, an individual experience, and reflects what happened only through his or her own account, without juxtaposing these accounts with the distorted images produced by the Nazis; they exist as human beings rather than as an accusative choir. In this manner they escape from History (with a capital "H") and reconstruct their own very personal history, which is the true fabric of the human experience. This move against the terrible simplifiers of doctrine and ideology is absent from *The Eighty-First Blow,* which shifts uneasily between an assertion of collective Jewish victimhood and a no less powerful assertion of collective Jewish resistance. Both lead to a redemptive finale, in the shape of the Jewish State established shortly after the Holocaust. Nor does the film provide any other types of contextual elements, such as historical analysis and documentation. It is, ultimately, a moving but one-dimensional pamphlet, modeled more on the sketches performed in schools and youth movements, accompanied by a song that seems to combine traditional lamentations with socialist kitsch. While the film is neither an authoritative nor a subtle statement on the relationships between complicity and resistance, and dehumanization and human nature, it ends up giving the impression of an incomprehensible tragedy—which occurred, as Ka-Tzetnik said in the courtroom, on "another planet"—yet one that must serve as an example and as the ultimate justification for Jewish nationalism.

The ideological tone of the film is set in the opening scene. Golda Meir (1898–1978), former prime minister of Israel (who is not identified specifically in the film), makes a speech to the viewers. Meir was born in Kiev, and in 1906 her family immigrated to Milwaukee, Wisconsin. Meir arrived in Palestine in 1921, rising to prominence as a spokesperson, diplomat, and politician of socialist Zionism and the Jewish State. Thus her words carry the weight of a veteran Zionist leader. But her speech is also related to the specific historical context in which it was recorded. *The Eighty-First Blow* was completed shortly after the disastrous 1973 Yom Kippur War, in which Israel, under Meir's premiership, was attacked by Egypt and Syria, sustaining such heavy initial losses and setbacks that even the normally cocky defense minister, Moshe Dayan (1915–1981), made apocalyptic statements to his generals about the looming destruction of the Third Temple.[49] Characteristically, Meir attempts to link the catastrophes of the past, the challenges of the present, and the eternal victimization of Jews, which necessitate the existence of an independent and powerful Israel:

> Friends, you are to see the Holocaust as it happened, as it was promised by Hitler that it would happen. . . . There are people who do not remember any more. There are people who wish to forget. And there is an entire generation of young men and women, who did not know, who were children, who were not yet born. For them too it is important that they see and realize what happened in the twentieth century. And there is one more reason why it is important that this film should be seen now. We are close to the end of the twentieth century, and the Protocols of the Elders of Zion, something that was fabricated in Czarist Russia, is being distributed, published and republished, in the Middle East, and distributed throughout Europe, mainly, and other places of the world. People say, mad, impossible, and yet, let us not forget, we have said before that it was impossible, and here it is again, spreading hatred, falsifications, practically toward the same aim that Hitler had. . . . For everybody's sake . . . let us not brush this terrible, awful lesson aside.[50]

Here, then, rather than being a cause for mourning and lamentation, the image of the "Jew" as victim is used to fortify its Jewish (Israeli) audience, suggesting that in order to look forward with hope one must also look backward with horror. According to this logic, terror of the past breeds courage in the present. The implied meaning of "never again" includes the suggestion that whoever is against us is allied with the Nazis, "practically toward the same aim that Hitler had." The "Jew" as victim is, then, the begetter of the "Jew" as hero. For if Hitler was the worst that could ever happen, but is always lurking in the future, then anything, anything at all, can and must be done to prevent his reappearance.

This rhetoric, however, is not carried through in the film. Just as it tries to confirm the victims' heart-wrenching testimonies by showing the perpetrators' cynical footage, so it seeks to assert Jewish nationalism by depicting Jewish humiliation. But one does not easily follow from the other. The consequences of nationalism born out of collective humiliation and degradation may be either deep repression and denial, mixed with animosity for the humiliated, or brutal retaliation against anyone perceived as a new potential perpetrator somehow linked in the mind with the figure of the Nazi.[51] Documentaries such as *The Eighty-First Blow*, or feature films based on historical episodes such as Andrzej Wajda's *Korczak* (1990), make use of footage taken by German propaganda companies of Jews dying in the Warsaw and Lodz ghettos. As noted above, this same footage was employed to depict them as subhuman in the rabidly antisemitic film *The Eternal Jew*.[52] Such citations of Nazi propaganda are meant to have the opposite effect from that originally intended. But one must wonder, would Hitler or Goebbels or Himmler have been offended or pleased by such material? And what does it mean that those who want to keep the memory of the atrocity alive, and to create something positive, even noble, out of it, rely so heavily on the sadistic films that the henchmen shot with such obvious glee?

Linking Jewish victimhood with both courage and helplessness, that is, making the "Jew" as victim into the "Jew" as hero, and vice versa, stripping the latter of his unique heroic mantle and turning him into merely one more instance of the former, is at the center of this representational conundrum (reflecting in turn the Jewish existential conundrum during the Holocaust). One of the most powerful testimonies given at the Eichmann trial, which we can hear in *The Eighty-First Blow* and see in *The Trial of Adolf Eichmann* (1997), served as an inspiration for an episode both in the book and the film *Schindler's List* (1993).[53] Here we have a witness who was a reserve officer, who obviously had respect for uniforms, discipline, and integrity. Hurled into a world turned upside down, he adheres to this ethos of bourgeois and military correctness and as a result loses his family:

> And they said, the men to the right with the children over fourteen years old, and the ladies to the left, with the boys and girls. And I stood with my son who was twelve. Suddenly someone arrived, dressed in a German army uniform, elegant. I did not know who it was. And he asked me what is my profession. I knew that [saying] lawyer was not agreeable, so I said former officer. He looked at me and said, how old is the boy? At that moment I could not lie and I said, twelve. Then he says [and here the witness switches from Hebrew to German]: "*Wo ist die Mutti? Antwortete ich, sie ist links gegangen. Sagte er, meinem Buben, also lauf nach Mutti*" [Where is the mom? I replied, she went to the left. He said, my boy, go run after mom]. [The witness continues in Hebrew:] "Run after mom." And I continued and then went to the right, and I saw the boy running. And I asked myself, how could he find his mother there? There are after all so many women there. How did I recognize her? My daughter was wearing some kind of red coat, and the red spot was the sign that she was there. And this spot became ever smaller. I went to the right and never saw them again.[54]

The former officer cannot lie to another uniformed member of the officer corps. Telling the truth, he loses his son. This Jewish man, still cutting an impressive figure when he gave this testimony some twenty years after the event, was characteristic of the newly assimilated European Jewry, a member of the military and professional elites, well educated and proud. At this moment he was transformed into a helpless victim. All that was left of his previous identity was the slowly diminishing red spot. The deception of the German officer, and his own inability to lie, must have forever shattered the sense of social, family, and personal pride of this witness, as indeed happened to thousands of other Jews.

But if Jewish masculine pride is destroyed, stories of other kinds of heroism emerge from the film. They are often about women; they are desperate acts that can end only in death; they are filled with anger and dignity; and they are remembered over generations. We find them cited in feature films, such as Wanda Jakubowska's Polish movie *The Last Stage* (1948) and in works of fiction, such as the Hebrew novel *The Name.*[55] But these Jewish heroes are doomed; they are the products of helplessness and hopelessness, not of any belief in the future. Their acts are carried out and indeed remembered as symbols of resistance and honor, but they can hardly serve as an example for the future, since their very context assumes that such a future does not exist:

> They took Mala and organized a huge roll call and Mala managed to hide a razor blade in her sleeve and cut her veins. Then the SS man walked up

to her and began mocking and cursing her so she struck his cheek with her bloody hand and said to him, "I will die as a hero and you will perish like a dog."[56]

They hanged four girls and the last word by Roza Robota heard by the girls standing at the roll call was "revenge."[57]

Yet such stories of female heroism are drowned in the film by tales of male submission and humiliation. Unlike the accounts of heroic women that are related by eyewitnesses, the men's stories are told by the men themselves, who in part survived precisely because they did not rebel:

> Sometimes we took the ashes from Crematorium 3 and in winter we had to use the ashes for the roads. And when we were done with the job and there was still time, the Kapo of the Sonderkommando pitied us and would say, "Well, children, it's cold outside, go warm yourselves up in the gas chambers." Sometimes of course it happened that when we got to the crematorium they said, "Now you can't go in, there are people inside."[58]

> We didn't want to undress, so they started shooting. We undressed and threw the clothes on the floor. Then one of the Sonderkommando who worked there walked up to us and said, "*Khevre,* don't show that you are anxious, *singt, khevre, singt* [Yiddish for "sing, lads, sing"]." Some were petrified and could not utter a sound, like me; some began praying, and some also sang. They moved us to a small hallway and opened a large door and got us into that hall. In the hall it was pitch dark. They shut the door behind us, and then I heard for the first time . . . crying. They opened the door again and ordered us to come out. Then the SS commander selected fifty lads. The rest of the children were sent back into the gas chamber, and we were ordered to get dressed and they took us to the train station and there ordered us to unload the potatoes and bury them in the ground.[59]

> We stayed alive. There was shame. We were ashamed of ourselves. Loneliness. The entire world had collapsed. The undergrounds had not yet begun in those days. There was no sign of light in the world. We knew that they would defeat us first. But we knew that they would pay a heavy price for our lives.[60]

These are testimonies of despair. Some of the very same men who survived by working as Sonderkommando members, pushing victims into the gas chambers and then clearing out and cremating their bodies, were also among those who rebelled against the SS. Similarly, the young women and men who rose up in the Warsaw Ghetto had seen the vast majority of the ghetto's population, including their parents, grandparents, younger siblings, and children, being taken away to the Umschlagplatz and transported from there to Treblinka. They were ashamed, they were lonely, and they had no hope. They only wanted to die fighting. On April 23, 1943, Mordechai Anielewicz, leader of the uprising, wrote in a letter to Yitzhak (Antek) Cukerman:

> Shalom Yitzhak. I don't know what to write you. I'll dispense this time with the personal details. I have only one expression to depict my own feelings and the feelings of my comrades. Something has happened that surpassed our most daring dreams. The Germans have escaped twice from the ghetto. Be well, my dear, perhaps we shall still meet. The main thing is that what we have dreamed of all our lives has become a reality. I was privileged to see Jewish defense in all its greatness and glory. Mordechai.[61]

And so, the legacy of the Holocaust that *The Eighty-First Blow* wishes its viewers to inherit is that of the birth of Jewish resistance, from which should flow the birth of the Jewish nation in its independent state. But can a live body emerge from the ashes of millions? And if such a phoenix were possible, what shape and form would it take? Or is it better to relegate the "Jew" as victim to an entirely different planet and let the new "Jew," the hero, emerge from the "virgin" land of his homeland? The film ends with the testimony by the writer Yehiel Dinur, known by his pen name Ka-Tzetnik, who stamped all subsequent representations of Auschwitz by describing it as "another planet":

> I was there about two years. Time there is not as it is here on Earth. Every fraction of a minute there passed on a different scale of time. And the inhabitants of this planet had no names, they had no parents nor did they have children. They did not dress in the way we dress here; they were not born there and did not give birth; they breathed according to different laws of nature. Their name was the number, "Kazetnik." . . . And I believe with perfect faith that I have to continue to bear this name so long as the world has not been aroused to wipe out this evil after this crucifixion of a nation, just as humanity was aroused after the crucifixion of one man. I believe with perfect faith that, just as in astrology the stars influence our destiny, so does this planet of ashes, Auschwitz, stand in opposition to our planet Earth, and influences it. If I am able to stand before you today and relate the events on that planet, if I, as a fallout from that planet, am able to be here at this time, then I believe with perfect faith that this is due to the oath I swore to them there. They gave me this strength. This oath was the armor that gave me the supernatural power to overcome the time of Auschwitz—the two years when I was a Musselman. For they left me, they always left me, they were parted from me, and this oath always appeared in their gaze. For close on two years they kept on taking leave of me and they always left me behind. I see them, they are staring at me, I see them, I saw them standing in the queue.[62]

But it is difficult to end a film that begins by celebrating the new State of Israel on this note. Hence the makers added two curious final captions. In the first, they "beg forgiveness from all those who were not seen and not heard," a remarkable statement considering that it was the filmmakers' own choice not to show the faces or provide the names of the witnesses. In the second, they "beg forgiveness . . . from the hundreds of thousands of unknown Jewish soldiers who sanctified the name of Israel under alien banners." Here it is difficult to understand why the filmmakers wish to be forgiven by those killed fighting the Nazis; why they are so certain that Jews fighting in British or Soviet or American or any other armies necessarily saw themselves as sanctifying the name of Israel rather than fighting for their respective homelands as patriots; and, finally, by what right the film-makers claim that—for the Jewish soldiers who fought under them—those were "alien banners." Rather, this is an attempt to add a final heroic flavor to a film that is, appropriately but against the grain, about Jewish victim-hood, despair, and destruction. In a sense, *The Eighty-First Blow* fabricates the "Jew" as a hero by hijacking his identity as a citizen of another country, taking away his flag, and recruiting him into the Zionist narrative.[63] Under-lying this exercise is the assumption or assertion that the Jewish victims would have survived, indeed, would have been transformed into heroes, had they abandoned the "alien banners" to which they belonged and come to the Promised Land. This may be hypothetically true, but historically it is meaningless. As a final, rhetorical attempt to reshape the victim as a hero, it is more than anything else indicative of the ambiguity of Jewish/Israeli documentation of the Shoah.

If *The Nazi Death Camps* makes the Jewish victims disappear, if *Shoah* converts them into its main protagonists, and if *The Eighty-First Blow* both employs their voices in a disjointed narrative of Nazi film footage and tries to convert them into heroes, then the German television documentary *Holokaust* (dir. Guido Knopp and Maurice Philip Remy, 2000) presents itself as an objective historical reconstruction. Apart from some ironic asides about Nazi leaders and some expressions of sympathy for the plight of the Jews, the film tries to maintain a dry and factual tone while offering a fair amount of original, previously unseen film material. Yet its juxtaposition of original footage with recent interviews tends to blur the differences between the perpetrators and their victims: the witnesses all appear framed against a similar dark background, all narrate their experiences with the same calm voice and composed features (only occasionally allowing their emotions to show through), and most speak very good or native German. Most important, they are all alive. It is difficult to reconcile this apparent similarity of the film's subjects with the vast gap between the appearance and mentality of the victims and the killers seen in the ample

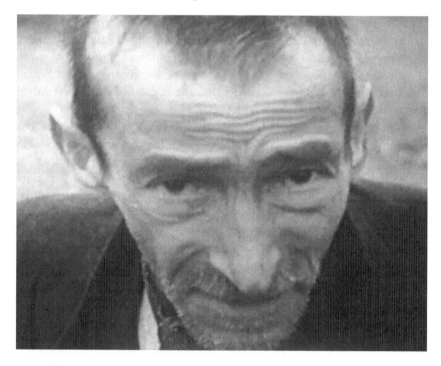

The Jew through the Nazi camera (*Holokaust*): A terrified Jewish man filmed as he is humiliated and beaten by Nazis and most probably killed shortly thereafter.

footage from the period. Moreover, in this meticulous historical documentary, there is a certain lack of awareness of its own limits. For this is an event which, by its very extremity and traumatic repercussions, must resist its own reconstruction. Listening to the testimonies of men and women from both sides of the divide, it is difficult to understand how they lived during the half-century following their experiences. If Lanzmann's obvious partiality in *Shoah* can be disturbing, it at least carries with it a certain sense of justice: one does not treat killers and victims in the same manner. In *Holokaust*, history becomes a compilation of documents and personal accounts that must be arranged in a manner that will explicate an event, which, on another level, is a site of chaos, terror, massacre, and destruction. In order to accomplish this ordering of reports and images from hell, an image of the "Jew" must emerge, not just as victim but as doomed from the very beginning, and precisely for that reason too alien for us to do anything but record his fate and move on. The person who narrates the story fifty years later may, of course, look and sound very much like the rest of us. But we cannot imagine him back into the images from the past, we cannot gain anything but the most superficial knowledge of factual data about the event and almost no insight into the mentalities of the people who lived through it or their subsequent fates. Technically remarkable, this film manifests all the faults of a documentary that fails to comprehend the very history it claims to reconstruct.

NON-JEWISH VICTIMS

Holokaust is, of course, a vast improvement on earlier German cinematic representations of the Nazi genocide. One should remember the shock and astonishment with which the NBC miniseries *Holocaust* (dir. Marvin Chomsky, 1978) was received when it was screened on German television in 1979. It was the first time that German audiences had to confront the fate of a German-Jewish family from the rise of the Nazis to the end of the war. While most Germans knew by then a great deal about Nazism and the Holocaust, they had not been offered an intimate look into the fate of individuals. *Holocaust* brought into German sitting rooms the individual victims of the somewhat abstract, though terrible, *Judenvernichtung* (extermination of the Jews). It is from that period, despite many complaints about the artistic quality and Hollywood nature of the miniseries, that the word "Holocaust" entered German usage. Just over twenty years earlier, one of the most popular representations of World War II in Germany was the film trilogy *08/15* (1954–1955). However, *08/15* portrays the main victim of the war, of Nazism, and of the general stupidity of the traditional German military to be the wretched German *Landser* (the equivalent of the American GI), whose delicate soul is crushed by a combination of idiotic discipline and Soviet armor. Not only does the film, lasting a total of three hundred minutes, fail to devote a single episode to the persecution and genocide of the Jews but also the only Jewish character appearing in it is a particularly unattractive soldier who arrives in Germany with the rest of the conquering, naive, and vindictive Americans. As this otherwise anonymous Jewish character throws his feet on the former German commander's desk, he is offered a sausage by a subservient German, who explains to him the merits of this delicacy. Revealing his distinctive "Jewish" profile, the American replies in perfect German: "I ate these when I didn't even know where America was." Is he a German traitor or an eternal alien who makes his home wherever things are good and sausages plentiful? This "Jew" is certainly not a victim, and his pose as arrogant victor only accentuates the victimhood of the Germans.

If in *08/15* the victim is simply German, an array of postwar feature films complicates and at times entirely undermines the figure of the "Jew" as victim; occasionally this figure turns out to be in fact a non-Jew. This is, of course, related in part to the desire to undermine the antisemitic view of the "Jew" as a paradigmatic "other." By depicting Jews who do not look "Jewish," or non-Jews who do, one may destabilize the essentialist, racist identification of appearance, character, and fate. By showing the other victims of Nazism, one may "save" the "Jew" from being depicted as the eternal victim; and by allowing Jews to play the role of Germans, even Nazis, one extracts the figure of the "Jew" from an assumed, innate innocence and introduces the function of circumstances in determining the actions and fortunes of individual human beings. But of course all of this may also have an apologetic or obfuscating effect. For while the "Jew" is a victim only as a stereotype, the historical episodes with which most of these films are concerned are ones in which Jews were indeed the primary victims.

A good example of effectively undermining the stereotype, while criticizing an entire policy that was based on precisely this assumption of essential difference, is Markus Imhoof's influential film *The Boat Is Full* (1981). In 1942, Switzerland declared that, since it had become akin to an overloaded lifeboat in the raging seas of war, it would no longer provide a haven to the refugees trying to cross its borders, apart from a few belonging to rigidly defined and enforced categories. This ban applied primarily to Jews fleeing from the Nazi murder machine. Imhoof exposes the implications of this policy, whereby thousands of desperate refugees were delivered by Swiss officials to the German authorities, by telling the story of one such group, thrown together by fate and coincidence, which seeks asylum in a Swiss village situated near the German border. Judith Krueger (Tina Engel) is a young German-Jewish woman whose non-Jewish husband, Hannes, is already detained by the Swiss. Judith seeks to join him and to save her teenaged brother, Olaf Landau (Martin Walz), who was hit by a bullet as they escaped from a German train. Lazar Ostrowskij (Curt Bois), an elderly Viennese Jew, reaches the village only with his granddaughter Gitty (Simone), his wife having been caught by the Germans on the train before he managed to escape.[64] Finally, there are Maurice (Laurent), a little boy who was left behind on the train and taken along by the group, and Karl Schneider (Gerd David), a Wehrmacht deserter.

This unlikely collection of refugees tries to constitute itself as a family, in the belief that this may help them gain permission to stay. Since Olaf cannot pass as his older sister's husband, he assumes the identity of the deserter, while Karl becomes Judith's spouse. Despite his protests, Lazar, a religious Jew, becomes the grandfather, which makes his granddaughter the child of a German soldier. Maurice, who speaks only French, is made their second child and told not to utter a sound. It turns out, however, that those in the village who advised them to become a "family" had misread the complex bureaucratic regulations as to who may stay and who must be deported. Furthermore, Olaf is hardly convincing as a German soldier; Maurice exposes his French identity; and Judith's desperate attempts to contact her husband cast suspicion on Karl, who reveals that he is the real deserter after discovering that the Swiss government will not deliver him to the Wehrmacht. The others, however, are all sent back across the border and perish at the hands of the Nazis.

Besides its role in triggering a national debate over the complicity of Switzerland in the Holocaust, *The Boat Is Full* reveals the insidious effects of defining individuals according to racial and ethnic criteria as well as the influence of traditional prejudice and xenophobia. What this group of individuals has in common is only their urgent need to escape a regime that has defined them as targets of genocide. For the Nazis, they are an abstract entity that must be removed. For the Swiss authorities, they are a burden that must be thrown overboard. To the locals in the village, they appear both as entirely normal human beings and as strange and vaguely threatening outsiders, not least because the authorities are obviously after them. Traditional antisemitism is mixed with the dynamics of a closed and isolated village community, whose inhabitants are suspicious of difference and resentful toward but also fearful of the representatives of the state. Nor are the refugees shown as free of prejudice and self-interest. On the face of it, Judith and Karl appear as a perfectly likely couple (after all her real husband is also a non-Jewish German), and the deserter seems to be in the same dire straits as the Jews in the group. But Lazar detests the idea of having a German in his "family," while Karl readily betrays them the moment he sees a better chance to survive. Meanwhile, Olaf is first abused as a German soldier and then, reverting to his true identity, perishes as a Jew.

Similarly, the effects of government policies on a small village community are subtly depicted. It is the local policeman—vain but insecure, cunning if not particularly intelligent, and somewhat vindictive—who interprets the regulations on asylum. Exhibiting no love for foreigners, be they Germans or Jews, though happy to take away their few remaining valuables, he is determined to get rid of them as soon as possible. The innkeepers Anna Flueckiger (Renate Steiger) and her husband Franz (Mathias Gnädiger) have the most complex and interesting relationship with the refugees. Initially Anna gives them food and shelter in spite of her husband's vehement protests. Then he relents and helps her care for them. As the authorities intervene, however, Anna wants to avoid any further trouble. But Franz, who has taken a liking to Judith, resents the policeman. Ashamed of his own cowardice, he tries to save them. Eventually he is also caught and imprisoned. From the perspective of the innkeepers, then, the brief presence of the refugees has disrupted a simple but secure life. Indeed, the entire community seems curious about these outsiders, both attracted to and repelled by their strangeness. The villagers are angry at the policeman's brutal attempts to drive them to the border, but most are also hardly welcoming to the Jews. Kindness, prejudice, opportunism, gossip, courage, and brutality are all mixed in this small community's reaction to the arrival of a few desperate people about to be murdered. When they leave, almost everyone is relieved.

Apart from a few subtle hints, such as Lazar's rejection of ham despite his evident hunger, there are hardly any indications of the refugees' Jewishness. But their status as foreigners and refugees, persecuted and ultimately desperate people who conceal their true identities and resort to lies and falsehood, marks them as Jews in the eyes of their environment. Still, for this little mountain community they are no more than a brief interlude: they arrive, create a bit of a stir, and then they vanish again, as if they had never existed. Hence, apart from its obvious political message, this film is about the "Jew" as an outsider, a figure of both unstable and yet innately different identity, and a troublemaker in the same sense that Kathy means in *Gentleman's Agreement,* when she says to Phil: "They always make trouble for everybody, even their friends, they force people to take sides against them." Thus the very status of the "Jew" as victim makes him a disruptive element, since whether we help, reject, or persecute him, we must act in a way that reveals something we may not want to know about ourselves or that others will use against us.

This notion of the "Jew" as a disruptive element precisely because of his status as a victim can be translated into a variety of representational modes. If the most distinctive characteristic of the "Jew" is his victimhood, then it follows that the victim must somehow contain "Jewish" characteristics, whatever his actual identity may be. Thus, for instance, in Lina Wertmüller's *Seven Beauties* (1976), Pasqualino ("Settebellezze") Frafuso (Giancarlo Giannini), a small-time Neapolitan crook who lives off the labor of his seven sisters, defends the honor of the family by killing his sister's pimp. The discovery of the murder takes him on a nightmarish journey into jail, an insane asylum, the Russian front, and a Nazi concentration camp. Upon returning home he finds that all his sisters, as well as the girl he loves, had meanwhile prostituted themselves to the American liberators. The central, most haunting, and most controversial scene in this movie is Pasqualino's desperate attempt to seduce the Nazi commandant (Shirley

Becoming the Jewish victim (*Seven Beauties*): Pasqualino ("Settebellezze")
Frafuso, Neapolitan crook and murderer, fascist soldier incarcerated by the
Germans in a concentration camp, tries to save his skin by seducing the Valkyrie-
like commandant, in a sadomasochistic fantasy that transforms Italian POWs into
Jewish Holocaust victims.

Stoler) as a means of saving his neck. As the tiny, famished, terrified Neapolitan worms his way up the commandant's huge, Amazonian legs, she
taps his buttocks impatiently with her horse whip, eventually feeding him
like a dog in hope that a portion of wurst and sauerkraut will revive his
manhood. Indeed, Pasqualino is eventually saved, but not before he plunges
into the very bottom of degradation by shooting his best friend in the head
in order to demonstrate his loyalty to the Germans.

Seven Beauties wishes to subvert conventional views about male–female
relations, to reveal the traps and falsehoods of the traditional ethos of
family honor, to examine the instinct of survival and the power of perver-
sion, and to do all this in situations of growing extremity of violence and
sadism. In this Wertmüller in some ways followed in the footsteps of Liliana
Cavani's *The Night Porter* (1974), which focuses on the relationship between a former SS officer and his past Jewish sexual slave who meet again
many years after the war. But what is intriguing about *Seven Beauties* is the
perceived need to bring Pasqualino into a Nazi concentration camp and
have him try to perform sex with a huge, Aryan SS officer. One cannot
think of a more radical situation, both in terms of reversing traditional

male–female power relations and in terms of the sheer sadism of the camp as an institution. In a sense, the best way to expose and shake up Pasqualino—a simultaneously likable and detestable character—is to turn him, the quintessential Neapolitan macho, into a "Jew" in a Nazi camp, the ultimate example of the non-human.

Using the Nazi camps as a site of sexual titillation and fantasy is of course an old trope that is still very much part of the pornographic scene.[65] Employing the Holocaust as a site of extremity, on which various theories of human behavior, representation, gender difference, philosophy, theology, and so forth can be tried out, is also a common (if not always gratifying) practice.[66] Utilizing the "Jew" as the epitome of victimhood, and ascribing this status to a non-Jew so that he may learn and gain from the experience, is nevertheless a somewhat disturbing undertaking in this context. This is not to say that Italians were not treated wretchedly by the Germans following the armistice signed with the Allies, but rather that the situation in which Pasqualino finds himself is entirely part of the fantasy of Jewish-Nazi humiliation.[67] We can look at this phenomenon also from the opposite side: if *Seven Beauties* is about an Italian who becomes a "Jew," Roberto Benigni's *Life Is Beautiful* (1998) is about a "Jew" who is entirely Italian. Here Guido Orefice (Roberto Benigni) becomes a "Jew" only because he is persecuted as one. Indeed, although his half-Jewish son Giosué (Giorgio Cantarini) and his non-Jewish wife Dora (Nicoletta Braschi) are also interned in a concentration camp, he is the only one to die there. Guido's "Jewish" attributes, just like those of Benigni, exist only to the extent that the physical stereotypes of Jews and Latins (especially among non-Latin Europeans) have a great deal in common. Whether a Jewish or a Catholic Italian, Guido as a "type" could look, speak, and behave in precisely the expected manner. It is also for this reason that the traditional antisemitic "anxiety of similarity"—the fear that Jews who do not look "Jewish" would be impossible to tell apart from non-Jews—failed to play a significant role in Italy. And yet, of course, the Italian fascist regime did distinguish between Jews and non-Jews, and thousands of Italian Jews were deported and murdered by the Nazis.

What is interesting about *Life Is Beautiful* in our context is the fact that Benigni's father was also incarcerated in a Nazi camp. But while quite a few Italian viewers of the film actually thought that Benigni himself was Jewish, the fact is that his father, a non-Jew, was arrested and sent to a camp by the Germans as a soldier in Mussolini's army following the armistice, which the Germans perceived as a betrayal by an ally in the war. In that sense, Benigni's father underwent the same fate as Wertmüller's Pasqualino. But

Benigni the son felt compelled to translate his father's untold (and ironic) story of a fascist soldier ending up in a Nazi camp into a more redeeming tale of an Italian "Jew"—that is, unlike his father, an entirely unambiguous victim—who saves not only his son's life but also his innocence by pretending to him that the hellish world into which they have been thrown is a mere game. Thus, while Guido is "playing" a concentration camp inmate for his son, Benigni is playing a "Jew" as a tribute to his father's unacknowledged victimhood as a fascist soldier. To be sure, Benigni has spoken of his father's experience and its impact on his film; but he apparently did not believe that he could achieve the same effects of victimhood, innocence, and altruism through the tale of a fascist soldier. Victimhood, it seems, demands to be represented by a Jewish concentration camp inmate, even if this particular inmate is so stereotypically Italian that he compels one to laugh and cry at the same time.[68]

The non-Jewish "Jewish" victim manifests himself in a variety of other guises, often dictated either by ideological or political constraints or by issues of taste, political correctness, and fashion. Jan Němec's Czech film *Diamonds of the Night* (1964), which is based on a story by Jewish-Czech writer Arnošt Lustig, is about two boys who jump off a train and escape into the forest, where they are eventually hunted down by a band of elderly ethnic-Germans.[69] In one version of the ending the boys are shot; in another, they are allowed to run away. The latter, more hopeful, dreamlike sequence of eventual survival characterizes several films that provide audiences with an illusion of rescue or reflect the director's insight into the minds of those killed at the instance of their murder. But there are hardly any direct indications of the two boys' identities in the film itself. This gives it a universal aspect, which is strengthened by the expressionist atmosphere, the sparse dialogue, the gap between natural beauty and human despair, and the contrast between the innocence and fine features of the boys and the degenerate, wrinkled, toothlessness of the crass and brutal hunters. But this is also an obvious obfuscation typical of films made in Communist-controlled Eastern Europe at a time when emphasis on the unique fate of the Jews was frowned upon by the authorities.[70] Hence the boys represent victimhood as an anonymous state: they are the universal victims of all that is ugly, old, obscene, and brutal; they are the hope for a better future that has almost been extinguished by the leftovers of a dying world. They are victims because they are victims: this is their only, overarching identity. In this sense, they are the "Jew" under Nazi occupation. But this is left unsaid. Rather, they appear merely as quarries for the hunters—breathless, hungry, and terrified. They represent what they are,

The Jew as quarry (*Diamonds of the Night*): Jumping off a train destined for an extermination camp, two starving (possibly but never explicitly defined as Jewish) boys run through the forest until they are caught and apparently executed by local ethnic Germans shortly after they feast on a loaf of bread.

and they are what they represent. Yet the train they are seen leaping from was presumably packed with Jews going to a death camp. This is what viewers may or may not assume, depending on who and where they are and when they watch the film.

This specific obfuscation of the victim's identity has to do both with aesthetic judgment and with ideological orientation and constraints. Němec said of Communist Czechoslovakia in the late 1960s:

> The moving force of all our activity to date has been "the struggle against the dark forces of reaction," to borrow a phrase from Stalin's history of the Bolshevik Party. . . . When one lives in a society that is essentially not free, it is the obligation of every thinking person to attack obstacles to freedom in every way at his disposal, which is what happened.[71]

But it is also clear that Lustig's story, which takes place in the Sudetenland during the Nazi occupation, has been turned into a powerful universal fable emptied of the specific content of the persecution of the Jews, yet using the figure of the "Jew" as a symbol of all the victims of history. Two other manners of approaching this dilemma may serve to illustrate the malleability of the relationship between the "Jew" as victim and the victim as "Jew." Relevant here are attempts to respond to the perceived need to credit certain categories of persecuted humanity with the status of victim, a need which may have been previously denied or insufficiently acknowledged. In order to accomplish this, it often seems necessary to diminish the centrality of the "Jew" as victim—since his victimhood allegedly overshadows all others. Indeed, at times the effect of handing this status over, so to speak, to other representatives of the persecuted of the world is even further enhanced by a complete transformation of roles, to the extent that the non-victim "Jew" now becomes the victimizer of the non-Jewish victim.

Thus in Max Färberböck's *Aimée & Jaguar* (1998), the core of the story is not the persecution and murder of the Jews, but rather the improbable love affair between a young Jewish woman trying to pass as an Aryan in wartime Berlin and a young Aryan mother of four sons whose husband is serving at the front. Based on the memoirs of Aimée, the name given to Lili Wust (Juliane Köhler) by her Jewish lover Felice Schragenheim (Maria Schrader), whose nickname is Jaguar, the film uses all the predictable cinematic devices to evoke the atmosphere of decadence, fear, destruction, sex, music, alcohol, and tobacco that comprise the popular image of the 1930s and 1940s.[72] Illicit both because it is a lesbian affair and because Felice is a so-called Jewish "U-Boot" or "submarine" (a term describing Jews hiding among the Aryan population under a false identity), the affair is obviously all the more exciting for the lethal consequences it must eventually bring. Indeed, Felice is finally arrested by the Gestapo and dies in the camps. She is, in this sense, the "Jewish" victim. But as we know, Lili's life, despite the fact that she survived well into old age, was wretched. In many ways, she had been victimized by her society and in some respects paid the price for what was apparently her only true relationship of love and passion. While the film could have been a powerful psychological drama about the love between two human beings who defy moral conventions and ideological taboos, it is made into a vulgar melodrama that can serve as a model for the capacity of Nazism and war to turn everything that represents them into kitsch.[73]

To be sure, there were such stories of rescue, and even of love, under Hitler's rule and the Allies' bombing raids. But, as the eighty-five-year-old Lili Wust said in an interview in 2000, "I would never have worn a cardigan like the one Juliane wears in the film."[74] The dramatic postures, the schmaltzy music, and the carefully staged sexual scenes are all intended to give the film the "right" atmosphere, making it appear cheap and false. The conventional beauty and mannerisms of the actresses seem to have little in common with the two historical subjects, whose less-glamorous appearance concealed far more interesting and complex characters than those exhibited by their cinematic doubles. Ultimately, this film constitutes one more attempt to hijack the fascination with fascism and war and sell it to an audience whose thirst for this kind of kitsch appears unquenchable. Added to this well-worn mix is the shift in emphasis, also present on the film's "official" Internet site, from those persecuted by the regime to the destruction of Germany.[75] The strategic bombing of Germany specifically, and the victimhood of the Germans at the end of World War II more generally, have recently become a new topic of conversation, representation, and historiography.[76] In some ways, *Aimée & Jaguar* anticipated this development. In this context, the "Jew" as victim—especially when, like Aimée, she is beautiful, sexy, and cool, sitting in glitzy bars next to handsome SS and Wehrmacht officers who do not know that under her flimsy dress lurks a Jew—is an especially alluring subject. This is precisely so because most of the time Aimée does not seem to feel herself as a victim and does not give a sense of her victimhood to the audience. In this manner, she facilitates— especially for a German audience—identification with the German victim, both specifically, in the form of her intellectually and socially inferior lover, and more generally, in the shape of the German capital torn asunder by American and British bombs. It is only appropriate that in this sea of kitsch the "Jew" gives birth to the resurrection of German victimhood.

A far superior yet problematic film, based on William Styron's important (and no less problematic) eponymous novel, is Alan J. Pakula's *Sophie's Choice* (1982).[77] In some respects, this is an intentional attempt to deconstruct the stereotype of the "Jew" as victim, thus exposing the self-guilt, self-recrimination, frustration, and rage among those Jews who lived relatively normal lives in some parts of the world while innumerable other Jews were butchered by the Nazis and their collaborators. The novel is a courageous undertaking, especially by a non-Jew, who employs the perspective of the young aspiring writer Stingo (Peter MacNicol), freshly arrived in late 1940s Brooklyn from the South, as a lens (akin to Styron's own gaze) through which to observe the passionate but violent relationship between Nathan Landau (Kevin Kline), a charismatic but disturbed American Jew, and Sophie Zawistowska (Meryl Streep), a Polish-Catholic survivor of Auschwitz.

The novel and the movie have some similarities with the novel by Isaac Bashevis Singer and the film based on it, Paul Mazursky's *Enemies, a Love Story* (1989), which I will discuss below.[78] But the difference in perspective is just as striking, expressed with particular force in the reversal of the relationship between the gentile woman and the Jewish man. In *Sophie's Choice*, Nathan saves the recently arrived Sophie from undernourishment and neglect in New York but cannot rid himself of the thought that while she, a gentile, had gone through the hell of Auschwitz, he, a Jew, had been spared it. He therefore victimizes her for the sins of her antisemitic and pro-Nazi father (who was murdered nevertheless by the Germans); for her utilitarian relationship with Rudolf Höss, the commandant of Auschwitz; and for the choice she made trying to save her son (who is subsequently murdered anyway) by letting the SS take away her younger daughter. Conversely, as we shall see, in *Enemies* it is the male Jewish survivor, Herman Broder (Ron Silver), who is saved by Jadwiga (Margaret Sophie Stein), a Polish-Catholic woman who was his family's servant. Nathan is obsessed with having "missed" the Holocaust; Herman cannot liberate himself from it. Nathan victimizes Sophie for having been a victim instead of him; Herman victimizes Jadwiga because he was a victim and can no longer find a place in the world for himself. Nathan is mentally ill; Herman is a torn personality because of the horrors he experienced. Both are profoundly unhappy men: one because of what had *not* happened to him and a raging illness that attacks his psyche, the other because of all that *had* happened to him and the unbearable clarity of its memory.

Not unlike *Aimée & Jaguar*, in *Sophie's Choice* there is a fair amount of atmospheric music, dress, drinking, and smoking, although it is much more pertinent in the latter and makes for more convincing cinema. But what is crucial about this film from the perspective of the present discussion is, of course, that it reverses the roles of victim and victimizer entirely, though without ever slipping into either antisemitic or apologetic discourse. Sophie—Polish, Catholic, blond, and blue-eyed—represents the victims of the Nazis. Nathan—handsome, dark, wildly passionate, and deeply disturbed—is out to destroy both of them as a kind of perverse punishment for the crimes of the Nazis. He wants to destroy Sophie, because she is the "wrong" victim, and he wants to destroy himself, because he failed to be a victim. Psychologically, this is a powerful drama. For here we see the destructive effect of the paradigmatic "Jew" as victim: the terrible burden of guilt and the helpless wrath in view of the inability to reverse history, undo the atrocity, or transport oneself into a time and a place not even accessible to the wildest imagination.

Historically, the story has some plausibility, since there is plenty of evidence to show the deleterious effects of the Holocaust on those Jews (and some non-Jews) who were spared it, and the impact on later generations of a "politics of identity" that presents the Jews collectively as victims.[79] The core of the story, however—the central theme, namely Sophie's fate and her "choice"—are troubling precisely because while this was indeed the fate of many Jewish women, it rarely, if at all, occurred in the case of Polish

Catholics. Stories and rumors about Jewish women forced to give up one or more of their children by the SS, as well as about young Jewish women who were forced into the role of sexual slaves of SS commandants such as Höss in Auschwitz and Amon Göth in Płaszów (reenacted in Steven Spielberg's *Schindler's List*), were common at the time and have since been repeated in various memoirs and testimonies.[80] But generally, Polish women who ended up in concentration camps were sent there because of Resistance activities, and they were rarely accompanied by their children. To be sure, some three million non-Jewish Poles were murdered by the Nazis, along with over three million Polish Jews. But Sophie's story is highly unlikely in its details.

Styron's artistic decision (and Pakula's cinematic rendition of it) to ascribe to Sophie what was in fact a typical "Jewish" choice cannot have been a simple literary device to intensify the drama of the story: it is so much at the heart of the matter that it calls for a more comprehensive interpretation. After all, this "Jewish" choice was at the very core of the Nazi worldview: it symbolized the urgent need to eradicate the "Jew" completely and to prevent the possibility of any future Jewish life. It therefore indicated the difference between the place of the "Jew" in the Nazi universe and that of all other "races" and nations, which were to be subjugated, exploited, and abused, but did not merit total extermination. Yet Styron and Pakula are concerned with another issue, even if their preoccupation blurs the central distinction of Nazism. For *Sophie's Choice* is fixated on the admittedly fascinating paradox of the non-victim "Jew" who longs with an increasingly maniacal passion to become a victim, and his encounter with a non-Jew whose victimhood can hardly be distinguished from that of the Jews.

Appropriating the victimhood of the Jews was a rather common feature of post-Holocaust politics of memory, commemoration, rhetoric, and historiography. The Soviet Union refused to recognize the unique fate of the Jews under German occupation; the Poles claimed that they too had six million victims (conveniently forgetting that half of them were Polish Jews and that many Poles had collaborated in their murder or stood passively by as it took place); the Germans insisted that the "catastrophe" that ended the "thousand-year Reich" made them into the moral equivalents of their victims; the French made the Jewish victims of Vichy vanish under the mantle of the heroic Resistance deportees; the Dutch made Anne Frank into a symbol of compassion rather than of denunciation and betrayal.[81] *Sophie's Choice* does not wish to be part of this discourse. But it is also not sufficiently sensitive to the implications of making the Jewish mother and her lost children (the representative par excellence of Jewish victimhood) into a Catholic—not least because of the religious connotations of the sacrifice of children, the murder of babies, and the birth of God that attach and divide Judaism and Christianity. In some ways, choosing Sophie as victim is akin to constructing a monastery in Auschwitz: an appropriation that comes close to distortion and can facilitate denial through an assertion of equal suffering.

At its best, *Sophie's Choice* inverts convenient distinctions and categories in a jarring and illuminating manner. Sophie, an emaciated and disheveled camp inmate, desperate to save her remaining child, tells Höss, the SS commandant responsible for murdering over a million Jews: "My father and I wrote the text that declared for the first time in Polish history the need for a final solution to the Jewish question," and she asserts, "I am an active campaigner in the war against the Jews."[82] Hence she too is both victim and potential victimizer; she is willing to join the devil in order to save her son. At other times, the film slips into cinematic conventions of which it may not even be aware. Tall, charming, handsome Nathan is, in fact, a fraud. Behind the facade of a successful, self-assured, brilliant scientist lurks a homicidal and suicidal madman. Everything about him is false: his profession, his identity, possibly even his love and friendship are mere figments of a sick mind. Nathan is only a victim of his own, unacknowledged disease. The real victim, then, is Sophie. But the "real" Sophie was, in fact, a Jew. To be sure, Sophie also lies: just as she tries to conceal the truth about her father's antisemitic activities from Nathan and Stingo, she pretends to have supported him when pleading with Höss. Indeed, by the end of the film it is hard to know what is true and what is false in her statements. But ultimately she is the prey of circumstances beyond her control, whereas Nathan's fantasies emanate from his own psyche. She is a historical victim, Nathan is a psychopath.

But in a deeper sense, Nathan's love or passion for Sophie symbolizes his sickness: what he longs for in her is the experience that she survived and that he was denied. She can never give it to him, and he can never wrench it out of her. For this he can forgive neither her nor himself. His wretched attempts to extract himself from this emotional cul-de-sac by demeaning her as a woman who saved herself by whoring with the Nazis only drives the two of them ever deeper into incomprehension and despair. The fantasy of the survivor as a prostitute haunted the guilt-ridden imaginations of numerous, powerless Jewish men during their early postwar encounters with young Jewish women who had emerged from an apocalypse that was supposed to have devoured all Jews.[83] But the fact that Sophie is both Catholic and the daughter of an antisemitic professor further complicates this male response to perceived pollution by evil. On the one hand, she is a more obvious target for rage than a Jewish survivor. On the other, this male Jewish passion for a gentile woman, an antisemitic trope and a much-discussed topic in Jewish writing and fantasy, adds yet another layer to the self-hate of the Jewish non-victim. This profusion of contradictory and violently clashing images of the "Jew" is what makes *Sophie's Choice* into a powerful, disturbing, but ultimately flawed film. On the face of it, Nathan is handsome and strong; underneath he is sick and murderous. Professing endless sorrow for the victims of the Holocaust, he victimizes the only survivor of the camps he knows. Starting off as a healer of physical and emotional wounds, he reveals himself to be an uncontrollable destructive force. Thus, while both the film and the novel courageously grapple with the image of the "Jew" as victim by making her distinctly both a victim and a non-Jew, they must contrast this non-Jewish victim with a non-victim, and victimizing, "Jew." This compulsion to invert both figures, while it gives the film much of its drive and energy, also leads it too far toward cliché and melodrama and deprives it of subtlety and deeper psychological insight.

A final transformation of the Jewish victim into its opposite (in the sense of being either a non-Jew or a non-victim) can be found in Eyal Sivan's *The Specialist* (1999). Based on over five hundred hours of footage originally filmed by the American documentary photographer Leo Hurwitz during Eichmann's trial in 1961, the film differs in some essential aspects from the ABC documentary *The Trial of Adolf Eichmann* (1997). In the latter, producer Daniel B. Polin and editors Benno Schoberth and Stan Warnow provide a reconstruction of the event based on recently rediscovered and restored videotapes which, until recently, had been dispersed in several sites in the United States and Israel. Their focus is on the testimonies given by the survivors, which indeed formed the core of the trial and the main strategy of Attorney General Gideon Hausner. For Hausner, and eventually for Israeli Prime Minister David Ben Gurion (1886–1973), the trial was to serve as an opportunity to teach the Israeli public, and especially the youth, about the Holocaust, while at the same time serving as the first occasion ever in which a perpetrator was specifically and exclusively placed on trial for the genocide of the Jews. The witnesses were thus not merely giving testimony that directly incriminated Eichmann, but rather painted a picture of the Holocaust as a whole. This was not much to the liking of the judges, who wanted to preserve the legal decorum of the trial and to focus solely on the evidence relevant to Eichmann's role in the Final Solution. But it was an effective strategy (despite the reaction of many critics, not least of whom was Hannah Arendt), in that it exposed the reality of the Holocaust through the oral testimony of some one hundred witnesses.[84] Thus this ABC production is in essence the reconstruction of the event as envisioned by Hausner, in which the Jews appear as the victims they were.

Conversely, Sivan's film devotes little time to the testimonies of the victims. Even when it does show them, they are edited in a manner that tends to merge one testimony with the next, a stream of tormented voices and anguished faces, a parade of human pain, sorrow, anger, and pity. *The Specialist* primarily focuses on the attorney general, the judges, and, most important, Eichmann himself. Here, then, in the first legal setting that established the "Jew" as the primary victim of Nazi policies, we find a Jewish prosecutor and Jewish judges determining the guilt of the man who embodies the regime that strove to make all Jews into victims. The prosecutor is shown in his most accusatory poses, railing against the defendant in long, not always perfectly coherent tirades, gesturing wildly, asking rhetorical questions, and generally appearing through the editing of the film as the stereotypical *Ostjude,* that proverbial Eastern Jew of German (and German-Jewish) fantasy and anxiety. The judges, who are all products of German education and speak the well-articulated and precise German of the prewar upper-middle-class, demonstrate in their remarks and body language their distaste for Hausner's tactics and style. They appear very much as the poised, somewhat authoritarian and aloof, but absolutely just and fair representatives of the Law, men of unquestionable integrity who insist on showing Israeli-Jewish justice in the best possible light to the rest of the world (known to be keenly following the proceedings). For the Israeli viewer, however, their distinct accent when they speak Hebrew, their perfect German, and their mannerisms make them almost into a parody of the Yekkes, the German-Jewish immigrants who came to Palestine in the 1930s. Retaining their love for the culture they left behind even as they had to flee Nazism, the Yekkes at times seemed to use those beloved fragments of a world that spat them out as their bulwark against what they derisively saw as the quasi-Oriental and quasi–East European culture of the majority of their new homeland's population.[85]

Eichmann (1906–1962), for his part, appears in this film precisely as the middle-ranking, low-middle-class bureaucrat that he indeed was. Nothing is left of the arrogant SS officer who had the power to ship millions of Jews to their deaths. Eichmann here is just as Hannah Arendt described him in her essay on the banality of evil: nervous, smirking, insisting on endless administrative details, stubborn yet obsequious, respectful of authority, and ever-mindful of his status.

The Jew as *Ostjude* (*The Specialist*): Attorney General Gideon Hausner, representing the State of Israel in the first-ever trial of a Nazi perpetrator for the genocide of the Jews, in a characteristic "Jewish" posture that embarrassed the scrupulously professional German-Jewish judges and elicited signs of anger from Adolf Eichmann.

This is the rub. In *The Specialist* Eichmann is clearly the social and educational inferior of the judges. While he shares their unexpressed but visible dislike of the *Ostjude* Hausner, he responds with the kind of respect to the judges that goes well beyond their power to convict him. They are clearly his superiors, as they would have been in pre-Nazi Germany. In this sense, the judges embody the "Jew" as judge, a higher category than that of the "Jew" as prosecutor. For, while the latter is indeed very "Jewish," the former are perfect specimens of the German educated upper-middle-class. The "Jew" as judge has therefore been transformed into the "Jew" as respectable (or *anständig*, as Himmler would have put it) German: the incarnation of German justice and authority. Conversely, while Eichmann figures as the ever meticulous and subservient *Schreibtischtäter* (desk murderer) that has come down to us as the typical Nazi bureaucratic perpetrator, he is also gradually transformed in this film into the stereotypical "Jew" of antisemitic representation. He murders without getting his hands dirty; he obfuscates, concealing his intentions and meanings by a thousand euphemisms; he never accepts responsibility for his actions; and he appears never to understand that behind his mask of bureaucratic respectability hides a mass murderer. Eichmann, then, is transformed into the "Jew" as perpetrator, into an antisemitic caricature of his victims.

Nothing reflects this better than some of the direct discussions between the judges and Eichmann, which are, incidentally, among the most fascinating documents about the Holocaust in existence. In a series of incisive questions, the judges query Eichmann about language, conscience, the manner in which the "Final Solution" unfolded, and the role of the Jews in their own destruction. In all this, despite his refusal and possibly his inability to cut through the thick euphemistic web that entangles his every word, Eichmann is quite frank (though one could hardly describe him as honest). The result, however, is devastating, for it creates a picture of language—the primary tool of human communication—as an instrument that means nothing (Eichmann the bureaucrat was the master of empty phrases) yet facilitates everything (Eichmann's instrument of genocide was the written word). It also creates a picture of conscience, not as the bulwark against criminal inclinations but as the shield that protects one from acknowledging the reality of atrocity; of genocide as an incremental process that is both unstoppable and invisible; and of victims as the facilitators of their own murders and their executioners' most decisive collaborators. In this manner, finally, the boundary between victim and perpetrator becomes blurred, just as the distinction between the "Jew" and the non-Jew is confused. Where language has multiple contradictory or unrelated meanings, conscience is separated from morality, events can neither be seen nor halted, and victims undertake their own victimization; where Jewish judges are the epitome of German justice and the defendant has all the makings of a shifty Jew, we are indeed in a world turned upside down.

Note, for instance, the conversation between Judge Yitzhak Raveh and Eichmann on the subject of the Wannsee Conference of January 20, 1942, in which the decision on the "final solution of the Jewish question" was discussed and coordinated with senior officials of the German Reich. The protocol of the meeting was written up by Eichmann shortly thereafter:

> RAVEH: Here in the protocol is a passage that says, "In conclusion the various types of possible solutions [*Lösungsmöglichkeiten*] were discussed." Do you remember this? Or do you want to see it?
>
> EICHMANN: I remember that it was there, Your Honor.
>
> RAVEH: Perhaps you still remember what was discussed there?
>
> [. . .]

EICHMANN: The various possibilities for killing [*verschiedene Tötungsmöglichkeiten*] were discussed.

RAVEH: *Verschiedene Tötungsmöglichkeiten?*

EICHMANN: Jawohl! [Somewhat equivalent to the military "Yes, Sir!"]

RAVEH: Now, you must explain to me why, after the conference, it was precisely these three men—[Reinhard] Heydrich [head of the Reich Security Main office, RSHA], [Heinrich] Müller [head of the Gestapo, the secret state police, that was part of the RSHA], and Eichmann—who stayed behind and celebrated.

EICHMANN: Why celebrate?

RAVEH: Heydrich and Müller, I understand. Why Eichmann, why also Eichmann?

[. . .]

EICHMANN: Because—we had only just been left alone, and no one else was there, and then Heydrich gave instructions as to how he wanted the protocol written up, and after he had listed these items, there was no further talk of these matters. Rather, I was invited to drink a glass of cognac . . . or two . . . or three. That's what happened.[86]

Here, then, is the cold bureaucrat describing how a decision was made to murder an estimated eleven million Jews (according to the population statistics presented at the Wannsee Conference), how the various killing methods were discussed, and how, having managed to assert his authority as the main architect of the Final Solution, Heydrich invited his two principal assistants to an unusual and thus memorable celebration. Several days later, the presiding judge, Moshe Landau, returns to this issue, pressing Eichmann on the question of these "killing methods" and striving to make him move from the passive form to a more direct form of speech that will name names and specify methods:

LANDAU: Now . . . in connection with the Wannsee Conference—you replied to my colleague, Judge Raveh, that in the part not referred to in the record, methods of killing were discussed.

EICHMANN: Jawohl!

LANDAU: Who talked about this subject?

EICHMANN: Today, I no longer have any detailed recollection of this matter, Your Honor, but I know that these gentlemen were sitting together and that they talked about it using . . . very blunt words, not the words I was later told to put in the protocol. Rather, they talked about it

82

in very blunt terms. Without any circumlocution. I certainly wouldn't remember this were it not for the fact that I said to myself, "Look at that [*schau, schau*], there's [State Secretary of the Interior Ministry Dr. Wilhelm] Stuckart, who is always so meticulous and . . . and a pettifogging stickler to the rules!" And at that moment his tone was . . . He was using a vocabulary far removed from legal language. This is the only thing, I would say, which has actually remained imprinted on my mind.

LANDAU: What did he say on the subject?

EICHMANN: In detail, Your Honor, I would like . . .

LANDAU: Not the details . . . in general!

EICHMANN: There was talk about killing, elimination, extermination. . . . Since I had to prepare the protocol, I couldn't stay and listen to what was said. But the words reached my ear. The room wasn't very big—and I could make out certain words.

[. . .]

LANDAU: And what was said about this important topic you claim to have completely forgotten?

EICHMANN: Your Honor, that's not . . . the more important point is . . .

[. . .]

LANDAU: You mean to say that the methods of killing [*Tötungsarten*] were an unimportant topic?

EICHMANN: Oh, the *methods* of killing [*die Tötung*sarten]?

LANDAU: That's what we are talking about! . . . At that time, was there talk of killing by gas?

EICHMANN: No, not with gas.[87]

Note that what makes Eichmann remember the language used to describe the killing methods is not the methods themselves, but rather that this crass language was used by a man he considered to be superior to himself by rank, education, and breeding. Stuckart's sudden brutality, therefore, not only demeaned him in Eichmann's eyes, but also legitimized for Eichmann the use of such methods in his subsequent actions. For if State Secretary Stuckart could speak like that, Eichmann, a mere SS official, certainly could and should. Yet in the courtroom Eichmann refuses to specify the details. This is not, of course, because he forgot them, or, as he implies later, because this is, to his mind, an unimportant issue— once a decision was made in principle on genocide, the methods and means of accomplishing it were mere technicalities. Rather, he avoids the details because of a combination of bureaucratic unease—Eichmann truly does not like calling a spade a spade if it can be given a euphemism—and, to be sure, in order to lessen his guilt by not associating himself directly with mass murder, or at least with talk about implementing it. At the most he is willing to admit eavesdropping on a conversation that in fact concerned a topic that later became his own primary responsibility. In other words, Eichmann presents himself as a passive observer and mere recorder of an event rather than as an active participant, and somehow he wishes to link this early passivity to his subsequent role as a main agent in the perpetration of genocide.

This position is also crucial to Eichmann's articulation of the concept of conscience. In a statement made during his pre-trial police interrogation, a recording of which was played at the trial (a scene also shown in *The Specialist*), Eichmann remarked on the extent to which the setting of the Wannsee Conference resolved any pangs of conscience he might have otherwise felt:

> It was the first time I attended a conference with the participation of such senior officials as secretaries of state. Everyone was very calm, very friendly, very courteous. Not very much was said and it didn't go on very long. We were served cognac before or afterward, and the affair was over. I felt satisfied as to my personal self-examination with regard to the result of the Wannsee Conference. At that moment I felt the kind of satisfaction Pontius Pilate must have felt, because I felt devoid of any guilt. The prominent figures of the Reich spoke at the Wannsee Conference. The Popes had given their orders. I had to obey. I kept this in mind throughout the following years.[88]

Now it is quite unlikely that the thought of personal guilt had even crossed Eichmann's mind during the Wannsee Conference, and thus he obviously did not need the sanction of the "Popes" in order to be liberated of it. Rather, Eichmann is referring here to guilt and conscience in the juridical sense. He knew that he would have to implement a crime. But since this was allowed and ordered by his superiors, he could no longer be blamed. Thus his conscience, as he understood it, would no longer be burdened. That he chose the analogy with Pontius Pilate is of course quite telling. Perhaps, in the back of his mind (he came from a practicing Protestant family), there was the same association suggested by the Polish woman filmed in Chełmno by Claude Lanzmann: "So Pilate washed his hands and said: 'Christ is innocent,' and he sent Barrabas. But the Jews cried out: 'Let his blood fall on our heads!'"[89]

During the trial, Judge Raveh pursues the matter of conscience further with Eichmann. He reminds Eichmann that while in an Israeli prison awaiting his trial, he had written the following: "Despite everything, I, of course, know that I cannot wash my hands of this, because the fact that I was a recipient of absolute orders definitely no longer means anything today." Raveh asks Eichmann how he can reconcile this statement with his assertion that he felt like Pontius Pilate. But for Eichmann there is a difference between his personal sense of innocence and his knowledge that under the law he may be found guilty. He responds by saying that "according to today's [law] . . . obviously the fact that one was a recipient of orders can no longer make any difference, and consequently, according to the existing paragraphs, I cannot wash my hands of things in innocence, but in fact am incriminated under these paragraphs." And yet, Eichmann believes himself to be innocent, as the following exchange indicates:

RAVEH: But I had always understood that Pontius Pilate's washing his hands was based on an introspective process.

EICHMANN: That is precisely what I wanted to refer to, Your Honor. But when it came to my innermost self—I in fact now had to search my soul, and of course one always searches one's soul—and this is where man judges himself. And I admit that this soul-searching and judging oneself may be a hard thing, depending on the mood and the prevailing influences on one—sometimes one is inclined to personal cowardice, and one would prefer to shirk this business of taking a clear-cut decision on oneself. I am aware of all this. But if I say to myself, if I remind myself how often I tried to get away and to obtain another posting . . . then I tell myself . . . Yes, I did everything I could have done. I was a tool in the hands of forces stronger than myself. I—let me put it in a somewhat vulgar way—I must wash my hands of it in innocence, as far as my innermost self is concerned. That is how I would understand this. As far as I am concerned, this does not involve external factors as much as my own soul-searching.

RAVEH: So when you washed your hands in 1942, it was a form of mental reservation?

EICHMANN: In 1942?

RAVEH: At the time of the Wannsee Conference!

EICHMANN: Oh, the Wannsee Conference.

RAVEH: Was it a form of mental reservation?

EICHMANN: Yes, well, here I said to myself—here are all the bigwigs together—there is nothing to be done.[90]

Thus Eichmann "washes his hands" in relief because the responsibility has been taken over by his seniors—which is of course precisely one of the reasons that Heydrich had convened the Wannsee Conference in the first place. His conundrum is that while he cannot admit to the court that from this point on he could proceed with the murder of millions without any pangs of conscience, he can also not admit moral reservations, since his point is that the legitimacy given his actions by the Reich's top officials relieved him of any responsibility. In fact, Eichmann gives little sign that he had had any moral reservations to start with. But at least after January 20, 1942, he also believed that he had no reason to worry about the illegality or criminality of his actions. The "Popes" had taken that upon themselves.

The most important moment in *The Specialist*, indeed, the most important moment in the trial itself, comes with Judge Benjamin Halevi's interrogation of Eichmann. Halevi was known already from the so-called Kasztner trial of 1954, in which Israel (Rudolf, Rezső) Kasztner, former head of the Hungarian-Jewish community and by the time of the trial a senior Israeli official, brought a libel suit against Malkiel Grünwald, who had accused Kasztner of complicity in the Holocaust in Hungary. In 1944 Kasztner had tried to delay or prevent the deportation of the Jews to Auschwitz through direct negotiations with Eichmann. Although his efforts failed, he did manage to save 1,685 Jews, including many members of his own family, who were safely sent off to Switzerland. Halevi found that Grünwald's accusation was not libelous, and instead accused Kasztner of "selling his soul to the Devil." The Israeli Supreme Court later reprimanded Halevi for his conduct in the trial and absolved Kasztner of all responsibility, noting that "there is collaboration that deserves praise and that, in any case, if it is not accompanied by malicious and evil intentions, it should not be condemned or seen as a moral failing." But Kasztner's reputation was destroyed and he was assassinated in 1957. This was also the reason that Halevi did not serve as the sole judge in the Eichmann trial but was a member of a three-judge panel presided over by Landau, who was a member of the Supreme Court.[91]

Now, however, was Halevi's opportunity to speak directly with one of the main facilitators of the Final Solution, and the man who had almost single-handedly organized the murder of Hungarian Jewry. He could now return to the very same issue that he had raised during the Kasztner affair: the nature of the crime, the motivation of the perpetrators, and the role of the victims. It is here, finally, that Eichmann himself is employed by an Israeli judge to elaborate his views on the complicity of his victims in an incremental process that culminated in unprecedented genocide:

> HALEVI: I shall also permit myself to depart from the normal practice by abandoning Hebrew for a moment to address the Accused in his [!] own language. [He switches from Hebrew to German, as Judge Raveh had also done.] . . . Did you ever experience a conflict . . . a—what one would call an inner conflict between your duty and your conscience?
>
> EICHMANN: It would be better to call it a split state.
>
> HALEVI: A split state [*Gespaltenheit*].
>
> EICHMANN: A form of splitting, where one fled from one side to the other, and vice versa.
>
> HALEVI: One had to renounce one's personal conscience?
>
> EICHMANN: Yes, one could say that. Because one could not determine and regulate it oneself.
>
> HALEVI: Unless one accepted personal consequences for oneself.
>
> EICHMANN: One could have shot oneself, or one could have simply said, "I am not going to do this any longer." But I don't know what would have happened then.
>
> HALEVI: But you did not try that, did you?
>
> EICHMANN: I did it differently, in my normal standard—my continuous requests to be transferred. . . .
>
> [. . .]
>
> HALEVI: If there had been more moral courage [*Zivilcourage,* courage of one's convictions], everything would have turned out differently. Do you agree with this?
>
> EICHMANN: Of course, if this moral courage had also been structured hierarchically, then that would have been quite clear.
>
> HALEVI: Then this wasn't fate, inevitable destiny?
>
> [. . .]
>
> EICHMANN: It's a question of human behavior, and definitely that is how things were, it was wartime, things were turbulent, every individual thought to himself: "There's no point in my being against it, it would be like a drop in the ocean, damn it, and there is no point, no sense, nor will it do any good nor any harm, nor anything." And so it must also be a question of the times, I think, times, education, that is ideological education, rigid

discipline, and all that kind of thing. . . . Because generally militarists, by definition, do not have moral courage.

HALEVI: Well then, if you are now examining your conscience seriously, must you not then admit that you lacked moral courage?

EICHMANN: I lacked this just as many others lacked it, in the entire army, just like most of those in uniform.

[. . .]

HALEVI: According to you, the idealist you claim to have been is defined as someone who executes the orders he receives from above to the best of his ability.

EICHMANN: Yes, I understood by this clinging to the National Socialism which was preached and, as a nationalist, to do my duty in accordance with my oath . . . Today I realize that every nationalism if taken to extremes leads to brute egoism, and from there, it is only a small step to radicalism.

HALEVI: At that time, it was very difficult for an individual to accept the consequences of refusing to obey orders?

EICHMANN: At that time people were living in a time of crime legalized by the state . . . and it was the responsibility of those who gave the orders.[92]

This discussion of conscience also takes place at several points during Eichmann's cross-examination by Attorney General Hausner, in which the presiding judge, Landau, also intervenes. Sivan has patched together these moments into what appears to be a single exchange, whereas in the transcript of the trial they are scattered over several sessions. This text provides another extraordinary insight into the mind of a perpetrator who feels that he has learned an important lesson that he could teach to posterity, a conviction he expresses with much greater certainty than any of his victims. Eichmann presents himself here as nothing less than an expert in genocide prevention. Here we find the perpetrator, who had already exterminated his victims, also annihilating the very possibility of the "Jew" as victim through his rejection of any responsibility for the "creation" of this victim. Since without a perpetrator we may logically never have a victim of human misdeeds, the victim ceases to exist and is replaced by the figure of the non-responsible organizer of the victim's extermination. In other words, with the undoing of conscience comes the erasure of the victim: this is the heart of the matter, or, perhaps more accurately, the void at the core of modern genocide:

Remorse is for little children.

The perpetrator as ersatz Jew (*The Specialist*): Eichmann positions himself at the forefront of fighting genocide: "Remorse changes nothing, it won't bring anyone back to life. Remorse is pointless. Remorse is for little children. What is more important is to find ways and means to prevent these things from happening in the future."

HAUSNER: Do you admit, therefore, that you were complicit in the murder of millions of Jews?

EICHMANN: From the legal point of view . . .

HAUSNER: My question is not juridical. In your conscience, do you consider yourself guilty of complicity in the murder of millions of Jews? Yes or no?

EICHMANN: In human terms, yes. Because I am guilty of organizing the deportations.[93] . . . Remorse changes nothing, it won't bring anyone back to life. Remorse is pointless. Remorse is for little children. What is more important is to find ways and means to prevent these things from happening in the future.[94] . . . And I intend to request permission, after the trial is over, to treat these matters in the form of a book, say, in which I can express myself freely, and I am prepared to call a spade a spade [*das Kind bei Namen zu nennen*] as a warning to present and future generations. . . .[95]

LANDAU: You must understand that it is your duty to say here everything which you would have written in this book you just mentioned—to call a spade a spade. . . .

EICHMANN: Jawohl. Since you have asked me, Your Honor, to give a clear answer here, I must state that I consider this murder, this extermination of the Jews, to be one of the most heinous crimes in the history of mankind. . . . In conclusion I would like to state that even at the time, I personally thought that this violent solution was not justified, already then I considered this to be a monstrous deed, where I regrettably, bound as I was by my oath of loyalty, had in my sector to deal with matters relating to transport aspects and could not be released from this oath. . . . So, deep down, I did not consider myself responsible before my own inner being, and I felt free of guilt. I was greatly relieved that I had nothing to do with the actual physical extermination. The part I was ordered to deal with was quite enough for me.[96]

Returning to Halevi's interrogation of Eichmann, having discussed and dismissed the question of conscience and responsibility, the judge then moves on to the process of genocide:

HALEVI: The general outlines, both strategic and tactical, of the extermination of the Jews . . . were planned as a military campaign, and also planned using psychological warfare, tactical deception of the opponent, and so on. . . .

EICHMANN: I believe this gradually crystallized during the course of events. And if necessary, Himmler gave orders directly. I do not think that right from the outset—how can I put it—there was a discussion of action to be taken, whereby the whole thing was dealt with in the minutest, finest detail, but that this automatically somehow resulted from events.

HALEVI: All right. So you are saying that this evolved—let us say organically, in the course of time.

EICHMANN: Yes, that is how I would describe it.[97]

Now that the Holocaust had been established as an incremental process (a point on which Halevi appears to agree with Eichmann), the judge proceeds to what is both for him and for Sivan the most critical issue, namely, the relationship between perpetrator and victim. If for the perpetrators moral courage was a meaningless concept, disobedience unthinkable, and resistance barred by the very fact that genocide had developed "organically" without any identifiable plan or program, what was the role of the victims' conduct in the process of extermination? It is at this point that the "Jew" as victim is transformed into his own executioner:

HALEVI: For example, first the Jewish communities in Vienna, then Prague, then Berlin, came under the supervision of the Gestapo, for the purpose of emigration.

[. . .]

EICHMANN: First centralization of the Jewish organizations took place together with their parent organizations.

HALEVI: I am talking about the supervision of the Gestapo.

EICHMANN: Yes, yes.

HALEVI: So that, for example, the Jewish functionaries were given the task of registering the members of their communities for the purpose of emigration, settling property matters, and exercising fairly stringent controls here, which greatly facilitated emigration.

EICHMANN: Yes, that's right [*Jawohl, das stimmt*]. . . .

HALEVI: Yes. And then that could be switched rapidly and smoothly to deportation.

EICHMANN: Jawohl.

HALEVI: Then there was the idea of the Jewish councils, especially in Poland.

EICHMANN: Jawohl.

HALEVI: And later also for Hungary, too? Before that, let us say for Holland? Possibly it started in Holland with the Jewish council in Amsterdam, then in Poland—or perhaps simultaneously—and finally in Hungary?

EICHMANN: Jawohl.

HALEVI: As instruments of German policy regarding the Jews, these Jewish councils—shall we say—considerably facilitated the implementation of measures taken against the Jews?

EICHMANN: Jawohl.

HALEVI: And saved a great deal of manpower and staff.

EICHMANN: Jawohl.

HALEVI: Both police and civil servants, too?

EICHMANN: Jawohl.

[. . .]

HALEVI: These made it possible, by misleading the victims, to facilitate the work, and also to harness the Jews themselves to work for their own extermination [*Diese ermöglichten durch Irreführung der Opfer, die Arbeit zu erleichtern und auch die Juden selber einzuspannen in den Dienst ihre eigenen Vernichtung].*

EICHMANN: Jawohl, das stimmt.[98]

This is an extraordinary moment. Here the judge, who speaks to the accused "in his own language" (which is of course the judge's mother tongue as well, even as he now represents his new and newly chosen Motherland), is Eichmann's social superior, *his* judge, and the man who will send him to his death; at the same time, he is on a quest for the logic, nature, and meaning of the genocide of his people (and the loss of his own previous identity as a German). His rage against those who had "sold their soul to the Devil" is hidden under his boyish looks and seemingly naive questions. Unlike Hausner, he almost seems to express a kind of understanding for Eichmann's predicament as a man caught up in the conventions and ideas of his time, the framework of a subservient bureaucracy, and the relentless logic of creeping, incremental inhumanity. Almost obscenely, the root of Halevi's wrath at the Jews is given factual confirmation by Eichmann, the engineer of their destruction. Thus the Jewish judge, who for the first time in history sits in judgment of his people's murderer, ends up creating the "Jew" as his own perpetrator in the guise of the Jewish councils manipulated by the Nazis to act as their instruments of destruction. A trial intended to bring some sort of redemption, along with knowledge, understanding, and justice, ends up on a very different note. For ultimately, as reflected in this "lost," "rediscovered," and, it must be said, digitally manipulated footage, the trial can be seen not only as a failed attempt at judicial redemption but also as a record of the failure of the human spirit, of human civilization, and of humanity as such. This failure cannot be made good in the courtroom: as we watch the images and hear the voices of these men and women, who were still young enough in 1961 for us to imagine what they might have looked like during the war, we must compare our position to that of Franz Kafka's K. at the gate of the Law: Perhaps there is some sort of redemptive justice on the other side of that gate, but we will never be allowed in. Most likely, however, the gate simply separates two moral voids.[99]

UNREDEEMED VICTIMS

Such major judicial events as the Nuremberg Tribunal and the Eichmann trial had, however, a built-in redemptive moment: the perpetrators were arrested, tried, and punished. Yet this moment belongs to everyone but those who matter most: the perpetrators and the victims. The perpetrators cannot be redeemed, both because of the enormity of their deeds and because of their inability to recognize their guilt, thus revealing their capacity to emerge from hell with their conscience intact. The victims cannot be redeemed, both because the kind of justice meted out to the perpetrators bears no relationship to the horror they experienced and because the perpetrators refuse to recognize them as their victims, thereby erasing the link between the crime and the criminal, the murdered and the murderer. If the victim exists in a different universe from that inhabited by the perpetrator, then the punishment of the latter (rare, belated, and often ludicrously light) can have no redemptive effect on the former.

Such absence of redemption for the victim is almost impossible to represent. The figure of the "Jew" as an unredeemed victim is unbearable precisely because he is the rare remnant of the millions who were murdered. We seek consolation in the presence of the survivor; for, after all, it is the survivors we see, not the "drowned." And in cinema, whose power lies in its ability to draw us into its world, the figure of the unredeemed victim has the same effect as that of a black hole: it sucks us in, obliterating all light, and leaving nothing behind. In a sense, it destroys itself and everything that comes into contact with it. This is also why films that do provide us with redemptive endings as a response to the catastrophe of the Holocaust so often appear false, their happy endings casting a long shadow even on their most truthful moments. Curiously, then, only irony, distance, and humor may at times relieve the cinematic "Jew"—in his capacity as the absolute victim—from the need for redemption without self-destruction, or allow a glimpse of redemption without turning into contrived exercises in moralistic deception.

Antonín Moskalyk's *Dita Saxová* (1967), which was based, like Zbyněk Brynych's *Transport from Paradise* (1963) and Jan Němec's *Diamonds of the Night* (1964), on a story by Arnošt Lustig, was a product of the liberalization of Czech cinema that swept that country in the 1960s. Following the Soviet invasion of 1968, this wave was quickly stemmed. Films dealing explicitly with the fate of the Jews were accused of Zionist tendencies. Since Lustig immigrated to the United States in the wake of the invasion, films based on his work were withdrawn from distribution. Ironically, it was only the liberalization of the arts in Czechoslovakia that allowed the making of films lacking almost any redemptive note, whereas communist aesthetics demanded an uplifting moment and condemned pessimism as a sign of decadence. But during those brief years of the new wave, Czech cinema at its best sometimes surpassed Polish cinema, which still often insisted on heroic sacrifice even if it moved away from the conventions of socialist representations. Thus precisely the hopes of "socialism with a human face" facilitated the making of films on the dehumanizing effects of racism, dogmatism, and war, and allowed for a focus on the "Jew" as the embodiment of victimhood. No less ironically, with the reassertion of dogmatic socialism in the 1970s, such a focus on the "Jew" as victim was again made anathema.[100]

Dita Saxová is a bleak and not entirely successful portrayal of several teenaged girls who lost everyone in the Holocaust and are trying to rebuild their lives in an uncaring, corrupt, and exploitative postwar Czechoslovakia. Some escape their hopeless dormitory existence through marriage; others emigrate; others die, whether by suicide or through illness. Influenced both by socialist realism and by the new French cinema of the time, the film lingers on mood, atmosphere, and pose. Dita, whose ephemeral beauty attracts men like moths to a flame, eventually burns herself out, driven into the snow by a deep and never-articulated despair. We see a glimpse of her as a young girl, walking hand-in-hand with her parents; they are heading to the train station, for deportation. This is her only memory of her parents, whom she will never see again. It is a powerful moment, reminiscent of Saul Friedländer's description of being led away from his parents by two nuns through the street of a southern French town.[101] But the film provides very little insight into the minds of these young women, their past, their hopes, their character. Even their Jewish identity is merely hinted at. Beautifully filmed, the movie itself is emotionally somewhat juvenile, unable to penetrate what lies behind Dita's striking eyes, and somewhat too self-consciously preoccupied with exposing the emptiness of socialist rhetoric and bourgeois hedonism.

If such an attempt to represent the unredeemed fate of youth after the Holocaust was a novelty of the Czech cinema, or any socialist cinema in the 1960s, it was even less likely to come from Hollywood, whose name became associated with obligatory happy endings. And yet, one of the most remarkable films ever made on the "Jew" as unredeemed victim was the product of the same industry that had by then churned out thousands of heroic tales and romances on the war that bore little similarity to its actual devastation. Interestingly, Sidney Lumet's *The Pawnbroker* (1965) shares with *Dita Saxová* an insistence on representing a Jewish protagonist with none of the stereotypical characteristics of the "Jew."[102] But both the ideological and cultural sources of this "untypical" Jew and the ramifications of this portrayal are quite different. Dita appears as a non-Jewish "Jew" because of a socialist predilection to obscure Jewish identity and suffering, and also because an antisemitic tradition makes it necessary to present Jewish fate as part of a larger context of misfortune so as to facilitate empathy. Sol Nazerman (Rod Steiger), the protagonist of *The Pawnbroker,* is, by appearance and mannerisms, "untypical," yet is thrown, both by fate and by choice, into the "typical" role of the "Jew," that of a pawnbroker in a black slum. Rather than juxtaposing an atrocious past with an idyllic present, the film merges them into a continuum of pain, suffering, exploitation, and deception. The few glimpses we have of Nazerman's prewar existence, when he was an assimilated academic, suggest that he was "untypical" also in his interaction with society, but that this had no effect on the destruction of his family and the ruination of his life.

It is precisely this fate that brings him to the frontier of racial and economic confrontation in Harlem. In a sense, Nazerman refuses to leave the Nazi universe and insists on finding its closest equivalent in the American slum of the 1960s. And here he "plays" the "Jew" that he never was, the "Jew" of antisemitic fantasy, the product of centuries of persecution, the figure into which the Nazis had made him and which he, in a self-hating, flagellating, inexpressible silent rage, has taken upon himself. His entire view of the "Jew" in history, the disillusioned view of the enlightened, assimilated, non-Jewish "Jew" whose world had been shattered by the Holocaust, is encapsulated in his response to a question by his assistant, Jesus Ortiz (Jaime Sanchez), who asks, "How come you people come to business so natural?":

> First of all, you start off with a period of several thousand years during which you have nothing to sustain you but a great bearded legend. No, my friend, you have no land to call your own or to grow food on or to hunt. You have nothing. . . . You're never in one place long enough to have a geography, or an army, or a land myth. All you have is a little brain . . . a little brain and a great bearded legend to sustain you and convince you that you are special, even in poverty.
>
> But this . . . little brain, that's the real key. You see, with this little brain, you go out and buy a little piece of cloth and you cut that cloth in two and you go out and sell it for a penny more than you paid for the one. . . . Then you run out and buy another piece of cloth. Cut it into three pieces, and sell it for three pennies profit. But, my friend, during that time you must never succumb to buying an extra piece of bread nor a toy for a child. . . . No, you must immediately run out and get yourself a still-larger piece of cloth, and so you repeat this process, over and over and suddenly you discover something. You no longer have any desire, any temptation to dig into the earth or grow food, or to gaze at a limitless land and call

it your own, no, no. You just go on and on and on repeating this process over the centuries, over and over, and suddenly, you make a great discovery: you have a mercantile heritage. You are a merchant. You're known as a usurer, a man with secret resources, a witch, a pawnbroker, a sheeny, a mockie, and a kike.[103]

To be sure, it is precisely because of the pernicious consequences of representing the "Jew" as a type, particularly in antisemitic discourse, that we find attempts to deprive Jewish protagonists of characteristic religious, cultural, physical, and behavioral traits while preserving their status as victims. Nor do such representations in and of themselves necessarily stretch the imagination or the historical reality of the events depicted. Certainly under the Nazis, but also in other instances in pre-Nazi Germany, France, the Soviet Union, and many other lands, men and women who had shed all or almost all of their Jewish traditions and sense of identity were nevertheless persecuted as Jews. It is this condition of being a non-Jewish Jewish victim that creates the representational tension often lacking in films whose protagonists, however historically authentic they may appear, correspond to the anticipated antisemitic imagery.[104]

While Nazerman's occupation in the (formerly Jewish but now black) ghetto is almost impossibly stereotypical, he derives no pleasure from it, evokes no sympathy, and seems to have no compassion for anyone. Having decided to kill all emotion in himself, he disdains sentimentality, nostalgia, pity, friendship, and love. Yet his hard crust cracks as he is beset by recurring flashbacks of his life before the disaster, the loss of his children and his wife, the endless humiliation he underwent, and his inability to remake himself as anything more than an empty shell. Nazerman's postwar world is hell, a life to be endured after death, not the paradise that we expect survivors to have felt themselves entering following their liberation. Nazerman is never liberated, and the universe he inhabits is as cruel, violent, and crooked as the one he left behind in Europe.[105]

When a young black woman offers herself to him for money so as to pay her pimp, Nazerman recollects being forced to see his wife turned into a sexual slave for the Nazis. Only then does he also realize that his own pawnshop is merely a cover for laundering drug money for the powerful local Mafioso, in the shape of an elegantly dressed black man. Traveling in the subway, Nazerman recalls his son slipping out of his grasp and being trampled to death on the transport to the camps. His unrelieved sense of guilt is compounded by the death of his assistant, Jesus, who shields him during a holdup. Jesus himself had organized the holdup as a logical conclusion of Nazerman's lesson that, "next to the speed of light, which

The Jew transformed (*The Pawnbroker*): Sol Nazerman, an assimilated European academic, is forced to watch his wife being turned into a whore for the SS. This is part of a flashback sequence triggered when a local prostitute in Harlem offers herself to him to pay her pimp, who is using Nazerman's pawnshop as a means to launder underworld profits.

Einstein says is the only absolute in the universe, second only to that, I rank money. . . . That's what life's all about."[106] Just as Nazerman is finally beginning to feel compassion for another human being—the former petty criminal Jesus, who treats him as a mentor and father figure—the brutality of an indifferent and arbitrary fate tears him away. Saved by his self-proclaimed "disciple," the shattered Nazerman presses his hand into the nail holding the sales receipts, literally crucifying himself. The Catholic Jesus has sacrificed himself for the Jewish Holocaust survivor Nazerman (the man of Nazareth, or Nazarene, the ancient name for Christ or Christian), and in turn the Jew crucifies himself for all the suffering of humanity. As Nazerman stumbles out of his shop into the bustling streets of Harlem, his mute scream accompanied by Quincy Jones's disjointed, jazzy score, there is perhaps a glimmer of hope that all the accumulated pain of the downtrodden will bring forth a small measure of compassion. In the face of the conundrum of representing the "Jew" as victim, Lumet manages to avoid falling into the trap of either antisemitic tropes or the banality of empathy.

The Jew's crucifixion (*The Pawnbroker*): After Nazerman is saved by his assistant, who staged a holdup of the pawnshop and was then killed protecting him from being shot, he presses his hand into the nail that holds the sales slips, in rage and despair over the endless cruelty of the world and the futility of goodness.

Lumet, himself the son of two actors on the Yiddish stage, uses the eponymous novel by American-Jewish author Edward Lewis Wallant to create a tale of possible, if tentative, Christian redemption.[107]

The strength of this film lies in its merciless exposure of the lingering impact of atrocity, its ability to distort the survivors and drive them to persecute others even as they never recover from their own pain. The impact of the film and its controversial status is a result of its uncompromising insistence on the injustice and suffering of the present, in which the survivor is complicit, but which also drives him to final despair. *The Pawnbroker* is a rare accomplishment for American cinema that has arguably never been matched since. It creates a non-Jewish Jewish victim who chooses to transform himself into the most persistent stereotype of the "Jew" as a response to a complete loss of faith in human civilization and progress; it sketches a repulsive yet crushed man whose suffering cannot arouse sympathy but whose condition is nonetheless heart-wrenching; and it depicts a world that remains indifferent to pain and sorrow and keeps producing more victims.

Another unredeemed but very Jewish victim is Herman Broder (Ron Silver), the protagonist of Paul Mazursky's no less extraordinary *Enemies, a Love Story* (1989). Unlike the black-and-white, dark, and relentlessly grim *The Pawnbroker,* Mazursky's film, faithful to Bashevis Singer's tone, is full of color and humor, even as it focuses on the tormented survivors of catastrophe. If Nazerman can move neither forward nor backward, weighed down as he is by his dead soul, Herman is in constant flux, always running away even as he breathlessly seeks happiness and fulfillment. Having lost his wife and children in Poland, Herman lives in the very Jewish neighborhood of Coney Island with Jadwiga (Margaret Sophie Stein), the family's former Catholic servant who saved his life. Although she converts to Judaism and Herman finally marries her out of gratitude, the blond, blue-eyed Jadwiga remains his adoring servant and cannot grasp his inner turmoil.

Indeed, Herman leads a second life with his mistress, Masha (Lena Olin), who is to him in a certain sense what Sophie is to Nathan in *Sophie's Choice.* Sexually obsessed with each other, these two survivors are completely incapable of achieving the normality they claim they long for: Herman, because he must always keep escaping; Masha, because her passion for life is always on the verge of being transformed into a suicidal urge. When Masha becomes pregnant, Herman marries her too, this time out of a sense of responsibility, as he understands it. Then his prewar wife Tamara (Anjelica Huston) turns up. Not too surprised by Herman's situation (as Bashevis Singer has written, the characters in this story are victims of their own personalities as much as they are of the Nazis), Tamara proposes to act as Herman's "manager," since he has obviously lost control of his existence.

Thus Herman finds himself married to three women, all of whom he feels obliged to and in his own fashion loves, but with none of whom can he actually live. His triple existence becomes a harried, intense, and increasingly blurry non-life, as he spends most of his time rushing from one to another, always evading himself. When Masha's mother dies, they plan to run off together, but know that they never will. The other option is suicide. Here, too, each acts according to his and her character. Masha kills herself, and Herman, whose urgent need to flee is motivated by a powerful urge to survive, vanishes forever. As Jadwiga gives birth, Tamara comes to assist her in the joint venture of raising their child. It is a kind of redemption after all: a new life is born, symbolic, perhaps, of reconciliation between Jews and gentiles; the mother who lost her children has been given a new family; the servant will now care for the child of her master-husband.[108] Herman will lead many more non-lives, never stopping until he falls; but his baby may have some hope of a relatively normal existence with two loving mothers, far from the horrors of the past.

In several ways, *Enemies, a Love Story* inverts the role of the "Jew" as victim in a manner that can be related to but is very different from *Sophie's Choice*. Despite the catastrophe, on the surface things seem to return to normal. Jadwiga is the servant again, Tamara manages her husband's life, and Herman has a mistress. But then Jadwiga is in fact Herman's savior, wife, and mother of his child; Tamara is the mother of his murdered children; Masha plunges into suicidal despair; and Herman will never stop running from his terrifying nightmares. The attempt to recreate the past is both false and impossible. Herman's domination of Jadwiga is out of place, for he will always remain in her debt. The transformation of Jadwiga into a Jew is both farcical and deeply sad, symbolizing a world turned upside down, a past that cannot be restored, and lives that cannot be mended. Normality will never be regained: personal biography and historical events cannot be erased, and their effects on one's mind are irreversible. Nor should one try to reach back to relations, habits, and beliefs that were at the root of the catastrophe that burned all bridges to the past.

In one sense, then, there is no redemption: much as Herman tries, he cannot return to his faith, cannot find happiness in a family, and can only be swept away momentarily by passion. The turmoil in his soul resembles in some ways the dark void of Nazerman's heart. Yet the characters here are very much part of a Jewish universe—including Jadwiga, who takes up her prewar role without pause. Their redemption, if one can call it that, is also very Jewish: life must continue, and that life is symbolized by the birth of a baby. If Nazerman crucifies himself, Herman plants his seed. The "Jew" as victim can escape from that fate only through a new generation that does not know the hell from which he emerged. Indeed, thousands of survivors acted precisely according to this logic as soon as they could after their liberation: they made a child.[109]

REDEMPTIVE NOSTALGIA

The "Jew" that Herman was has been torn out of everything that gave his existence meaning: the social, cultural, and religious milieu without which he cannot define or find himself. The qualified redemption through the second generation, a Jewish-gentile child with a Jewish-gentile mother, is all that we can hope for in *Enemies*. Whatever we may say about Herman, he is no hero. Always on the run, he will do everything to avoid confrontation, to please everyone, until he finally snaps and vanishes without a trace. For a discussion of redemption through heroism, in which the "Jew" sheds his characteristic mode of shirking confrontation and replaces his status of victim with that of hero—with varying degrees of success—we will wait for the next chapter. This is one figure that grew from the ashes of the Holocaust. But let us conclude the discussion of the "Jew" as victim with a few words on that other characteristic mode, or mood, of post-catastrophe representation, namely, redemptive nostalgia.

Numerous postwar films exhibit an urge to use the figure of the "Jew" both as a historical embodiment of the victim and as a liberating tool for the present—whether by recognizing past sins, omissions, and repressions, or by humanizing a present reality perceived as cold and insensitive precisely because it no longer contains this "Jew." Perhaps because the burden of this double role is too great, such films often end up caricaturing the very figure they intend to bring back to life. In a sense, they become implicated in the antisemitic discourse on the "Jew" even as they believe themselves to be in the process of undermining it.

In chapter 1, I argued that films depicting the "Jew" as perpetrator draw on self-representations of Jews as victims; this indicates that such self-representations are one of the most valuable sources of antisemitic imagery. But for post-1945 cinema, the predilection of movies depicting the "Jew" as victim to appropriate certain antisemitic tropes is much more significant, not least because in the West (unlike in the former Communist Block and the present-day Middle East), both cinematic depictions and public discourse have eschewed overt antisemitism, tending to present Jews in a positive light. Hence, while the use of negative stereotypes has greatly diminished, they have often been replaced by positive stereotypes that are similarly one-sided. This can be understood only if we keep in mind the sources of such imagery, best revealed in antisemitic films and other forms of popular representation. From this perspective, while it is true that the harvest of overtly antisemitic cinema was qualitatively and quantitatively poor, its long-term impact has been substantial, particularly because, for the most part, it was and remains unconscious.[110]

The Holocaust made the "Jew" into the epitome of victimhood. But how does one represent the "Jew" as victim, or the victim as a "Jew," while neither slipping into a racist and essentialist discourse that attributes to the "Jew" innate cultural and physical traits, nor asserting that the "Jew" is a mere construction of the antisemitic fantasy with no independent existence outside the perpetrator's murderous gaze? In the former case, one becomes complicit in the argument that no amount of assimilation will entirely erase the taint of cultural and racial foreignness. Hence the "Jew" will never truly come out of the ghetto. In the latter case, the very notion of Jewish identity is denied. Hence the removal of antisemitism simultaneously annihilates the "Jew." And, if some Jews insist on being Jewish independently of antisemitism, that is, if they assert their identity despite the absence of the antisemitic fantasy that allegedly constructs them, they may well be suspected of avowing the kind of unique and immutable essence that was at the root of the Holocaust in the first place. Conversely, if the "Jew" is the symbolic embodiment of victimhood (rather than "simply" a victim), then by extension all victims become Jews, for the only distinguishing mark of the "Jew" is victimization.[111]

Not surprisingly perhaps, some of the least self-conscious and most jarring examples of this slippage from philosemitism to antisemitism can be found in post–World War II Germany.[112] Didi Danquart's film *Jew-boy Levi* (1999), based on Swiss playwright Thomas Strittmatter's 1982 text (*Viehjud Levi*), is one example of the new and well-meaning German cinema, which appears entirely unaware of reproducing old stereotypes even as it tries to depict the "Jew" as an innocent victim of ideologues, bigots, opportunists, and weaklings. In Strittmatter's original thirty-page play, the itinerant cattle dealer Hirsch Levi arrives at a small Black Forest village in the mid-1930s, where he encounters the peasant Andreas Horger, his wife Krescencia, and other inhabitants and temporary visitors. Levi is humiliated by railroad workers from the north and is later found dead. The play suggests that he was either murdered by the villagers or committed suicide.[113]

Danquart and his scriptwriter Martina Döcker use the basic ingredients of the play to create a more dramatic narrative. Levi (Bruno Cathomas) is provided with all the trappings of a "Jew" so that the German audience would have no difficulty in recognizing him as such. Appropriately dressed in black clothes and a black hat, he "performs" his "Jewishness" in front of an audience of one—his inseparable travel companion, Jankel the rabbit—by chanting a Yiddish song and breaking out in a little "Hasidic" dance. Always trying to please everyone, Levi is a keen but kind haggler. He is also very keen—in his hopelessly inept, not to say pathetic way—to marry the Horgers' daughter Lisbeth (Caroline Ebner). But this is hardly a realistic or "natural" option, quite apart from the (unmentioned) racial laws of the Nazi regime. Lisbeth is in love with the virile Paul Braxmaier (Bernd Michael Lade) who, despite his handsome Aryan looks, is strongly opposed to the "invaders" from the north. These other outsiders are embodied by the Nazi engineer Kohler—who doubles as a magician in a faint citation of Thomas Mann's parable on fascism, "Mario and the Magician"—and his sexy female assistant.[114]

The fake Jew (*Jew-boy Levi*): The itinerant cattle dealer Hirsch Levi "performs" his Jewishness in front of his inseparable travel companion, Jankel the rabbit, chanting a Yiddish song and breaking out in a little "Hasidic" dance in the midst of the German forest.

Thus the cast of characters is set up for a sentimental tale concerning love and social exclusion, the warmth but also narrow-mindedness of village life, the evils of modernity (represented by the Nazi engineer and railroad workers), and the now-lost but once-endearing "Jews," who roamed Germany's lands before Nazism cast its evil spell. To be sure, there may still have been some itinerant Jewish cattle dealers in the Black Forest in 1935, although most Jews who stayed in Germany were by then concentrating in the cities and were unlikely to look and sound as "Jewish" as Levi. Indeed, the main complaint of the Nazis was that they could not easily tell who was a Jew, a problem eventually resolved by introducing the yellow star (*Judenstern*). Similarly, the rate of intermarriage between German Jews and Christians before the Nazi regime was very high and—with the exception of the Nazis—many Germans did not view such unions as "unnatural" as Levi's aspiration appears in the film. Conversely, by 1935, intermarriage was hardly a reasonable expectation, not because the two "looked" so different, but because of the Nuremberg Laws, which forbade any sexual contact between Aryans and Jews.[115] Nor does Danquart seem to be aware of the fact that such liaisons between Jewish men and Aryan women play a central role in the antisemitic imagination. Lisbeth is in fact attracted to Levi, perhaps precisely because he is so different and "exotic." But she will "obviously" not become his wife. Instead, she saves his life by facilitating his escape from rowdy Nazis in the tavern where she works. Fortunately for Levi, in the film he is not murdered, but merely vanishes into the night.

Danquart's focus in the film is on the manner in which the villagers turn against "their" Jew once representatives of the outside world, that is, Nazi Berlin, appear on the scene. But in fact, the "Jew" appears to be inherently foreign to the village even before the Nazis arrive. Indeed, his bizarre relationship with Jankel the rabbit accentuates his status as a wandering Jew who travels from one location to another, apparently without a home, a family, a *Heimat*. Unlike the real "cattle-Jews" who had lived in Germany for centuries until the Nazis murdered them, Levi speaks with a foreign accent and sings Eastern European Jewish songs, as if he had just stepped off the train from Galicia. Thus, when the good-hearted Lisbeth finally manages to persuade Levi to leave, his departure seems quite natural, since he never belonged to the village in the first place, and one expects that he will continue on his way to yet another foreign land, as he obviously has no home to return to.

Danquart has remarked that "when I tell a story about 1935 in 1997, it must be a 'modern' story."[116] The film critic Gerhart Waegner noted in response that the "film sheds light on the mechanism of mass psychology that casts out fellow-citizens, but implicitly does not confine this process to the antisemitism of the 1930s. Despite its cautious opening toward the present the film remains faithful to the basic thought of the play: Strittmatter called his play 'a reflection about my concept of Heimat.' In this sense Didi Danquart's film has become a Heimat film against the grain— perhaps in Fassbinder's sense."[117]

This is an interesting observation, because the film is in fact both a critique of the nostalgic view of the German *Heimat* (as depicted most famously in Edgar Reitz's film saga *Heimat* [1984]) and, in a less conscious manner, also embraces precisely those elements that define this genre. For Levi is not simply "cast out" in a process the Germans call *Ausgrenzung*, or being put on the other side of the border. Levi in fact never belonged to that *Heimat* in the first place. He may be a "fellow citizen" (*Mitbürger*), but he is obviously neither an inherent part of the village community nor "essentially" German. He is an outsider who should have been accepted yet never belonged. Thus the nostalgia expressed in this film for such colorful characters as Levi—with his dark hair and black clothes–has an obviously redeeming feature for its German viewers, who can feel how much more tolerant of foreigners they have become since the bad old days of Nazism, without noticing perhaps that these foreign fellow-citizens are still being defined as non-German precisely by the fact that one tolerates (or does not tolerate) their presence.

Jew-boy Levi is only one of several films that have tried to provide a sympathetic perspective of the "Jew" as victim and in the process have fallen into the trap of antisemitic representational discourse. This is not simply a question of the limits of a specific filmmaker's creative talent or the imaginative capacity of a society still grappling with the issue of accommodating outsiders. Rather, it reveals the extent to which antisemitic imagery has polluted our representational universe. The attempt to create an "authentic" cattle-Jew ends up in a caricature that fails to retain any semblance of authenticity. Precisely the urge to condemn antisemitic prejudice culminates in the introduction of such an unmistakably "Jewish" figure that his environment's reaction to him as an outsider must be viewed with a certain degree of understanding and even sympathy. The prevalence of this dilemma can be demonstrated by reference to several other films emanating from entirely different cinematic and cultural milieus. Thus, for instance, Steven Spielberg's box-office success *Schindler's List* (1993), which I will discuss in greater detail in the next chapter, includes several scenes where Jewish characters seem very close to their images in the Nazi propaganda of the time, while the main protagonist is a handsome and fearless gentile.[118]

In some films on the Nazi period, Jews do not appear as victims at all. Rainer Werner Fassbinder, referred to positively in Waegner's above-cited review of *Jew-boy Levi*, was heavily criticized for his play "Garbage, the City, and Death" (1976), which was perceived by many critics as blatantly antisemitic and was performed only once on the German stage in 1985.[119] But in another case, Fassbinder's film *Lili Marleen* (1980) uses the figure of the "Jew" to highlight in a subtler manner the victimhood of the Germans (and the role played by the "Jew" in this fate). Attacked by critics mainly as a sellout to Hollywood because of its lavish aestheticization of Nazi "culture" and war, it hardly drew attention for its representation of Jews. Here the German singer Wilkie (Hanna Schygulla), who makes her living working in Swiss bars, falls in love with Robert Mendelsson (Giancarlo Giannini), a young Jewish composer. But Robert's rich father manages to send Wilkie back to Germany, thus separating the couple. As the war breaks out, Wilkie becomes a star with her song, "Lili Marleen," and she soon enters the glitziest circles of the Third Reich. In the end, Robert marries a Jewish woman and becomes a famous conductor, while Wilkie returns to the anonymous existence she led before the war. Based on the autobiography by singer Lale Andersen (nicknamed "Angel of the Soldiers"), who made

"Lili Marleen" into the greatest hit of World War II, the film presents Wilkie as the true victim of the period—of the Nazis, the war, and the Jews—whereas the dubious Jewish characters who fleetingly reappear at the end of the movie seem not only to have survived but to have made a neat profit from the war.[120]

Fassbinder, it might be said, is mostly concerned with German redemption. In this he is hardly alone among German filmmakers. Such well-known directors as Volker Schlöndorff, Alexander Kluge, and Wim Wenders are also preoccupied with German fate, history, and loss.[121] The difference between Fassbinder and other German filmmakers is that his films often contain a "foreign" character, not infrequently a "Jew," who somehow is at the root of the disasters that eventually call for redemption. In most German films, the "Jew," even if he does not appear in person but is only a memory, or even a mere echo, serves as the facilitator of redemption rather than the cause of disaster. This can be seen, for instance, in Caroline Link's *Beyond Silence* (1996), the story of Lara Bischoff (Tatjana Trieb, then Sylvie Testud), the daughter of two deaf parents who becomes infatuated with playing the clarinet. Initially, her love for music creates a rift between Lara and her father, to whom it is inaccessible. But eventually, especially after Lara "discovers" klezmer music, the link between daughter and father is reestablished. Thus the eminently "foreign" klezmer music, which first acts as a barrier, turns out to be a facilitator of communication between the musically gifted young woman and her deaf father; by extension, this music has the potential of reestablishing the long-obstructed links between the generations of postwar and post-unification German society.

Beyond Silence is therefore one in a long series of German films concerned with the manner in which all that is deaf, emotionally dead, and spiritually barren in the postwar German soul might be released from its chains of silence and repression; only this time, liberation is achieved through the medium of traditional Eastern European Jewish music, the music of a culture and a people that was eradicated by the Germans. (The context of this newly discovered tool of liberation is, of course, the recent revival of klezmer music and its numerous derivatives in Europe, the United States, and Israel.)[122] This is one of the best examples of what I have called elsewhere the representation of absence, the redemptive quality of the absent Jew as the representative of all that is emotionally vital, whose "departure" deprived Germany of its ability to communicate with itself and whose return, however elusive and incorporeal, may bring back the links to the soul that were lost when the Jews "went away."[123] This link between

The Jew's necessary absence (*Beyond Silence*): With Chagall's lovers in the background, Lara Bischoff, whose parents are deaf, meets klezmer master Giora Feidman, through whom she discovers the communicative powers of Jewish music in a Germany bereft of both Jews and emotions: "It's from the heart and it's joyful and wild and at the same time it's sad and not truly free."

the return of Jewish absence through its musical echoes and its capacity to bring back to life an emotionally desolate and incommunicative present is introduced in *Beyond Silence* with a fair degree of subtlety. Yet, when the absent "Jew" finally and briefly surfaces toward the end of the film, he cannot but evoke all the old philosemitic clichés that merely reflect the prevalence of their obverse aspect.

Thus, when Lara comes to a performance of Giora Feidman (who also played much of the background music in *Schindler's List*), she actually meets the Argentine-born Israeli clarinetist and klezmer master on the stage, in front of a projected image of one of Marc Chagall's famous shtetl depictions.[124] Preceded by his heavily accented, awkward, but expressive English, Feidman emerges from the darkness, his "typical" Jewish features juxtaposed with Lara's well-illuminated Aryan face and wide-open, trusting blue eyes, while Chagall's lost world of surreal reds and blues flickers all around them. It is at this moment that the communicative power of (Jewish) music is "transmitted" to Lara:

FEIDMAN: Listen [*sic*] the sound of the picture. Can you hear it? Is a great artist, Chagall. He know, that el mundo is music. You want to know the truth of music?

LARA: Yes, I want to learn.

FEIDMAN: Learn? You don't need it. You have it inside. Listen to the song inside.

At this point Feidman is called to prepare for the show. But Lara has heard something that will resonate in her mind as she comes to the audition at the music academy. Here the appropriately severe and humorless examiner goes straight to the heart of the matter, and for the first and only time in the film calls Lara's favorite music by its name:

EXAMINER: Miss Bischoff, in your application you write that you're interested, among other things, in traditional klezmer music. What interests you in this musical direction?

LARA: That's hard for me to say. It's a feeling, perhaps because it's so emotional.

EXAMINER: Emotional? Oh, well . . .

LARA: I mean, it's from the heart and it's joyful and wild and at the same time it's sad and not truly free. And this is a connection that I can well understand. Do you know what I mean?

Now Lara's father unexpectedly arrives in the back of the room. Lara plays her music (a modern work, in fact, rather than klezmer music) and then converses in sign language with her father just before the film's titles appear.

FATHER: So that's your music?

LARA: Yes, it's my music. Do you think you'll ever be able to understand it?

FATHER: Maybe I can't hear it, but I'll try to "understand" it. Have I lost you?

LARA: I've loved you ever since I was born. You'll never lose me.[125]

In this manner, without ever mentioning Jews, and only once indicating Lara's instrument of liberation and redemption specifically as klezmer music, the "Jew" as the unnamed healer of postwar German emotional paralysis makes his melodious appearance. Curiously, this central, if subtle, motif in the film seems to have escaped its reviewers. Perhaps, indeed, even the filmmaker herself was unaware of the implications of her own work: Both that the "Jew" as victim had taken away with him Germany's soul, and that the recovery or "discovery" of the "lost" world of the Jews through their music will deliver Germany's soul back to it and facilitate the human interaction that had been barred by the eradication of the Jews themselves.[126]

Redemptive nostalgia of a different kind characterizes Yolande Zauberman's French-Russian co-production *Ivan and Abraham* (1993), a sensitive but somewhat contrived evocation of life in a "typical" shtetl in eastern Poland on the eve of World War II. In a general sense, this film belongs to the same trend that made klezmer into the bon ton of the musical scene in the 1990s, along with the discovery of music from Europe's former colonial empires. But in this case, the evident nostalgia for the vanished world of Europe's eastern borderlands, with its mix of languages and customs, beauty and savagery, derives its redemptive fantasy from the friendship between fourteen-year-old Ivan (Sasha Iakovlev), a Christian apprentice to a Jewish family, and nine-year-old Abraham (Roma Alexandrovitch), the Jewish grandson of the tyrannical estate manager Nachman.

The French-born daughter of Polish Jews who survived the Holocaust, Zauberman employs an almost exclusively non-Jewish cast of Russian actors (the one exception is Zinoviy Gerdt, who plays Zalman, the father of the handsome young Jewish communist Aaron [Vladimir Mashkov]).[127] The actors were taught to speak Yiddish, and the film also features Polish and Romany characters who are supposed to add to the texture of this black-and-white film as a quasi-realistic fantasy of a world on the brink of an abyss. For those unfamiliar with the languages spoken in the film or with the actors who try to speak them, the illusion may be more effective. Paradoxically, then, the less the audience knows about this world, the more authentic it will appear. Just as Abraham can transform himself from a Jew to a Gypsy simply by cutting his hair and sidelocks, so the well-known Russian actor Rolan Bykov can become the stereotypical Jewish estate manager for a bankrupt Polish prince by assuming the kind of mannerisms displayed by Ferdinand Marian in *Jew Süss* five decades earlier. If one is willing to ignore some glaring anachronisms and the not entirely convincing linguistic mélange, the film does provide some insight into Jewish-gentile relations on the eve of a pogrom, revealing the Jews to be vulnerable outsiders within their own environment and victims of their own neighbors. This is indeed the prelude to Nazi policies of "resettlement" and genocide and to Soviet border changes and deportations that erased a centuries-long legacy of multiethnic (if at times violent) cohabitation.[128]

Somewhat reminiscent of Sholem Aleichem's *Tevye the Dairyman* (*Tevye der milkhiker*) (1894–1916), the traditional structure of Abraham's family disintegrates under the combined weight of modern times and anti-Jewish violence.[129] Abraham's only friend is the gentile Ivan; his sister Rachel (Maria Lipkina) is in love with Aaron; and Nachman is abandoned by the Polish prince who was his employer and protector. To her credit, Zauberman has gone to great lengths to recreate life in the borderlands of the 1930s by shooting the film in Ukraine. She has also attempted to go against conventions by focusing on the friendship between Ivan and Abraham, who escape from the town at the beginning of the movie so as to be able to stay together, and return to it at the end of the film, only to find that the entire community had been murdered by the local peasants. Thus the friendship of the two boys is set against the relentless and merciless logic of religious hatred and ethnic incitement. If a beautiful peasant girl tells the two boys that the Jews drink the blood of Christian babies, Abraham is saved from the wrath of the villagers, who believe that as a Gypsy he has cast an evil spell, only by admitting that he is a Jew. Indeed, Zauberman plays with this ambiguity of Abraham's character by endowing him with an uncanny ability to communicate with horses, thereby exemplifying his instinctive links to nature, a quality denied the Jews in the antisemitic imagination. Somewhat awkwardly, then, the film tries to break down the stereotypes of appearance and conduct, both through its cast and by its narrative. Yet it is difficult to avoid thinking of antisemitic films in which actors strove to appear "Jewish" by use of exaggerated gesticulations and foreign-sounding speech, and it is no less troubling that the nostalgia for this mythical borderland on the eve of destruction must highlight the redemptive element of a gentile-Jewish comradeship that was so sorely lacking in the far more sordid reality of the period.[130]

To be sure, *Ivan and Abraham* is not far from the truth by depicting a world in which innocence, ignorance, habit, and tradition breed aggression and violence, while the refusal to obey conventions and follow the old ways opens up people's eyes and hearts. There are no real villains in this film, but there is no lack of perpetrators. The peasants murder the Jews because they believe they stole the land whose proceeds were in fact wasted by the Polish prince. They perceive the Jews as magicians and servants of demons hiding immense riches inside their homes, whereas in fact the Jews live in poverty that is only marginally less wretched than that of their gentile neighbors. The social fabric of the Jewish community is rapidly coming apart largely because of the intrusion of the modern world and not only because of antisemitic violence: while the old men still pray fervently

The Jew as Gypsy (*Ivan and Abraham*): As Abraham cuts off his sidelocks and escapes from home to the countryside, he reveals an uncanny ability to communicate with horses. But he is suspected by the villagers of being a Gypsy who consorts with demons, thereby discovering that endless fields and fast horses notwithstanding, his margins of liberty are as constricted as his shtetl.

in the synagogue, the children play soccer in the yard. Moreover, the world outside the confines of the shtetl to which Abraham and Ivan flee— somewhat akin to the world outside the ghetto in *The Golem*—is distinguished by a combination of physical beauty and human brutality. Finally, if the friendship between Ivan and Abraham is a doomed remnant of human sentiment in a world torn by ethnic and religious strife, the only ray of hope for a better future is represented by Rachel and Aaron, who flee to Paris, where they will presumably take up the ideological fight against racism and prejudice (though under the flag of a communism that was to subject those regions to dictatorial rule for many decades after their liberation from German occupation).

This escape to Paris—the capital of human rights and Enlightenment values—was also the path belatedly taken by Zauberman's own parents. Yet *Ivan and Abraham* may in fact demonstrate how difficult it is to employ that very Western perspective in an attempt to reconstitute the fragments of the lost world of Eastern European Jewry. For now the "Jew" of those formerly multiethnic borderlands is a Russian who learned Yiddish in the studio and who uses "Jewish" gestures borrowed from Jewish self-representations and antisemitic caricatures. Just as these borderlands are now littered with

111

ruined synagogues and desecrated cemeteries, so too this film is not a recreation of a past and a memory but a manifestation of absence and erasure resurrected as fantasy and the longing for a world that never was.

The redemptive qualities of children, especially Jewish children, play a particularly important role in tales of horror and evil. Since the Jewish child has come to represent the victim par excellence in much of European, American, and Israeli depictions of victimhood, such children appeal both to the makers of images and to the producers of nostalgia, both to those who wish to shock and traumatize and to those who strive to humanize and empathize. The memory of child victims is the most difficult to bear. Yet it may also have a redeeming effect, whether by dint of survival and rebirth, or thanks to the innocence and purity of the victims. Precisely because of the extreme tension between the guiltlessness and naiveté of childhood and the horror of genocide, such tales are especially moving and troubling; they also tend to be appropriated by others as the most desirable, because it is the most terrible, form of victimhood. We can think here of such diverse works as the beautiful, heart-wrenching, yet somewhat detached memoirs of Saul Friedländer on the erasure and reconstruction of the self; Louis Begely's fictionalized memoir on survival through identity fraud and the inability to regain the child that was; the faux-memoir by Binjamin Wilkomirski, who imagined himself into a Holocaust childhood; films that will be discussed below, such as Andrzej Wajda's *Korczak,* on the man-child who went with his orphans to Treblinka, and Orna Ben-Dor Niv's *Newland,* on the remaking of child survivors in Israel; and many others.[131]

Michel Tournier's novel *The Ogre* (1970), which took its title and central theme from Johann Wolfgang von Goethe's poem *The Erl-King,* served in turn as the basis for Volker Schlöndorff's film *The Ogre* (1996).[132] This is the tale of a terrible yet innocent monster, Abel Tiffauges (John Malkovich), a French orphan whose only friends are children. Accused by a girl of having molested her, Abel is offered redemption through service in the army on the eve of World War II, and is soon thereafter taken prisoner by the Germans. It is in the service of the Nazis that Abel's life—inscribed as it is with the Mark of Cain for his original sin—assumes its most ambivalent and disturbing quality. Ending up in the paramilitary elite school Kaltenborn, Abel finds himself playing the role of that infamous Erl-King, stealing children from the Masurian Lakes in East Prussia to serve as cannon fodder for Hitler's voracious army. And yet, having become the caretaker of hundreds of beautiful Aryan boys, Abel is also in his own private, albeit doomed paradise. The arrival of the Red Army heralds the collapse of his

The Jew as redeemer (*The Ogre*): Abel Tiffauges, French prisoner of war and child-snatcher for an elite Nazi school, is led away from the last battle into the Masurian bogs by Holocaust child-survivor Ephraim, in a reversal of Goethe's *Erl-King* and in ironic reference to the legend of St. Christopher, the "bearer of the Christ-child."

idyll. The Nazi commanders order the children to fight, knowing full well that they will all be slaughtered in a grotesque and macabre bloodbath. But Abel has meanwhile found the agent of his redemption: a Jewish child he rescues from a death march that passes by the school on its way from that other, unarticulated hell of the Holocaust. Ephraim (Ilya Smolyanski) is thin, dark, and determined to survive at any price. Riding on Abel's shoulders, Ephraim leads him through the battle raging in the school into the endless expanse of half-frozen lakes. As they sink into the marshes, it seems that Abel's tormented soul may have finally been redeemed by this act of martyrdom. In Goethe's poem the child arrives at the castle dead in his father's arms, for the Erl-King had stolen his soul as they rode through the forest. In the film, however, it is the child who cleanses the ogre's soul and erases the mark of sin on his forehead, even as he leads Abel into an icy grave in the swamps of ancient Germandom.[133]

The Ogre unfortunately does not measure up to some of Schlöndorff's greater films, and fails to do justice to Tournier's complex and deeply disturbing novel, which won him the Prix Goncourt in 1970.[134] While the film is dedicated to Louis Malle, its treatment of child victims—admittedly profoundly troubling also in Tournier's novel—lacks the subtlety and insights of Malle's melancholy and low-key masterpiece, *Au revoir, les enfants* (1987).[135] In many ways, the film exploits the Jewish child victim to bring about Abel's final epiphany. As he evolves from victimized child to victimizer of children, his erotic fascination with young Aryan bodies makes him complicit with fascist aesthetics, manifesting that mélange of evil and naiveté that was at the heart of the Nazi annihilatory endeavor, even as Abel himself is the most unmanly of men and manifests a deep aversion to violence of any kind.[136] Abel's sexual attraction to boys is reminiscent, of course, of Luchino Visconti's *The Damned* (1969), where the filmmaker lingers on the beautifully sculpted bodies of innocently juvenile, savagely violent, and utterly doomed homosexual representatives of Aryan manhood, half-stripped of their Nazi storm-trooper uniforms. Abel's schoolboys and would-be executioners are cut down by the Soviets, just as Ernst Röhm's Storm Troopers are massacred by the SS: their youth, beauty, and helplessness transform them into innocent victims (and children are *always* innocent victims).

The only boy to survive this slaughter of children, riding Abel into his watery grave, is Ephraim, the Jewish survivor of his people's destruction. In saving Ephraim, Abel must die; for Ephraim is the tool of his deliverance and death. In Günter Grass's *The Tin Drum,* also made into a film by Schlöndorff in 1979, Oskar Matzerath is transformed from an eternally three-year-old child, who drums and shrieks his way through the Third Reich, into a monstrous dwarf in the Federal Republic of Germany.[137] In Schlöndorff's remaking of Tournier, the child victim turned child-eating ogre Abel is redeemed by the embodiment of victimhood, a Jewish child-victim of the Holocaust. Does Ephraim now reverse the role of the Erl-King by giving his own soul to the Nazis' faithful soul-snatcher, Abel, just before drowning him in those Masurian Lakes where the Germanic warriors of old are still lying encased in armor and mud? Or has Ephraim been transformed from the epitome of the "Jew" as victim into Christ Himself, transforming Abel in turn into St. Christopher, the "bearer of the Christ-child," as in Hieronymus Bosch's famous painting of 1480, the giant who defied both king and Satan until Christ Himself led him to martyrdom through a raging stream? Ephraim the redeemer of Satan's servant, turned into the savior of souls, may appear to be a strange figure indeed. In fact, the metamorphosis of the Jewish victim into a Christ-like figure, and the accompanying transformation of his persecutor into a saint, is part and parcel of the European imagination of the Holocaust, deeply rooted in the role allotted to Jews in Christian theology, tradition, and fantasy.[138]

Schlöndorff's somewhat heavy-handed treatment of this theme cannot but itself evoke images of Wagnerian götterdämmerung, a fascination with doom and destruction that appears in many of his other films as well. The link between Schlöndorff's and Tournier's understanding of human fate and redemption has much to do with their background. Born in 1939, the German filmmaker's predilection for Christian motifs was probably influenced by his years as a student in a Jesuit boarding school in Brittany in the 1950s (he also completed a degree in political science in Paris). The French writer's fascination with the culture on the right bank of the Rhine began with his parents, who had studied German at the Sorbonne, and taught him the language at an early age. Born in 1924, Tournier spent many summers during the 1930s vacationing with his mother in Hitler's Germany, while also attending several private religious schools. Immediately after the end of World War II, he spent four years at the University of Tübinbgen.[139]

Such dark and generally humorless fascination with evil, in which the "Jew" plays Christ to his murderers and the fabricated false grandeur of fascism combines horror and nostalgia, is turned on its head in the recent, deceptively light Czech tragicomedy, *Divided We Fall* (2000). Eschewing all pomposity about fate and victimhood, sacrifice and glory, the film paints a picture of general complicity, compromised humanism, and unwilling heroism. But this is not a cynical tale of a terrible time. Instead, the film subtly weaves in the Christian motif of the birth of Jesus as the Jewish Messiah under the most unexpected circumstances and with the assistance of the most unlikely Magi. For while God is absent from the film, His son is fathered by David, the single survivor of his local Jewish family, and is borne by the devoutly Catholic Marie, who remains barren (and thus in a sense a virgin) to her goodhearted, bungling, and sterile husband Josef. Since according to the Jewish tradition, the Messiah will be a descendant of the house of King David, the baby produced combines Christ, the Jewish Messiah, and, in the most literal sense, the continuation of (partly Jewish) life and hope after the catastrophe of war and genocide. In a far more subtle and slightly ironic manner, then, the baby, who is the product of a spontaneous, if hardly unambiguous, act of goodness, signifies the tentative, practical, in some ways opportunistic, yet absolutely necessary redemption of a segment of humanity that is corrupt, petty-minded, often mean, sometimes murderous but never truly evil, and on occasion even kind, caring, and courageous.

There are no real heroes in this film, just as there are no absolute villains. Directed by Jan Hřebejk (born in 1967), and based on a screenplay and novel by Petr Jarchovský (born in 1966), this film was made by a generation far removed from the events of World War II, and whose contributions to cinema began on the eve of the final dissolution of communist rule. Nevertheless, *Divided We Fall* is very much part of a far older tradition of Czech fiction and film, going back as far as Jaroslav Hašek's *The Good Soldier Schweik* (1926) through Milos Forman's *Loves of a Blond* (1965) and Jirí Menzel's *Closely Watched Trains* (1966), and of course such novels as Milan Kundera's *The Joke* (1967) and *The Book of Laughter and Forgetting* (1979). If Hašek recalled the horrors of World War I, Forman—whose father was Jewish—lost both parents in Nazi camps, Menzel was closely watched by the communist authorities, and Kundera went into exile in France after 1968. Conversely, the young makers of *Divided We Fall* are at the forefront of Czech (and Slovak) post-communist fiction, theater, and cinema.[140]

In *Divided We Fall*, Josef Cizek (Boleslav Polivka) and Marie Cizkova (Anna Siskova), a childless couple who had hoped to witness the war from behind firmly shut windows in their little Bohemian town, find themselves more or less forced to shelter young David Wiener (Csongor Kassai), the son of Josef's former Jewish employer, who escaped from the camps in Poland where the rest of his family was murdered. Terrified of denunciation by their neighbors, they are also under constant threat of being found out by their self-declared friend Horst Prohaska (Jaroslav Dušek), the Wieners' former chauffer, an ethnic-German who now prospers under the occupation and is infatuated with Marie. Josef attempts to keep Horst at bay by working with him for the Germans, sorting out stolen Jewish property, thereby making himself into a collaborator as well as a rescuer. But when Marie rejects Horst's advances, he seeks revenge by trying to impose on the couple a local Nazi bureaucrat, Albrecht Kepke (Martin Huba), the loss of whose sons on the Eastern Front has left him mentally unbalanced. This potentially catastrophic imposition is thwarted by Marie's declaration that she is pregnant, and since Josef has just been informed by the doctor of his infertility, there is no choice but to have her inseminated by David. Marie is in labor just as the Russians arrive. But who will deliver the baby now that the doctor is dead? Josef remembers that Horst had delivered his own children, and rescues him from prison and execution claiming that he is a doctor. As Horst delivers the baby, Josef is denounced as a collaborator by a neighbor who had previously refused to shelter David but is now parading as a partisan. About to be shot by a Czech Red Army officer, Josef is released when David appears at the last moment and attests that this is his rescuer, establishing the authenticity of his own identity as Jewish victim by showing the number tattooed on his arm with indelible ink (the officer checks it, saying that this is a common trick to escape just retribu-

The Jew as alibi (*Divided We Fall*): A much-relieved Josef Cizek, about to be executed for collaboration, discovers David Wiener hiding on the roof. He shows a skeptical Soviet-Czech officer, who just liberated the town, that "his" Jew has a number tattooed on his arm.

tion). In the last scene, Josef walks through the ruins of the town with the baby in a stroller. Seeing the murdered Wiener family having a picnic together with the last Kepke boy, who was shot for desertion from the front, he proudly shows off the baby, the lower part of whose body is exposed. As he wipes the baby's urine from his hand, we are left to wonder whether this Messiah, son of David, has also been miraculously circumcised.

The predilection for Christian religious symbolism in films about the "Jew" as victim is one of the most significant aspects of cinematic representations of the Holocaust, and we shall see more examples of it in the following chapters. This film, however, uses this symbolism neither in an apologetic mode nor in order to mock it. Marie, who keeps a painting of the Virgin Mary and Baby Jesus on the wall despite Josef's derision of her faith, does not commit adultery but saves one life and creates another. Josef, who by disposition is a coward, and prefers the life he has—as employee of the Jews, working for the Germans, or submitting to the communists—to any future ideal or sacrifice, finds his crowning achievement and moment of greatest happiness with the baby he never wanted to have. The characters are all transformed with the arrival of the baby, even Horst, who is generally an unsavory character; the particularly despicable neighbor, who betrayed both David and Josef and then put on the insignia of a partisan; and the brutal Czech Red Army officer. The sight of a new, innocent life brought into a cruel and cynical world has a redeeming effect even on the most jaded and compromised. David, who had been exposed by the neighbor, does not denounce him; Horst, who had saved David earlier from a German raid, is now saved in turn by David, who testifies that the former had helped the couple hide him. And, perhaps, there is even a grain of truth in this assertion, since Horst preferred to exploit this unmentioned presence of David to pressure Marie to spend more time with him.

Thus everyone is lying, yet everyone also has a certain measure of goodness, even old Kepke, whose sorrow at the death of his sons culminates in an incapacitating stroke. The tales of resistance and liberation are stripped of their heroic garb: the few remaining Germans and collaborators are humiliated and killed by those who refused any help to their victims. And yet, in the midst of all this betrayal, accommodation, opportunism, and cowardice, a young man is saved and a new life is brought into the world thanks to the ambivalent heroism and shards of goodness of a few undistinguished people. This compromised and yet somehow effective heroism is akin to what Tzvetan Todorov has called the fragility of goodness, the moment at which imperfect people decide to make a stand and become inextricably complicit in good despite their many faults, just as others become inextricably complicit in evil without entirely lacking in virtue.[141]

Fundamentally, however, *Divided We Fall* is neither about the "Jew" as victim nor the "Jew" as hero. Rather, the "Jew" provides here an opportunity to glimpse the compromised yet lifesaving heroism of the bystanders. One could almost say that David, the obliging and never accusatory victim, is there as a test for the rest of the community, revealing much more about the gentiles than about the Jews, who ultimately all disappear at the end of the war, as does he—without his son, who is left as his unclaimed progeny with Josef and Marie. The "Jew" here is thus less a person than a symbol, neither of good nor of evil, but of the manner in which extremity makes people display either their worst or their best aspects, and most often both at the same time. In one sense, the "Jew" here is the ultimate symbol of the victim, the victim of all humanity who had taken its sins upon himself so as to redeem it. In other words, it is the "Jew" as Christ, which makes the "Jew" into the absolute victim precisely by unmaking him as a Jew. In another sense, the "Jew" provides humanity with an opportunity to do good precisely because of his extreme victimization. In this sense, by saving him from crucifixion—in fantasy if not in reality—the gentiles can remain

The Jew as Messiah (*Divided We Fall*): Josef Cizek shows off the son born to his wife Marie and David, the Jew they hid—a coincidence of names and circumstances indicating that the boy represents the second coming—to the ghosts of David's family enjoying a picnic in the ruins.

Christian and the "Jew" can remain a Jew. Finally, whether David's son was (at least symbolically) circumcised or not, we know that he will be raised as a good Catholic by Marie, while David Wiener, his father, will figure only in the stories that the townspeople will tell about the years of occupation, some more truthful than others. It will take another generation, born long after these events, to evoke the memory of the flesh-and-blood victims who vanished forever from the scene. And, when finally evoked, they will all-too-often return under the guise of nostalgia for the better and simpler times of the past and the redemption they brought in some mysterious manner to those who witnessed their murder.

[3]

THE "JEW" AS HERO

JEWISH HEROES

The emergence of the "Jew" as hero from the ashes of the Holocaust was a profoundly paradoxical process. After all, the most distinguishing mark of the Shoah was the systematic destruction of masses of helpless and defenseless Jews. No wonder that the "Jew" as victim plays such a major role in post–World War II cinema. Yet it was precisely the scale of national humiliation, the bleak despair evoked by mass murder, and the shadow that genocide cast over the belief in goodness and progress that generated the need to create the postwar heroic "Jew." From the reality of starving ghettoes, overcrowded freight cars, and airtight gas chambers came an imaginary hero charting a path to liberty and self-assertion. In a world where the future had been obliterated, heroic fantasies were needed in order to forge a livable destiny.

Heroic Jews in cinema existed long before the Holocaust, of course, whether as ancient biblical figures of quasi-superhuman dimensions, or as modern characters who exemplified social integration and patriotism, especially through courageous service in their nations' wars. This was certainly the case on the American screen, both in the interwar and the pre-1914 periods.[1] But the nature of the heroic "Jew" has been irreversibly transformed by the event of the Holocaust and its exposure of the devastating effects of antisemitism, prejudice, racism, and exclusion. To be sure, the "Jew" as hero has emerged in the service of very different and often conflicting needs and agendas; he therefore wears a variety of masks and costumes. He may be a typical "Jew," cast in a heroic rather than depreciating mode, but still preserving either the comical aspects of Jewish self-representation or the protean nature attributed to the "Jew," whether as a menacing, endearing, or even admirable characteristic. He may be the end product of a transformation from a typical "Jew" to a national figure—a process in which he sheds his Jewish characteristics and takes on all the attributes of heroism, patriotism, and sacrifice venerated by his country or its dominant ideology. In some of the most breathtaking metamorphoses of this genre, the heroic "Jew" appears as a cross between Christ, a biblical hero, and a member of the revolutionary proletariat. Finally, he may take up some of the ancient Hebrew warrior's traits in the context of the struggle over the Jewish State in the immediate wake of the Holocaust, and in another spectacular mélange he may simultaneously display many of the qualities of the American cinematic superman.

Whatever features the "Jew" of post-Holocaust film displays, there is little doubt that he is, overtly or implicitly, the obverse of the "Jew" as victim, a response and a challenge to that searing indictment of the Jews who "went like sheep to the slaughter." By being the opposite of the victim, however, the heroic "Jew" takes up certain attributes that have often been associated with the perpetrator. From this interplay between the extremes of helpless, tragic victimhood and active, ruthless heroism, the heroic "Jew" eventually emerges as a figure that bears a disturbing resemblance to the persecutor himself: callous, brutal, humorless, and deadly.

Frank Beyer's *Jacob the Liar* (1974), based on Jurek Becker's literary masterpiece of the same name, is the quintessential Jewish hero caught in the net of Nazi extermination policies, for which even the rich history of Jewish persecution provides no precedent.[2] Sent to the Gestapo office in the Polish ghetto to receive his "just punishment" for being outdoors during curfew, Jacob Heym (Vlastimil Brodský) overhears a German radio announcement that the Russians have taken over a nearby town. But no one believes that a Jew could have listened to the radio in the lion's den and emerged unscathed. Jacob therefore invents an imaginary radio that he supposedly keeps hidden, and from that point on he becomes the only ray of hope in a community about to be totally destroyed. The steady stream of fictitious good news received by the invented radio creates new relations between people; gives them strength to endure their daily routine of slave labor, constant hunger, and frequent humiliation; and forges a deep link between Jacob and Lina (Manuela Simon), the young girl he cares for.

Jacob's lies are a source of hope, even as the future he invents is doomed never to happen. The courage of imagining a different end, and of giving people the strength to hold out for just a little while longer, makes Jacob into the reluctant hero of a condemned community. The goodness of lying and the falsity of truth that the film exposes provide the context for this instance of a very specific and very Jewish kind of heroism. For while the truth is that everyone will be sent to the gas, this truth is such a distortion of the laws of nature and such a breach of the moral order that it cannot but be rooted in a lie, the lie that some people must die because they belong to a category slated a priori for destruction. And while both the radio and the news it delivers are false, the lie they are based on is in fact a vehicle of truth, the truth that people should not be murdered, that this evil system will ultimately be dismantled, and that people cannot live without believing in some distant possibility of rescue and justice.

What makes *Jacob the Liar* a truthful film is not only the fact that the lie helps, but also that ultimately it does not matter. The lie alleviates the suffering of the spirit for a brief moment but cannot bring any change to the relentless logic of the perpetrators. Ultimately, neither lies nor truth make a difference; the victims will die just as surely as the perpetrators will kill them. But they will have had some hope, will have allowed themselves some happiness; they will have lived before they were murdered. The heroism manifested by Jacob is the antithesis of the perpetrators' idea of heroism. It is based on weakness, deceit, illusion, and fantasy. It is a small and insignificant stick in the spokes of the relentless wheel of homicidal fate, but it is a stifled cry of humanity and compassion, and as such it sheds a scorching light onto the legions of "honest," humorless assassins.[3]

Another instance of "typical" Jewish heroism is provided by Roberto Benigni's *Life Is Beautiful* (1998). As I noted in the previous chapter, Guido Orefice may have been made into a "Jew" by Benigni precisely because this was the only manner in which to highlight the tragic fate of a father who was in fact a soldier in Mussolini's fascist army, thus having a much more ambiguous claim on victimhood. But in another sense, Benigni's film is an Italian-slapstick take on the same theme explored long before by Becker and Beyer (and of course, as I will note below, also indebted to Charlie Chaplin and Ernst Lubitsch). The incensed American reviewers of *Life Is Beautiful*, who claimed self-righteously that one could not make a comedy about the Holocaust, seem to have had very little idea about the Jewish tradition of humor and its relationship to pain and persecution, about the specific role humor and fantasy played in attempts to survive or at least maintain a semblance of normality and humanity during the Holocaust, and about the tradition of "black," "gallows," or "concentration camp humor" in literary and cinematic representations of the Holocaust and other horrors of modern warfare, going back at least to the aftermath of World War I.[4]

The determination of the Italian-Jewish waiter Guido to save his son Giosué (Giorgio Cantarini) both physically and spiritually from the atrocity of the camp calls for a deception not unlike that orchestrated by Jacob, especially in the latter's relationship with Lina, who is more or less the same age as Giosué. Here too the web of lies Guido relentlessly spins affirms love and humanity, while the blinding truth of reality represents atrocity and inhumanity. Thus the argument that the film is unrealistic is not only beside the point but demonstrates a profound misunderstanding of the relationship between reality and truth established in the film and the extent to which it reveals a deeper truth about the Holocaust itself. *Life Is Beautiful* may not be as successful as *Jacob the Liar,* but to assert, as some have, that it is false (as well as flippant and irresponsible) is to say that the only manner to represent the Holocaust is by depicting it "as it really was," as if that were either possible or desirable. Ultimately, the film's authenticity lies not in the conditions it recreates, but in its insistence on the power of love to transform reality.[5]

Guido pretends to Giosué that they are merely involved in some elaborate game that can eventually be won by strength of imagination and will. Thus Guido's heroic quality is not his struggle with the perpetrators or even his struggle to survive, but his entirely altruistic devotion to his son's survival as an innocent child in a world that has seemingly shattered innocence forever. Relying on trickery, humor, dissimulation, and quick-wittedness, Guido shares some qualities with such characters as Menachem Mendel in *Jewish Luck,* but his enemies are deadlier and his task is more difficult: saving the soul of a child. Indeed, if *The Ogre* is a Wagnerian drama about a soul-snatcher, *Life Is Beautiful* is a heart-wrenching comedy about a soul-savior. Whereas Ephraim rides Abel into the Masurian lakes, Giosué rides an American tank into his mother's arms. In the former, the powers of darkness predominate even at the moment of redemption; in the latter, the power of love predominates, even at the moment of (Guido's) death.

To be sure, neither love, even the most intense and self-sacrificial, nor humor, however crazy and infectious, is known to have actually saved anyone in the Holocaust. But love and humor are among the most human of all qualities, and devotion to saving the soul of a child is the most noble of all sacrifices. In this sense Guido has absolutely nothing in common with his foes; indeed, he is precisely and intentionally their stark opposite. That he succeeds in his mission, while sacrificing himself, is more fantasy than reality. But this is a fantasy well-worth recreating, whereas attempts to recreate the reality of the camps all too often turn into obscene failures, precisely because they fool us into believing that they are authentic depictions of a reality we cannot even imagine.

Thus, by censoring the trope of humor in representing the Holocaust, one curiously veers to the side of the perpetrators. For the Jews, humor was often their last resort. Conversely, the Nazis took themselves and their project of extermination with deadly seriousness. They saw nothing funny in what they were doing (if anything made them laugh, it was the tortured bodies of their victims). It was the sheer humorless nature of the German bureaucratic extermination apparatus that made it so extraordinarily lethal. Had he known about Auschwitz, Charlie Chaplin may not have made *The Great Dictator* (1940) with a portrayal of Hitler as a ridiculous little man.[6] But while more people should have taken Hitler seriously before it became too late, it would have also helped if there was ridicule toward the fanatical earnestness with which the Nazis perceived themselves, and if some Germans could have seen through the facade of apocalyptical visions and exposed its fatal barrenness.

Benigni's Guido is the same bumbling, ludicrous, impossible character caught in the throes of a universal destructive convulsion as Jaroslav Hašek's protagonist in *The Good Soldier Schweik* (1926) and so many other European heroes-in-spite-of-themselves. Benigni makes no attempt to provide Guido with any familiar Jewish traits, thereby transforming him into a universal figure whose cultural specificity is, if anything, Italian rather than Jewish. And yet nothing captures this type of non-heroic hero (rather than anti-hero) more than the classical Yiddish *nebech*, that unfortunate, somewhat pathetic, yet endearing, endlessly resourceful, and resilient character immortalized in the person of Menachem Mendel the matchmaker. On the eve of the Six Day War, when some predicted that the Jewish State would become the site of a second Holocaust, and just before a swift victory catapulted Israel to the status of a regional superpower, prime minister Levi Eshkol described his little country as "*Shimshon der nebechdikker*" (Samson the nerd). Here was a depiction of a national character that combined the heroic strength of a Samson—clearly associated with the macho Sabra—and the cunning and whining of the Diaspora Jew: a rather unstable, volatile mix of which, in different measures, both Eshkol and his defense minister, the often cocky but at times apocalyptic Moshe Dayan, were perfectly good representatives.[7]

There is, however, a very different kind of Jewish hero, the active, aggressive, vengeful, and dangerous fighter who confronts force with force and killing with killing. Some of these heroes also retain their Jewish qualities. As early as January 1942, the Jewish Pioneer Youth Group in Vilna issued a manifesto calling for resistance and urging the Jews in the ghettos not to go "like sheep to the slaughter." But in his testimony at the Eichmann trial in 1961, Abba Kovner, former commander of the United Partisans Organization in the Vilna Ghetto and author of the manifesto, insisted that for "those beyond despair, subjugated, and those tortured to the extreme . . . [and] deprived of their human image, it was not an easy matter for this manifesto to be accepted" [and that this was] "not accidental and . . . not to be wondered at. On the contrary," he stressed, "it is astonishing that . . . a fighting force existed at all, that there was armed reaction, that there was a revolt. That is what was not rational."[8]

Others may replace their traditional Jewish traits with a Zionist/Israeli identity that makes them into "new" Jews, rather than non-Jews, a process that facilitates the transmission to future generations of certain qualities attributed to the Diaspora, though increasingly diluted with local values and experiences. Thus, the young Israeli soldiers who fought in 1967, and especially those who came from super-secular socialist kibbutzim and served in elite combat units, subsequently lamented the perceived need to kill their enemies (and suppressed some of the atrocities they experienced in the war). This came to be know as the "shooting and weeping" syndrome of the "state generation" (those born after Israel was founded in 1947), and while the weeping was supposedly an expression of socialist humanism, it also carried undertones of the Jewish *nebech* whose masculinity was constantly cast into doubt by his predilection to sigh and sob.[9]

None of these weaknesses of spirit or body appear to plague Jan Wiener, the real-life protagonist of Amir Bar-Lev's documentary *Fighter* (2001). Here is a living legend, a tough, seventy-seven-year-old man born in Hamburg to Czech parents, who escaped from German-occupied Prague to Yugoslavia in 1939, went on to Italy after his father's suicide in 1940, and was incarcerated by the fascists in an Italian concentration camp until his escape in 1943. Then after his escape, he joined the Royal Air Force, became a colonel in its Czech contingent, and flew bombing missions over Germany. Returning as a hero to liberated Czechoslovakia, he was sentenced in 1950 by the communist authorities to five years in a labor camp. Wiener subsequently left Czechoslovakia, has taught at universities in several countries, and now lives in Massachusetts. His hobby is boxing, and he can still throw punches that echo menacingly in the garage where he trains.[10]

Wiener is, of course, a survivor of this century's cruelest regimes. In this sense, his life, and the manner in which it is depicted in *Fighter,* resembles that of Heda Margolius Kovály, as told in her extraordinary memoir, *Under a Cruel Star,* as well as the fictional life of W. G. Sebald's mysterious protagonist in his no less remarkable novel *Austerlitz.*[11] But unlike so many who linger on their suffering, Wiener is entirely focused on the fight: not merely the struggle for survival but the fight for vengeance, honor, self-respect, and pride. Paradoxically, of course, the only aspect of Wiener's personality that can be described as Jewish is his victimhood—the fact that he had been persecuted and hunted as a Jew by both the Nazis and the communists. But his reaction to this is not that of the typical "Jew," but rather much more akin to the philosophy preached by Zionist prophets of "muscular Judaism": do not turn the other cheek and certainly do not bow your head, but hit back, with all your might, whatever the consequences.[12] This was the heroic stance of the Polish uprising of 1944, which differed from the Warsaw Ghetto revolt of the previous year not by being any less suicidal, but because it was generated by pride more than by despair.[13]

But Wiener is portrayed in this film not merely as an admirably heroic Jew who lacks all Jewish qualities but as one who has an ability (almost in spite of himself) to survive. He is also shown with his old friend and double compatriot, Arnošt Lustig, as they retrace their steps from their current homeland, the United States, back to Prague, the city of their youth. Lustig, who survived both Theresienstadt and Auschwitz and wrote a great deal of fiction related to his experiences in the Holocaust, is the "Jewish" foil against which Wiener's lean and powerful figure is sketched. Wiener wants to tell his story "as it really happened"; Lustig wants to imagine other possibilities or perspectives. Wiener wants to identify culprits and punish the guilty; Lustig is interested in complex motivations and degrees of complicity. Ultimately, Wiener can no longer suffer his old friend's predilection to fantasize about or even romanticize the past, which in Lustig's case also includes supporting the Czech communist regime at the same time that Wiener was imprisoned by it. This becomes all the more difficult for Wiener because his insistence on the bare, hard facts of the past is confronted by the fragility of his own memory and the ephemeral nature of things: no one remembers him, either because they forgot or because they are no longer alive. In a sense, Lustig's fiction is destined to a longer life than Wiener's memory of his own fate.

But the final price for Wiener's un-Jewish heroism is his inability to feel. On the one hand he insists: "Boxing taught me the noble art of self-defense. You have to keep to the rules that are strict, very similar to life." But on the other hand, as Lustig observes, precisely because what motivated Wiener was hate and vengeance, he has lost the ability to love, to empathize, to feel. He has encased himself in a hard, muscular shell that is immune to everything including his own emotions. Of course, says Lustig, "No one who survived the war is normal, it's impossible." But Wiener's "abnormality" is of a different kind. Strong and proud, he remorselessly punches his way through life, but he can no longer understand it. He cannot grasp the things of the past as they disintegrate both materially and in his mind, and he cannot look at the present without the hate and bitterness of the past. Encrusted in his solitude, he stands in his garage and punches his punching bag. And only the memory of his father, who preferred to kill himself rather than live a life on the run, brings tears to his eyes: perhaps because he cannot forgive his father for not having kept up the fight, and perhaps because now, many years older than his father was then, he appreciates the price of the fight and wishes—even though he may never admit it to himself—that such a choice had not been forced on him. And yet, as the end of *Fighter* suggests, he may have learned something about the power of suppleness and pliability after all: in the last shot of the film, Wiener's wife is teaching him tai chi.

PROTEAN HEROES

Jan Wiener's solid, never-changing identity is what makes him into a classical non-Jewish hero. He does not adapt to circumstances but fights against them with the same relentless determination throughout his life. He is thus the precise opposite of the protean "Jew," that central trope of antisemitic phobia, with its nightmarish visions of unrecognizable Jews who lurk behind a facade of non-Jewish respectability while they plot to pollute and destroy society. (Of course Wiener's non-Jewishness is precisely what such thinking would find so insidious about him.) This was the core idea behind *Jew Süss*, the most effective and popular antisemitic film produced by the Third Reich. But in 1940, the very same year that Veit Harlan's tale of Jewish penetration into the Aryan body was shown in German cinemas, another film was screened in the United States that turned the trope of the protean "Jew" on its head. Charlie Chaplin's *The Great Dictator*, rather than depicting the "Jew" as a fraud and a cheat who must be unmasked, presented Hitler, thinly disguised as the dictator Adenoid Hynkel, not only as a brutal, ranting buffoon but also as the exact physical replica of an otherwise morally superior and courageous little Jewish barber. The moment of unmasking in *The Great Dictator* does not expose the hidden "Jew" to the sunlight and reveal him to be the rat that he always was (as was most viciously depicted in *The Eternal Jew*), but rather exposes the dictator as a villain.

Far more disturbing, however, is the discovery that no one can tell who is who: Where does Hynkel end and the "Jew" begin? Essentially, what distinguishes one from the other is not their appearance but their moral qualities. For while this time it is the "Jew" who uncovers the dictator, he does so by literally taking his place, and then making a passionate speech to the masses of "Tomania." Just as Hynkel had won their support earlier, now the "Jew" sways them to his side in the name of love and humanity:

> I'm sorry but I don't want to be an emperor—that's not my business—I don't want to rule or conquer anyone. I should like to help everyone if possible. Jew, gentile, black man, white. We all want to help one another, human beings are like that. We all want to live by each other's happiness, not by each other's misery. We don't want to hate and despise one another. In this world there is room for everyone and the earth is rich and can provide for everyone. . . . Don't give yourselves to these unnatural men, machine men, with machine minds and machine hearts. You are not machines. You are not cattle. You are men. You have the love of humanity in your hearts. Don't hate—only the unloved hate. Only the unloved and the unnatural. Soldiers—don't fight for slavery, fight for liberty.

To be sure, the speech was Chaplin's, not the Jewish tailor's, made in his very first talkie, and unlike Hitler's speeches, its only visible effect was on the fictitious population of "Tomania." Despite the popularity of the film, it could not win any hearts in Germany, where only Hitler and his paladins are said to have watched it. In fact, it got Chaplin into a great deal of trouble and in some ways signaled the end of his career as one of the most successful filmmakers in the United States. Some attacked Chaplin for making a comedy about dictatorship and persecution; others disliked the introduction of an earnest political speech into what they saw as an otherwise entertaining movie. Suspected of communist sympathies because of his support for a second front during the war, as well as his empathy for the victims of capitalism, Chaplin left the United States in 1952, under pressure from the FBI (which failed to find any proof that he had ever been a member of the Communist Party), and made his home in Switzerland. He vowed never to come back to America, but returned just once to receive a special Academy Award in 1972 "for the incalculable effect he has had in making motion pictures the art of this century."[14] That year the former head of the FBI, J. Edgar Hoover, died. The humorless Senator McCarthy was long gone, and the taste for black comedy was defined by such novels as Joseph Heller's *Catch-22* (1961) and Francis Ford Coppola's film *Apocalypse Now,* released after several years of shooting in 1979.[15] *The Great Dictator* has remained a classic evocation of the little hero who, despite himself but also thanks to his courage and moral convictions, defeats evil. But the realities of world war and totalitarianism made this type appear as quaint as Don Quixote.

Yet it is the confusion of identities between the little Jew and the great dictator that remains so intriguing. Chaplin embodied some of the qualities of the protean "Jew" depicted in film. It was difficult to deny his likeness to Hitler (or vice versa). Born in London on April 15, 1889, only five days before the future Führer of the Reich, and known to the entire world for the same moustache that became Hitler's trademark, he was also considered to be a Jew by the Nazis (which he was not), and indeed he was depicted as one in *The Eternal Jew*.[16] Chaplin made it his life's mission to mock and undermine everything that Nazism and fascism stood for: militarism, fanaticism, prejudice, and a cult of murder and death. The very possibility that Chaplin and Hitler, and not just Hynkel and the Jewish barber, could be confused with each other was distinctly disturbing precisely to those who associated physical appearance with moral or "racial" qualities. To be sure, *The Great Dictator* intentionally used this real and fictional similarity—especially troubling for those who insisted on Chaplin's Jewishness—in order to ridicule the whole notion of racial purity. But from another perspective, the film unintentionally suggested precisely that uniquely Jewish trait of changing one's exterior (looking like the Führer) while remaining the same on the inside (propagating racial equality), personified much later in Woody Allen's *Zelig* (1983), the "human chameleon." In terms of linking motivation and phobia, this means that while some social psychologists would propose that a little Hitler lurks in everyone, the antisemitic fantasy would proclaim (both apologetically and aggressively) that in every Hitler lurks a little Jew.

The unity of opposites can also be interpreted as suggesting that Chaplin's little tailor was Hynkel's good side, his "Jewish" alter ego, so to speak. Even the great dictator can discover within himself the spirit of Beethoven's *Fidelio* and "Ode to Freedom," and establish his heroism not on hate and mayhem but on humanism and love. Nevertheless, the little Jew's uncanny ability to look and behave just like the leader, and to sway the masses just as effectively, was disquieting. Was this, ultimately, not a case of mistaken identity, or of a doppelgänger, but of Dr. Jekyll and Mr. Hyde? Could the heroic little tailor be the "real" dictator, just as Chaplin was the "real" Jew, never mind his assertions to the contrary? Could the Jews, as some of the antisemitic fantasies asserted, have fabricated their own destruction so as to bring down Germany, or Europe, or bring in the Bolshevik-Slavic hordes? Was Hitler, finally, merely a stooge of the Jews?

The complexities of representation in the figure of the "Jew" as a protean hero were not explored in *The Great Dictator,* whose main goal was both to deride the Nazi fetishization of race and to mobilize Americans for the inevitable fight against Germany. Interviewed by the *New York Times* in October 1940, Chaplin commented: "It would be a sad moment if we couldn't laugh now. I believe there is more promise and sign of victory if we in America can laugh about them [the Nazis]. I've always felt that the nation which can laugh is the nearest to being sane." Later that month Chaplin published a response to his critics in the same paper, where he stated again: "As to Hitler being funny, I can only say that if we can't sometimes laugh at Hitler then we are further gone than we think. There is a healthy thing in laughter, laughter at the grimmest things in life, laughter at death even."[17] For the real Hynkel, Adolf Hitler, this was no laughing matter, even though his favorite pastime in the days before he ignited the fire that destroyed Europe was to watch Hollywood comedies. For Hitler, Jewish humor was grounds enough for wiping out the entire "race." On January 30, 1939, he spoke on this subject at the Reichstag, saying that while "during the time of my struggle for power it was . . . only the Jewish race that received my prophecies with laughter when I said that I would one day . . . settle the Jewish problem . . . for some time now they have been laughing on the other side of their face." It was this derision for the little man who fancied himself a great dictator, this unmasking of a self-proclaimed hero of the Aryan race as a mere buffoon, that made Hitler make his final, and all too accurate prophecy that day: that the outcome of the next war would be nothing less than "the annihilation of the Jewish race in Europe!" After that, whatever else one might say about the Führer, no one would make fun of him.[18]

Indeed, Hitler has not been the butt of many jokes since 1945. His biographers, even as they expose his evil, tend to perceive him in heroic dimensions, if only because of his monumental destructive capacities.[19] One of the most influential films about him, Hans-Jürgen Syberberg's *Hitler, ein Film aus Deutschland* ("Hitler, a Film from Germany," also titled "Our Hitler" [1977]), combined a cabaret setting with apocalyptical tones

130

and an ironic, even sarcastic perspective tinged with a certain reluctant glorification of this "man without qualities."[20] None of this would have gone down well with that other great émigré filmmaker and master of comedy, Ernst Lubitsch, whose *To Be or Not to Be* (1942) caused an even greater uproar than *The Great Dictator.* Two years after Chaplin's film, much more was known of the Nazi regime's brutality. A comedy about the occupation of Poland and the resistance to German rule seemed all the more out of place. Following the destruction of Warsaw, critics were incensed with the lines given to German colonel Ehrhardt, who responds to the question whether he had ever heard of "that great, *great* Polish actor, Josef Tura" by saying, "What they [Tura and his troupe] did to Shakespeare, we are doing now to Poland." By that stage in the war, poking fun at the Nazis was almost as unacceptable as ridiculing their victims. The war was a deadly serious affair, and while humor was useful in lifting up the morale of the troops and the home front, political satire of the type offered by Lubitsch was deemed inappropriate.[21]

In fact, of course, the film was about much more than ridicule. Lubitsch claimed in his own defense that in *To Be or Not to Be* he had "referred to the destruction of Warsaw . . . in all seriousness," and that there could not be "any doubt in the spectator's mind what my point of view and attitude are toward these acts of horror." Rather, what he "satirized in this picture are the Nazis and their ridiculous ideology . . . [and] the attitude of actors who always remain actors regardless of how dangerous the situation might be."[22] Indeed, just as in *The Great Dictator,* Lubitsch's film is focused on two main motifs. First, despite its light tone, it is a call for action against tyranny, oppression, and racism. It demands and glorifies resistance and sacrifice, but does so in a manner that also reveals all the human weaknesses that may either prevent people from resisting evil or spur them to heroism. In other words, it depicts heroism as the outcome of both fear and courage, weakness as well as strength, and consequently it creates the hero as an ordinary rather than unique and rare individual.

Second, the film strives to undermine all racial and national prejudices by creating a comedy of mistaken identities, an endless masked ball in which the representatives of the Master Race and their allegedly subhuman subjects can never be told apart. Lubitsch thus slams directly into the rhetoric of essential difference, whereby the external appearance of human beings reveals their value and thus determines the manner in which they ought to be treated. The fact that *To Be or Not to Be* is a play within a play, and that the actors in the play must become actors on a larger stage—the film studio, which both imitates reality and concedes that it is merely a simulacrum of that reality—is the crucial core of the film: not because it is dismissive of the atrocities taking place in the world, but because it links these atrocities to the falsehood of the Nazi view of humanity, the idea that some lives are unworthy of life and can easily be determined as such.

At the center of the film are two famous Shakespearean soliloquies. The first, after which the film is named, is one of the most eloquent calls for action ever written. Unlike, for instance, King Henry V's exhortation to his soldiers to fight for their country and for the manner in which their progeny will remember them, Hamlet's lines are about self-motivation: the knowledge that all action may lead to disaster and death, and the fear of the unknown beyond death's gates. It is an appeal to the thoughtful, the weak, and the fearful, the reluctant heroes that litter the battlefields of history. Is one to live in shame or die for a good cause? How can one know that the cause is good? How can one choose to die not knowing what death is? Yet how can one decide to extend a life of humiliation and indignity?[23]

To be sure, while Josef Tura (Jack Benny) is declaiming Hamlet's famous soliloquy, Lieutenant Sobinski (Robert Stack), the handsome Polish pilot, takes action and visits Josef's wife Maria (Carole Lombard) in her dressing room. Josef is, after all, an actor, and he prefers to act the hero rather than risk his neck as one. But he too must eventually opt for action, and a much more decisive and dangerous kind of action than making love to another man's wife. Hamlet's call for action, which always heralds some of the funniest moments in the film, is also deadly serious. Josef may stumble on his lines whenever he sees the young aviator rise from his seat and head toward backstage, but he plays (indeed overplays) his role as a Nazi officer. Similarly, Maria, who had planned to wear an evening dress for her role on stage as a concentration camp inmate (she responds to the director's astonishment by saying, "think of me being flogged in the darkness, suddenly the lights go on and the audience discovers me on the floor in this gorgeous dress"), manages to fool the spy Professor Alexander Siletsky (Stanley Ridges) by sweetly whispering "Heil Hitler" in his ear.

The second soliloquy in the film is repeated three times by Greenberg (Felix Bressart, who was a refugee from Hitler's Germany), the most obviously Jewish-looking member of the theater troupe around which the film revolves. His life's dream is to play Shylock, and he first delivers the famous lines backstage with no hope of ever being called upon to perform them. Then, when he sees the ruins of Warsaw and the mistreatment of the Jews, he delivers them again, this time as a reflection not of his desire to play the role but of his sorrow at the mistreatment of his people. Finally, in a fit of rage, he delivers the soliloquy to Hitler himself—or rather, to an actor in

The protean Jew as comedy (*To Be or Not to Be*): Greenberg defiantly performs his Shylock soliloquy, which he was never allowed to deliver on stage, to Bronski, Hitler impersonator, surrounded by "real" Nazis, suggesting that while Hitler is a fraud, he is a real Jew and hero.

his troupe who was supposed to impersonate Hitler in a play that could not be performed, and now plays the Führer "for real" as part of a complex Resistance plot against the occupying Germans.[24]

This third performance of the famous lines is the very climax of the film and constitutes its most crucial moment. For while up to now *To Be or Not to Be* exposed the emptiness of Nazi rhetoric by turning actors into Nazis and Nazis into fools, now the film devises a confrontation between Hitler—in the person of the actor Bronski (Tom Dugan), who bears an uncanny resemblance to the Führer—and Greenberg, in the role of his life as Shylock, who, despite being surrounded by "real" Nazi soldiers, stands up to Hitler with all the desperate defiance of a victimized yet heroic Jew. To be sure, this is Lubitsch at his best. Bronski (as Hitler) is actually part of the plot against the Germans; Greenberg knows it, and his impulsive Shylock personification, which almost ruins the plot, is both an expression of real anguish at the sight of "Hitler" and a mere instinct of an actor who feels that the time has come to deliver his soliloquy. Everyone is playing a role.

But while Hitler is shown to be a fraud (since he is merely Bronski), Greenberg plays himself: the times have changed, and the role he always wanted has become a reality. There is nothing protean any longer with this Jewish hero—he is what he is, defiantly standing up to the (false) leader of his persecutors.

To Be or Not to Be begins with Hitler touring Warsaw and terrifying the entire population, until a little girl uncovers him as none other than the actor Bronski (just like the little boy who called out that the emperor has no clothes), a little man with a moustache. Anyone can play the Führer, and adults rarely listen to children who see through the rhetoric and pomp. The film ends with Greenberg calling for compassion and staring "Hitler" straight in the face. There are not many such Greenbergs, Lubitsch seems to be saying. But however few, pathetic, and ultimately ineffectual they may be, they are real, not actors, their pain is real, not simulated, and their urge to speak out is heroic and admirable. This is very much a view from the midst of the fight, when little was known about the actual fate of European Jewry but minds were focused on doing battle. With the distance of time, the memory of the pressures and needs of war diminished, and the knowledge of the atrocity greatly increased. Such films as those made by Chaplin and Lubitsch were no longer possible. But could one still make a comedy about Jewish heroism? Could one still create the hero as a "Jew," without slipping into stereotype and melodrama, cliché and kitsch?

Fantasies about Jewish survival and heroism after the Holocaust are, by the nature of things, much more fantastic than any made before the event or before the details of the destruction became know. The hopes that could still be expressed in *The Great Dictator* and *To Be or Not to Be* were dashed by the growing statistics of murder. The horror of the Holocaust, which only gradually seeped into the mind in all its magnitude and enormity, made the very notion of comedy and farce appear obscene. If American and British films poked fun at stereotypically fat and stupid German sergeants and retained a certain awe vis-à-vis the stereotypically elegant but sinister SS officer, the "Jew" in the clutches of the Nazis evoked neither mirth nor empathy, and hardly was featured as a hero. As Radu Mihaileanu, who had worked in the Bucharest Yiddish Theater before fleeing the Ceausescu regime in 1980, said about the making of *Train of Life* (1998), his film was in large part a reaction to Steven Spielberg's *Schindler's List:*

> On the one hand, I was very moved by it. At the same time, I began to feel that we can no longer keep telling the same story of the Shoah in the same way, solely in the context of tears and horror. . . . My theory was to change the language but not the context. I wanted to tell the tragedy

through the most Jewish language there is—the tradition of bittersweet comedy. It was a desire to go beyond the Shoah—not to deny or forget the dead, but to re-create their lives in a new and vivid way.[25]

Although it received little attention in the United States, *Train of Life* is, to my mind, a better—and, if one may say so, both more hilarious and more disturbing—film than *Life Is Beautiful*, precisely because it is framed entirely as a fantasy without any pretension whatsoever to reflect reality. It is, in a true sense, a dream of and a hope for a past that never happened and never could have happened. It depicts an idyllic shtetl of the kind that existed only in Jewish tales and fiction, and instills in it the kind of life that is derived more from I. L. Peretz and Sholem Aleichem than from present-day nostalgia. It captures the spirit of Jewish fairy tales about ingenious survival against all odds, which emanated precisely from an acceptance of the fact that reality was far more sordid and hopeless and survival was tenuous at best. And then it transfers all this to the terrain of the Holocaust, whose very totality and relentlessness makes this shtetl's scheme appear all the more absurd. Finally, it places at the center of this fable a protean Jewish hero in the best tradition of Jewish self-representation, conceived, however, in the wake of a tragedy known by the viewers to have shattered the very possibility of fantasy by the sheer scope of its genocidal reach.

In order to survive, the inhabitants of an Eastern European shtetl decide to deport themselves as far away from the approaching Nazis as possible. They buy a train, make Nazi uniforms, and drive off to the east, where they hope to encounter the Red Army. While some of them remain what they always were, Shtetl Jews, others must play the role of Nazis, at the head of whom is Mordechai the Woodworker (Rufus Narcy), now transformed into an SS officer. On the way they undergo various adventures, including almost being killed by partisans, who desist from shooting at the last moment when they realize that the Nazi soldiers are praying like Jews with the strings of their prayer vests showing under their uniforms. Eventually they are stopped by a group of Germans but, as it quickly transpires, these are in fact Gypsies who have employed the same strategy to escape their persecutors. Finally they reach the front, but just before they are liberated by the Russians we realize that this was all a dream, conjured up by Shlomo the Fool (Lionel Abelanski), who is fantasizing the rescue of his shtetl from behind the barbed wire of a concentration camp. Filled with klezmer-like music composed by Goran Bregovic—the son of a Croatian father and a Serbian mother, who also composed the score for Emir Kusturica's own cinematic fable, *Time of the Gypsies* (1989)—this film is in some ways the post-Holocaust, Technicolor remake of *Jewish Luck*. It is a mad comedy of

The protean Jew as farce (*Train of Life*): Mordechai the Woodworker, complete with Nazi uniform and yarmulke, alongside the rabbi of the shtetl that decided to transport itself away from the Germans rather than be shipped by them to the extermination camps, moments before they discover that they have been liberated by the Red Army and we find out that this was all a dream conjured up by Shlomo the Fool, now incarcerated in a concentration camp.

the absurd, which totally disregards the reality of the past it depicts, thus managing to provide a glimpse of a culture—and its fictions—that was annihilated in the Holocaust along with its vain hopes, impossible dreams, and love of life.[26]

There is, however, another aspect to *Train of Life* that places it squarely within the rubric of the protean hero. What makes this film into a true fantasy is not merely that the shtetl manages (in Shlomo the Fool's imagination) to escape the Nazis. After all, individuals did manage to escape the Nazis, including some who in fact put on Nazi uniforms. Rather, it is that the premise on which this story is constructed suggests that the only way for the Jews to survive the Nazis was to acquire the qualities of their persecutors. The fantasy, then, is that such an exchange of identities is possible, that is, that one can both become a Nazi and at the same time remain a Jew. This is precisely what Mordechai the Woodworker tries to do—as he explains to his "prisoners," he must behave with them like a Nazi; otherwise no one will believe them. Better to suffer a little under Mordechai than to fall into the hands of Haman. In reality, of course, the "Jew" cannot become a Nazi without being destroyed as a Jew, but without becoming a Nazi he will be murdered in any case. The fantasy of the shtetl's heroism is thus rooted in its ability to remain a Jewish community despite the transformation it must undergo in order to survive: for the protean Jewish hero in the Holocaust is either the victim of his previous identity or the prisoner of his newly acquired one. Rescue is possible only as a dream. If Chaplin could transform himself from Jewish tailor to great dictator, and if Lubitsch could let Greenberg confront the (faux) Führer with his Shylock, then here the shtetl will survive as a living Jewish community only if Mordechai keeps his yarmulke under his officer's cap—and only if the Germans encountered are all either fools, in the tradition of postwar Hollywood, or cross-dressing Gypsies, whose affinity with the Jews is not merely their status as the persecuted but also their music, provided by composer Bregovic.

When reading accounts of the Holocaust, and perhaps even more so when watching footage from the period, one is sometimes overcome with the urge to save the people who have long been dead. Some respond as Hausner did during the Eichmann trial, asking rhetorically and at times cruelly, "Why did you not resist?" Others invent for themselves stories of resistance and rescue, fantasizing as did the children to whom Primo Levi lectured on his incarceration in Auschwitz: How would one have jumped over the fence, dug a tunnel, killed a guard. . . .[27] These fantasies are now part and parcel of our imagination and memory of the Holocaust. They combine with other types of often ignorant if well-meaning nostalgia for a world we did not and could not know. *Train of Life* plays on these themes. Its Jews are, of course, caricatures, but they are Jewish caricatures taken from Jewish tales: they are as real as were the fictional characters of Yiddish literature. The Jews' survival scheme is, of course, absurd, but precisely for that reason it recalls the impossible schemes desperately thought up by the Jews at the time of their destruction. This is therefore a truthful film just because it is a self-acknowledged fantasy: a fantasy from and about the past, and a fantasy that all those who wish that the past could be undone sometimes secretly entertain even if, especially as grown-ups, they dare not reveal it to others.

Children adapt to circumstances more easily, and fantasize about their identity more readily, than adults. To be sure, small children, if they were not sheltered by gentiles or hidden away in Christian institutions, had very little chance of surviving the Holocaust, several miraculous stories of survival under the most horrendous conditions notwithstanding. Louis Malle's film *Au revoir les enfants* (1987), Saul Friedländer's memoir *When Memory Comes* (1978), Shlomo Breznitz's memoir *Memory Fields* (1986), and Louis

Begley's novel *Wartime Lies* (1991) are among the best-known works about children who underwent drastic changes of identity, often more than once, in order to survive. These works suggest the profound effects such transformations had on their subsequent lives or, as in the case of Malle's film, on the lives of those who knew them.[28] Somewhat older teenagers often had to fend for themselves. It was from among such young men and women, both in Eastern and Western Europe, that partisans and Resistance fighters were recruited. Josh Waletsky's *Partisans of Vilna* (1986) and Mosco Boucault's *Terrorists in Retirement* (2001) are among the most remarkable documentaries on these extraordinarily brave youngsters (who in the latter case also included Armenians).

Yet there is little doubt that one of the most improbable and definitely one of the most protean Jewish heroes of postwar cinema is Agnieszka Holland's Solly, the main protagonist of her film *Europa, Europa,* known in Germany by the more ironic title *Hitlerjunge Salomon* (1991). Based on the actual experience of Salomon (Shlomo) Perel, this is the tale of a young German Jew (born in 1925) who ends up being a hero in the Wehrmacht and an outstanding student in a school for Hitler Youth cadets.[29] The film is somewhat akin to *Schindler's List* in that it recounts a true story (with numerous modifications due to cinematic requirements and possibly also ideological restraints or inclinations) that is so incredible as to be representative only of itself and certainly not of the fate of Jews under Nazi rule and occupation.[30]

The notion of Jewish heroism as finding expression only in a Nazi uniform is of course an extreme version of the entire discourse on Jewish degeneration, masculinity, and passivity that formed an important element of antisemitic, Zionist, and post-Holocaust discourse.[31] It is especially interesting to see this presentation of a heroic Jew in a film by a director who had for many years worked with Andrzej Wajda, whose own representations of Jewish heroism were far more imbued with a combination of Christian and socialist motifs.[32] Holland's hero is in some ways much more like Woody Allen's Zelig than like Wajda's Samson. He fits into every role imposed on him and seems to have few loyalties to anyone or anything apart from himself. His urge to survive is tremendous. Unlike Solly, Holland expresses her scorn for communism, her contempt for Nazism, and her view of the affinity between the two through stark cinematic images, which include a fantasy of Hitler and Stalin waltzing with each other in a communist school classroom. But Solly shares none of these sentiments, nor does he betray any inner conflict regarding his Jewish identity. Rather, his greatest desire is to be accepted, even if only as an Aryan lad in the heart

The protean Jew as communist (*Europa, Europa*): Solly Perel, who escapes Germany and ends up in the Soviet Union, is eager to be accepted and even more so to survive: Here he is in his incarnation as a faithful member of the Komsomol, the Soviet youth moment.

of the Nazi Reich, at least so he can win the heart (and body) of a girl he has fallen for.

As long as he is a Jew, Solly plays the familiar role of a victim escaping persecution. But once he joins the other side, whether as a Komsomol member, a German soldier, or a Hitler Youth, he excels not only intellectually but also physically. The one area in which he cannot perform is sex—although he is the target of both homosexual and heterosexual desire—since he cannot reveal his circumcised penis. Thus Solly's circumcision becomes the last barrier to his desire to merge; or, seen differently, it serves precisely the role for which it was intended by protecting his Jewish identity even when he is entirely willing to give it up. Just like Bertolt Brecht's slogan on the wall, circumcision cannot be erased, and any attempt to "correct" it only enhances his pain and sense of exclusion. It is this that keeps him from being wholly transformed from victim to perpetrator, this "fault" that erects a moral hurdle to becoming a Nazi.[33]

Solly's protean hero comes close to constituting the precise counter-image of the antisemitic fantasy's stereotypical "Jew Süss." Indeed, *Europa, Europa* pokes fun at the entire racist undertaking, demonstrating the fluidity

The protean Jew as Nazi (*Europa, Europa*): Having been captured by the Wehrmacht and declaring himself to be an ethnic German, Solly Perel serves on the other side of the front and is eventually sworn in as a member of the Hitler Youth.

of both cultural and physical traits, as Solly easily transforms himself from a Jewish boy to a communist student to a Hitler Youth, and is even proclaimed to have pronounced Aryan features by the Nazi school's racial expert (an experience recounted by several other Jews who went to school in 1930s Germany).[34] But matters are complicated by the fact that Solly is heroic only in his incarnation as a non-Jew, especially when he becomes the absolute opposite of the "Jew," a Wehrmacht soldier or a Hitler Youth. Moreover, Solly is both a hero-in-spite-of-himself—for in a better world, he would rather have not gone through these role changes—and also is a more willing hero than his circumstances permit, for he must keep hidden that sign of identity that prevents him from performing the masculine role dictated by his heroic status. If Süss Oppenheimer presents a sexual danger but lacks the required martial qualities of the Aryan, Solly is a perfectly good fighter who is barred by his own "deficiency" from having sex with an Aryan maiden. Would he have fully joined in had he been able to "repair" that Jewish "fault"? Clearly his striving for acceptance and popularity makes that into a distinct possibility. In this case, rather than "polluting" the Aryan body, as is Süss's intent, he would have been swallowed up and polluted by Nazism, possibly dying a heroic death for Führer and Volk.

The Jew as gay Wehrmacht soldier (*Europa, Europa*): Unlike the ardent Nazi girl with whom he can never have sex because of his "handicap," the gay Wehrmacht soldier who discovers Solly's circumcision makes their shared threatened status a basis for solidarity: If Solly can be a Hitler Youth, a gay soldier can be (and is almost by definition) a Jew.

Nevertheless, Solly does not go through the complete transformation of character that we will encounter in István Szabó's *Sunshine* (2000). He never insists on his chosen role, and his actions are determined more than anything else on his urgent desire to survive. His swift transformation from Jew to communist to Nazi and back to Jew is not at all a matter of commitment or identity but merely of play-acting. Once the war was over, as we know, Perel went to Israel. But one is never convinced, from the film, whether his Jewish identity was any stronger than all the other identities he tacked on to himself. In this sense, being a hero was also merely dictated by circumstances. In essence, then, Solly's character is no character at all. In that sense, he is indeed a "human chameleon"; underneath his various facades one finds nothing at all, neither heroic nor insidious, but merely an instinct of survival that instantly transforms him into whatever it is that would make him least vulnerable: Jew or German, coward or hero. From this perspective, Solly is hardly the contradiction of the antisemitic stereotype, but merely one of its variations, that of the eternal parasite hiding under a thousand masks.

In a final, ironic twist to this tale of mixed identities, the German Oscar Committee refused to submit *Europa, Europa* for a Best Foreign Film Academy Award, arguing that while it was a Franco-German co-production, its director was Polish. Instead, Holland was nominated for her screenplay. A similar irony can be observed in the case of the recent film by Roman Polanski, *The Pianist* (2002). Born in Paris in 1933 to Polish-Jewish parents, Polanski barely survived the Holocaust in Poland, during which his mother was murdered. Trained at the Polish Film School in Lodz, he subsequently moved to Paris, London, and Hollywood. Since 1977, he has not been able to live in the United States due to the threat of legal action for statutory rape of a minor.[35] *The Pianist* was thus produced and shot in Europe, although considering the lavish production, whose cost ran up to some $35 million, and the fact that it is primarily in English—the one language that none of the protagonists would have spoken—this is a very American film.

The Pianist was greatly praised by American film critics, whose reviews betrayed a certain discomfort that Polanski was barred from returning to the United States. Unlike *Europa, Europa, The Pianist* won three academy awards, including Best Director for Polanski, as well as winning the Palme d'Or at the Cannes Film Festival. Conversely, although Polanski left Poland decades ago and created an English-language rendition of a Polish-language memoir in which a largely Yiddish-speaking community was murdered by Germans, *The Pianist* was greeted in Poland as a truly Polish film and as such was enthusiastically endorsed by critics and audiences alike. Indeed, in a certain sense, this is Polanski's most autobiographical film, since it deals with a period that he experienced as a child and with a character whose devotion to his craft, not unlike his own, supersedes any of the experiences he undergoes. But as can be said about many of his previous films, Polanski chooses to detach himself from this experience by telling the real story of another person, thereby avoiding any direct autobiographical link and preserving an emotional distance.

Moreover, Władysław Szpilman's memoir, on which the film is based, is itself distinguished by an emotional aloofness that seems to suit Polanski's style.[36] Szpilman's eye is like a camera, recording events with very little emotional involvement. His one means of expression is the piano's keyboard, and when that keyboard is missing, he can only report his journey—from the radio studio into a man-made hell and back into the studio—as accurately and as dryly as possible. This seems to be the ideal script for Polanski, who fills it with all the violence, suffering, and destruction of those years but—with the exception of music—adheres to the emotional numbness that characterizes the memoir and appeals just as much to the filmmaker.

Szpilman is as fanatically dedicated to his art as a pianist as Polanski is to filmmaking. Throughout their lives, these two men have made their art into the center of their existence, an emotional and psychological focus that, in a process of inversion, enables them to distance themselves from the rest of the world and to protect themselves from all the suffering and loss they have experienced and observed. This may be the result of their childhood and youth in the Holocaust; it may have even earlier origins. Presumably, Polanski could never make a film about his own, no less re- markable experience during the war. But because he insists on this dis- tance, *The Pianist* lacks precisely that emotional core that transforms the cinematic depiction of horror and devastation from a meticulous recre- ation into a human tragedy.

Whether Szpilman survives thanks to his skills, determination, or sheer luck does not really matter. What matters is that six years after he was bombed out of the recording studio in Warsaw, a period during which he lost his entire family and witnessed the extermination of the Jews and the murder of millions of Catholic Poles, he is back where he started, playing Chopin's "Nocturne in C sharp minor" as if nothing had happened, creat- ing normality where all that was normal had been torn to shreds. Szpilman wrote his memoir shortly after the war, as his son writes, "for himself rather than humanity in general. It enabled him to work through his shattering experience and free his mind and emotions to continue with his life."[37] Polanski waited for five decades before he told his own story of horror, and then he decided to tell it through the eyes of Szpilman, as a true allegory of a childhood he would not film.[38]

This may also be the reason that *The Pianist* has been seen by Poles as a Polish film. In a certain sense, Polanski's Szpilman is the most acceptable type of Jewish hero for all concerned—entirely protean in his unrelenting will to survive (and in this he is just like Solly), at the same time he is entirely devoted to one aspect of his character, an aspect which is beyond or prior to any national, racial, or ethnic characteristics: his art. Szpilman does not survive as a Jew, or as a Pole, and he does not draw any personal conclusions from his experience. Unlike many other surviving Polish Jews, he does not become a Zionist, or immigrate to the United States, or join the Communist Party. He survives as an artist, a pianist, and goes back to the same "Nocturne" whose playing was so rudely interrupted by the war. *The Pianist*, then, is ultimately a film about the artist as hero; and as such, it provides us with an admirable example of total dedication, avoiding any confrontation with the troubling questions of identity transformation, loyalty to one's own or to another's culture and existence, guilt, denial, and erasure. It is, finally, a story of triumph, the triumph of art over barbarism. How can anyone criticize that?

There is, of course, another hero in this story. Both in the memoir and in the film, the German officer who saved Szpilman's life in the last harrowing weeks of the fighting in Warsaw receives very little time and yet is made into a centerpiece of the entire narrative. Captain Wilm Hosenfeld had already served as a lieutenant in World War I, and was thus not a young man by the time he was taken prisoner by the Soviets toward the end of the war. He died in captivity seven years later. A devout Catholic, Hosenfeld was by all accounts a brave man who seems to have saved several Jews and Poles. This figure of the "good German" played a problematic role in Szpilman's tale from the very beginning. In the original version of the memoir, published in Poland in 1946 under the title *Death of City* (it was soon thereafter withdrawn from publication in compliance with Stalin's view that the Jewish genocide should not be highlighted), Hosenfeld had to be presented as an Austrian so as not to grate against Polish anti-German sentiments.[39] Conversely, in Polanski's film, made almost six decades later, it is Hosenfeld's tragic end in a Soviet POW camp that is highlighted. To be sure, we know that Szpilman's family, along with a quarter-million other Warsaw Jews, died in the ghetto, in Treblinka, and in other camps. But the only name mentioned at the end of the film is that of the "good German." The polarity of the two heroes, the Jewish artist and the German officer (who saves him after hearing him play Chopin's "Nocturne"), therefore becomes the other core of the film: the heroism of survival versus the heroism of rescue, both rooted in an almost religious dedication to music, the most abstract and therefore perhaps also the most spiritual of all arts.[40]

Polanski's Szpilman is a protean hero in that his feat of survival, accomplished through endless transformations, is of a most extraordinary type. In another sense, his type of heroism is set against other heroes, be they the "good German" or the "good Poles" who help him. Whereas Hosenfeld in fact was most of the time bemoaning his inability to act against the Nazis, in the film he plays an active role. This is also the case with the Poles who give shelter and food to Szpilman, although in fact most Poles stood by passively as the Jews were murdered. Thus heroic Jewish survival is essentially passive in this film, while heroic Polish and German rescue is by definition active. Interestingly, Polanski also introduces a Polish character who is a synthesis of various Polish women mentioned in the memoir, and he extends her relationship with Szpilman to before the ghettoization of the Jews, although no such relationship is mentioned in the memoir. Szpilman returns not to Poland but to the piano and the recording studio. But the film, as it was seen by Polish audiences at least, seems to indicate that Szpilman returned to Poland, not least because it was Poland that helped him survive. In this sense, the main protean heroes of this film are Szpilman's rescuers rather than the protagonist himself: on the screen they reveal the good aspect that was so often hidden in reality—the Wehrmacht officer and the Polish intellectual joining hands to save the Jews from the evil Nazis. We can almost see them all sitting at the concert hall and listening to one of Szpilman's postwar recitals, congratulating themselves on their courage and resourcefulness. Perhaps, after all, it would have been better had Polanski told his own story. Perhaps coming closer to himself, he would have been compelled to recall that most of the Jews, for most of the time, saw a very different aspect of their Polish neighbors and German occupiers. Had it been otherwise, perhaps more of them would have been left to tell their tales.

Very few people were left to tell the tale of the uprising by the most deeply complicit and at the same time the most heroic Jews of the Holocaust: the Sonderkommando of Birkenau. Primo Levi called them "the ravens," those strong young men who hovered on the outer limits of the "gray zone" as they prepared the transports for the gassing and then incinerated their lifeless bodies in vast numbers.[41] It is also an almost impossible story to tell, for who can delve into the depths of despair, degradation, and horror in which these men lived? Who can empathize with their precarious balance between facilitating the murder of endless thousands of innocents, momentarily enjoying the riches of food and clothing robbed from the doomed, and knowing that their turn would soon come to be treated in the same manner by the next team of newly selected Sonderkommandos? And who can gauge the courage that led these men to stage the only full-scale revolt ever attempted at Birkenau, that vast factory of death, torture, and slave labor, and to blow up the facilities that were devouring the remnants of European Jewry? How can the imagination penetrate these regions, how can the camera try to capture the reconstructed reality that should never have been allowed to exist in the first place?

The recent attempt to provide a cinematic representation of this most sinister locus of the entire Nazi genocidal enterprise, where the Jews were intentionally made (temporary and under threat of instant death, always eventually carried out) into the allies and colleagues of their own and their families' and communities' executioners, and where they, the lowest of the low, revolted against the masters of that anus mundi, brings us to the very extremes of the "Jew" as a protean hero. For here indeed the "Jew" is both a perpetrator—of the murder of his own people—and a hero—fighting a hopeless battle against the exterminators of the Jews. It would seem just as impossible to depict the gas chambers from within, as it is to create a credible picture of the Sonderkommando men's moral debasement and mixed motivations—often hardly heroic—to stage a revolt, indeed, to transform themselves, if only for a brief moment, from Satan's apprentices to his nemesis. Tim Blakes's *The Grey Zone* (2002), adapted from his own Obie-winning play, and based on Miklós Nyiszli's memoir, *Auschwitz, a Doctor's Eyewitness Account*, along with other diaries written by Sonderkommando members and found hidden in the death camps after the war, is in many ways a unique film precisely because it tries to do the impossible. While it succeeds beyond expectations, it ultimately cannot but be flawed precisely because its ambition is confined by the limitations of the medium.[42]

In some ways, *The Grey Zone* provides the same stark depiction of gratuitous, indifferent, at times even playful violence that we find also in *The Pianist*.[43] The relentless, merciless realism of these films shrugs off any more suggestive, indirect references to violence and brutality of earlier generations of movies on the Holocaust, a new trend begun perhaps most famously (but less starkly) by Spielberg's *Schindler's List*. This almost hyperrealist representation of violence is of course also related to the new genre of war films and other cinematic depictions of violence unrelated to the Holocaust. The association between violence and entertainment made by such films, and their links to depictions of the Holocaust, is disturbing not least because the Nazi perpetrators themselves often found the violence they "staged" to be highly entertaining. (At the screening of *The Grey Zone* I attended—it swiftly disappeared from the theaters—quite a few members of the audience were excitedly munching popcorn for much of the movie.)

Yet the difference between *The Pianist* and *The Grey Zone* is just as evident. In *The Pianist*, not only does the victim/hero survive, he survives in a certain important sense entirely unscathed. Obsessed with preserving his hands and fingers during the Holocaust (as Szpilman repeatedly mentions in his memoirs), he puts them to good use after the end of the war: indeed, his musical abilities are neither diminished nor does his musical taste change in any marked way. Conversely, in *The Grey Zone*, everyone is simply shot at the end of the rebellion. Thus we have here two entirely different narratives of victimhood and heroism. For Polanski, Szpilman's heroism is his ability to survive and then pick up his trade and ply it again. In the course of this battle for survival he will transform himself into whatever figure and form is necessary so as to be able to come out on the other side entirely unchanged, the same artist he was when he tumbled into hell. In *The Grey Zone*, the Sonderkommando have been transformed from perfectly ordinary young men into beasts, and they struggle to maintain their physical existence even as their human image is distorted through the conscious effort of the SS. But then they decide to change course: they transform themselves by sheer power of will back into human beings, despite their hellish existence, and with the knowledge that by becoming human again they are doomed to die.

Their heroism, then, is their refusal to accept the transformation imposed on them by their masters. It is, of course, mixed with fear—for they know that they may be sent to the gas chambers at any moment—and also by the hope that perhaps, somehow, they will be able to break out nevertheless. Yet their main motivation is different. It is to prove to themselves that they are men and not beasts, and quite concretely, it is to put an end to the endless slaughter of Hungarian Jews who are streaming into the gas chambers from the transports organized so efficiently by Adolf Eichmann in Budapest. Thus, when they die, they die as men; it is those who shoot them who have irrevocably been consigned to the regions of hell, despite their effort to blur the distinction between themselves and their victims.[44] If the film does not entirely succeed in presenting this dilemma in all its depth, it is because film is a medium unsuited to such purposes. It must become somehow complicit in the pornography of violence that was at the core of the Nazi exterminationist enterprise, despite every effort to avoid this effect. If we don't see a depiction of an event, we can wish it away from our minds; but if we watch it on the screen, we feel that the director has both recreated what must not exist and has made us, the audience, into voyeurs of a universe beyond our imaginative capacities. But within these constraints, *The Grey Zone* is nevertheless one of the most honest representations of Jewish heroism in the Holocaust—the greatest heroism of all, that of transforming oneself from slave to rebel, from beast to man, from a raven that feeds on human flesh to an eagle that soars to freedom.

NON-JEWISH HEROES

In the case of the protean hero, the "Jew" goes through a series of transformations that both characterize him as a Jew—by manifesting the adaptive, unstable nature of a chameleon—and enable him to become a hero—as one of his numerous aspects. In other cases, however, the cinematic "Jew" undergoes a conversion that permanently changes his nature and determines his fate. This can be the case with Jews who convert—symbolically or literally—and are thus transformed in a manner that enables them to become the heroes they could not have been prior to their conversion. Or we can see the reverse, non-Jews who—this time without literal conversion—come to share the fate of the Jews and act as ersatz heroes for those who are innately blocked from taking up this role. In both cases, therefore, the heroic "Jew" is the outcome of metamorphosis: either of a Jew into a non-Jew, or of a non-Jew into a Jew. In other words, the underlying assumption in the case of such cinematic representation is that heroism and the "Jew" is a contradiction in terms that can only be resolved through some act of transformation.

Andrzej Wajda's *Samson* (1961), which is based on the eponymous novel by the Jewish Polish writer Kazimierz Brandys, is a good example of the first type, making the "Jew" into a hero by transforming him out of his Jewishness.[45] Samson is of course the Jewish, or rather Hebrew, hero par excellence. In Jewish tradition he is always referred to as "Samson the Hero." In the biblical tale there are, of course, several ironic twists. First, Samson's strength has been given to him by God. Because its source is divine, it can always be taken away from him. Moreover, Samson is so powerful that in fact he needs no courage. From this perspective, he is not at all a hero, if by that one means courageous; rather, he is heroic only in the Greek or Hollywood sense of being a superman. Finally, Samson's weakness of character ends up as his source of true heroism, that is, of courage in the face of unequal odds. Samson loses his strength by letting Delilah, the gentile, cut off his hair, where his strength resides. Having "unmanned" him in this manner (the loss of hair symbolizing the loss of his masculinity, that is, his potency and strength), Delilah delivers him to his enemies the Philistines, who blind and chain him. Only now does Samson's true moment of heroism arrive. He appeals to God to give him strength one last time, asks to be led to the pillars that support the Philistine temple, and with the cry, "May my soul die with the Philistines," topples the temple over his enemies in an act of courageous suicide. (It is curious to think of this act, which has passed through generations of Jewish lore as one of national martyrdom, in the light of the recent spate of suicide bombings by Palestinian youths venerated by their society as "shahids" or martyrs for killing hundreds of Israeli civilians. But it must also be noted that such acts of mass suicide as that of the Jewish defenders of Masada were frowned upon by Jewish authorities until modern Zionism revived the story told by Josephus Flavius as an act of national heroism.)[46]

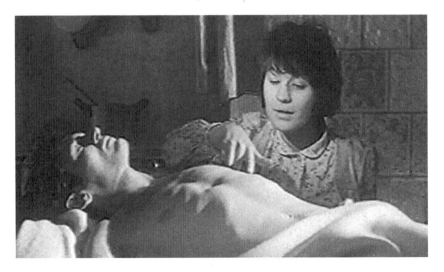

The Jew as Christ (*Samson*): The adoration of Jakub Gold by Kazia, in whose Warsaw house he is hiding from the Germans.

Samson's moment of true heroism is therefore the moment of his greatest weakness. Herein lies the tragic significance of this figure. The arrogance of inhuman strength makes him vulnerable to female wiles, while the humiliation of powerlessness and imprisonment brings out the self-sacrificing hero. Wajda turns all of this around and adds to the story a strong Catholic tinge, mixed—not as surprisingly as may appear today—with communist bravado. We should recall such immensely influential films as Roberto Rossellini's neorealist *Rome, Open City* (1945), in which the communists and the clergy join hands in fighting the fascists. In the present context, it is of more than passing interest that neorealism often had little to do with even the most recent historical reality (the Vatican was hardly an opponent of fascism), and that some of the most influential Italian filmmakers and writers of the postwar era began their careers under the auspices of the regime whose rejection they later made into the focus of their works.[47] For what we have with Wajda's *Samson* is an attempt by this gifted director to confront the question of Polish attitudes toward Jews while, at the same time, exhibiting some of the prejudices his film is intended to negate.

Jakub Gold (Serge Merlin) is jailed by the Polish authorities for having unintentionally killed a fellow Polish student who had in fact tried to protect him from an antisemitic attack. Released from prison with the

German invasion of 1939, he soon finds himself in the Warsaw Ghetto, where conditions are rapidly deteriorating. Again Jakub escapes his prison. First he is sheltered by Lucyna (Alina Janowska), a Polish society lady with a well-appointed residence and elegant intellectual guests. It soon turns out that she is in fact also a Jew hiding under a false identity. Both Jakub and the viewers lose track of Lucyna, and next he is hidden in the cellar of Malina (Jan Ciecierski), whom he had known in jail before the war. Malina's niece Kazia (Elżbieta Kepinska) quickly comes to worship the emaciated Jakub, whose condition deteriorates further after Malina dies, presumably because he had been sheltering a Jew. Finally Jakub breaks out of this last prison and tries to return to the ghetto. But the ghetto is no more, just a vast field of smoking rubble guarded by German soldiers and dogs. This is the moment of Jakub's liberation. He joins a communist resistance group headed by Pankrat (Tadeusz Bartosik), another acquaintance from his days in jail. In an effort to save the cell from being uncovered by the Germans, he throws a string of grenades at a Wehrmacht unit searching their hideout. As the Germans are buried under the collapsing masonry, Jakub dies with an expression of happiness on his tortured face.[48]

Several important points need to be stressed here. First, it is clear that all those who help Jakub end up badly. The student who comes to his rescue is killed (inadvertently by Jakub himself). Malina dies because he hides him. Pankrat's cell is uncovered when Jakub joins it. This is a running theme in many of Wajda's films, namely, not only that Poles suffered under the Germans just as badly as the Jews, and that Poles helped Jews more than the Jews are willing to concede, but also that such help often entailed further tragedy for the Poles. Linking Polish suffering to Jewish suffering by way of showing the former helping the latter, and often suggesting the Jews' ingratitude to the Poles, their indifference to Polish victimhood, and even their urge for revenge, is part of the Polish discourse on the German occupation and the Holocaust. In this sense, Wajda reflects—through a variety of transformations dating back to postwar Stalinism, the "Thaw," martial law, and finally post-communism—his nation's sentiments, engagement, and apologetics about the fate of Polish Jewry. Interestingly, this was reflected in a kind of remake of *Samson*, Wajda's *Holy Week* (1995), based on an early postwar story by Jerzy Andrzejewski (who also wrote *Ashes and Diamonds,* on which Wajda's celebrated film of the same name was based).

Holy Week also tells the story of a Jew, this time a woman, who is sheltered by a Polish-Catholic family. As the reviewer Tadeusz Sobolewski wrote, the tragic irony in this tale is that Jan Malecki (Wojciech Malajkat) and his family "act in the best of faith, according to the ideals of civic duty, patrio-

The Jew as Polish-Communist martyr (*Samson*): Having had his hair shorn by Kazia, and discovering that the ghetto has been wiped out, Jakub joins an underground group and is transformed into a Samson-like figure by sacrificing himself in an act of suicidal heroism in which he kills the Germans who have discovered their hideout.

tism and honor. They do everything a good Pole should. But face to face with the Holocaust this 'everything' turns out to be nothing. The world of traditional values is crushed by a strange, bloody order." Rather than juxtaposing those who make "facile charges against the Poles accusing them of collective guilt or collaboration" with those who wish to "acquit the nation as a whole, setting the Shoah against the huge number of Polish victims," Sobolewski seems to agree with Wajda by proposing to take "a disillusioned view of human nature, based on the Christian notion of guilt."

Yet as the critic relates the narrative, we discover that it was the Poles who were the heroes. For the "Malecki family represents the best qualities of Polish patriotic intelligentsia: Jan's brother with a group of scouts goes forth to help the ghetto; . . . his pregnant wife, all of whose siblings were killed during the fights and in concentration camps, takes care of Irena; and Malecki dies, trying to find her a better hiding place." Conversely, Irena, the Jewish woman whom they shelter, while being the direct cause of the disasters that befall her rescuers, never shows an iota of gratitude. She is "disillusioned, ungrateful, careless, [and] simply begs disaster." To be sure, Sobolewski notes that precisely because the actress Beata Fudalej "underscores Irena's unpleasant traits, making us feel excruciating pity half mixed with irritation," she enables the viewers "to discern in ourselves the shameful reaction of people for whom Irena was 'trouble.'" But he simultaneously stresses that this was "a challenge calling for a sacrifice which nobody could meet. Which—even if met—could only be made in vain."[49]

Thus the heroes of *Holy Week* are definitely the Poles, even if the film takes place during the Warsaw Ghetto rebellion of 1943 that coincided with the Jewish holiday of Passover (the Nazis liked using Jewish holidays as occasions for mass killings) and coincidentally also with Easter. The uprising, the first full-scale rebellion against the Germans anywhere in occupied Europe, was an entirely Jewish affair. Not only did it not entail Polish heroism, it actually reflected the isolation of the Jews even as they and the Catholic Poles faced the same enemy. While some Poles rejoiced at the destruction of the Jews, and others looked on passively, the much-better-armed Polish Resistance saved its weapons for its "own" fight against the Germans, more than a year later, and offered only minimal and reluctant help to the desperate Jews.[50] But these historical facts have to be weighed against collective memory and self-perception. Between 1961 and 1995, the "Jew" remains a passive shelter-seeker in Wajda's treatment of the topic, while the Poles who help him are doomed precisely because they do so, and are thus both victims and heroes at the same time, a status denied the "Jew" by his passivity.

True to this pattern Jakub finally becomes a hero only with his Samson-like act of killing himself together with the Germans. This is most probably a moment derived from socialist influence. Like all other Jewish characters in Wajda's films about the Holocaust, Jakub's Jewishness is merely encapsulated in his victimhood—he has no other Jewish traits, links, or language. But he becomes fully a Pole, that is, a non-Jew, at the moment of his decision to stand by the communist resistance cell, protect his comrades, and die cheerfully as a fighter for his (Polish) people. He does not take part, however, in the Jewish uprising, which he reaches only after it has been put down. Conversely, in *Holy Week*, no such moment of heroic reassertion and redefinition is given to Irena. Heroism has returned completely to the Catholic Poles.

There is, however, another important point to be made about *Samson* that has interestingly not been given much attention by critics. To be sure, Jakub is a Jew only because he carries a Star of David on his jacket and is hunted down by antisemites and Nazis. His "Jewish looks" are curiously based on Wajda's choice to use a French actor for this role. And yet, underneath the explicit socialist narrative that fits in with the spirit of the time in which the film was made, there is a deeper and more important level. This was hinted at by Sobolewski in his reference to the "Christian notion of guilt," but it receives a crucial twist in Wajda's *Samson*. For here the biblical hero is worshipped as Christ by Kazia, the simple Polish girl whom he meets for the first time as they sit down for a Christmas dinner at his friend Malina's apartment. That night, Kazia sneaks into Jakub's room and traces her fingers over his thin, tortured chest. As she looks at him in the semidarkness, what we see is not mere love or desire, but adoration. This notion of the victimized Jew as symbolizing Christ was not uncommon in Poland at the time, and it seems to have coincided with traditional Polish antisemitism, on the one hand, and with the Nazi persecution of the Jews, on the other. The Jews were being punished for their murder of Christ—but at the same time, they were being crucified themselves, as the first step before the anticipated slaughter of Poland, the Christ of all nations.

This image of Jakub as Christ is an important phase in his transformation from Jew into Pole and from passive victim to non-Jewish hero. Kazia's adoration of him increases as he hides in the cellar, where she keeps him almost as her prisoner and as the object of her passion. It is, interestingly, only after she cuts his hair that he finally breaks loose and races back to the destroyed ghetto. This transformative moment, which changes him again from a dying Christ to a fighting—and suicidal—Samson, is filled with the kind of Polish symbolism that has little to do with the historical past or the Jewish memory of events. In her role now as Delilah rather than as Magdalena, Kazia has facilitated Jakub's final emergence from Jewishness into heroism. And, with his hair shorn and the ghetto destroyed, he can finally become a true Polish hero (fighting in this case also for the communist cause).[51]

A very different non-Jewish Jewish hero was created by Wajda in the film *Korczak* (1990), with a screenplay written by Agnieszka Holland. The film depicts the last years of Henryk Goldszmit, known to the world and celebrated in Poland as the great and self-sacrificing pedagogue Janusz Korczak (1879–1942). In many ways, this is one of the most moving cinematic works on the fate of Polish Jewry, portraying the deep bond between an educator and the most innocent of all victims, the Jewish orphans whom Korczak eventually accompanies on their last trip to Treblinka. Here is indeed a true hero, a man of peace, a lover of nature, and a dedicated teacher, whose extraordinary charisma went hand-in-hand with an unmatched ability for empathy, both for those discarded by the rest of humanity and (astonishingly, considering the circumstances of the time) even for their henchmen.[52]

Korczak was an acceptable, indeed, glorified hero within Polish as well as Jewish memory from the very beginning. It would thus seem that this was a sure way to link the two perceptions of the past through a figure admired and even worshipped by all. And yet, as Wajda himself conceded, the film met with tremendous criticism right from the beginning. As the director writes, "I committed to *Dr. Korczak* all of my talents and skills," but "the official screening at Cannes during the 1990 festival, followed by the standing ovation in the Festival Palace was, regrettably, the last success of *Dr. Korczak*. By the next morning, the review in *Le Monde* had transformed me into an anti-Semite, and none of the major film distributors would agree to circulate the film outside Poland. My good intentions were useless."[53] Why did this happen? Was Wajda completely misunderstood by his critics or was something else at play here?

Writing in *L'Humanité* on May 12, 1990, critic Jean Ray was full of praise for the "flawless script by Agnieszka Holland, the black-and-white photography, amazingly intensifying the cruelest details of life in the ghetto," and for Wojciech Pszoniak's interpretation of Korczak, "full of dignity, [which] gives this battle for humanity the magnitude it calls for. . . . Respect, that is the word which spontaneously comes to mind."[54] But the following day, Daniéle Heymann savaged the movie in *Le Monde:*

> The film is well made. . . . One could almost believe it. . . . [Wajda's] charismatic intensity inescapably draws us into the overall illusion of truth. . . . And what do we see? Germans (brutal, they must be brutal) and Jews, in collaboration. Poles—none. The Warsaw Ghetto? A matter between the Germans and the Jews. This is what a Pole is telling us. The embarrassment which accompanies us from the start . . . changes into distaste. Until the epilogue, which almost makes us faint. . . . The liquidation of the ghetto is underway. Under the Star of David, the children and Dr. Korczak enter the sealed carriage singing. And then the doors swing open—a coda to a sleepy, disgusting dream on the edge of revisionism— and we see how the little victims, energetic and joyful, emerge in slow-motion from the train of death. Treblinka as the salvation of murdered Jewish children. No . . . Not ever.[55]

Let us note, first, that the criticism of the last scene of the film was misplaced. As Betty Jean Lifton, who introduced the Korczak diaries and authored his biography, wrote in the *New York Times* on May 5, 1991:

> Those critics who detect only a Christian vision in the final ethereal scene (Korczak and the children leap off the train in slow-motion and fade into a misty countryside) are unfair to Wajda. After the war there were rumors that the carriage with the transport from the orphanage became miraculously unlinked from the train. Villagers throughout Poland recognized the "old doctor" and his children. It could be that, like Wajda, they wanted to believe that people like Korczak are indestructible. . . . Instead

The Jew in Paradise (*Korczak*): In a dream sequence that closes the film, the cattle car carrying Janusz Korczak and his orphans to Treblinka is miraculously detached from the rest of the train: they cheerfully leap off it and run to the forest. Heavily criticized, this scene reflects the refusal to accept the reality of murdering children and the hope against hope that it never actually happened.

of stirring up Polish-Jewish antagonisms, we should rather be thankful for the sincere sympathy with which Wajda attempts to recreate this modern Jewish hero who died—like he lived—for his children.[56]

Other critics, such as Elisabeth de Fontenay, writing for *Messager Européen*, stressed that "Korczak was profoundly Polish; before the war he accepted into his orphanage both Jewish and non-Jewish children. What's more, his concept of children's rights, even though based on time-honored principles of justice and compassion, has remained alien to Judaic tradition [!]." She thus insisted that *Korczak* "might be [one of] the first signals of a Polish-Jewish symbiosis which would be the Nazis' final defeat."[57]

The question then, to a large extent, is not whether the film accurately portrays Korczak's heroism, the life in the ghetto, or the death of the doctor and his orphans. There is little doubt about Korczak's heroism, all the more because he was given various opportunities both by the Jewish police and by the Germans to evade deportation. The question is, rather, whether he is a Jewish or a Polish hero. Blaming Wajda, for instance, for depicting Korczak staging Rabindranath Tagore's play with his children rather than "introducing them to the prospect of a happy afterlife with the Jewish God," is also entirely beside the point, since Korczak actually writes in his diary about putting on this play with his children, and the event was indeed remembered as having "produced a staggering impression" on those present.[58] Instead, what is crucial both to understanding Korczak's unique status in Polish memory and to his place within Wajda's cinematic representation of Polish-Jewish relations is the fact that, ultimately, Korczak embodies the non-Jewish Jewish hero par excellence.[59] From this perspective, Korczak provides an almost precise inversion of Jakub's figure in *Samson*. Whereas the latter *must* shed his Jewish traits in order to perform a heroic deed, the former *chooses* to become a Jew without, however, shedding those Polish characteristics that are by definition heroic.

In other words, Korczak is Polish through and through, and behaves as a Pole even when he chooses of his own volition to join the Jews. Just as he refuses to take off his Polish officer's uniform after the victory of the Germans despite the danger this poses to his own safety, so too he initially refuses to wear the Jewish Star on his arm when he (voluntarily) enters the ghetto. In both cases he behaves as a proud Pole and rejects the idea that anyone can dictate his identity to him. To be sure, Wajda has been blamed more generally for presenting only Jewish characters that lack any specifically Jewish cultural traits (such as religious faith or use of Yiddish). Indeed, one critic has argued that "there is absolutely no difference in accent or pronunciation between the Polish spoken by Poles and Jews in Wajda's films about the Holocaust."[60] But, of course, choosing the opposite tactic by making Jews appear particularly "Jewish" may give rise to at least as much criticism. Certainly it would have made little sense to ask the actor Pszoniak to speak Polish with the Jewish accent that Korczak never had, even if most of the well over three million Jews living in Poland in 1939 did speak Yiddish as their first language.[61]

Yet the main issue resides elsewhere; for whether the cinematic Korczak speaks as a Pole or as a Jew, he is clearly presented in the film—and remembered by the Poles—as a Pole who *chose* to share the fate of the Jews in the heroic manner befitting his nation. It is for this reason that his final choice to go with the children to Treblinka is so crucial. It is precisely because he *had* a choice, while the "real" Jews did not, that he becomes a hero, and, even more important, that he comes to embody the self-sacrificial nature of Polish heroism vis-à-vis the Jews that was largely fabricated by postwar representation.

In reality, Korczak was much more concerned with his Jewishness than Wajda allows for. Even as the movie is closely based on the doctor's diary, it both suppresses his inner conflict about his identity and superimposes a

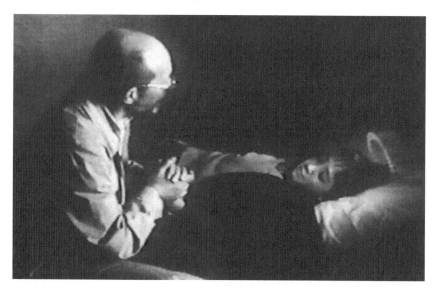

The Jew as saint (*Korczak*): As Janusz Korczak comforts a child ridden with guilt feelings for his mother's murder by the Nazis, director Andrzej Wajda paints a halo over the Jewish boy's head that can be seen only when this segment is digitalized: It is his statement, introduced subliminally, on the status of the Jewish victim as Christian saint.

deeply Christian element on the narrative that is entirely lacking from his writings.[62] Clearly the suppression of Korczak's Jewishness is a precondition for his conversion not merely into a Polish hero but also into a Christlike figure. But even more crucially, in a moment apparently missed by all critics, Wajda manages to convert the ultimate victim of Nazism, the innocent Jewish child, into a saint. This scene, which is given a typically ironic yet deeply moving treatment in Korczak's diary, is transformed into a powerful pietà in the film, with an added subliminal twist that has remained largely known only to Wajda himself.[63]

After much persuasion, a child agrees to leave his dying mother's bedside and go with Korczak. When his mother dies he is filled with guilt. Korczak tries to soothe him, lays him in bed, bends over him, and holds his hands. And then, for the duration of a single frame, visible only when digitalized, a clearly drawn halo appears over the boy's head. This orphaned, famished, emaciated child, who cannot forgive himself for having "abandoned" his mother, and is destined soon thereafter to be murdered himself, this wretched representative of a million-and-a-half murdered

Jewish children, enters our subconscious in the form of a Christian saint. Here is the invisible core of Wajda's non-Jewish "Jewish" hero: victimized as a Jew, he is glorified as a Pole and worshipped as a saint.[64]

Wajda's Jewish heroes therefore must peel off their Jewish identity in order to fit into the Polish pantheon.[65] Conversely, in István Szabó's sprawling cinematic saga *Sunshine* (2000), the converted Jew enters the realm of tragic heroism, not as a victorious gentile but only when he prefers to die a horrible death rather than concede his Jewish origins and relinquish his newly attained status as a Christian, an officer, and an Olympic champion. This is not just a reversal of Wajda's perspective, taking a very Jewish look at a condition seen entirely differently through the Polish filmmaker's lens. It is also an ironic remake of the tale of Rabbi Akiva, who refused to deny his Jewish faith even as the Romans tore off his flesh with red-hot pitchforks, calling out the holiest prayer of the Jews, "Shema Yisrael," asserting the monotheistic core of Judaism. For Szabó's film is ultimately about the loss of that core, the tragic consequences of becoming a non-Jewish Jew, and the wasted courage of those who clung to an identity that could become a reality only when accepted by a society obsessed with "uncovering" and eliminating its newly integrated Jews. Szabó has spoken of this process as the sinking of the Titanic—his metaphor for Jewish assimilation and European culture—into the raging seas of war, fascism, and communism. He laments the abandonment of religion, tradition, and civilization in the name of revolution, glory, and nation. In the final analysis, after all the fighting and killing, Szabó sees a society ruled by what he calls the "vulgar people"—the faceless bureaucrats of modern authoritarian regimes—and doomed to live in a dreary, empty reality of shattered hopes and devastated cities.[66]

If Szabó's saga of the assimilation and destruction of a Jewish family in Budapest is told entirely from a Jewish perspective, that perspective becomes increasingly non-Jewish precisely because the Sonnenschein ("sunshine" in German) family, which soon changes its name to Sors ("fate" in Hungarian), seems to have abandoned all remnants of Jewish identity. But of course, the success of assimilation is measured by the views of others; the closer the non-Jewish Jews come to their goal of complete integration, the greater the hostility of the "real" non-Jews. Cut off from its roots, the family is nevertheless increasingly identified as different, alien, and pernicious, and it is ultimately uprooted and destroyed.

Unlike Wajda's deeply Christian view of conversion, Szabó—who is Jewish—presents it as entirely functional and opportunistic, very much in the spirit of the late Habsburg Empire. Conversion serves neither as a cover

The Jew as national hero (*Sunshine*): Ádám Sors, converted Jew and grandson of the founder of the Sonnenschein family fortune, celebrated by his Hungarian national fencing teammates as Olympic champion after defeating the German contender in 1936.

for continued loyalty to the Jewish faith, nor as an expression of true spirituality. Rather, its goal is simply to facilitate entry into secular, bourgeois, gentile society. Jewish patriotism for the Habsburg Empire and loyalty to Kaiser Franz Josef was based on a convergence of interests: integral nationalism threatened the Jews just as much as it posed a mortal danger to the multiethnic empire. Indeed, while the emerging Jewish middle class, which in large part invented Central European bourgeois culture, collaborated with the Magyar aristocracy in creating modern Hungary, it was finally that very nation that turned against the Jews as foreigners who must be excised in order to complete the formation of the Hungarian nation-state.[67]

In *Sunshine*, the Sonnenschein family comes from an East Galician shtetl to Budapest in the mid-nineteenth century, armed only with a unique liqueur recipe. The rise of the Sonnenschein family symbolizes the rise of the Jewish middle class. Emmanuel Sonnenschein (David De Keyser), the founder of the family's fortunes, establishes a distillery where he manufactures his famous tonic, known as "A Taste of Sunshine" (*A napfény íze*, the film's Hungarian title). Emmanuel's son Ignatz (Ralph Fiennes, who also plays the grandson and great-grandson) becomes a prominent jurist. In order to be appointed a judge, he changes his name to the more Magyar-sounding "Sors." Symbolically, Ignatz dies shortly after the collapse of his beloved Habsburg Empire (just as the death of his biological Jewish father and of the Kaiser, his political father, are closely juxtaposed in the film). His son Ádám makes the next crucial step by converting to Catholicism, this time so as to be able to join the officers' fencing club.

By 1936, Ádám is a confirmed national hero, having defeated his German opponent in the Olympic games in Berlin. But in 1941, Ádám and his teenaged son Ivan are hauled into forced labor under the rule of an openly antisemitic and collaborationist Hungarian government. Challenged by a brutal Hungarian gendarme to admit that he is a Jew—his white armband indicates that he is a convert—Ádám repeatedly declares himself to be "an officer in the Hungarian army and Olympic gold-medal winner," even as he is stripped naked, beaten savagely, hanged by his arms from a tree, and then sprayed with water until he turns into a statue of ice in the freezing winter air. His son Ivan survives the Holocaust, in which Hungarian Jewry was largely murdered by the Nazis with local fascist collaboration. Following the end of the war, Ivan joins the communist secret police but leaves it after Stalin launches his antisemitic campaign in 1952. By 1956, he is one of the leaders of the failed uprising against Soviet rule. After several years in prison, Ivan decides to "return" to his Jewish identity and changes his name back to Sonnenschein.[68]

While Ivan's fate both links this tale to the present and brings the last survivor of this family back to his "roots," there is in fact only one tragic hero in this ambitious but somewhat flawed film.[69] For clearly it is Ádám's horrible death that constitutes the centerpiece of *Sunshine*: not because it is elevating, but because it is so stupid and meaningless, and precisely for that reason also profoundly tragic in its blind and stubborn courage. Ádám dies for a lost—and false—cause. Unlike his son, Ádám never realizes that he devoted, and sacrificed, his life to the kind of patriotism that could only become a reality if shared by those who become his murderers.

This is a central issue for Szabó, who has always been concerned with the tragic fate of outcasts and opportunists in the face of nationalism and dogmatism. "Nationalism," he has said, "means to me that you are full of hate for everyone else," whereas patriotism means that "you love everybody and your place and your world. So I am for patriots and against nationalists."[70] This kind of Herder-like, romantic patriotism may sound naive; indeed, it is somewhat reminiscent of Ádám's own fantasy. But it clearly identifies the truly tragic aspect of the patriotic, non-Jewish Jew who has transformed himself into an entity for whom there is no place, and who

The Jew as betrayed hero (*Sunshine*): Ádám Sors, taken into a forced-labor brigade by Hungarian fascists, is beaten, suspended by his arms from a tree, and sprayed with a water hose in subzero temperatures and frozen to death, all for refusing to admit his Jewish heritage and insisting on his status as an officer in the Hungarian army and an Olympic gold-medal winner.

sacrifices himself in the name of a belief that everyone around him has long rejected.

Jewish role reversals—such as Solly's in *Europa, Europa*—are often born of the need to survive at all cost. They also carry the stigma of antisemitic views of the "Jew" as an insubstantial, protean parasite. In *Sunshine*, however, it is precisely the decision to hold on to this new identity, despite its lethal price, that makes the figure of Ádám so compelling. Both a Hungarian national hero and a Jewish victim, he ends up being martyred as a convert in a quintessential act of displaced heroism. In this he embodies the calamity of modern Jewish assimilation in much of early- and mid-twentieth-century Europe. But the model for this heroism is gentile society. One becomes a hero by joining one's enemies, either through fraud or by more gradual assimilation. Heroism is associated with those who exclude, persecute, or even murder the Jews. In other words, this is not at all Jewish heroism, but rather the heroism of others assumed by Jews.

Precisely the opposite occurs in *The Last Butterfly* (released in 1990 in Europe, 1993 in the United States), an English-language film by Czech director Karel Kachyna. This is the story of Antoine Moreau (Tom Courtenay), a well-known but declining French pantomime artist who attracts the attention of the Gestapo, first when he mimics the Nazi salute in one of his shows and then when his mistress turns out to be a member of the Resistance. Initially, the Gestapo believe that he is Jewish—otherwise why would he mock the Nazis and make even German soldiers burst out laughing in the theater? The truth is quickly established by the sure method of forcing him to drop his pants in front of a Gestapo official who carefully examines his penis. Nevertheless, speculations about his background remain an important motif throughout the film. Threatened with imprisonment, Moreau accepts a Gestapo proposal to travel as a guest performer to the Jewish ghetto of Terezín.

Upon arriving there, Moreau is shocked by the terrible misery in which the Jews live as they await their turn to be transported to death camps in the east. He also grasps that his "visit" is part of a German ploy to fool the Red Cross, scheduled to visit the ghetto, into thinking that this is nothing but an ideal city for the Jews, where nourishing food and outdoor sports combine with cultural events and even performances by internationally famous artists. At this point Moreau, whose initial inclination was to get back to Paris as soon as possible, is transformed. He insists on employing as many children and musicians as possible, knowing that this will at least temporarily save them from deportation. With their help he then choreographs a new version of *Hansel and Gretel*, whereby the witch shoves the children, all wearing yellow Stars of David, into a blazing oven, to the accompaniment of Jacques Offenbach's *Orphée aux enfers*.[71] The gentlemen from the Red Cross, of course, do not get the point. But the SS officers do, and soon thereafter Moreau himself, along with Stella (Linda Jablonká), the little girl he has befriended and saved, are sent to the transport.[72] There he performs his mime of the Nazi salute for the last time, to the great annoyance of the Germans and the merriment of the Jews, after which they all disappear behind the locked doors of the cattle cars.

Although *The Last Butterfly* hardly had the same impact on audiences throughout the world as Steven Spielberg's blockbuster *Schindler's List* (1993),[73] several reviewers have compared the two films. Quite apart from the fact that the films came out in the theaters at almost the same time, the comparison relates to their focus on a non-Jewish hero, whose empathy for the Jews transforms him into a savior figure for a largely passive community already reconciled to its looming destruction. Significantly, however, while their narratives are anchored in reality, only Schindler's fantastic tale is entirely true (with several cinematic modifications), whereas Kachyna recreates the reality of Terezín to spin a possible tale that did not happen.[74]

The imagination, therefore, ends up closer to the truth than the historical reality. Oskar Schindler's successful rescue of "his" Jews would have been entirely incredible had it not actually occurred. The fictional attempt by Moreau to save the Jews of Terezín, or at least to expose the Nazi extermination policies to the rest of the world, predictably fails. In this sense, Kachyna's fiction is inherently more authentic than Spielberg's documentary-like recreation of an actual event. Both films share the merit of depicting the possibility of action—motivated by empathy—by those who in almost all cases remained mere bystanders. But Kachyna insists that ultimately such action entailed the sacrifice of the intervening bystander rather than the rescue of the victims. Moreau's understanding that empathy may mean sharing the fate of the doomed and his willingness to persist makes him into a greater hero than Schindler. The latter's success in actually saving the Jews facilitates a happy ending to a Holocaust tale, which appeals to audiences but distorts the overall narrative of a genocide that spared very few of those it targeted.[75]

In *Schindler's List* we have a crook turned guardian angel. In *The Last Butterfly* we encounter the most un-heroic of men, a selfish womanizer, drinker, and fading artist whose innate goodness and courage are awakened only upon contact with Jewish victims, through an empathy so overwhelming that he cannot help but be transformed into a Jew himself. And yet it is he, the non-Jewish Jew, who acts with greater defiance and courage than any of them. This is indeed reminiscent of Spielberg's film, where Schindler (played by the Aryan-looking Liam Neeson) confronts camp commandant Amon Göth (played, ironically, by the no less Aryan-looking Ralph Fiennes, who starred as a converted Jew in *Sunshine*), in a battle of giants over the fate of the Jews, represented best by the accountant Stern (played by the Jewish-looking Ben Kingsley). But while Schindler almost forces the Jews to survive through his own willpower and cunning, Moreau's deeper empathy is reflected in his ability to save souls rather than lives. Schindler brings "his" Jews to the Promised Land (literally to Jerusalem in Spielberg's version), whereas Moreau joins "his" Jews on their last journey to the death camp. Indeed, while he initially insists to the inmates of

The Jew as target (*Schindler's List*): Amon Göth, sadistic commandant of the
Płaszów concentration camp, during morning rifle practice on "his" Jews, over
whom he struggles with Oskar Schindler, who succeeds in saving "his" Jews
from the Nazis' clutches.

Terezín that he is not a Jew (which they find hard to believe, since why else
would he be there), he ultimately ends up dying as one.[76]

Schindler became a kind of "honorary Jew" after the war, but there was
never any doubt about his non-Jewishness. Moreau, who never existed,
remains a vaguely Jewish character after all: being a mime, he comes into
his own only when he plays someone or something else. His actor's predilection to empathize with all living creatures, even with the imaginary
dying butterflies on his palm, is what ultimately makes him Jewish. He
cannot fight the Nazis with lists and production lines, drinking bouts and
macho demonstrations, but only with love and laughter. In this he joins the
tradition of Menachem Mendel in *Jewish Luck* and escapes the logic of
destruction forced on the opponents of evil. But this same quality must
also ultimately bring him to that last, lonely railroad track to Auschwitz.

If the transformation of the Jew into a non-Jew facilitates heroic acts, the
transformation of the non-Jew into a Jew may also elicit action and courage. Conversely, cinematic Jewish Jews who are not transformed one way or
another will at best—and by definition—display heroic qualities of a very

Jewish nature, such as dissimulation (as in *Jacob the Liar*) or constant changes of identity (as in *Europa, Europa*). In this sense, too, Moreau, however much he insists on not being Jewish, is a "Jew" precisely because panto-mime is the art of make-believe par excellence, and the mime makes one see what is never there. *The Last Butterfly* is about an event that never happened, told through the perspective of an art that ignores material reality, at a site where some of the most original artists of Europe were concentrated by the Nazis, exploited to fool the entire world about the reality of genocide, and then blown away into extinction just like the make-believe butterflies on Moreau's palm.[77]

APPROPRIATED HEROES

As already noted, Terezín has attracted numerous filmmakers, starting with the Nazi propaganda film *The Führer Gives a City to the Jews*. This fascina-tion with the tension between facade and reality, facile lies and terrible truths, was already evident in an earlier Czech film, Zbyněk Brynych's *Transport from Paradise* (1963). Both Brynych and Kachyna show the entry into the "model city" through the windshield of an official German Mer-cedes; both show the pathetic figures of Jewish council members breath-lessly chasing the German commander's car through the streets of this former garrison town; both use as the focus of their plot the approaching visit by the Red Cross and the elaborate camouflage operation orches-trated by the Germans, including the shooting of the Nazi propaganda film in Terezín. (Similarly, Wajda in *Korczak* and Polanski in *The Pianist* recreate the German cameramen who penetrated the cellars of the ghetto and uncovered the dying women and children there, and Wajda actually uses the very same footage that was screened to audiences in the Reich as a portrayal of Jewish subhumanity in *The Eternal Jew*.)

This preoccupation—with the layers of deceit and dissimulation, reality and fabrication, documentation and propaganda—must be at the center of any cinematic endeavor about the Holocaust. It is also part and parcel of representations of the "Jew" in film. Precisely because of its enormity, the Holocaust should arguably be represented in a straightforward, em-pirical, no-nonsense manner. But it resists this kind of representation, invariably making it appear false and contrived. Similarly, precisely be-cause of the catastrophe of the Jewish genocide, there is an urge to repre-sent the Jewish hero as having just one aspect, one identity, and one goal. But such attempts tend to make him into a non-Jewish Jew, depriving him of the complexities and ambiguities of Jewish existence, heritage, and memory; or, they create him as an empathizing non-Jew, who may share Jewish fate but can retain the simplicity of mind and determination of will required of heroes. In this sense, just like Moreau in *The Last Butterfly,* the Jewish hero can only exist as something that he is not, as a flicker of the imagination or as a non-Jewish "Jew."

An entirely different alternative is the appropriation of Jewish heroism for other ideological purposes. This is the perspective ultimately taken in Brynych's *Transport from Paradise.* To be sure, his own skill as a filmmaker, and the fact that the screenplay is an adaptation of Arnošt Lustig's story *Night and Hope,* somewhat ameliorate the ideological tone evidently necessitated by the constraints of the communist regime in Czechoslovakia of the early 1960s. The film focuses on events in Terezín during a brief inspection by a German general sent to ensure preparations for the visit of the International Red Cross. The main cinematic tension is created by two polar responses to the Nazi policies of humiliation, deprivation, and transportation to death camps. Most of the inhabitants act—as one of the characters in the film mutters to himself—"like sheep." A few, however, rebel.

One compromised rebel is Löwenbach (Zdyněk Štěpánek), head of the Jewish council, who had already put together the deportation list but now, having heard (apparently from the Resistance) that the trains are taking people to be murdered in gas chambers, refuses to sign it. He represents the old world of the civilized, liberal middle class, who can only hope for eventual progress as they find themselves torn between the general inclination to obey authority and the realization that they have become complicit in a monstrous crime. Thrown into a dungeon, Löwenbach is visited by the commandant, Obersturmbannführer von Holler (Jaroslav Raušer):

> VON HOLLER: Löwenbach, the game's up. We've found the printing press. We've got the whole gang. The transport leaves in a few hours. And you are going with it. You know what to expect.
>
> LÖWENBACH: Yes, I know. Gas chambers, crematoria . . . I know. . . . But I know too that you will lose the war. The whole world is against you, Herr Offizier.
>
> VON HOLLER: Aren't you afraid of us at all, then, Löwenbach? We lost already one war, and still we are masters of world history. We know how to remind people of their fear.
>
> LÖWENBACH: The history of the world teaches us that tyrants always go under.

The future, however, belongs to the young generation and the more radical elements. Although their Resistance activities are uncovered by the

Germans, they are certain that the camp will soon be liberated by the Soviets. They are not compromised by any previous collaboration, and while they are doomed to die, their actions herald a different, uncompromising, heroic future. Conversely, although Löwenbach is swiftly replaced by his deputy Marmulstaub (Čestmír Řanda), the latter's corruption and depravity clearly indicate that he is a mere remnant of a lamentable past.

The film strives to complicate and humanize the simplifications of the communist narrative by means of several moving scenes. Thus, when the visiting general agrees to meet a group of prominent inmates about to be transported to the death camps (including a former Reich minister and Saxon prime minister, and a former French minister of commerce and the navy), he decides to strike off the list a certain retired major general now employed in cleaning saddles at the German military school. But someone else must fill the vacated slot. Ironically, the new victim is none other than the very man who had earlier insisted never again to go like sheep to the slaughter, whose lone struggle against the Germans is easily overcome. In another scene, the youths, who know that they are about to be sent to Auschwitz the following morning, ask one of the women to have sex with them, and one by one climb to the top bunk in their room where she receives them.[78]

Still, the film contains all the necessary ingredients of a forward-looking depiction of the fight between good and evil, where justice and the future must inevitably join hands. Its heroes emerge as determined, unrelenting, and morally superior; its villains are mean, crass, corrupt, and brutal. Although the train leaves for the gas chambers, the trajectory drawn by the film is essentially uplifting. To be sure, the Jews will be largely excluded from this better future because they have been murdered; but this was not the main concern of films made at that time in the communist block. It is in this sense that the heroic Jew is appropriated by the communist narrative, both as victim and as hero. What matters here is not the destruction of the Jews but the defeat of tyranny; and this defeat will be accomplished, as the rebels indicate, by the forces of good advancing from the east. When one of the young resisters is carried off to his death, his fists clenched in a communist salute and his handsome, blond features twisted in hate, he calls out that the incriminating material found on his body was delivered by the Russians. It is thanks to his heroism that evil will presumably be destroyed. By the time the film was made, however, everyone knew that one tyrant had merely been replaced by another. Thus, rather than focusing on Jewish victimhood and sacrifice, the depiction of rebellious heroism in *Transport from Paradise* served at least in part to justify the continued occupation of Czechoslovakia by a communist dictatorship almost two decades after its liberation from the Germans.[79]

Polish cinema has had its share of attempts to reconcile a series of contradictory narratives: the German occupation, resistance, and collaboration; the "competition of victimhood" between Jews and Poles; the liberation (with or without quotes) by the Red Army; and the postwar role of Jews in Polish society, either as a once-more victimized minority or as perceived allies of the Soviets and the main sponsors of the new communist dictatorship.[80] One of the first cinematic confrontations with this issue, in which the Jewish heroine was entirely incorporated into the narrative of Polish nationalism and communist sacrifice, is Wanda Jakubowska's *The Last Stage* (1948).

In many ways, this is a remarkable film. Shot on site in a somewhat "reconstructed" part of Auschwitz-Birkenau, *The Last Stage* had a tremendous impact on subsequent cinematic representations of Nazi extermination policies. Such films as Alain Resnais's *Night and Fog* (1955), Andrzej Munk's *The Passenger* (1963), and Steven Spielberg's *Schindler's List* (1993) obviously owe a heavy debt to this first attempt to recreate the reality of a death camp. It is also distinguished by its (rather ambivalent) attempt to portray the different fate of Jewish inmates in Birkenau despite the general suffering of all other inmates; its insistence on the international nature of the victims (which works to "correct" any semblance of uniquely Jewish victimhood); and, not least, by its focus on the women's camp and thus on women as victims, perpetrators, and heroes. In the more conservative era of filmmaking that followed, this last motif by and large disappeared from representations of the Holocaust and most especially from depictions of inmate heroism (and perpetrator barbarism), a domain that came to be dominated by men.

All of this clearly had to do with Jakubowska's own background. Born in 1907 (d. 1998) in the Russian part of divided Poland, Jakubowska began making films in the early 1930s. In 1943 she was arrested by the Germans and spent the rest of the war in Auschwitz-Birkenau.[81] Thus not only was *The Last Stage* shot on the spot where the events took place, it was also directed by a woman who had only recently experienced these atrocities. Nevertheless, from the very first moments of the film, in which an assertion of authenticity is flashed on the screen, we become aware of the contradictions between a desire to tell the truth about the recent past and the constraints within which the film was made:

> The prisoners, the SS men and SS women, the guards and block seniors, are played by Polish actors and inhabitants of Auschwitz. The film is based on authentic events, which represent a small fraction of the truth

about the concentration camp in Auschwitz. We remind the viewers that 4,500,000 people from all countries under the Nazi occupation were murdered and exterminated in Auschwitz.[82]

Quite apart from the obvious need to remind Polish audiences that the hated Germans in the film are merely Polish actors, this short statement both provides erroneous facts and suppresses crucial evidence. As we now know, the total number of victims in Auschwitz probably did not exceed 1.5 million, of whom the vast majority were Jews. The inflated figure cited in the film universalizes the victims while failing to mention that the main task of Auschwitz was, in fact, the extermination of the Jews. Indeed, rather than offering a straightforward reconstruction of the reality of women's experience in Auschwitz, *The Last Stage* provided a model for other numerous, ideologically oriented representations of victimhood and heroism under Nazi rule.[83]

Watching this film more than half a century after it was made, one cannot but be struck by the fact that the exposure of the lies and fabrications that underlay Nazi ideology and policies was already predicated on a new series of lies and fabrications meant to facilitate the reestablishment of Polish nationalism and to legitimize communist domination.[84] Ironically, however, the main victim of this new narrative was none other than the Nazis' own main target of annihilation, even as this rescripting of the past was intended to erase all competing perceptions. Indeed, the redefinition of the "Jew" was at the very core of this process of replacing one discourse by another.

The Last Stage begins with a stark depiction of life in the women's barracks of Birkenau. The action is concentrated around the activities of the heroic Russian doctor Eugenia (Tatjana Górecka), who comforts the sick, encourages the weak, and forms the core of the Resistance. The arrival of a transport of Jews brings with it another central character, Marta Weiss (Barbara Drapińska), who is saved from the gas chambers thanks to her fluency in German. She becomes the camp commandant's interpreter. The Resistance manages to smuggle information about the camp to the outside world, prompting a visit by an international committee. The Nazis try to camouflage the real nature of Birkenau, but Eugenia bravely reveals the truth to the visitors. She is consequently tortured and killed.[85]

The action then moves to Marta, who has meanwhile encountered Tadek (Stanisław Zaczyk), her former Polish lover, in the camp. Tadek had apparently spurned her before the war because of her Jewish background (an event only obliquely referred to in the film).[86] Now both realize that they must work together for the Resistance. They escape from the camp with incriminating documents about its impending destruction by the SS, but

The Jew as Polish hero (*The Last Stage*): Marta Weiss, modeled on the legendary Mala Zimmetbaum—a Belgian Jew of Polish extraction who stood up to the Nazis—as representative victim of a postwar politics of memory that converted her into a Polish-Communist hero and played down her Jewish identity.

they are eventually caught. Tadek is tortured to death whereas Marta is to be hanged in front of the entire inmate population. However, she is given a knife by the hangman, cuts her veins, and heroically cries out to the prisoners: "Don't be afraid! They cannot do us any harm. Hold on.... The Red Army is near!" As the camp commandant (Władysław Brochwicz) runs toward her, she mocks him with a hand gesture: "You will be this little very soon," and then she slaps him on his face, crying: "You will not hang me!" Just then a fleet of bombers passes overhead (critics of the film dispute whether these are American or Russian aircraft).[87] The SS men flee, and Marta dies in the hands of a comrade with the words: "May Auschwitz never happen again . . . never again!"

Marta Weiss is not an unknown character in the myth and lore of Auschwitz: stories about her circulated even before the camp was liberated. In the Eichmann trial she appears in one of the survivors' testimonies as Mala Zimmetbaum, who had escaped from Auschwitz with a Polish inmate in summer 1944, carrying incriminating documents about the camp. Both were caught and tortured before their execution. According to one version she indeed cut her wrists with a razor blade before she could be hanged and then slapped an SS man who was mocking her with her bloody hand, crying out, "I will die as a hero and you will perish like a dog." She was then apparently beaten so savagely that she died on the cart that carried her to the crematorium.[88] But in *The Last Stage* her identity as a Belgian Jew of Polish origins, who was remembered by the survivors of the camp as the only person ever to have stood up to the SS with such courage, is appropriated in the service of another cause.

As is common in Eastern European films of the period, the Germans are portrayed as mere caricatures, even if in this film some of the characters are based on real figures. The commandant is fat, self-important, stupid, and brutal; the camp doctor (Edward Dziewoński) is thin, elegant, sinister, and sadistic; and the female superintendent of the women's camp (Aleksandra Śląska), is blond, sexy, and cruel.[89] But what is remarkable in the case of the latter is that she bears an uncanny resemblance to Marta Weiss even as she serves as her precise opposite. For Marta too is blond, sexy, and speaks perfect German. There is absolutely nothing in her looks, manners, or conversation to suggest that she is Jewish. In this sense, the two of them are completely interchangeable. To be sure, one is a cruel Nazi and the other a heroic Jew. But because there are very few indications of Marta's background, she seems more like the positive incarnation of the same type (German, Polish) than the representative of a people that was exterminated for its allegedly alien and insidious race.

But Marta does not merely look like a German and "pass" as a Pole. She also becomes part of the communist conspiracy. She thus does not die as a Jew but as a Polish and communist resistance fighter. The link between national liberation and ideological allegiance is established early on in the film. As the leading resisters gather, one of the women reads aloud a proclamation just smuggled into the camp:

> Hitler's henchmen have covered Europe with gallows and concentration camps. They have made Europe into a prison for entire nations and they call it "New Order Europe." We know the perpetrators of these infamous deeds. Their names are known to tens of thousands of tortured human beings. Let them know that they'll not escape responsibility for their crimes, nor avoid punishment by the tortured nations. Long live the liberation of Europe from Hitler's tyranny! A day will come full of joy and glory for us. STALIN.[90]

As the Soviet dictator's name is uttered, one of the women sighs in admiration: "Stalin!" This clear juxtaposition between Stalin, the "liberator of nations," and Hitler, their exterminator, is all the more important

because it is immediately followed by a discussion at the camp commandant's office that establishes a second crucial element in the film's recreation of the past. Here the issue is the common fate of the victims. As the
debate indicates, while the Jews may be the first to be targeted, everyone is
ultimately slated for extermination. There is thus supposedly no sense in
distinguishing between genocide for racial reasons and repression of political resistance, nor between Jewish and non-Jewish victims:

> SS OFFICER: Due to the rapid and victorious advances of our troops on all
> fronts, new transports from Poland, the Netherlands, Norway, France,
> and so forth, will come to our camp. From the eastern territories alone
> we have to reckon with 20 to 25 million.[91] As you know, a variety of
> attempts were made to bring down to a minimum the time and cost of
> gassing and cremating.
>
> BUSINESSMAN: Just a moment, please. I believe you are not approaching
> the solution to this problem correctly. You see it only in one way: brutal
> extermination! Are we barbarians? Due to the immense extension of our
> battle lines we are forced to take German workers out of our factories.
> But among the transports, which you send directly from the station to the
> gassing facilities, certainly 70 percent are fit to work. If you exterminate
> them immediately, you will profit only from the personal belongings that
> these people bring with them. If you pass them on first to the relevant
> factories, however, you will gain a significant additional labor force.
>
> FEMALE SUPERINTENDENT: Gentlemen! I think you have not yet quite
> understood the greatness of our task. The Führer has given our camp,
> that is, has placed on our shoulders, the great goal first and foremost of
> purging Europe of all racially and politically inferior elements. Extermi-
> nation, that is the right way. And this endless back and forth about those
> who are fit to work and those who are not, about Jews and non-Jews, this
> I simply cannot understand!

The female superintendent immediately puts into practice her understanding of the camp's goal, and sends the entire cohort of female Jewish
inmates to the gas chambers. As the women are gathered, we are given two
swift glimpses of a Star of David on the striped shirt of one of the inmates.
But this action is soon followed by another selection, in which many of the
non-Jewish women are also sent to the gas. As one of the women cries, "I'm
not Jewish!" the SS man responds: "Doesn't matter, you bitch, hurry up!"
Moreover, if the Jewish women go to their deaths in silence, the French
contingent sings the Marseillaise on the truck carrying them to the crematoria. As a gesture of solidarity, the Polish women then offer a Catholic
prayer for those who were murdered, and soon thereafter both Poles and

Russians break out in national and communist songs and dances as they celebrate the German defeat in Stalingrad. As fellow sufferers, some of the inmates have distinguishing religious, national, and political marks. The Jews, however, though they may be victimized as such, have no language, religion, or culture of their own. And, if they happen to manifest particularly striking heroism, they must be assimilated into the national-communist camp.

The stark distinction made in the film between good and evil among the inmates is also based entirely on political lines. Thus the Polish Kapos (camp inmates in charge of fellow-prisoners) are particularly repulsive characters. One of them uses a Jewish menorah to light up her room and a Gypsy inmate to entertain her. They adorn themselves with clothes and stuff themselves with food taken from Jewish transports. Upon hearing that the Russians are getting closer, one of them exclaims: "I would prefer ten years in the camp to living with the Bolsheviks!" Conversely, the heroism of the resisters is just as clearly linked to their political sympathies. When Anna (Antonina Górecka), the long-term political inmate, is exposed as a member of the Resistance, the female superintendent fumes: "You damned red pack . . . it's still not over with us. . . . We are still the masters!" All of this serves to show that Polish nationalism, communist allegiance, and resistance to the Nazis were synonymous. The cinematic resisters proclaim: "We shall not die without fighting. . . . We must organize the resistance . . . we shall fight no matter what the outcome may be." In fact, however, although there was indeed an organized Polish Resistance in Auschwitz-Birkenau, the only recorded uprising of some consequence that occurred there was the rebellion of the Jewish Sonderkommando in the crematoria.[92]

As Stuart Liebman has shown, *The Last Stage* is in part an attempt by the Polish authorities to deny the popular perception of communist rule as the consequence of a Jewish-Bolshevik conspiracy against Polish nationalism, Catholicism, and the peasantry. The view that the party was disproportionately populated by Jews despite the fact that for a while it had seemed as if the Nazis had finally "solved" the "Jewish question," and the perceived links between an unloved minority and the hated Russian invaders, all made this an urgent issue that Polish cinema was called upon to engage. In this sense, *The Last Stage* actually tries to rehabilitate the Jews as members of the Polish nation while presenting the communists as the liberators of Poland from Nazi rule (making no reference, for instance, to the passivity of the Red Army on the eastern bank of the Vistula as the Germans obliterated the Polish uprising in Warsaw in August 1944).[93] But this kind of rehabilitation is predicated on denying the disproportionate toll of Jewish victimhood, the singularity of Jewish heroism, and the very existence of Jewish identity, all of which must be subsumed under the ideological dictates of Polish communism.

Political conditions in Poland had significantly changed by the time the Polish-Jewish avant-garde filmmaker Andrzej Munk (1921–1961) began shooting *The Passenger*. Munk had taken part in the Resistance during the German occupation, and following the war became one of the founders of the "new wave" in the Polish cinema of the 1950s, and a major influence on such filmmakers as Roman Polanski, who called him "my teacher and mentor." *The Passenger* is Munk's last and most influential film, despite the fact that he did not live to complete it. In 1961, driving back from Auschwitz, where some of the scenes were shot (Munk actually lived in former camp-commandant Rudolf Höss's office), the director was killed in a car accident. His absurd death seemed to mirror the black humor and irony of his films.[94] The film was put together by Munk's collaborator Witold Lesiewicz and finally screened in 1963. Making use both of footage and still photographs taken by Munk during the shooting, Lesiewicz also left gaps in the narrative to indicate both the absence of the original director and the impossibility of penetrating into the minds of the protagonists or of completely understanding the nature of the events that unfold on the screen.

De-Stalinization facilitated the emergence of a more experimental and less social-realist cinema in Poland, and Munk's work was certainly one of the best representatives of this trend. Yet the memory of the Nazi occupation, the glorification of the Resistance, the shame of collaboration, the trauma of the camps, and the unresolved questions surrounding Polish-Jewish relations continued to haunt Polish filmmakers. Indeed, despite significant differences between these two films, *The Last Stage* and *The Passenger* exhibit some remarkable similarities, especially as regards the increasing trend of appropriating Jewish heroism. As I noted, during the immediate postwar years Jewish cinematic heroes were permissible, even encouraged, albeit in a highly modified form as Polish patriots or committed communists. But Stalin's antisemitic campaign of the early 1950s, followed by the return in 1956 of Polish national-communism under Władysław Gomułka in the wake of the Soviet dictator's death, transformed such representations, partly due to political control and partly as a matter of choice by filmmakers. This shift can be seen especially well by comparing Jakubowska's and Munk's important films.

The Passenger provides two possible versions of a single event, both through the perspective of Liza (Alexandra Śląska), an SS overseer at the women's camp in Auschwitz-Birkenau. Traveling from North America back to Europe on a luxury liner with her new husband, Liza encounters a woman who may or may not be Marta (Anna Ciepielewska), a former Polish inmate under her direct supervision in Birkenau. In the first version of the story, Liza admits to her husband: "I wasn't a prisoner, I was an overseer" (implying that up to that point she had masqueraded as a survivor). She then quickly shifts to a familiar apologetic mode, asserting: "I didn't hurt anyone, and if Marta is alive it's only because of me." She goes on to claim that she brought Marta together with her fiancé, Tadeusz, and explains the latter's subsequent death and Marta's punishment as the consequence of circumstances entirely out of her control.

In a second version, which is silently remembered but not told by Liza, she recreates in her mind the relationship of exploitation, cruelty, jealousy, and finally murderous revenge that she developed with Marta. Here we find that Liza envied Marta for having a lover while she, an SS overseer, was alone; that she had an unacknowledged attraction to Marta, whom she wanted to control and humiliate but also to possess and preserve for herself (Liza's plan to take her along to a new posting is foiled by Marta's "betrayal"); that she intentionally set out to destroy Tadeusz; and that her final perceived humiliation and consequent decision to punish Marta came upon discovering that the latter was smuggling information about the camp to the outside world as a member of the Resistance. Hence her shock upon encountering Marta two decades later is triggered by a mixture of deep-seated guilt and a newly awakened sense of loss.[95]

This is a remarkable film, both because it uncharacteristically takes up the perspective of the perpetrator with at least a certain degree of empathy, and because its fragmented structure and Rashomon-like multiple perspectives are quite unique for a representation of an event that is normally presented in black-and-white terms of good and evil. While it is very much a moral tale, it is also a complex psychological drama that refuses to come down on the "truth" of the past precisely because it insists that the Nazi camps are not just part of history but intimately linked to the present. Liza's last words in the film, uttered just after she slaps Marta and presumably sends her to what she expects would be a certain death, are: "She forced me to do it. She wanted to destroy me, and I had to defend myself." As the background commentator observes,

> Those last words are not very clear to us. How did Liza defend herself? And how did she influence Marta's subsequent fate, the fate she first recounted to her husband, and now prefers to say nothing about? And why does she break off her own story before its climax? But we should not

demand too much of a camp overseer. She has admitted quite enough. And if she always sought to justify herself, that's only human.[96]

The commentator then closes the film with the following statement—reminiscent of Alain Resnais's rhetoric in *Night and Fog*—intended to associate the erasure of past criminality and complicity with the perpetuation of atrocity in the contemporary world:

> What is this recollection of a game played between the overseer and the chosen prisoner? Is it a vast apology, an escape? A flight into a web of human motives, a flight into a world of cruelty and evil? In the vague, unreal background, there are always human beings dying, silently, casually, anonymously. Dying, while Liza performed her duty, victims trodden into mud, people over whom she walked unseeing. This story, centered on a liner, which is an island in time, can be concluded easily. The brush with the past did not last long. And Marta, or someone resembling Marta, disembarked at the next port of call. The ship sails on. It's doubtful if the two women will ever meet again. And even more doubtful if Liza will be challenged with truths now buried in the mud of Auschwitz. Nothing can disturb Liza's life among people who prefer not to remember yesterday's crimes, among people who even today . . .

Despite its modernist structure and greater ideological detachment, however, there can be little doubt about the conspicuous similarity between the narratives of *The Passenger* and *The Last Stage*. To this must be added the stark realism of the scenes, shot by Munk on site, in what appears to be not just an attempt to imitate reality but a conscious citation of Jakubowska's pioneering film, yet infused with more irony and reflecting greater emotional and aesthetic complexity. We see the children descending quietly, almost ceremoniously, into the gas chamber, speaking softly with each other; a young girl pats the head of a German shepherd held by a smiling German soldier, who then quickly stiffens and she joins the procession; another soldier, wearing a gas mask, matter-of-factly punctures a can of gas pellets and pours the contents into the ventilation openings at the roof of the gas chamber; the chimneys of the crematoria belch out black smoke; the victims' luggage is piled by the now-empty rail tracks. We see the brutal, terrifying selections, as naked women run past the examining SS officer; a hound mauls a prisoner by the electrified fence; an inmate orchestra plays a violin concerto as another transport arrives.

Yet most striking is the similarity in the relationship between the two main female characters in both films. Since Munk died before he completed his movie, it is impossible to tell what he might have had in mind by reworking precisely the same theme of perpetrator-victim relationship already introduced by Jakubowska. But the fact that he chose the appropriately older Śląska, who played the SS superintendent in *The Last Stage,* for the role of Liza in *The Passenger,* can hardly have been a coincidence. Paradoxically, Munk's more sophisticated, multilayered, and intricate film accentuates some of the elements that were already present in *The Last Stage.* The thematic relationship of similarities and polarities between the SS woman and her prisoner in Jakubowska's film becomes an overt and ultimately destructive link of attraction and dependence in *The Passenger*—somewhat reminiscent of but less sensationalist than Liliana Cavani's *The Night Porter* (1974), not least because it continues beyond the war years. Conversely, while Jakubowska still allows Marta Weiss to retain a tenuous identity as a Jew, Munk's Marta has lost this identity altogether. The only mention of Jews in the film occurs when Liza complains, "Marta made me a silent accomplice in an effort to save a Jewish child." But then she asserts: "I am German and she is a Pole."

In both films Marta's heroism has the same sources: it is the product of love (to Tadek or Tadeusz) as well as of devotion to the cause (communism or Polish nationalism). Indeed, this heroism is even expressed in relation to the very same (nonexistent) international commission that visits the camp. If in *The Last Stage* love and ideological sacrifice are overtly linked, in *The Passenger* Marta translates (echoing Marta Weiss's role as interpreter) the incriminating note that reveals her work for the Resistance as a love letter from her fiancé. Thus Munk creates the same relationship of interchangeable victim and perpetrator that we found in Jakubowska: two young, attractive, charismatic, and dedicated women who ended up on opposite sides of the ideological divide because of fate and upbringing. All four are essentially the same character; but while Jakubowska's heroic prisoner is given a (vague) Jewish identity, Munk's has already been transformed into a (universal) Pole.

To be sure, Munk's film is both about the reality of the past and the effects of memory—distorted, suppressed, exploited, and cherished—on the present. One can only assume that he meant to make a statement also about the celebration of Polish heroism and victimhood and the denial of the specific Jewish memory of the war. But in the film as we have it, there is no sign of that. Had Munk lived, he would have soon thereafter been exposed to the antisemitic campaign by the Gomułka regime that led to the final exodus of the remnants of Polish Jewry from the country. One would like to believe that he was already conscious of that potential when he made *The Passenger,* and that in the final version this other aspect of the past, not merely the suppression of Jewish victimhood but the appropriation of Jewish heroism, the transformation of Marta from Jew to Pole, would have been given the kind of wry and ironic expression of which Munk was such a master.

There is a well-contained but keenly felt anger and bitterness in Munk's film. It opens with Liza reading a book entitled *Zu Hause in Ruhe* (At home in peace); it ends with the uncompleted sentence, "Nothing can disturb Liza's life among people who prefer not to remember yesterday's crimes, among people who even today . . ." Yet as it is, *The Passenger* remains an extraordinary film on the horrors of the camps and their long-term traumatic effects while simultaneously reflecting just that preference to expunge from memory and representation the very core of that experience. It is, in a way, the Polish equivalent but also the exact inverse of Alain Resnais's *Night and Fog*. Resnais's film turns all the victims of Nazism into heroes of the Resistance, thereby using heroism as a means to incorporate the genocide of the Jews into the larger tale of European sacrifice, and burying the singular memory of the Shoah under a rhetorical mountain of generalized sorrow and official bombast. Jakubowska's film takes over Jewish heroism and transforms it into a manifestation of Polish patriotism and communist dedication, masking the difference between Polish and Jewish fates, as well as masking Polish collaboration and communist perfidy by uniting an attenuated Jewish identity with vigorous nationalism and socialism in the figure of a legendary inmate hero. Munk's *The Passenger* goes one step further, depriving his hero entirely of her Jewish identity and interpreting her resistance to evil in terms of universal sacrifice and devotion. Thus the original Jewish hero has become the embodiment of the power of love and the eternal quest for justice in the midst of evil. Munk uses Marta's story to appeal to a distracted, forgetful world to remember the horrors of the past so as not to repeat them. But his own appeal leaves out the ultimate targets of the atrocity. All that is left of the true victims of Auschwitz is the faint cry of a Jewish baby that was briefly saved, and row upon row of empty strollers whose inhabitants went up in smoke. Why Munk chose this path is not clear. But as we can see from the following example, he must have been well aware of the traps and pitfalls of the alternative.

Within the Polish context, the alternative was to directly confront the issue of Polish-Jewish relations in a manner that, while hardly reflecting the reality of the war, served the perceived needs of postwar society. This was accomplished by depicting the emergence of the heroic Jew as part of his transformation into a patriotic, working-class, socialist Pole, on the one hand, and showing the erosion of mutual prejudices and the eventual solidarity between the two communities in the face of the danger posed to

all Polish citizens by Nazi barbarism, on the other. No film was more successful in weaving these themes into a dramatic cinematic tale than Aleksander Ford's influential *Border Street* (*Ulica Graniczna*, 1948, distributed in
the United States under the title *That Others May Live*, and in France as *La
Vérité n'a pas de frontière*).

Born into a Jewish family in Lodz in 1908, Ford began making films in
the 1930s, including a movie shot in Palestine (*Chalutzim* or *Sabra* [1934])
and a documentary about Jewish children in interwar Poland (*Children
Must Laugh* or *Mir Kumen On* [1935]). With the outbreak of World War II,
Ford fled to the Soviet Union, where he became head of the film studio of
the Polish army, whose members included several other Jews and communists who had already worked with Ford before the war on social-realist
productions. In 1944 Ford shot the very first documentary on the Holocaust ever made, *Extermination Camp Majdanek: The Cemetery of Europe.*[97]
Following the end of the war, Ford became director of Film Polski, the
government-controlled production studios in Lodz. Despite his communist credentials and the fact that he became one of the leading figures of
postwar Polish cinema and a major influence on such younger filmmakers
as Andrzej Wajda, Ford's increasing criticism of the regime, expressed in
such films as *Eighth Day of the Week* (1958), got him into increasing trouble
with the authorities. As probably would have happened to the younger
Munk had he lived, Ford was forced out of Poland in 1968 by the antisemitic campaign of the Gomułka regime. He spent two years in Israel, and
then moved to Denmark, where he made *The First Circle* (1973), based on
the eponymous novel by Aleksandr Solzhenitsyn, a critical perspective on
Stalinist Russia. Ford eventually settled in the United States and died in
Los Angeles in 1980.

Members of the same generation and sharing the same ideological inclinations, Ford and Jakubowska had a great deal in common. Yet *Border Street*
is distinguished from *The Last Stage* by its direct and insistent focus on
Jewish-Polish relations and its depiction of the life of a Jewish family. Not
surprisingly, Joseph Stalin disapproved of this film because to his mind it
overemphasized the Jewish experience and neglected to deal with the
communist Armia Ludowa (People's Army), providing instead an example
of a Polish hero who seems to be much closer to the nationalist Armia
Krajowa (Home Army). Nevertheless, Ford's film was hardly a call for
either Jewish nationalism or for Polish anticommunism. Rather, it envisioned the struggle against the Nazis as the melting pot of a new Polish
society where Catholic and Jewish Poles would be able to live side by side
as equals. To be sure, the political circumstances of the immediate postwar

period in Poland, already mentioned in reference to *The Last Stage,* played a role in this very first cinematic representation of the Warsaw Ghetto uprising. But as one can see from the significant differences between the two films, responses to these circumstances on the screen could be strikingly distinct. Notably, one of the central elements in this response was the manner in which the emergence of the "Jew" as hero was depicted.[98]

The Warsaw Ghetto uprising of April 1943 that constitutes the climax of *Border Street* clearly served two contradictory purposes at the time the film was made. First, it was an opportunity to extol Jewish heroism, showing that the Jews were "just as heroic" as the Poles and asserting that Jews and Poles had united in resisting the Germans. Second, it served as an ersatz depiction of what most Poles experienced as a far more traumatic, but equally heroic event, the Polish Warsaw uprising of August 1944. Contrary to the expectations of the Polish Resistance, the Red Army, then camped along the east bank of the Vistula, did not attack across the river but waited until the Wehrmacht had totally destroyed the Armia Krajowa, eliminating thereby precisely those forces that would have resisted communist domination. Only then did the Soviets move to the ruined city where hundreds of thousands of Poles had died. (The destruction of Poland was so thorough that *Border Street* had to be made in Czechoslovakia.)

In the circumstances of 1948, this was not an event that could be publicly celebrated or mourned. The first important cinematic treatment of the Polish uprising was made only a decade later by Ford's former assistant Andrzej Wajda, in his film *Kanal* (1957). Thus, just as Nathan Rapoport's memorial to the Warsaw Ghetto uprising became the rallying point of anticommunist protesters lacking any concrete representation of the 1944 rebellion, so, too, Ford's film could be seen as a cinematic monument to a trauma that was barred from any celluloid representation. In other words, in this film, Jewish heroism plays a direct and specific role as an officially legitimate representative of Polish nationalism.[99]

All of this may explain both the strengths of *Border Street* and the numerous compromises it had to make. The film tells the story of several families living on the same street in Warsaw through the children's perspective. Unlike Jakubowska's movie, almost all the main characters are Jews. Just as the film opens we encounter casual and malicious prewar antisemitism among some of the block's children. Dawidek Liberman (Jerzy Złotnicki), a religious Jewish boy, is playing soccer with some of the neighbors. As he stumbles and falls into a tub of water, one of the other lads, Władek Wojtan (D. Ilczenko), laughs: "Let the little Jew bathe once in his life. . . ."[100] He is joined by Fredek Kuśmirak (Eugeniusz Kruk), who tries to push Dawidek back into the tub, shouting: "The little Jew won't bathe himself. We must help him. . . ." Then a taller teenager, Bronek Cieplikowski (Tadeusz Fijewski), steps in and puts an end to the confrontation.

The children represent different classes and faiths in Polish society. Dawidek shares a basement room with his religious grandfather (Władysław Godik), who works as a tailor; his widowed mother; his aunt; and his Uncle Natan (Stefan Śródka), an electrician with socialist leanings. Władek's father, Kazimierz, is a nationalist and antisemitic banker; Fredek's father (J. Munclingr) is the ethnic-German owner of the bar; and Bronek's father (Władysław Walter) drives a horse-drawn wagon. Finally, another important figure that soon joins in is Jadzia Białek (Maria Broniewska), whose father (Jerzy Leszczyński) is a well-respected doctor. Once the Germans take over, everyone falls into their anticipated roles. The Jewish family is humiliated and soon driven to the ghetto. Kazimierz Wojtan joins the Resistance. Mr. Kuśmirak becomes a lackey of the Germans. Moreover, having discovered that Dr. Białek's grandfather was in fact a Jew called Bialer, the Kuśmiraks drive him out and take over his apartment. As Fredek's sister Wanda says: "They will go to the ghetto . . . and their beautiful flat will be ours."

Jadzia, who was staying with an aunt in the countryside, returns to find her father dying of typhus in the ghetto. Bronek, a straight and honest working-class lad, immediately offers her shelter. Like all other youths in the film, Bronek takes after his father, who displays similar altruistic inclinations. When Mr. Cieplikowski—who refuses to work for the Germans—helps the Libermans move to the ghetto, Mr. Kuśmirak mocks him: "What, are you going to the ghetto too . . . ?" Cieplikowski is quick to answer: "Neither to the ghetto nor to Berlin . . . Why are you reproaching me? Because I am helping my neighbors? One helps, and one will be helped in return."

Władek, for his part, has been contaminated by his father's bourgeois antisemitism. Initially Mr. Wojtan tells his son not to play "with such dirty children" as Dawidek, and opines that "the war, of course, won't break out. . . . The Jews only encourage such gossip to make better business." But good, patriotic Poles are not beyond repair. Following the German occupation, when Władek secretly meets his now-heroic father in a cafe, Mr. Wojtan tells him that Grandfather Liberman had actually saved his life: "I left my battledress in the workshop . . . The policemen beat him so terribly that many a young man would have broken down and betrayed me. The Jews are not all alike, and we have our Kuśmiraks, too."

Indeed, if the Wojtans can eventually be made to see the light, ethnic-Germans such as the Kuśmiraks are beyond the pale. The moment the

Germans arrive, Mr. Kuśmirak trims his moustache and combs his hair in a manner that makes him look remarkably like the Führer. His son is morally corrupt and joins the fascist youth. His daughter flirts with the Wehrmacht officer Hans (Robert Vrchota). But even such bad apples would have been harmless without the evil influence of the Germans. As Hans says to Wanda about their newly acquired apartment: "See? You didn't want to do it, you were sorry for him and I was sure that Mr. Bialer would agree!" Thus while the film delegitimizes antisemitism, it simultaneously depicts it as a marginal phenomenon limited to the most unsavory and essentially foreign elements of society. Even though it may occasionally infect true patriots, it rapidly vanishes once the Jews show themselves to be as brave and self-sacrificing as the Poles.

And this is the core of the film. Ford depicts a variety of Jewish reactions to the new circumstances. Some, like Dr. Białek, try to hide under an "Aryan" identity but are doomed to be betrayed. Others, like Grandfather Liberman, hold on to their faith and will perish in its name. Others still, represented by Uncle Natan, are proud, strong, and determined fighters. Returning exhausted from a prisoner-of-war camp, Natan already knows that the Germans plan to exterminate the Jews. But he believes in the unity of Jews and Poles and in the need to fight together against the Nazis.

NATAN: They will make a ghetto.

GRANDFATHER LIBERMAN: Maybe it will be better for the Jews to be separate.

NATAN: If the Germans organize a ghetto it is not in order to do us good.

ESTHER (Dawidek's mother): But in the ghetto we shall all be equal.

NATAN: Oh, yes, they will exterminate us equally. Don't you see? They intend to separate us from the Poles. It will be much easier to exterminate the Poles and the Jews separately. It is their policy. I heard in the POW camp people saying that we [Jews and Poles] should be together, and struggle!

GRANDFATHER LIBERMAN: Struggle? Who? You? My son-in-law? Jewish electrician? He will go to fight. . . . You have fought enough. Ha . . . Hitler laughs at you. What will you fight with? Your bare hands?

NATAN: Yes, with our bare fists! The Poles will surely fight, and I shall go with them.

DAWIDEK: I shall fight the Germans, too.

GRANDFATHER LIBERMAN: You have one more fighter.

REGINA (Natan's wife): Natan is right, Father.

For the faith in you...

The Jew as Jewish victim (*Border Street*): Grandfather Liberman, an orthodox Jewish tailor driven insane by suffering, consigns himself to God in the burning Warsaw Ghetto, dying as Jews have died through the ages, wrapped in his prayer shawl, saying Kaddish for his murdered family, and calling out the holiest prayer of the Jews, Shema Yisrael, as he is engulfed in flames.

The Jews, who traditionally eschew fighting, should therefore be as brave as the Poles, who are expected to fight as a matter of course.[101] The young generation, and especially such skilled laborers as Natan, is beginning a process that will turn them into warriors, in other words, into Poles. Moreover, in this unequal battle the Jews must join hands with the Poles in a united struggle against occupation and the perceived plan of the Germans to separate the two groups so as to exterminate them one by one. The Jews may be the first victims, but the Poles are sure to follow. Paradoxically, then, Jewish heroism must model itself on Polish heroism, for "the Poles will surely fight." But at the same time, Jewish sacrifice must precede Polish sacrifice, for the Jews are first in line for extermination. The Poles must learn that they and the Jews are on the same front against a common enemy. The obvious conclusion that, as Mr. Cieplikowski says, "one helps, and one will be helped in return," is even understood by the hound Rolf, trained by his master Hans to hunt down Jews. Saved by Jadzia from bleeding to death from a gunshot wound when she and Dawidek flee from the Germans into the sewers, this dog, whose name is Polonized into "Wind" (*Wicher*), returns the favor by saving her from Hans when he tries to kill the Jewish girl.

The transformation of the Jews entails empathy for the Poles, just as the Poles must learn to care for the Jews. At the last Shabbat dinner before they move to the ghetto, Grandfather Liberman says, "Children, children, terrible times are coming to the Jews. . . ." But Natan responds, "Not only to the Jews." This recognition of the other side's misfortune also dictates one's actions. As the Jewish uprising breaks out, Grandfather Liberman dies as Jews have died for centuries, wrapped in his prayer shawl, saying Kaddish (the Jewish prayer for the dead) for his murdered family, and calling out the holiest prayer of the Jews, Shema Yisrael, as he is engulfed by flames. Having lived as a traditional Jew he also dies as one. Defying the Germans as Rabbi Akiva had defied the Romans two thousand years earlier, he remains segregated by choice from the Poles and will not offer even token resistance to the murderers apart from his fanatical determination to hold on to his faith: "And as we perish for the sanctity of your name, take us to your kingdom and allow us to be there with those we loved, who died and who are now dying."

Natan's reaction is diametrically opposed to that of his father-in-law. First we hear him singing the Yiddish song "Our Shtetl Is Burning," a lament over past pogroms. But then the mournful tune changes into a military march, a call to arms. Natan urges his fellow workers to strike back: "Jews . . . look . . . there on the roofs. Polish and Jewish flags of war have been hoisted. . . . Brothers, the Jewish organization calls you to fight!" Thus, even as he dies fighting the Germans, Natan represents the future. But which future? As he stands at the top of a burning building, throwing his last grenade at the advancing enemy, we do indeed see two flags fluttering behind him, but both are the Polish national flag.[102]

An even younger generation now joins the hopeless battle. Dawidek, who has been sent back with Jadzia to reach the "Aryan" side through the sewers, encounters Jewish fighters making their way toward the besieged and burning ghetto. The young boy decides to go back with them into the fray. His friends attempt to stop him, but he persists:

> JADZIA: Wait Dawidek, don't go there. I won't allow you. You will die there.

> DAWIDEK: My grandpa and my uncle Natan are there, I have nobody but them.

The Jew as Polish hero (*Border Street*): Uncle Natan, married to Liberman's daughter, a veteran soldier in the Polish army, socialist laborer, and leader of the uprising in the Warsaw Ghetto, throwing his last grenade at the advancing Germans, flanked by two Polish national flags. Such flags were never flown by the Jewish resisters, who felt betrayed by the Polish underground's reluctance to supply them with arms.

BRONEK: Stay with us, you can rely on us.

JADZIA: I won't let you go.

DAWIDEK: I have to go there.

WŁADEK (offering Dawidek a pistol): It is the dearest thing I have from my father. Take it.

DAWIDEK: Władek, thank you.

Having learned from his father that (some of) the Jews are as brave as the Poles, Władek offers Dawidek the means to fight back. To be sure, the pistol will at best facilitate a heroic death, but in this manner the balance of Jewish and Polish heroism will supposedly be maintained. Yet this is a post factum, ideologically constructed balance, which even the plot of the film cannot fully sustain. The death of Władek's father raises no questions: His last words before he is executed by the Germans are: "Long Live Poland!" But for what and in the name of which cause is Natan dying? In whose name is Dawidek about to fall? The film cannot resolve this question. The Polish youths who wave to Dawidek as he marches back with the Jewish fighters do not propose to join the battle for the ghetto. They honor and respect the "little Jew's" courage. But this is not their war.

Indeed, the fighters of the ghetto did not raise Polish banners but rather the Jewish Star of David. In the film, a heroic Polish fireman who tries to put out the fire in the ghetto is shot down by a German soldier. In reality, the Jews fought and the Poles watched. Natan and Dawidek thus die as Jews; but posthumously, and especially under the circumstances of the immediate postwar period, they are transformed into heroic Poles. During the occupation itself transformations of this sort were anything but common, certainly not for such "Jewish-looking" individuals as are all the members of Dawidek's family. Only some, represented by the blond, clear-eyed Jadzia, could opt for one identity or another. Raised as a Pole, and benefiting from what was called at the time the "good looks" of an Aryan appearance, she is a Jew only from the perspective of the Nazis and their collaborators. Faced with the choice, she decides to live as a Pole rather than die as a Jew.[103]

As the three blond youths watch Dawidek vanish in the darkness of the sewers, Bronek says to Jadzia, "Don't cry . . . he cannot die, he won't die." Then a final voiceover provides viewers with the lesson they should draw from this little boy's appropriated heroism:

> Farewell, Dawidek. . . . We believe, too, that you won't die, that at the other side of the Border Street everybody will fight: Władek, and Bronek, and everyone who knows that there are no borders between the people and that all people are equal to one another.

The Jews knew well enough that they were being persecuted, ghettoized, starved, tortured, and murdered as Jews. And when they rose up against the Germans, in the first organized military action against the occupation anywhere in Europe, they did so as Jews, not as Poles. Beyond the enormity of mass extermination, what makes the uprising all the more tragic is that it never fulfilled the hopes expressed by Ford and his cinematic spokesman Natan. For while Jewish heroism was readily appropriated by the postwar regime for its own purposes, it was never assimilated into the Polish narrative of the past as part of the common struggle against oppression and injustice. There was far too much guilt and recrimination about collaboration with the Germans; too much relief about the disappearance of the Jews; and too much resentment about alleged Jewish-communist control for the hopeful sentiments expressed at the end of the film to have more than a passing effect.

JEWISH SUPERMEN

It may seem hardly surprising that the "Jew" as hero emerged in his purest and least complicated embodiment in the land that invented Superman. Although the original *Übermensch* could scarcely be suspected of any Jewish heritage, the gradual normalization in the status of American Jews in the first postwar decades was bound to entail also a shift in their cinematic representation. Between the 1940s and 1960s, the "Jew" as an individual who is trying to fit in, thereby becoming invisible as a Jew, was transformed into one whose identity is not a cause of embarrassment or a defect that needs repair but rather a source of either real pain or justifiable pride (or both).[104]

The Shoah, on the one hand, and the establishment of the State of Israel, on the other, became the focus of more open discussion and, eventually, fascination to growing numbers of American Jews and subsequently to the American public at large during this period. If the Holocaust did not sit well with an American cinematic tradition that reflected a more optimistic and upbeat view of the world than that afforded by the wholesale genocide of the Jews, the establishment of the State of Israel seemed to provide the necessary corrective. In fact, through the perspective of the Zionist success story (and Israel's own official view of the Shoah as an event of national martyrdom and heroism), Hollywood could fabricate the Jewish catastrophe as a morality tale about the victory of good over evil without having to come to terms with its legacy as an irreversible crime against humanity that betrayed the very principles on which modern civilization is predicated.[105]

To be sure, as such films as *The Pawnbroker* (1965) and *Enemies, a Love Story* (1989) amply demonstrate, Hollywood at its best has been able to produce extraordinary representations of the "Jew" as victim. This accomplishment is all the more remarkable because of the general predilection of popular culture in the United States and elsewhere to make the Holocaust into a profitable industry of kitsch or to exploit it as the new focus for a Jewish identity anchored in a self-perception of individual, collective, and vicarious victimhood.[106] But what interests me in the present context is the creation of the "Jew" as a typical Hollywood hero who is nevertheless Jewish. Indeed, because Hollywood is the largest and most popular producer of cinematic images in the Western world, the type of heroic Jew it manufactures has significance far beyond the frontiers of the United States or the English-speaking world.

As we shall see, while this type was modeled on American perceptions of the struggle between good and evil, justice and injustice, freedom and oppression, a closer look at some of Hollywood's most influential films reveals a somewhat more complex characterization despite the constraints of an industry catering to the popular taste. Nevertheless, there is little doubt that the ideal type of the post–World War II Jewish hero was forged in Hollywood. Indeed, although some of these productions were filmed in Israel and employed Israeli actors, Israeli cinema itself could never rival Hollywood in the fabrication of such ideal types. Moreover, thanks to a more intimate knowledge of reality, as well as European cinematic and literary influences, as early as the 1960s Israeli filmmakers and audiences became increasingly uncomfortable with one-dimensional, heroic Sabras or "new Jews."[107] Thus, somewhat paradoxically, the most blatant examples of the "Jew" as Superman were produced by the film moguls of Los Angeles rather than by the Jewish State that served as the setting for these sagas of heroism and redemption.

Perhaps the most successful and influential film ever made on the link between Jewish victimhood in the Holocaust and Jewish heroism in Palestine/Israel is Otto Preminger's *Exodus* (1960).[108] Loosely based on the story of the refugee ship *Exodus,* which carried forty-five hundred Holocaust survivors from France to British-Mandate Palestine in 1947, and also on several other events related to the period, the film depicts the Jewish State's struggle for independence through the perspective of two amorous relationships.[109] Ari Ben Canaan (Paul Newman), a Haganah (the pre-state Jewish defense organization in Palestine) leader, is sent to Cyprus to smuggle Holocaust survivors incarcerated there by the British into Palestine. There he encounters Catherine (Kitty) Freemont (Eva Marie Saint), a widowed American nurse, who wants to adopt the young survivor Karen (Jill Haworth). Karen, however, is determined to go to Palestine, not least because she is falling in love with Dov Landau (Sal Mineo), another young survivor.

Under pressure of a hunger strike the British finally let the ship sail off to the Promised Land. Dov joins the Irgun (the more radical right-wing Jewish Resistance organization), whose chief Akiva (David Opatoshu) happens to be Ari's uncle, and participates in the Irgun bombing of the King David Hotel. While Dov manages to escape the British, Akiva and many other members of this terrorist organization are arrested and face execution by the British in the Athlit prison. In a daring raid Ari frees the prisoners, despite their status as bitter rivals of the Haganah, but is badly wounded. Finally the United Nations votes to partition Palestine and the State of Israel is declared, but the Arabs immediately unleash war against it. Ari's kibbutz, Gan Dafna, where Karen and Kitty are now living, is attacked. Shortly after she is reunited with Dov, who arrives to help the besieged kibbutz, Karen is murdered. That same night Ari's Arab friend Taha (John Derek), who had sheltered Ari from the British while he was recovering from his injuries, is killed by his own people in the nearby village for alleged collaboration with the Jews. As they bury the two side by side, Kitty, who has meanwhile fallen in love with Ari, vows to join the Jews in the struggle.

Many of the events depicted in the film are based on historical fact. This includes not only specific incidents such as the bombing of the King David Hotel and the raid on the Athlit prison, but also the larger historical context. The plight of the Jewish displaced persons, British policies against illegal immigration, the ideological tensions between the Irgun and the Haganah, and the Arab refusal to accept the United Nations partition resolution and subsequent attack on the newly declared Israeli state are by and large accurately, though simplistically, represented in the film (which is nevertheless over two hundred minutes long). It is generally acknowledged that *Exodus* played an enormous role in popularizing Israel's view of the events leading to its establishment and its war of independence. It was particularly effective with American audiences, not least because it employed the well-tried model of heroic sagas. At the center of this tale is Ari, who embodies the traditional superhero. Yet Ari's thematic relationship with Dov—the compromised and in many ways more authentic and interesting hero—and his emotional relationship with the non-Jewish Kitty—who questions some of his dogmas even as she ends up on his side—complicate his otherwise one-sided persona, even as his character is ultimately folded back into the conventional mold of the American western.

Casting the handsome, blue-eyed, and muscular Paul Newman in the role of Ari, a self-assured, individualistic, and indomitable fighter for a good cause, supported by a platinum-blond American lover, made Hollywood's new Jewish hero into a strangely familiar figure despite his involvement in a far-off and not entirely explicable conflict. This necessitated numerous compromises with the historical reality of the time. Haganah leaders were hardly likely to wear well-cut summer suits or to sip martinis and smoke expensive English cigarettes with elegant ladies on the balcony of the King David Hotel. The attempt to combine in one character a stylish ladies' man, a Jew, and a rough and ready Sabra is hardly convincing despite Newman's immense charm. At one point, Ari asks the waiter for "some of your very good champagne," indicating that he is quite a connoisseur of the hotel's restaurant (visited mainly by British army officers). As the drinks are served, however, and after exchanging a few meaningful glances with Kitty, he quickly asserts his Jewish/Israeli identity: "I'll teach you a Hebrew toast: Lechayim!"

The familiarity that American viewers may have felt with this kind of hero, who conformed to the rules of Hollywood cinematic characterization, may have been paralleled by the reaction of Jewish audiences, especially in the United States, who were finally provided with a Jewish character who was so recognizably and unambiguously heroic. After all, if Newman could be Ari, then there could be no difference between Jewish and non-Jewish heroes. But this grafting of an American-type hero onto the story of Jewish resurrection and nationalism was also related to the Zionist perspective. Quite independently from American imagery and Hollywood representations, the ideal Sabra of Zionist-Israeli lore and fiction tended to look strikingly similar to the Aryan heroes of the European imagination.[110] The Jews who had begun constructing the idea of their nationhood in Europe created an image of a hero, combining the attributes of a Germanic warrior, a Cossack horseman, and a Bedouin nomad into a stylized ancient Israelite. From this perspective, we can say that Newman actually managed to fulfill this contradictory role, including a Hollywood version of an appropriately loyal and self-sacrificing Delilah at his side—who doubled as the object of Jewish male fantasies about gentile women.

Moreover, the fact that Newman was in fact partly Jewish, despite his perfect Aryan looks, may well have been on some Jewish viewers' minds.[111] To be sure, in order to prevent any confusion, considering the fact that Newman's physique did not immediately evoke any stereotypes of the "Jew," the film provides him with a large Star of David hanging from a chain on his well-developed chest. The irony of this Aryan-looking Jewish hero played by a partly Jewish actor reaches its climax when Ari, disguised as a British officer, discusses the ease of identifying Jews with a fellow officer. It is this scene in particular that demonstrates how well suited Newman was for this role, especially when complemented by Dov as his alter ego:

> MAJOR CALDWELL [Peter Lawford]: Well, Bowen, I see you are going to be getting rid of some Jews for us, eh?
>
> ARI [disguised as British Captain Bowen]: Yes, sir, shipping the whole caboodle back to Hamburg.
>
> MAJOR CALDWELL: In my opinion, that's where they belong. It's a German matter. Let the Germans handle it. . . . We should have started this policy two years ago. Oh, I don't care about the Jews one way or the other. But they are troublemakers, aren't they?

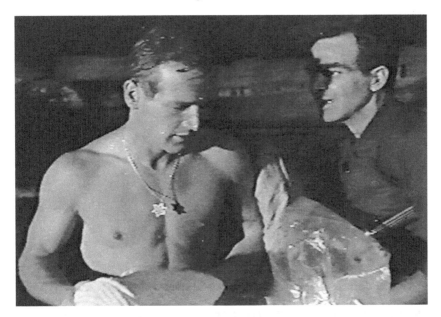

The Jew as hero born from the sea (*Exodus*): Ari Ben Canaan emerges from the sea on the Cyprus Coast in order to smuggle Jewish Holocaust survivors incarcerated in a British concentration camp, his shiny Star of David ensuring that he will be recognized as a proud Jewish warrior.

ARI: Oh, no question about it, sir. You get two of them together and you've got a debate on your hands you'd think you've got to put out a revolution.

MAJOR CALDWELL: Half of them are communists anyway.

ARI: And the other half—pawnbrokers.

MAJOR CALDWELL: They look funny, too. I can spot one a mile away.

ARI: Would you mind looking into my eye, sir? It feels like a cinder.

MAJOR CALDWELL [while closely examining Ari's eye]: You know, a lot of them try to hide under gentile names. But one look at that face, you just know.

ARI: With a little experience, you can even smell them out.

MAJOR CALDWELL [abandoning his examination]: I'm sorry Bowen, I can't find a thing.

ARI: It must have been my imagination. Thanks.[112]

The Jew as Aryan comrade (*Exodus*): Ari Ben Canaan, disguised as a British officer, asks Major Caldwell to examine his eye as the latter comments that he needs just "one look at that face" to recognize a Jew and Ari agreeing that "with a little experience, you can even smell them out."

Here all the common antisemitic tropes are visited: the Jews are communists, pawnbrokers, revolutionaries, talkers rather than doers, they look funny, and they smell bad. All of this is thrown at Ari's face and he, being Newman, need only stand there in his immaculate British uniform, ironically even adding fuel to the fire, to make the entire barrage of prejudices appear entirely ridiculous (hearing it in a British accent helps avoid any direct attack on American antisemitism and racism). This is a gratifying moment for American Jews just as it is for Zionist sentiments. When Major Caldwell is asked by General Sutherland, his commanding officer, what this Captain Bowen—who had just "stolen" a ship full of Jews from the British army—looks like, he answers: "Look like? Well set up sort of chap. Proper bearing. Decent decorations. Like any of us."

Nevertheless, the film treads risky territory with this dissimulation of identity, a major component of the conventional antisemitic discourse. To be sure, Ari remains himself, being neither a protean hero like Solly nor a parasitic infiltrator into gentile society like Süss. Ari disguises himself as a British officer in order to save the innocent, victimized Jews from the evil—or at least misguided—British. His goal is to transform the Jews into fighters for their homeland, that is, to make Diaspora Jews into proud Israeli nationalists akin to all other uncomplicated and one-dimensional patriots. And yet, the echo of dissimulation remains. Ari can look more British than the very epitome of the Englishman, the British officer. How solid can the identity of such a master of disguise truly be?

Similarly, Ari's association with Kitty, while "normalizing" the narrative by way of providing an American outsider's perspective, also carries with it echoes of the antisemitic charge of the male Jew as the polluter of Aryan female bodies. On the one hand, Kitty's progressive engagement in the dramatic struggle for Jewish independence provides an opportunity for American audiences to empathize with the Zionists. On the other hand, and despite the two actors' handsome "American" features, the compulsive and dangerous link between the dogmatic Jewish nationalist and the liberal, open-minded gentile can almost be seen as a rewriting of *Jew Süss*, only this time told from the standpoint of heroic Zionism. This tension is managed in the film by way of an interesting dialogue between Kitty and Ari as he shows her the kibbutz in which he was born, a neat little agricultural settlement nestled in the Jezreel Valley and overlooked by Mount Tabor:

ARI: I just wanted you to know that I am a Jew. This is my country.

KITTY: I do know. I understand.

ARI: Sometimes it's not that easy.

KITTY: It's the easiest thing in the world, Ari. All these differences between people are made up. People are the same no matter what they are called.

ARI: Don't ever believe it. People are different. They have a right to be different. They like to be different. It's no good pretending that differences don't exist. They do. They have to be recognized and respected.

KITTY: I recognize and I respect them. Don't you understand that you make me feel like a Presbyterian when you can't just for a minute or two forget that you are a Jew? You are wrong Ari. There are no differences. [They kiss passionately.]

Ultimately, the film accepts both points of view. The Jews are different, and because of that they want a land of their own. But their desire for independence is normal, and therefore they are essentially just like the Americans: pioneering, brave, pragmatic, and with a deeply ingrained sense of justice. Ari and Kitty are different. But she chooses to stay with him (which appears quite normal) and to share his fate. And thus they erase the differences between them.

If the relationship between Ari and Kitty provides the narrative of Israel's establishment with a familiar Hollywood twist, the case of Dov and Karen acts as a foil to the newly fabricated Jewish hero cum Israeli cowboy. Dov is a different kind of hero. He is young and erratic, lacking in confidence but recklessly brave. His decision to join the secretive terrorist Irgun seems to fit his inclinations. But before being accepted, the dark, "Jewish-looking" Dov is mercilessly interrogated by Akiva, who will not take him in until he reveals the terrible secret of his past. This revelation both compromises his heroic stature and makes him into a much more "Jewish" hero—directly related to the tragedy of the Holocaust—than Ari, whose handsome blond heroism is almost entirely free of dark spots and troubling memories:[113]

AKIVA: So you want to blow up British installations for the Irgun?

DOV: Yes.

AKIVA: You are an expert in dynamite, true?

DOV: Just try me.

AKIVA: There's still a point or two we do not completely understand. . . . First I will ask you please to recreate for me again how it was in Auschwitz. . . . For instance, how it was that people were chosen to live or to be killed.

DOV: Well, first you undressed, and then they clipped your hair. And then you all lined up and went to the station room . . . and then the doctor examined you and told you what gate to take. There were three gates, and if you were to be killed, you went through the left gate.

AKIVA: Which most of them did?

DOV: Yes, most. But if you were strong enough to work, you went through the right gate.

AKIVA: Which you did?

DOV: Yes. And then they assigned you to a . . .

AKIVA: You said there were three gates. Who went through the third gate?

DOV: Girls.

AKIVA: All the girls?

DOV: No, only if they were young and pretty.

AKIVA: And what happened to them?

DOV: Well, the SS guards kept some of them, and the rest were sent around to army camps, for the soldiers. . . .

AKIVA: Now . . . how was the killing accomplished in Auschwitz?

DOV: They went in to take showers, two, three thousand at a time. And the doors were locked, and then came the gas.

AKIVA: Very professional. One thing I overlooked. You say you got this dynamiting experience in the Warsaw Ghetto fighting Nazis?

DOV: That's right.

AKIVA: You blew up quite a few Nazis with this dynamite?

DOV: All I could!

AKIVA: Good. Now, return to Auschwitz please. From the gas chambers the bodies went where?

DOV: The ovens.

AKIVA: At Auschwitz they had crematoriums only at the last . . . I mean before the installation of the ovens what happened to the bodies?

DOV: They buried them.

AKIVA: How?

DOV: In trenches and in holes.

AKIVA: Who dug the holes?

DOV: I don't know

AKIVA: I ask you again. Who dug the graves?

DOV: I don't know. . . . They had demolition squads. At least, sometimes they did. To blow holes in the ground and then dump the bodies in.

AKIVA: That is correct. Now, may I tell you something, Dov Landau? At no time did the Jews use dynamite in the Warsaw Ghetto. They had no dynamite. Do you remember better now?

DOV: Maybe . . .

AKIVA: So it was not possible for you to learn the use of dynamite in the Warsaw Ghetto. You learned about dynamite in Auschwitz, making mass graves to receive the dead bodies of your people, true? Hundreds and hundreds of thousands of them. And you saved your own life by working in that camp as a Sonderkommando, correct? It was the duty of those Jews who became Sonderkommandos to shave the heads of other Jews, to remove dead bodies from the gas chambers, to collect gold fillings from their teeth. . . .

DOV: Yes . . . [sobbing] what can I do, what can I do?

AKIVA: Take into consideration that you were less than thirteen when you went to Auschwitz. Even so we must have the truth. Is there anything else?

DOV: Yes.

AKIVA: Then tell us!

DOV: No, I won't tell you. Please don't make me tell you. Kill me, I don't care, I won't tell you. . . .

AKIVA: Tell us!

DOV: [hiding his head between his hands and sobbing] They . . . they used me, they used me like you use a woman.

At this point Akiva helps Dov to his feet, brings him to a wall covered with a map of Jerusalem, and, by the light of a menorah, has him swear an oath of allegiance to the Irgun on a pistol and a Bible.

This is a remarkable scene that has not received much attention by critics. For here we have the compromised, wounded, humiliated Jew who then becomes not just a fighter but also a terrorist, willing to blow up a hotel full of innocent people in the name of freedom and vengeance. Rather than being a heroic Resistance fighter in Warsaw, Dov was a Sonderkommando who helped the Nazis carry out mass murder. Having presented himself as the embodiment of soldierly virility, Dov is revealed to have been used as a sexual slave. In his first testimony, Dov recreates the past as he wishes it had been: He longs to have a memory of blowing up Nazis. In fact, however, he learned his demolition skills from mass burials of Jews. His unfulfilled desire to kill Nazis will now be turned against the British and the Arabs. For Dov, the war in Palestine is a direct continuation of the Holocaust.

This is also a curiously inaccurate depiction of Auschwitz. Jewish Sonderkommandos would have hardly been allowed to handle dynamite. Indeed, the only time that dynamite (smuggled by the Resistance in the camp) was used by the Sonderkommandos was during their uprising, in which they blew up one of the crematoria.[114] Dov could have therefore been a Holocaust hero after all. But the logic of the film does not provide for this. In order to become the new Israeli hero, Dov must first be the humiliated and collaborating Jew of Auschwitz. Only upon landing on the shores of the Promised Land can he be remade in the shape of the ancient biblical heroes or the contemporary freedom fighters of all other nations. In other words, only then can he be recast in the shape of Ari.

Similarly, while there certainly was a great deal of both female and male prostitution in the camps, at no time was there a triple selection on the ramp at Auschwitz, or a "gate" for young women chosen as sexual slaves for the SS and the Wehrmacht (sexual intercourse with Jews was officially forbidden for racial reasons). Rather, this "fact" is invented by the film for the sake of highlighting Dov's own compromised masculinity in Auschwitz, where he was used "as a woman," and in order to distinguish between his Diaspora identity and his emerging Israeli/heroic nature which, by definition, must also include a "healthy" sexual relationship.[115]

Dov's "healthy" relationship is with Karen. A German-Jewish girl hidden in Denmark during the war, Karen has even more pronounced Aryan looks than Kitty. This time, however, she loves Dov not only for his strength but also for his weakness. Apart from conforming to the aesthetic ideals of early 1960s Hollywood, Karen's strikingly non-Jewish features create an interesting balance between Dov and Ari. For Dov, Ari is a model of heroism that he must emulate. But on a deeper level, Dov is the justification for Ari. As Dov evolves into a "new" Jew, he brings with him the historical context and the psychological complexity that Ari lacks. Similarly, Karen emulates the older Kitty and is tempted to follow her to the United States. But by the end of the film, it is Kitty who takes up Karen's commitment to Zionism and who has internalized both the pain and the ideals of the murdered teenager. Just as Dov's tortured soul enriches Ari's character, so Karen's innocence and idealism transform Kitty's detached liberalism into a more profound engagement with an existential cause. Finally, the characters merge: Ari integrates the darkness of Dov's past that Hollywood convention would not have permitted him to experience himself, and Kitty integrates Karen's Jewishness, which for conventional aesthetic reasons must retain a blond facade.

Heroism in films about Israel must be expressed in fighting the Arabs. True to the model of the western film, the Arabs take up the role of the Indians. They may be either noble savages or cunning and murderous primitives; they are endowed with certain Oriental romantic features, but must eventually either submit or be destroyed. Yet in films such as *Exodus* there is a historical element missing from the classical western. For while Dov avenges the Germans by fighting the Arabs, the Arabs who fight the Jews are seen as somehow connected to the Nazis. When Taha, Ari's devoted Arab friend, is hanged by his fellow villagers, they mark his chest with a Star of David and paint a large swastika on the wall. And just as the Nazis are associated with sexual violation, it is suggested that the Arabs behave in a similar manner. While Karen is murdered at night by an unknown assailant, and the viewers are shown no marks of physical injury, a clear association is made with Dafna, her model of heroism and Ari's first love, who was horribly mutilated by the Arabs. Allowing for the strict rules of language and presentation in Hollywood at the time, every hint is given that both girls were raped.

Behind its facade of conventionality and conformism, *Exodus* attempts to provide a more complex representation of the emerging "Jew" as hero. In the end, however, it must retreat to convention. As Ari speaks over the common grave of Taha (the good Arab) and Karen (the innocent "Aryan-looking" Jewish girl) in the closing scene of the movie, his plea for peace is rooted in a justification of Jewish self-affirmation and fighting heroism:

> This is Taha. Mukhtar [village chief] of Abu Yesha. And this is Karen, secretary of the rooms' committee, Bungalow 12, Gan Dafna. We have no qadi to pray for Taha's soul, and we have no rabbi to pray over Karen. Taha should have lived a long life, surrounded by his people, and his sons, and death should have come to him as an old friend offering the gift of sleep. It came instead as a maniac. And Karen, who loved her life, and who lived it as purely as a flame, why did God forget her? Why did she have to stumble unto death so young, and all alone, and in the dark? We of all people should no longer be surprised when death reaches out to us, with the world's insanity, and our slaughtered millions, we should be used to senseless killing. But I am not used to it, I cannot get used to it, I will not get used to it! I look at these two people and I want to howl like a dog, I want to shout and murder, so that the whole world will hear it and never forget it. It's right that these two people should lie side by side in this grave, because they will share it in peace, but the dead always share the earth in peace, and that's not enough. It's time for the living to have a turn. A few miles from here there are people who are fighting and dying and we must join them. But I swear on the bodies of these two people that the day will come when Arab and Jew will share in peaceful life this land that they always shared in death. Taha, old friend and very dear brother, Karen, child of light, daughter of Israel, Shalom![116]

This is the idealized vision of the heroic Jew, a combination of the white settler in the Wild West and the righteous victim of persecution seeking justice through war and peace. His loyal Friday is maliciously murdered by the natives, yet he seeks compromise rather than destruction. His innocent children are slain, yet he still believes in a common future. But behind this transformation of the heroic Jew into an American Superman lurk the shadows of other figures, of phobias and prejudices that remain immune even to the blinding sun of the new Jewish State. The other side of the proud, blue-eyed Ari is the humiliated, vengeful, and violent Dov; the other side of the newly committed Presbyterian Kitty is the murdered Karen, the angelic blond who cannot conceivably survive this cruel land and its dark-eyed inhabitants. Finally, the other side of Ari's brotherly

friendship with Taha is the association of the Arabs with the Nazis, signify-
ing the emergence of the heroic blond Israeli—now divorced from his
Jewish past—who faces the deceitful and murderous dark Arab, now associated with the Jews' most lethal enemies in Europe, but transformed
through the distorting mirror of an antisemitic imagery into a perfidious,
Jew-like figure.[117]

If *Exodus* launched the Jewish Superman as a Zionist commander, Melville Shavelson's *Cast a Giant Shadow* (1966) brought to the screen an
American hero who discovers his Jewish identity on the bloody road to
Jerusalem. Based on Ted Berkman's novel of the same name, this star-
studded movie cast some of Hollywood's most celebrated machos as Israeli
freedom fighters or their courageous American supporters.[118] Erroneously
described by some critics as the first commander of the Israeli armed
forces, Colonel David Marcus was in fact a U.S. army colonel who volun-
teered to help the Jews in Palestine under the nom de guerre Mickey
Stone.[119] Appointed supreme commander of the Jerusalem front by Israel's
prime minister and minister of defense, David Ben-Gurion, on May 28,
1948, Colonel Marcus initially tried to break the siege of Jerusalem by
launching an attack on the former British police fort in Latrun that strad-
dled the road to the city. The costly attack was repelled by the superior
firepower of the well-trained Arab Legion. Colonel Marcus then headed
the opening of a bypass road—subsequently named the Burma Road, after
the World War II supply route from Burma to China—to the besieged
capital. The successful operation finally brought in supplies and reinforce-
ments and saved the western part of the city (which remained divided until
1967) from falling into the hands of the Arabs. But on June 11, while
staying the night with an elite Palmach battalion near the monastery of
Abu Gosh, Colonel Marcus left the perimeter of the camp to relieve himself. Not knowing Hebrew, he did not respond to a sentry's demand for the
password, and was shot to death.[120]

The story of Colonel Marcus had to be reworked and embellished so as
to appeal to American viewers. Adjustments had to cater not only to public
taste but also to views about identity and loyalty. Rather than being killed
as he returns from answering the call of nature, the cinematic Marcus
(Kirk Douglas) dies after a dramatic farewell from his sensuous Jewish
mistress, Magda Simon (Senta Berger). Thus he is shot after proclaiming
his intention to go back to his American wife, Emma (Angie Dickinson),
and the conventional life he had left behind when he set out to single-
handedly save the Jewish State. This "correction" of the historical record,
which transforms a stupid, accidental death into a moving, sentimental

ending, plays a central role in the film's somewhat awkward attempt to maneuver between stressing the heroism of an American Jew and presenting him as a man of double loyalties and split patriotism.

In some ways, Douglas's Marcus cuts a more credible figure than Newman's Ari. For one thing, Marcus actually did play a brief but crucial part in the history of Israel. For another, Newman seems quite odd as a Haganah commander, whereas Douglas can retain all the attributes of an American soldier in a foreign land. Moreover, the actor's own biography and persona provide some interesting overlap with the cinematic protagonist. Born Issur Danielovitch (later changed to Isidore Demsky) to illiterate Russian-Jewish parents, Douglas was a tough young man who worked as a wrestler and an usher to pay for his studies. He served in the U.S. navy in World War II before launching his career in the movies.[121] In this sense, Douglas was precisely the type of "muscular Jew" already called for by the early Zionists and required by Hollywood's new penchant for heroic Jews. This tension between having a Jewish background yet neither looking nor behaving like a stereotypical Jew links Douglas with Marcus, who is a Jew in America and an American in Palestine (although initially more readily accepted as an American in the former than as a Jew in the latter).[122]

Unfortunately, the film does not succeed in making productive use of this tension. While shooting in Israel and paying attention to historical detail could have provided the movie with some measure of authenticity, casting actors of non-American origin in the roles of some key Israeli figures at times verges on the ridiculous.[123] Thus Haganah commander Asher Gonen (somewhat reminiscent of the historical Yigael Yadin) is played by Yul Brynner, a Hollywood tough guy of Russian and Gypsy origin; the youthful Palmach brigade commander Ram Oren (possibly based on Yitzhak Rabin) is played by the relatively unknown Greek actor Stathis Giallelis; and the sexy Jewish Holocaust survivor and fighting Israeli Magda is played by the ample Austrian actress Senta Berger. For the crucial battle in the Negev Desert, these heroes are joined by Frank Sinatra, in the role of an American pilot who saves the day by throwing bottles of seltzer water on the advancing Egyptian armored column. Finally, the Arab sheikh who helps the Jews is caricatured in a rather embarrassing manner by the Israeli actor Haym Topol, otherwise known for his role as Tevye the Milkman in *Fiddler on the Roof* (1971).

But the failure goes much deeper than fuzzy casting. It has primarily to do with Shavelson's uncertain, even timid handling of the central theme: The case of an American World War II hero who decides to fight another country's war as a Jewish nationalist. By filtering this dilemma through

Marcus's relationship with two women, the film ends up as a sappy romance rather than as an examination of the problematic links between heroism and identity. Moreover, by introducing an exotic local beauty who threatens to tear the hero away from his faithful wife, the film unconsciously slips into the antisemitic convention of the dangerous Jewish female who lures the hero to his doom by her wiles and uncontrolled sexuality.

Cast a Giant Shadow thus features the American Marcus in danger of being taken over and transformed into a Jew by the temptress Magda. On the one hand, Marcus asserts that he has now found his true identity as a Jew and his true home in Palestine. On the other, he ultimately decides to retain his original identity as faithful husband and patriotic American by returning to his homeland and hearth. Marcus thus inexplicably sheds precisely those attributes of Jewish nationalism and solidarity he had just declared to be the newly found core of his identity. Finally, his untimely death saves him from having to face the consequences of his decision. Hence we are faced with the apparent paradox that making an American-Jewish hero (Marcus/Douglas) into a fighter for the Jewish cause in Palestine is a far more problematic cinematic exercise (at least for Hollywood) than employing an American actor in the role of a heroic Israeli (Ari/Newman).

One can easily illustrate the film's shifting foci, from one pole of identity to another, by examining how the film shows Marcus's complete loyalty to the United States even as it tries to depict his growing commitment to the cause of the Jewish State. Approached by Major Safir (James Donald) of the Haganah to help the Jews in their desperate struggle, Marcus initially refuses to express any solidarity with the Zionist cause:

MARCUS: Would you give up everything you love to fight an insane war for a little country that'll get its brains blown out in a few weeks?

SAFIR: If it were my country.

MARCUS: Maybe it's yours, but it isn't mine.

SAFIR: But you're a Jew.

MARCUS: I'm an American, major. That's my religion. Last time I was in temple I was thirteen years old. . . . [walks off]

SAFIR [chasing after him]: Colonel, I'm asking you as an American. What is it you say in your schools when you salute your flag? "Liberty and justice for all"? Is it only for all of you?

MARCUS: Don't give me history lessons!

SAFIR: Six million of our people have recently been murdered, Colonel Marcus. Would you like us to try for seven?[124]

The mention of the Holocaust at the beginning of the film is no coincidence. Without quite deciding how to deal with this theme, the genocide of the Jews keeps appearing as the clinching argument whenever anyone has any doubts about the Zionist cause. When a senior British officer threatens to shoot illegal immigrants landing on the shores of Palestine, a younger officer says: "Now's the time to find out if we're bloody Nazis or not, isn't it." In her first encounter with him Magda tells Marcus that her husband, André (who is conveniently killed shortly thereafter), "has a number tattooed on his right arm . . . in this country, it's unfortunately not unusual." And yet, as the conversations between Marcus and his wife, Emma, seem to indicate, his decision to go to Palestine has to do more with his love of adventure than with any ideological commitment. Indeed, Emma believes that war "gets you more excited than I do, doesn't it?" Significantly, Marcus is urged to recognize his deeper link to the emerging Jewish State by his former World War II commander, the "blood-and-guts," Patton-like General Mike Randolph, played by the epitome of the American hero, John Wayne. Thus the legitimization of a split loyalty is delivered by the man and actor whose statements about heroism no one would dare contradict.

Marcus encounters the general during World War II. Initially he explains his insubordination as motivated by his urge to keep "knocking off guys who were making soap out of my relatives." Later on, he takes the general on a tour of Dachau. Without ever mentioning the word "Jew," Marcus says to the general: "Those that are alive weigh an average of eighty-five pounds. Over there's a building filled with ovens, still warm. No one ever baked any bread in them. Here there are thirty-two hundred corpses, near as we can tell, that they didn't have time to bury." Visibly moved, the general blurts out: "Give this insubordinate son of a bitch every truck and blanket in the Third Army. And I don't care who you have to steal them from." Thus the encounter with the camps increasingly makes both Marcus and the general into Zionists. When Marcus returns angry and frustrated from his first stint in Palestine, the British ambassador (Michael Hordern) comments that the Jews in Palestine "are, as the Bible says, 'a stiff-necked people,'" and urges Marcus to "persuade them that it's better to bend a little, if those necks are going to be saved at all." It is at this point that the general delivers the decisive pep talk to the bitter and torn Marcus:

> You don't give any of the rest of us credit for being human beings. I saw Dachau too, remember? And if anybody ever deserved a home on the basis of sheer gallantry, it's those poor devils from those camps. And you have friends too, Mickey, although it'll probably upset you to find it out.

... But what about you? Are you too big to go back and help your own people unless they bow down and kiss your West Point ring? ... What happened to that insubordinate SOB that jumped out of one of my planes over Normandy? Who won the Distinguished Service Medal? Are you proud of that medal, and ashamed you might win the Star of David? Stand up and be counted, Mickey. And there's a lot of us who'll stand up with you. Lechayim.

Having been given the general's blessing, Marcus returns to Palestine. He is there to help the Jews fight, but he is there also because he loves Magda. And between bouts of fighting and loving he learns the meaning of being Jewish. When he proposes to the minister of defense Jacob Zion (Luther Adler, playing a thinly veiled David Ben-Gurion) that Jerusalem would need to be abandoned to save the southern part of the country, since "it doesn't make sense to risk everything you've got to save the other half," Zion responds: "Did it make sense for a fellow with a nice steady job building pyramids to march his friends into the Red Sea?" At which point Zion appoints Marcus general (*Aluf*) and charges him with saving what he calls "the heart of Israel." Marcus's learning curve as a Jew continues even as he teaches the Jews how to fight like the gentiles. As he watches newly arrived immigrants being driven in buses directly to the front, he hears them singing. Turning to Asher, the Haganah commander, he asks, "Where do they come from?"

> ASHER: Belsen, Auschwitz, Buchenwald, by way of [British concentration camps in] Cyprus.
>
> MARCUS: What are they singing?
>
> ASHER: The same song they used to sing on the way to the gas chambers. And as most of our songs, it begins, "next year in Jerusalem."

It is, indeed, after the failure to capture the fort of Latrun that Marcus finally seems to feel that he has become part of the emerging state rather than a foreign advisor:

> MARCUS: We're all worn out, but we'll do it. We made it across the Red Sea, didn't we?
>
> ASHER: Mickey, it's the first time I ever heard you say "we."
>
> MARCUS: Yeah ... You people. Pipsqueak nation ... Tin-can army that fights with seltzer bottles. "We." All my life I've been looking for where I belong. Turns out it's here. The Catskill Mountains with Arabs. I've been so angry at the world ever since I was circumcised without my permission.

All of a sudden I find out that I'm not so special after all. Everybody here is in the same boat and nobody's bellyaching. Okay. "Stand up and be counted," the man said. "Grow up," is more like it. I'm not fighting anymore because I'm ashamed of being a Jew. I'm fighting because I'm stiff-necked and proud of it. Next week, Asher. Next week in Jerusalem.

But this revelation is followed by a rapid retreat. Having discovered where he belongs and asserting his pride in being a member of a stiff-necked people, Marcus's final decision as a "grown-up" is not to stay in Israel with Magda but to go back to his middle-class life as a lawyer with Emma. How this transformation can be reconciled, beyond his recognition of his love for Emma, is unclear. In fact, this is not merely Marcus's withdrawal to the safety of his base across the ocean. It is also Shavelson's flight from what would have otherwise threatened to be a statement about the essential difference between true American heroes (such as General Randolph, who naturally ends up in the Pentagon) and American-Jewish heroes who are always liable to discover a new loyalty to another nation.

MARCUS: Magda, I've fallen in love.

MAGDA: Your wife, I know. What has that got to do with us?

MARCUS: You're being very European.

MAGDA: I am European. I live with what is, not what I would like it to be.

MARCUS: I can't live that way. Not anymore. See, when Emma said I could go I knew it was time to stop running after everything. Excitement, war . . . I'm going home, Magda, for good. For damn good. I guess I've been in love with Emma all my life, and I wouldn't admit it. [He kisses Magda.] Now I'm picking a rose for her. I'll take it to her as if I were the schnook lawyer she always wanted me to be. Run Magda. Run for your life. The schnooks are taking over the world.[125]

TRUE HEROES

With all its fanfare of heroic battles, stirring music, and famous stars, *Cast a Giant Shadow* was thus itself somewhat of a compromise with the schnooks who had taken over the world. No wonder that it had very little impact on either side of the Atlantic. Things were very different in the case of the NBC television miniseries *Holocaust* (1978). Produced by Herbert Brodkin and directed by Marvin Chomsky using a screenplay by Gerald Green, *Holocaust* evoked unprecedented empathy for the fate of Jewish victims even—and most important—in what Albert Einstein had called "the land of the perpetrators." Yet the miniseries presented the Jews not only as victims but also as engaged in a heroic struggle for survival, which culminates in their actual fighting as resisters in the Warsaw Ghetto and as partisans in Ukraine, increasingly motivated by a Zionist spirit.[126] Furthermore, *Holocaust* presented a new type of Nazi perpetrator, who differed dramatically from the brutal and vulgar characters of earlier Eastern European and American films, yet was shown to have evolved from an "ordinary" German into an organizer of genocide intimately involved in the details and realities of mass murder to an extent not previously seen in German representations of "desk-killers."

The common assertion in the Federal Republic was—and to some extent remains—that precisely because of the extremity of the Holocaust, neither perpetrators nor victims could or should be represented in a manner conducive to empathy. The perpetrators were obviously so despicable that one could not create them as "normal" human beings on the screen—despite the well-known fact that many real perpetrators had quickly reverted to the role of "ordinary" Germans after the war. Similarly, it was argued that because of the wholesale dehumanization of the victims, any attempt to empathize with them would divert attention from the detached analysis of the event that was required, replacing it with empty expressions of sorrow and pity evoked through kitsch and nostalgia. To be sure, behind such assertions was the simpler reality that Germans wanted to distance themselves both from the murderers—who were seen as un-German—and from the victims, who were viewed as an abstraction rather than as real people. Conversely, *Holocaust* presented both killers and those they killed as "normal" people; indeed, it showed them as "ordinary" Germans. And, because the film was made in English, and the Jewish family at its center seemed as eminently assimilated as any American-Jewish family, the miniseries also spoke directly to viewers in the United States.

Holocaust played an important role in changing attitudes about both the reality and the representation of the mass murder of the Jews, first in large sectors of the public and eventually even among some of the most diehard intellectuals and scholars. By telling the story of the Holocaust through the saga of a single German-Jewish family as it is gradually destroyed by Hitler's regime, the film compelled viewers to identify with those who had all too often been marginalized or generalized as faceless victims. And by telling the parallel story of a timid young German who is gradually transformed into a mass killer, the miniseries also gave substance and individuality to the instruments of the regime, who had been equally pushed away from people's consciousness as faceless "perpetrators." Despite the many weaknesses of a TV miniseries based on the model of a soap opera, *Holocaust* succeeded where many others had failed in humanizing the victims while at the same time providing some unusually perceptive insights into the making of a mass murderer.

Docudramas such as *Holocaust* obviously suffer from severe limitations. While the creation of a generic Jewish family did no harm to the historical record—which is full of such accounts—the introduction of a fictional character into the well-known and not very extensive top hierarchy of the SS is much more problematic. Erik Dorf (Michael Moriarty) is a composite of several figures who played a crucial role in planning and implementing the so-called Final Solution of the Jewish question. But because he represents both most of them and none of them, his presence necessarily distorts the historical record and has irritated quite a number of those familiar with the finer details of Heinrich Himmler's and Reinhard Heydrich's genocidal apparatus. Yet, as I will note below, Dorf plays an enormously important role in the miniseries, since he represents a type of Nazi desk-murderer who was crucial to the implementation of genocide but received little attention in previous representations. For while cinema preferred the figure of the brutal, sadistic caricature of a Prussian drill officer, by the time *Holocaust* was made most scholars had accepted Hannah Arendt's portrayal of *Schreibtischtäter*, or desk-perpetrators, such as Adolf Eichmann as representative of the "banality of evil" at the core of Nazism.

Dorf, however, negates both types; indeed, his figure approximates much better the actual members of the Reich Security Main Office (RSHA) portrayed in recent scholarship.[127] They were well-educated young men, often lawyers, of middle-class origins, who came to see themselves as the cutting edge of the new Nazi state, and perceived their most important goal as the destruction of the Jews in a cold, calculated, and efficient manner. Nor were these men simply "desk-killers." Many of them went out to the killing fields either as inspectors, supervisors, or commanders of the murder "operations" and subsequent extermination camps. The introduction of Dorf, who is reminiscent of such characters as Eichmann, Werner Best, Otto Ohlendorf, and others, is thus one of the greatest accomplishments of *Holocaust,* and shows how much ahead of its time this miniseries was, despite the necessary (and sometimes unnecessary) historical inaccuracies this entailed.[128]

If scholars attacked the miniseries for its historical inaccuracies, prominent survivors and writers rejected it as demeaning the victims, and filmmakers despised it as Hollywood kitsch. Nevertheless, even some of its most vehement critics agreed that *Holocaust* had a generally salutary impact on German viewers and, subsequently, even on German scholarship and filmmaking. This is all the more remarkable considering the blistering attacks on the miniseries from several members of the German intelligentsia. Filmmaker Edgar Reitz fumed that "with *Holocaust* the Americans have taken away our history."[129] This alleged theft was all the more threatening since, to his mind, Americans and Jews were synonymous, as evidenced by the fact that "the Jews, since time immemorial 'people who go away' [*Weggeher*], fit well into this American culture" that produced *Holocaust*.[130] His reaction was to make *Heimat* (1984), a sixteen-hour cinematic saga on a "real" German family in the twentieth century. The Wagnerian scale of Reitz's saga was obviously meant to overshadow *Holocaust*'s "mere" 450 minutes. Moreover, with its focus on the tragedy and eventual disintegration of an "authentic" rural community, *Heimat* was clearly intended to demonstrate that German history belonged to Germans, be they filmmakers or their villager protagonists, and not to (Jewish) American filmmakers or even their urban (Jewish) German protagonists.

Similarly, German filmmaker Hans-Jürgen Syberberg, known especially for his monumental film *Hitler, a Film from Germany* (1977), asserted following the screening of the miniseries on German television that "America now has its own reparations to pay after this *Holocaust* from Hollywood in the German media."[131] No less telling was the official response to what seemed a politically sensitive issue raised by the miniseries. Initially aired in 1979 by the regional West German network WDR well after primetime, *Holocaust* met with tremendous popular success. Nevertheless, the network decided to delete the last uplifting moments of the show since they contained what appeared to be a blatant Zionist message. Heinz Kühn, acting board chairman of WDR, explained this decision by pointing out that "any apologetics for the Jewish homeland would have been undesirable."[132]

In hindsight, most critics in Europe, the United States, and Israel have concluded that while *Holocaust* was a "typical" Hollywood product, it should nevertheless be remembered for having facilitated greater empathy, especially in Germany, for the Jewish victims of Hitler's genocidal policies. The miniseries was also credited with having begun a wave of preoccupation with the circumstances under which these former "fellow citizens" were made to "go away" and "disappear" from the midst of German society. In other words, it was argued that *Holocaust* should be remembered more for its effects than for its own inherent merits.[133] But watching the miniseries a quarter of a century after it was first aired, one might be surprised to find that it offers far more insights into the history of the event and the psychology of its protagonists than it was given credit for at the time.

Perhaps this conclusion reflects the lamentable quality of much that has been produced since then. Perhaps, however, it also bespeaks the greater sense of responsibility felt at the time by the makers of *Holocaust,* the considerable research and care that went into its production, and the feeling that this would be very much a first, and therefore a determining, venture into the dangerous terrain of docudrama representation of the Holocaust.[134] The very fact that the miniseries resisted using big stars (though many of the actors subsequently had brilliant careers) is an indication. One may take issue with the author of the screenplay, Gerald Green, who argued that "there's more truthful, documented history in *Holocaust* than in anything I have ever seen about the Nazi destruction of the Jews."[135] But as a powerful, historically probable, and immensely influential cinematic representation of the fate of a single family during the Holocaust, and notwithstanding its aesthetic limitations and occasional lapses into kitsch, this is one of the best cinematic productions ever made on this allegedly unrepresentable event.[136]

Holocaust begins with a family wedding in 1935 and ends with an encounter between the last survivor of the family and his dead brother's wife and child in 1945. The Weiss family consists of Josef (Fritz Weaver), who came from Warsaw to study medicine in Berlin and established a medical practice there; his wife Berta (Rosemary Harris); and their three children: Karl (James Woods), Rudi (Joseph Bottoms), and Anna (Blanche Baker). Karl's marriage to the Catholic Inga (Meryl Streep) is the last happy moment the family experiences. Soon thereafter the Nuremberg Laws are passed. Karl, who is an artist, is arrested and taken to Buchenwald. Inga manages to smuggle letters to him but at the price of sleeping with her parents' friend, Heinz Müller (Anthony Haygarth), who is now a sergeant in the SS. In the *Kristallnacht* pogrom of November 1938, Berta's father, Heinrich Palitz (Marius Goring), a bookstore owner and decorated World War I veteran, is beaten and humiliated. Dr. Weiss, who is no longer allowed to treat "Aryans," is deported to Poland. As the family is ejected from their home, Berta's parents commit suicide. Inga shelters the family at her home despite her parents' protestations. Going out one night, Anna is raped by several SA men (storm troopers). Traumatized by the event, she is taken to the "sanatorium" Hadamar, where she is gassed as part of the "euthanasia" program of murdering the mentally handicapped. Now Rudi escapes from Germany and makes his way to Prague, where he meets and falls in love with Helena Slomova (Tovah Feldshuh).

As the war breaks out Berta is deported to the Warsaw Ghetto, where she meets her husband, who is now a member of the Jewish Council, together

Making the Jewish hero (*Holocaust*): Mordechai Anielewicz teaching a boy in the Warsaw Ghetto how to use a pistol, with Josef Weiss and his brother Moses—members of the Judenrat converted to the side of the underground—looking on, as Jewish heroism is translated into Zionist terms of armed resistance in the name of a national Jewish cause.

with his brother Moses (Sam Wanamaker). With the acceleration of the transports to Treblinka, Josef and Moses join the Zionist Resistance, despite the objections of Jewish Council Chairman Kohn (Charles Korvin). But Josef and Berta are deported to Auschwitz just before the uprising, commanded by Mordechai Anielewicz (Murray Salem). Moses participates bravely in the fighting and is finally executed. Berta and Josef are gassed in Birkenau. Meanwhile Karl has been moved to Terezín, where together with other artists he secretly makes drawings of the reality behind the facade of the town Hitler "gave to the Jews." Inga gets herself arrested so as to join him there. But the paintings are discovered, and Karl is tortured and sent to Auschwitz, where he dies, not before learning from Inga that she is carrying his baby. Now only Rudi is left. Having joined Jewish partisans in Ukraine, he marries Helena, but she is killed in an attack and he is captured and taken to Sobibór. There he joins the uprising and survives the war. At the end of the miniseries he meets Inga, who is now with Karl's little boy. He then decides to join the Zionists and smuggle children into British Mandate Palestine.

Parallel to this story is the tale of Erik Dorf, a young, unemployed lawyer, the son of a baker with socialist leanings who committed suicide when he lost his business during the Depression. Erik takes his wife Marta (Deborah Norton) to be examined by Dr. Weiss, who recommends rest. Instead, Marta relentlessly pushes Erik to join the SS, where he soon becomes a close associate of Reinhard Heydrich (David Warner). A master of euphemisms, Dorf helps Heydrich enforce the anti-Jewish policies of the regime, and later becomes one of the architects of the Final Solution. We see him at various crucial points of the events. He warns Father Lichtenberg (Llewellyn Rees) not to persist in his sermons about the Jews (a historical figure, Lichtenberg was arrested and died in Dachau). He meets Eichmann (Tom Bell) in Vienna; visits the mass shootings by Einsatzgruppen in Russia, including Babi Yar; participates in the Wannsee Conference; examines killing methods with gas vans and Zyklon B prussic acid; and visits Rudolf Höss at Auschwitz. His life intersects at several points with members of the Weiss family. He also periodically meets his uncle, Kurt Dorf (Robert Stephens), an anti-Nazi engineer who is nevertheless constructing roads for the regime with Jewish slave labor. Kurt serves as a kind of conscience or foil but has no effect on Dorf, whose only source of chagrin is that Heydrich's successor, Ernst Kaltenbrunner (Hans Meyer), treats him with disdain. At the end of the war he is interrogated by an American intelligence officer, and then commits suicide.

A central feature of *Holocaust* is the clear distinction it makes between German/Nazi and Jewish heroism. The former is false, a mere facade for deceit, delusion, greed, and cowardice. The latter is true, emanating from existential need, a moral perception of the world, and nobility of spirit. Depending on the circumstances and nature of the Jewish protagonists, their heroism can be expressed in survival, sacrifice, or resistance. Finally, *Holocaust* identifies the heroism of Germans who stand up to the Nazi persecution of the Jews. But rather than present this as true *German* heroism—as opposed to the false heroism of the Nazis—the miniseries assimilates these non-Jewish German heroes into the saga of *Jewish* fate. That is, the few true German heroes gain their status precisely because they associate their destiny with that of the Jews and not because of any other actions against the regime.

In this sense, *Holocaust* is uninterested in such German heroes as the conspirators of the Bomb Plot of July 20, 1944, since their actions were primarily motivated not by the extermination of the Jews (largely completed by then) but by the approaching destruction of the Reich. Thus they acted as patriots, whereas the German heroes of *Holocaust* act as humanists, whether in a more abstract sense, as does Father Lichtenberg, or in the most concrete sense, as does Inga. This may also explain some of the unspoken resistance to the miniseries by German intellectuals, who have always obsessed over German fate, and have often represented it in precisely these terms of survival, sacrifice, and resistance. Thus German representations of Nazism, even when their makers condemn it entirely, are all about German heroism (and, if mentioned at all, Jewish victimhood). *Holocaust* not only focuses entirely on Jewish heroism, it simply rejects the very possibility of German heroism. German heroes in *Holocaust* are not portrayed as heroes but as cowards, opportunists, and murderers, or they are not German, since their integration into Jewish fate transforms them into an essential component of the Jewish narrative of the event. Moreover, these German/Jewish heroes act as a foil to the false heroes of the German narrative, exemplifying by their very existence that any assertion of heroism by those who facilitated genocide either by active participation or by a refusal to help the victims is fundamentally a lie.[137]

In other words, the underlying assumption of *Holocaust,* which is as disturbing to Germans today as it was a half-century ago, is that there was only one type of action under the Third Reich that could be considered heroic: intervening on behalf of the regime's victims, most especially the Jews. Rather than engage in a so-called competition of victimhood (since *Holocaust* dismisses any such option for Germans, with the exception of the few who did act on behalf of the regime's victims), the miniseries establishes a definition of heroism that turns on its head the conventional view of Jews as passive victims and Germans as in some sense heroic if tragic fighters. This is, to my mind, a crucial contribution. It is all the more remarkable in that it includes an understanding of the worldview of that most Nazi of all Nazi organizations, the group of SS men who planned the Final Solution. It shows that these men did indeed develop a perverted notion of their heroism, not by denying to others or to themselves their participation in genocide, but by being exceedingly proud of it. And it not only unmasks the moral perversity of this notion, but also demonstrates how it nevertheless seeped into and permeated much of the rest of German society, polluting the minds and souls of multitudes of otherwise "decent" men and women and negating any possibility of attributing to them such qualities as heroism or victimhood in anything but a highly diluted and compromised form.[138]

The manner in which the miniseries elaborates the points made above can be easily illustrated. I will begin with the negation of German heroism. The shy, self-effacing, but brilliant Dorf, who was among the top ten of his class in law school, quickly finds an affinity with Heydrich. The two men agree that the best approach to the Jewish "problem" is to remain "neutral, analytical, and cold."[139] Interestingly, this was precisely the view of Heydrich's deputy and SS ideologue, Werner Best, who believed that one had to "exterminate the [Jewish] opponent without hating him."[140]

The tension between the appearance of heroism and the reality of murder is revealed early on. As Dorf puts on his dashing new SS uniform for the first time, his children retreat from him in fear. But his wife Marta exclaims, "Erik, you look heroic!" Dorf's path to becoming a mass murderer is paved with a potent mix of euphemisms, insights, and calculation. Following the *Kristallnacht* pogrom of November 1938 (misconstrued in the miniseries as initiated by the SS rather than, as was actually the case, by Joseph Goebbels), Heydrich asks Dorf whether by this action "we stirred up a hornets' nest." Dorf's response shows that his thinking has clearly evolved. First he notes that "few governments will stick their necks out for Jews." Then, as an afterthought, he adds: "It's almost as if there's a moral precedent for punishing them."

The view that Nazi anti-Jewish policies had deep cultural and religious roots, which *Holocaust* strongly embraces, was supported even by such scholars as Raul Hilberg, who was among the first to interpret the Final Solution as a largely bureaucratic rather than ideological undertaking.[141] As part of Dorf's education as a budding mass murderer, Heydrich lectures him on the Christian antecedents of Nazism and the binding effects of antisemitism:

> HEYDRICH: Do the Jews serve a purpose? Tell me Dorf, how much is conviction and how much opportunism?
>
> DORF: I'm no psychologist, sir.
>
> HEYDRICH: Do I believe the Jews have to be removed from society? Of course. But supposing this racial stuff were nonsense? Jews have intermarried with Aryans for centuries.
>
> DORF: Then why are we so adamant on eliminating Jews?
>
> HEYDRICH: The practical side. Antisemitism is the cement that binds us together. Christians may disagree on a number of things but as men of conscience they can unite in their hatred of Jews.
>
> DORF: Yes, but haven't the Jews earned that hatred?
>
> HEYDRICH: Of course. Christ killers, well poisoners, agents of Satan, murderers of Christian children. Well, Himmler may believe that garbage but you and I know that this is medieval crap. Lies. But politically useful lies. In a way the ground has been prepared for us.

DORF: So, ideology, or the old traditions, go hand-in-hand with practical modern policies.

HEYDRICH: Precisely. Why do you think we've had no opposition? Why do you think the French and English barely protest? Because deep down, they have a sneaking admiration for the way we are handling the Jews.

Thus, Dorf learns the elemental truth behind the persecution of the Jews. Not only is it justified by the entire legacy of Christian Europe, it is also a practical political measure that brings Germans together and even lends them the passive support of their enemies. Yet there is a vast difference between such abstract discussions and layers of euphemisms, on the one hand, and exposure to actual mass murder, on the other. Having inspected the workings of a gas van and the killing facilities at Auschwitz, Dorf has difficulties sleeping. It is at this point, precisely when he realizes that he is an important cog in the machine of mass murder, that he fabricates for himself a heroic self-image as a protection from nagging doubts and pangs of conscience. In a late-night conversation with his wife he tells her:

Marta, the war is lost. . . . Some day people will tell monstrous lies about what we did in Poland and in Russia. . . . You must tell yourself and the children that I was always a good servant of the Reich, I was only an honorable man who did nothing but obey orders, orders from the very top.

Dorf fears that if his wife were ever to find out what his "honorable" deeds really were, she would be horrified. Now that his protector Heydrich has been replaced by Kaltenbrunner, and knowing that the war will end in defeat, Dorf is torn between feelings of shame, terror, and pride. To his shock—and relief—when Marta does discover his role in mass murder, it is she who provides him with the argument that will sustain him to the end:

MARTA: I suspected for a long time. . . . You were so adamant about people telling lies about you I knew something must be wrong. . . .

DORF: None of this matters anymore, Marta. . . . The walls are tumbling. . . .

MARTA: Don't say that! . . . No wonder your career is in ruins. Erik, it's evident . . . that you are sick of your work, you're ashamed of it.

DORF: Maybe I am sometimes.

MARTA: But you can't let yourself be. Do what you are told till the end. That will convince people that what you are doing is right!

DORF: Marta, my gentle Marta. How I've misread you. I thought you'd be furious. I've been supervising the killing of women and children and all you are outraged over is that I'm not prouder of my work!

MARTA: Erik, I'm afraid we'll be punished . . . all of us.

DORF: You've done nothing wrong, Marta. And I've been a good soldier.

MARTA: The naked people, the gas chambers, the funeral pyres. That's why they must be done away with. So that no one knows. So that no one can tell lies about you.

Dorf is, in fact, confronted with a different view on his actions, when he encounters his uncle, Kurt. Not only does Kurt try to shake him out of the comforting euphemisms that enable Dorf to avoid coming to terms with the reality of genocide, he also presents him with a different view on heroism. The true heroes, he tells him, are not the German Master Race, but rather the Jewish *Untermenschen*. Yet Dorf has now internalized Marta's logic. One must keep killing in order to avoid guilt:

DORF: Your roads are most important to us. As are sanitary precautions. Prevention of contagion. Great deal of disease in Auschwitz.

KURT: As much among those who run it as among the prisoners, I imagine. Disease of the spirit, perhaps, or of the soul itself.

DORF: You've become even more, what should I say, righteously indignant than ever. What we do, we do out of necessity.

KURT: Stop it! Save those lies for the Jews you've been murdering. Lying to them until the last moment. Why do you have to strip them naked? Can't you at least in the name of God let them die with some dignity? I've seen your SS louts grinning at the naked women.

DORF: They are criminals and enemies and they are sent to the processing plant naked for sanitary reasons.

KURT: Jews in the Warsaw Ghetto are fighting back. Think of that. Those despised, unarmed people in Warsaw, defying the Master Race. Almost restores one's faith in divine Providence. . . . How many dead will satisfy you? A million? Two million?

DORF: We must keep on killing them, don't you see? If we stop it's an admission of guilt. But if we go on we prove to the world that we had total dedication to our mission, that what we did were moral and historical necessities. Try to understand that.

At a final meeting with the top hierarchy of the SS, Dorf finally seems to surpass even his homicidal colleagues in his insistence on the rightness of their cause. Here he carries to the extreme the logic of genocide that even Heinrich Himmler (Ian Holm) had attempted to avoid:

HIMMLER: I would welcome suggestions from all of you on plans for the future dismantling of the camps. . . . Our job will soon be finished, a Jew-free Europe.

DORF: Why erase the evidence? . . . Would it not be more fitting to let them stand as monuments to our great service to mankind? . . . The Führer himself said that we were here to complete the work of Christianity, defending Western culture. . . .

HIMMLER: The Jews will lie about us. . . .

DORF: Not if we tell the world the truth! . . . We must explain logically and persuasively why it was a moral and a racial necessity to do what we did. We have committed no crimes. We have merely followed the logic of European history, and eminent philosophers and churchmen can be called upon to defend us. A case can be made for Auschwitz. . . . No shame, gentlemen, no apologies. . . . We must make clear to the world that we stood between civilization and the Jewish plot to dominate the world, to destroy decency. . . . We alone . . . were courageous enough. . . . [leaves the room]

HIMMLER [smirking]: The major may have a point. Let us be certain in our hearts that we fulfilled these tasks for the love of our own people. . . . We have remained decent and loving men. For that we may be proud.

Thus, while the cinematic Himmler is given the lines the commander of the SS actually uttered in his notorious Posen speech of October 1943, Dorf remains adamant even in the face of capitulation that "a case can be made for Auschwitz." It was, of course, Himmler who had insisted that there is no greater heroism than that of the SS, who could carry out genocide and yet remain "decent." But Himmler was, as *Holocaust* rightly points out, inconsistent, trying to cover up the traces of a crime he claimed was an act of heroism that would come down as "a glorious page in our history," yet as "one that has never been written and can never be written."[142] It is this ambivalence that Dorf rejects by insisting on the heroic nature of his deeds and the possibility of "selling" them as such to the world. And precisely through this insistence, devoid of any apologetics and manipulation, he reveals that German heroism and mass murder were synonymous.

The case of Jewish heroism is created in *Holocaust* first through its negative image, the Nazi view of Jewish compliance and passivity. This was, of course, also the view that Jewish Resistance leaders tried to combat, and the image that has haunted the memory of the event ever since. Yet *Holocaust* refuses to accept the simple dichotomy between the minority that fought back and the majority who went "like sheep to the slaughter," even as it depicts the various reactions by Jews to the genocidal onslaught of the Nazis.

Already during Dorf's first visit to a mass execution site, Paul Blobel (T. P. McKenna), commander of Sonderkommando 4a of Einsatzgruppe C, remarks about the victims' behavior: "No protest, no fight, nothing. Himmler was right. The bastards are subhuman." Similarly, when watching the mass executions at Babi Yar, Dorf comments: "It's astonishing how they cooperate." Blobel responds: "Which proves they don't deserve to live." Finally, when Himmler asks, were there "reports of rebellions, Jews fighting back?" Eichmann answers: "The Jews seem as intent as any of us on their annihilation."

Holocaust, however, strives to dispel this widespread prejudice about the Jewish willingness to collaborate in their own murder, with all its pseudoreligious connotations of sacrificial offering and atonement for past sins. Even as it portrays collaboration, the miniseries depicts its transformation into resistance. Thus both Josef and Moses Weiss, who become members of the Jewish Council of the Warsaw Ghetto, begin to have doubts about their function as soon as they perceive the real intent of German policies. As Josef says to his brother, "I'm not sure I like this business of being on the Jewish Council. Deciding who gets so much to eat, who gets a place to sleep, who will live, who is to die." The more conciliatory position is represented by the chairman of the Jewish Council, Dr. Kohn, who argues for continued cooperation with the Germans:

> At least a ghetto is something we can understand; we'll be allowed our schools, our hospitals, an administration. They need us. . . . We have no option but to cooperate. . . . We are what we have always been, victims. . . . We must obey orders, we must crack down on smugglers and resisters. Resistance is foolish, foolish. We can only pray for things to get better.

But when Sturmbannführer Hans Höfle (Sean Arnold) orders Kohn (who is obviously modeled on Adam Czerniaków [1880–1942], the historical head of the Warsaw *Judenrat,* who eventually committed suicide but left behind an important diary), to put together lists of Jews for deportation to the "east," council members begin to rebel against further collaboration.[143]

HÖFLE: Six thousand a day . . .

JOSEF WEISS: But what do we tell them?

HÖFLE: The truth. They are being transported to family camps in Russia. . . . Fresh air. Good food. Parents and children together. It's better than staying in this stink hole you've let Warsaw become.

JOSEF WEISS: People may resist.

HÖFLE: You people have not resisted yet. You realize that after the murder of Heydrich we can't be as merciful as we have been.

MOSES WEISS: But at the rate of six thousand a day the ghetto will be emptied.

HÖFLE: Nonsense, we just want to drain off the excess. People like you, officials, police, doctors, you'll stay. Understand?

To be sure, by the time the uprising actually took place, 85 percent of the ghetto had already been emptied, most of its inhabitants being sent to the gas chambers in nearby Treblinka. The lie that collaborating functionaries would be spared had its effect. *Holocaust* somewhat masks the degree of corruption and opportunism among the official Jewish leadership in the ghetto, and certainly fails to provide a sufficiently vivid picture of the horrifying conditions in which the Jews were living. Nevertheless, the miniseries successfully portrays the emergence of armed resistance, whose heroism was only magnified by the desperate lack of arms and training, the absence of any substantial support by the Polish Home Army, and the overwhelming military superiority of the Germans.

The conflict between the "rational" view of continued collaboration and the "heroic" perspective of resistance is presented in a confrontation between the youthful Anielewicz, who demands to smuggle weapons into the ghetto, and the elderly Kohn, who is outraged by the mere notion of outright opposition to the Germans:

KOHN: Such talk will guarantee our deaths. I can see us half-starved Jews taking on the German army. Anielewicz, the Germans cleaned up the Polish army in one month and they are rolling through the Soviet Union annihilating Stalin's divisions, and we, we are going to resist them?

ANIELEWICZ: We must!

KOHN: Young man, that's not the Jewish way. We have survived by accommodating. Give a little here, make a bargain there, find an ally, some prince, some cardinal, some politician.

ANIELEWICZ: You are not dealing with politicians or cardinals. The Nazis are mass murderers. No matter what we do, how obedient we are, how hard we work, they will kill us. . . . If this council is too cowardly to give the order, the Zionists will. We don't intend to die without a fight.

Ultimately, it is the impetuous Anielewicz who grasps the logic of genocide and not the cautious and experienced Kohn. The reality of the situation is finally driven home by Kovel (Toby Salaman, clearly modeled on Resistance leader and poet Abba Kovner), who arrives from Vilna. Kovel tells the council:

Don't believe anything the Germans tell you about ghettoes or work camps. . . . They mean to murder every Jew in Europe. . . . There were once eighty thousand Jews in the Vilna Ghetto. Today there are less than twenty thousand, . . . Undressed, searched, lined up in the ditches, shot with machine guns. They stood there. No tears. No resistance. . . . Ghetto after ghetto are being wiped out. . . . Resist. You can start with this: "Let us not go to our death like lambs to the slaughter. . . . It is Hitler's plan to annihilate the Jews. . . . Brothers, rather die fighting than live by the grace of the slaughterer."[144]

Thus *Holocaust* takes viewers from traditional attempts of accommodation with the Germans to the final Warsaw Ghetto uprising, which breaks out on Passover Eve, April 19, 1943. Unlike such Polish films as *Border Street*, here there is no doubt about the nature of the revolt and the motivation of the fighters. The Jewish flag is flown on the screen as it was flown in the ghetto. There is no trace of Polish patriotism among the rebels, and no assistance from the Polish resistance is forthcoming. To be sure, as the Jewish fighters concede: "We have four hundred armed, a few thousand who will support us, the rest of the fifty thousand terrified. . . ." They also note that "our miserable Ghetto police" are still on the side of the Germans. But the uprising is clearly presented as a transformation in Jewish consciousness. As Moses says: "I've never been a brave man. But I learned something. We all die. So why not make it worthwhile?" Having repelled the first German attack, he rejoices: "We have smitten the Philistines hip and thigh." It will be recalled that in *Border Street*, Grandfather Liberman dies passively praying, while his son-in-law Natan dies fighting with Polish flags in the background. But when Moses Weiss is about to be executed with the last survivors of the uprising, he recites the Jewish prayer Shema Yisrael. He dies, therefore, as a Jewish hero.

In a certain sense, however, it is Karl's fate that reflects this transition most powerfully. While Karl does not fight, his resistance is expressed in the will to preserve a record of the atrocity, a will that even the most inhuman torture cannot break. Through his figure, *Holocaust* succeeds in depicting the entire extraordinary phenomenon of individual and collective efforts by Jews to record the genocide even as the perpetrators did all they could not only to murder the Jews but also to erase all traces of their crimes. Interrogated by Eichmann, Karl maintains that "the function of art is to enhance life." By that he does not mean a false beautification of reality (which is how Eichmann understands it) but rather exposure of the horrors concealed from the world by the facade of normality at Terezín and the mountains of euphemisms erected by the perpetrators. He persists in his struggle to the very end, even after his hands are smashed. He dies as he sketches a last image of the tortured musselman—the camps' symbol of the living dead—that he himself had become. But his is not a passive death. And what he leaves behind is perhaps the only possible manner of representing the truth of the Holocaust: the destruction of the human soul.

The most innate, almost unquestioning resister in *Holocaust* is Rudi. In a certain sense, precisely because fighting comes so naturally to him, Rudi may be the least heroic Jewish character. His acts of bravery, his will to hit back, and his physical prowess make his transition from persecuted victim to active partisan seem self-evident. Thus Rudi's victimhood is expressed more in the loss of his family and his newly wedded wife than in his own personal fate. Although he is the only one to survive, Rudi may be the least memorable and the least authentic character in *Holocaust*. When Anielewicz and Kovel call the Jews to fight, they are as tortured and traumatized as those they address. Rudi displays none of these emotional scars. His difficulty in killing the enemy in his first military encounter has nothing to do with his Jewish identity; it is the initial shock felt by any soldier who enters combat for the first time. By the time Rudi disguises himself as a German soldier, it is impossible to tell him apart from the Wehrmacht troops he ultimately kills.

Still, Rudi is unlike Solly in *Europa, Europa,* since he has only one identity and has no thought of changing it. He is also almost the precise inverse of Jakub in *Samson.* Rudi is a fighter, and thus the circumstances in which he finds himself are in a sense perfectly appropriate to his natural inclinations. As his father says, had Rudi ended up in the Warsaw Ghetto, he would have been among the first to organize resistance there. Rudi does not do battle because he is a Jew being hunted down by everyone around him, but because fighting is in his nature. In this Rudi may be closest to Jan Wiener in *Fighter,* who is still confronting the world—even his friends— half a century after the end of the war. If Rudi undergoes any transformation, it is not from victim to resister, or from Jew to non-Jew, but rather from being an assimilated Berlin Jew into a Zionist on his way to Palestine. But once more, this transformation appears quite seamless, a logical consequence of the character's predilections and experience. His decision to go to Palestine is also a token of his love for Helena, who dreamed of going there before being killed. Helena's image of Palestine is a mirage rather than reality. But this makes the connection of war, love, and the Promised Land all the more potent. She tells him: "We will go to Palestine . . . we will live to go there. Orange groves, cedar trees, little farming villages, and a

blue sea . . . a life for us, where they cannot jail us, or beat us, or kill us. . . ."
And precisely because Rudi knows that there too the fight will have to
continue, he is even more inclined to go: the Zionist as a romantic warrior.

But it is also precisely because of this predictable trajectory that Rudi's
character seems far too wholesome, healthy, confident, and optimistic for
a survivor of the Holocaust. The horrors of the event, the choices one was
forced to make, the compromises and sacrifices, deceptions and betrayals,
pain suffered and inflicted, humiliation and oppression, all seem to wash
over him without leaving a trace. Even when Rudi finds himself in Sobibór,
the death camp that devoured hundreds of thousands of Jews, he is immediately taken in by the Resistance, and within what seems to be a mere few
hours storms the fences heroically and is back in the forest. We see none
of the terror of the camp, none of the moral degradation of the Sonderkommandos who facilitated the mass murder before their remnants rose
up against the Germans. This is far too simplistic a view of Jewish heroism
to be either convincing or moving.[145]

Conversely, the most powerful condemnation of German society during
the Shoah, and the most potent negation of any claims of German heroism, is provided by two non-Jewish characters in the film. The first appears
only briefly, yet plays a major role in underlining not merely the guilt of the
perpetrators but the complicity of those who one would have expected to
exercise their moral authority and influence against the crimes committed
right in front of their eyes. Nothing highlights this condemnation of official Christianity more than the brief encounter between Father Lichtenberg and Dorf, following the former's sermon calling his parishioners
(most of whom leave the church long before he is finished) to pray for the
persecuted Jews.

> DORF: I listened to your sermon with much interest.
>
> FATHER LICHTENBERG: And what did you learn from it, my son?
>
> DORF: That you are a kind man but misinformed.
>
> FATHER LICHTENBERG: But I know what is happening to the Jews.
>
> DORF: Father, Pope Pius signed a concordat with Hitler, the Vatican re-
> gards us as the last bastion between Christian Europe and Bolshevism.
>
> FATHER LICHTENBERG: But that does not justify tormenting the innocent.
>
> DORF: No one is being tormented.
>
> FATHER LICHTENBERG: But I've seen Jews beaten on the streets, sent off to
> prisons for no reason. . . .

DORF: They are enemies of the state and we are engaged in a war, Father.

FATHER LICHTENBERG: A war against armed enemies or against defenseless Jews?

DORF: Father, I appeal to you to be more temperate in your remarks.

FATHER LICHTENBERG: I will follow my conscience.

DORF: Don't let it lead you astray. You must be aware that almost to a man church leaders are actively supporting our policies.

FATHER LICHTENBERG: Well, in that case I must draw a distinction between what Christianity teaches and how some people distort and betray that teaching.

And, indeed, unlike the hierarchy in Germany and the Vatican, and more persistently than the clergy in France, Father Lichtenberg continued to condemn Nazi policies against the Jews and paid the price for a risk that others were unwilling to take.[146] But his death in Dachau was significant not only because he stood up to the Nazis. Many other Christian leaders resisted various aspects of the regime's policies, especially where they threatened the churches.[147] Rather, what distinguishes Father Lichtenberg is that his opposition to the Nazis focused on the persecution of the Jews, whereas even those Catholic and Protestant leaders who openly opposed Hitler's regime were in most cases unwilling to criticize its antisemitism. As the celebrated case of Bishop Clemens von Galen demonstrated, while he bravely condemned the "euthanasia" campaign, he uttered not a single public word about the genocide of the Jews.[148] Father Lichtenberg therefore provides *Holocaust* with one of its central themes. If the Nazi persecution of the Jews was deeply rooted in a Christian-European tradition, then Christianity, when liberated from political calculation and individual opportunism, was also a source of great moral courage. Such moral courage could best be displayed vis-à-vis the Jews. Hence Father Lichtenberg's role is not merely to show how one ought to have behaved, but to demonstrate the moral bankruptcy of the official church and the vacuity of its postwar claims of heroism and sacrifice under Nazism.

The most important non-Jewish heroic character in *Holocaust* is, however, Inga. Here we are no longer dealing with abstract morality but with the most (seemingly) self-evident and natural responses of one human being toward another. Being Karl's wife, Inga is committed to him and to his family with every fiber of her existence. She is not slavish or deferential. On the contrary, Inga is much more active and enterprising than her husband and sees the writing on the wall long before her in-laws. In some ways, she is the non-Jewish equivalent of Rudi, whose own recklessness and adventurousness make him appear almost non-Jewish. Inga is willing to sacrifice everything for Karl to an extent that even Karl himself cannot contemplate or understand. She is, in this sense, the incarnation of selfless love and altruism, in the face of which all talk about race, status, political interest, or fear of punishment and suffering simply loses all meaning. But because Inga is the only non-Jewish German in *Holocaust* who behaves in this manner, her very presence throws into sharp relief the inability of most others to behave in the same manner, revealing the limitations of empathy and identification.

Inga's heroism is so natural that, like Rudi's, it almost seems un-heroic. But unlike Rudi, Inga's actions are entirely voluntary, a matter of choice and not necessity. Her choice is all the more extraordinary not because devotion to another person and empathy with the plight of the persecuted should be so remarkable, but because in practice it was so exceedingly rare. Hence Inga's very presence in the film condemns all other "ordinary" Germans, not just for participating in the killing or even for sharing the "ideas" of the regime, but for their simple inability to empathize, lend a hand, or give even temporary shelter to those who had been their neighbors, friends, or even family members. In this Inga's figure can be compared to the all-too-few Aryan wives of Jewish men who protested in front of the Gestapo jail in Berlin's Rosenstrasse in November 1943 when their husbands were arrested, and may have thereby saved them from deportation.[149] It took an American historian to expose the story of the Rosenstrasse protest to an international audience, and it took an American TV miniseries to highlight the indifference of the Germans to the fate of the Jews by telling the fictional story of one woman who cared. Inga's heroism, so natural and unreflective, is thus not a manifestation of German heroism but becomes entirely integrated into the fate of the Jews as a condemnation of the profound lack of civic courage in Hitler's Germany. Nothing highlights better the emptiness of German claims of heroism than Inga's sacrifice.

By choosing to put themselves in the place of another's victimhood, by making a moral commitment of devotion, rooted in love to an individual or in an ethical obligation to humanity, Inga and Father Lichtenberg become the conscience of *Holocaust*. Their legacy is one of pain and censure, not of reconciliation and forgiveness. Karl's heroism is directly associated with Inga's. She is the source of his strength and the key to his survival. Inga first sacrifices her body to keep him alive by sleeping with Müller. She then gets herself sent to Terezín—historically a highly improbable case—where she becomes for Karl what Antoine Moreau becomes for the children of

Terezín in *The Last Butterfly:* she is the gentile whose total empathy with the fate of the persecuted and tortured makes her into a Jew. And, as in *Divided We Fall* and *Enemies, a Love Story,* Inga also becomes the vehicle of Jewish continuity by carrying Karl's child in her and out of the hell of genocide.

When Karl is allowed to meet Inga for the last time before being transferred to Auschwitz, where he will soon die, she tells him that she is pregnant. Karl's hands have been smashed so that he will never be able to paint again; he has been tortured endlessly yet has refused to reveal the existence of more drawings of the atrocities in the camps. Thanks to Inga, Karl has become the true hero of *Holocaust,* the keeper of the memory of an atrocity whose perpetrators wanted to be buried and incinerated together with their victims. But he is doomed. The future lies with his brother Rudi, who is on the way to become an Israeli, and with his Catholic wife. The future of Jewish existence in Europe is in Inga's womb. Unlike Edith Stein, the converted Jew who was canonized by the Pope,[150] Inga is a Catholic who becomes a Jewish saint, a righteous gentile who gives birth to the future of Jewish existence in Europe, precarious and tentative though it may seem:

> INGA: Your child is in me.
>
> KARL: You mustn't have it. . . . If you love me, end its life before it ever sees this wretched place.
>
> INGA: I will not. Karl, please, I want your blessing for our child.
>
> KARL: I want no child.
>
> INGA: The rabbis say that every life is sanctification, a holy spark.
>
> KARL: Show him the drawings when he is old enough to understand.

The essence of heroism, ultimately, is the salvation of life, granting the possibility of birth and thereby of goodness and beauty even from the devastation of atrocity. It is Inga who facilitates this resurrection, in the face of the millions of the dead and the endless multitudes of the indifferent, passive bystanders. For she who saves one soul, saves the entire world.

[4]

INVERTING STEREOTYPES

The canonical anti-hero of American cinema is doubtlessly Woody Allen, who in some ways continued the tradition of the hapless yet unyielding tramp begun by Charlie Chaplin. But Allen's character is distinguished by being essentially and unambiguously Jewish (that is, if lack of ambiguity can be ascribed to any of his cinematic personae). Of course, antisemitic opinion held that Chaplin too was a Jew, which he was not. And it is true that his tramp seemed to be influenced by Eastern European Jewish self-representation as the eternal victims of misfortune, whose condition compels them to evolve a peculiar, bittersweet, ironic, and self-deprecating sense of humor that shields them from their humorless persecutors.[1] But Chaplin's character is not concerned with his Jewish identity, even in his most blatantly anti-antisemitic film, *The Great Dictator.* Allen is all about Jewish identity.

And yet, Allen's films and concerns do not fit into the framework of my discussion here. This is partly to his credit, but it also indicates, to my mind, his limitations as filmmaker. Allen has repeatedly brought to the screen the question of Jewish assimilation into American society in a manner that is both full of empathy and often outrageously funny. He has studiously avoided creating a Jewish character that is more than the victim of his own hang-ups, background, cultural heritage, and personal phobias. Conversely, Allen's Jew is so stereotypically Jewish that very soon he can hardly do anything that will surprise us. Whether it is his lust for gentile women; his endless, nervous energy; his combination of relentless ambition and bottomless inner conflicts; or being an alien in his society and yet the epitome of the American intellectual New Yorker—Allen eventually ends up as a stereotype that resembles too many individuals and for that very reason fits no one in particular. Moreover, Allen's focus on the assimilating, but non-assimilated, American Jew—who has served as a model for innumerable non-Jews aspiring to become tormented New York intellectuals—has missed out on some of the central themes of the representation of the "Jew" in twentieth-century cinema.

It is true that in what may be his best film, *Annie Hall* (1977), Allen (as Alvy Singer) is obsessed with the film *The Sorrow and the Pity* and thereby seems to display an obsession with the Holocaust.[2] But even in this case, and very much unlike, for instance, *Sophie's Choice,* the compulsion of the American Jew to fixate on the genocide that he "missed" is not translated into anything more than his own (predictably unsuccessful) struggle to assimilate into WASP America. Ultimately we find that there is no need for such relentless assimilation: The "Jew" does not need to become a WASP since the WASP often aspires to become a "Jew." Philip Roth's distinction between "the Jewish Jew" and the "non-Jewish Jew" is, I think, somewhat misleading.[3] The "Jewish Jew" is, in fact, the orthodox Jew (Alvy imagines himself as one while dining with Annie's family, but he, of course, is anything but orthodox). The "non-Jewish Jew" encompasses a range that includes Allen's type, who is unmistakably Jewish but no longer constrained by any dietary, social, or religious limitation, as well as the successfully assimilated Jew, who nevertheless has not entirely disappeared as a Jew by maintaining some sort of link to that identity. The distinction that Roth makes between the paranoid, defensive, victimized, sensitive, and denial-prone "Jewish Jew," on the one hand, and the healthy, vigorous, gregarious, and aggressive "non-Jewish Jew," on the other hand, describes in fact both aspects of the same character. This can clearly be seen in Allen's films and in Jewish films depicting the traditional Shtetl Yiddle—the heroic little Jew immortalized in Solomon Mikhoels's *Jewish Luck* (1925) and Joseph Green's *Yiddle with His Fiddle* (1936)—or, for that matter, in anti-semitic representations.

Allen's films, however, lack tragedy. This is no coincidence. By studiously avoiding the main concern of Jewish existence in the modern world—or rather dancing around it, making fun of it, suffering from it, but never looking it in the face—Allen remains a notch or two below greatness, even as he has been universally acknowledged as possibly the most influential maker of films on the American "Jew." Trapped in Manhattan (or Brooklyn), Allen and his Jews assimilate into a milieu that has in many ways assimilated itself into their own world. This is a rather happy outcome; it can be funny, curious, bizarre at times, conflicted perhaps, but it is ultimately a reflection of modern society as such. This is an example of what is now fashionably called "hybridity": One merges into something else while keeping all the stereotypical attributes that originally hindered such assimilation and now make it all the more appealing.

My concern here is with an entirely different type of anti-hero. I want to look at the effects of the presentation of the "Jew" as either perennial victim or superhero on late-twentieth-century depictions of the "Jew" in a world where he could no longer claim to be either. I want to see how the stereotypes of the "Jew" have created a backlash, often productive but also at times shrill, overly political, didactic, and somewhat uncritical. Finally, I want to examine to what extent the original stereotype of the "Jew" as perpetrator has returned to the screen, after making its tortuous path through the last century. The "Jew" as anti-hero in this context, then, is not Woody Allen in Manhattan, it is the Jew who breaks down the stereotypes but at times falls into others: the saintly Jewish whore, the guilt-ridden Jewish rabbi, the untransformed Sabra, the homicidal Israeli. Finally, there is the blind and ignorant suction of Jewish victimhood in the Holocaust, which pulls Israelis and Palestinians alike into a black hole of mutual destruction.

It is hard to think of a less heroic figure than that of the retired Jewish prostitute who dominates Moshe Mizrahi's *Madame Rosa* (1977). All the stereotypes of Western bourgeois society—concerning the relationship between Jews and gentiles, Arabs and Europeans, respectability and depravity, victims and perpetrators, those who survive and those who succumb—are done away with. The core of such stereotypes (which, incidentally, is the core of Allen's films) is that there are certain types, whether racial or cultural, ethnic or genetic, male or female, who must inevitably look and act in a certain manner that gives away their identity. The core of *Madame Rosa*, and much more so, of the book on which it is based, is the assertion that there is no such essence, that identity is a malleable, fragile, protean entity, often determined by a fate beyond its control, but also by choices that reflect the measure of goodness in an individual's soul rather than the predetermined traits of an often invented and imagined ancestry.

The female Jewish survivor was often suspected—not least in Palestine/Israel in the immediate aftermath of the Holocaust and the years leading to Israeli statehood—of having saved herself through prostitution. The allure of forbidden sexuality mingled with the allegation of literally sleeping with the enemy. The fantasy of illicit sex, sadomasochism, and a concentrationary universe, where the unimaginable became routine, also served as the background for several cinematic forays that probably sought and certainly provoked minor scandals, such as Luchino Visconti's *The Damned,* Liliana Cavani's *The Night Porter,* Lina Wertmuller's *Seven Beauties,* and others. Pornographic literature and, nowadays, pornographic websites have found Nazi concentration camps an especially attractive setting for their tales of subjugation, violence, and exploitation. And, of course, the tradition of antisemitism, which has so often portrayed Jewish women as both sexually irresistible and destructive, fits perfectly into a universe where, after all, Jews were the main targets of extermination.[4]

The combination of talents, identities, and fates that went into the making of *Madame Rosa* ensured that this murky soup of prejudices and fantasies would be stirred sufficiently to expose its lies and deception. The film, titled *La Vie devant soi* in France, was based on the eponymous novel by the young French writer Émile Ajar, whose true identity was unknown at the time. The novel, which appeared in English as *The Life before Us,* was an instant success, won its author the prestigious Prix Goncourt, sold over a million copies, and was translated into twenty-three languages.[5] Ajar, who had published an earlier, well-received novel, went on to write two more under his pseudonym before his identity was finally uncovered. But the mystery went much deeper than the seemingly lighthearted game of identities it initially appeared to have been. In 1980 the respected writer Romain Gary, whose literary career had somewhat diminished in his later years, committed suicide, shortly after his former wife and mother of his son, Jean Seberg, was found dead in her car, also the result of an apparent suicide. It was only through the publication of his testament, *The Life and Death of Émile Ajar,* that Gary, who was born in 1914, admitted to having created the young writer of presumed Arab origins from his own imagination. As he wrote to Ajar, posthumously "assassinating" his alter ego: "I had a good time. Good bye and thank you."[6]

But who was Romain Gary? His origins are as obscure, complex, and contradictory as those of many others of his generation, whose lives spanned the greatest disasters, highest hopes, and deepest disillusions of the twentieth century. Born as Roman Kacew in Moscow to the minor actress Nina Borisovskaia (her theatrical name), he claimed to have never discovered his father's identity. In 1917 his mother fled with him from the Revolution, first to Wilno, then to Warsaw, and finally settled down with him in Nice, France in 1927. By then Romain was thirteen years old. This is not the only version of Gary's childhood, however, since he himself liked to speculate about, if not intentionally mystify, his origins. It has been suggested, for instance, that he was actually born in Wilno to a Russian father and French mother, although his mother spoke with a heavy Russian accent. It is also clear that he had Jewish ancestry, and both he and his mother were registered as Jews in France although they had no contact with the Jewish community. The Kacews, it was said, were "Russians in Nice, Jews within Russian circles, atheists among the Jews, belonging to none of these groups: They lived for each other, alone, on the margins of all fraternities of exile."[7]

Raised by his mother as a French patriot, Gary joined the Free French forces in World War II as a pilot and served in Europe and North Africa. Unable to visit his mother during the war, he regularly received letters from her, only to discover when he finally returned that she had passed away years earlier. Knowing his deep attachment to her, she had written an entire corpus of letters shortly before her death and arranged for them to be sent to him at regular intervals. Here was another origin of Gary's complex relationship with the living and the dead, fantasy and reality, truth and fiction. After the war, Gary was employed by the French diplomatic service for two decades, serving in Bulgaria, Switzerland, Bolivia, and Los Angeles. He also lived in South Africa and Paris. All this time he wrote numerous novels, some of which were also made into films. His book *The Roots of Heaven* (1956) received the Prix Goncourt, an award that can be given to a writer only once in his or her lifetime.[8] Gary was always known for his predilection to change his identity, whether by reinventing his origins or by transforming his appearance. But it was at the end of an illustrious career as patriot, diplomat, and author that Gary decided to recreate himself entirely as a youthful, angry, semi-educated, but brilliant Arabic writer. It was his way of getting back at critics who had claimed that his powers as an author had waned. But it was also his way of exposing the hypocrisy of his own society and tearing down the facade of respectability from which he himself had profited by creating an imaginary author who could tell the truth.

One of the few films of its genre whose protagonist is a woman, *Madame Rosa* depicts the last months in the life of a retired prostitute and former inmate of Auschwitz who now takes care of the children of younger prostitutes. Told from the perspective of Muhammad, or Momo, an Arabic boy who becomes almost obsessively devoted to her, the film shatters all the taboos and stereotypes associated with the depiction of Jewish victims. Although Madame Rosa (Simone Signoret) maintains a "Jewish hideaway" in the basement and occasionally mutters a few Yiddish and Hebrew words, she is otherwise entirely innocent of stereotypical Jewish characteristics. To her, raising a boy as Moïse or Muhammad is merely a matter of choice. But underneath her bravado, as her illness progresses, she increasingly succumbs to the trauma of the past. Suddenly we realize that all this time she is still waiting to be taken away to the camps, ready to pack and go at an instant's notice. But raising half-abandoned children in a dilapidated apartment in a working-class, largely Arabic neighborhood, Madame Rosa neither lingers consciously on her fate nor retains any prejudices. If the war destroyed her own life, she lives in the midst of newly ruined young lives and finds a path to the soul of a fragile, rejected boy. A hard and tough woman, unlike Nazerman in *The Pawnbroker,* she is entirely at home in her milieu; like him, she is desperately lonely, deeply scarred, and forlorn. But she gives life to Momo, and in return he mourns her for all those who would have done so had they not all been murdered decades earlier.

Because it tells this story from the perspective and in the distinct language of Momo, the film (and book) is often hilarious and at the same time succeeds in preventing its tragic backdrop from leading it toward sappy sentimentalism or nostalgia. Momo is deeply attached to this woman who is the only mother he has ever known, a rough customer if ever there was one but equally dedicated to him. When she dies, Momo locks himself with her corpse in the basement that she had designated "my secondary residence . . . my Jewish hole . . . where I go to hide when I am afraid." It is hard for Momo to believe that Madame Rosa would be afraid of anything. But she tells him: "It's not necessary to have reasons in order to have fear, Momo." "This," the older Muhammad remarks in retrospect, "I never forgot, because it was the most truthful thing I ever heard." He fills the space with perfumes to keep out the smell of her decomposing body, and prepares to die with her, surrounded by the little bits and pieces that recall the remnants of her Jewish heritage. After three weeks, when the neighbors break down the door to see where the smell is coming from, Momo realizes that "they cried for help oh what horror but they never thought of crying earlier because life has no smell."[9]

Although the novel is superior to the film, the movie's success is at least in part the result of a mélange of identities among its cast, which closely resembles that of Gary/Ajar. Moshe Mizrahi was born in Egypt in 1931, immigrated to Palestine in 1946, served in the Israeli Defense Forces in the Israeli War of Independence, and lived in a kibbutz until he moved to France in 1958. Simone Signoret was born in Wiesbaden, Germany in 1921, was raised in Paris, and had to support her family during the German occupation when her Jewish father fled to London and joined Charles de Gaulle's Free French Forces.[10] Sami ben Youb, who plays Momo, does not seem to have continued his acting career, but he is clearly an Arab of North African origin.

The world in which Momo grows up has little in common with the bourgeois reality of modern Paris. His friends are the mostly Arab and African prostitutes and their children, a Jewish doctor who occasionally makes a visit, and the North African porters who carry him up the numerous flights of stairs to look in on Madame Rosa when she is sick. His encounter with the middle-class family that eventually adopts him resembles a meeting between alien civilizations—despite their education they can understand him even less well than he can see through them. The mix of identities, cultures, religions, and ethnicities of his working-class neighborhood is hardly romanticized; but it is a world that is turned upon itself, where what matters is not identity but survival, and where compassion can save lives rather than merely making people feel good about themselves.

When Momo asks Madame Rosa what she is afraid of, her answer does not imply that there is nothing to fear, that fear is merely a product of the imagination. Rather, she simply states that her fear of what happened in the past has never dissipated, even if the event can now threaten only her psyche and no longer exists as objective reality. Madame Rosa is afraid of Auschwitz. As her senility takes over, she is constantly packing her bags. Is she preparing to go again to Auschwitz or to escape her persecutors? She is trapped within the memory of an atrocity that happened forty years ago. But her atrocity also becomes that of Momo, even as it makes for the powerful link between them: his natural empathy for her pain and sorrow, her effortless understanding of his solitude and need for love. For, as Momo says, life has no smell to call attention to itself. No one will come to help either him or her until it is too late, until their decomposing bodies will disturb the public peace and trigger some action, even if it may simply consist of the removal of their remains.

It is the "Arab" Ajar who writes about the Jewish fear and empathizes with this decrepit and coarse retired harlot to the point of wishing to die at her side. He can tolerate the stink of her body that finally makes the forces of peace and order take action and cart her away. It is through Ajar that Gary comes closer to the tragedy of our era than in any of the books he wrote under his own name. In Ajar's *The Anxiety of King Solomon,* a story told by a chauffeur who sounds like a French version of a grown-up Momo, an elderly Jew is haunted by the period he spent in hiding during the German occupation of France, protected by a chansonnier who was simultaneously having an affair with an SS man. But unlike Boris Schreiber's novel, *The Descent to the Cradle,* which came out a few years later and also dealt with the trauma of hiding and persecution, Gary/Ajar writes about love and compassion, not hate and revenge, and the core of the tale is the unbreakable bond between the "king" and his little singer.[11] In *The Life before Us,* it is the Jewish prostitute and the Arab orphan who perceive the continuing misery of existence in a world that turns away from them—they don't smell—a world whose greatest cries of dismay and anger are evoked by events that can no longer be reversed, even as it displays an appalling indifference to the mayhem and wretchedness of the present. Gary employed his own mongrel background to create Ajar who, in turn, created Momo and Madame Rosa, those keen observers of society's lies and misdemeanors who never utter a single word of complaint. How much more should we admire Gary's writing today, when we are constantly exposed to the demagogy of a "war of civilizations" and the "defense of our way of life," the murderous fanatical passions of Islamic fundamentalists, and the self-righteous liberal rhetoric of love and compassion preached mostly in fashionable cafes and manicured campuses.

Gary has only derision for the seemingly empathic yet actively indifferent and distancing politically correct prism, through which bourgeois intellectuals view minorities, the "underclass," foreigners, orphans, prostitutes, drug addicts, and all other unsettling elements on the fringes of respectable society. But he is just as pitiless about the insistence on firm identity by those whose objective marginality cannot excuse their criminality. This is powerfully expressed in one of the best scenes in the film, when Momo's presumed father comes to take him back. In precise opposition to Allen's insistence on the inborn characteristics of the "Jew" or the WASP, here all is mixed up and confused. Is Momo an Arab or a Jew? Does this matter? What are his loyalties, and where should they lie? It is in this scene that Momo, the child of a woman murdered by her pimp, becomes an "honorary" Jew, not through recognition as a righteous gentile or through donation from a Jewish agency, but thanks to his total empathy with Madame Rosa, the survivor of a world of indifferent hatred and hateful indifference. This identification is not intellectual and certainly not political. It is identification through experience: his experience of her suffering, and his experience of his own marginality and total lack of importance, not as a stateless person in Hannah Arendt's sense, but even worse, as a person not seen, not heard, and not smelled until his corpse begins to stink. Momo has no consciousness of victimhood or persecution because he was born into it and it is his only reality. But through Madame Rosa he becomes its modern variant. Whether this makes him Jew or Arab makes no difference. His love for Madame Rosa makes the child, who could have grown up without conscience and empathy, into a human being in a world where people are legion and humanity scarce.

This subtle, irreverent, and almost outrageously courageous dismantling of stereotypes, this exposure of the stupidity, heartlessness, and violence at the root of all politics of identity and bombast about roots, blood allegiance, and ethnic belonging, deserves to be quoted in full:

> KADIR: Eleven years ago I entrusted my son to your care. I haven't been in touch sooner, because I've been in a psychiatric hospital. I got the receipt from my brother-in-law. My wife had a tragic death as you know. They let me out this morning. I picked up the receipt and came right over. My name is Kadir Youssef and I've come to see my son, Muhammad. I want to say hello to him.
>
> MADAME ROSA: What's this again?
>
> KADIR: Madame, I'm a sick man.
>
> MADAME ROSA: Aren't we all?
>
> KADIR: Madame, for eleven years I was locked up in a psychiatric hospital after the newspapers wrote that I wasn't in my right mind.
>
> MADAME ROSA: What did you say your son's name was?
>
> KADIR: Muhammad.
>
> MADAME ROSA: And you remember what the mother's name was?
>
> KADIR: Madame, you know that I am mentally defective ["irresponsible" in the original French]. I was officially recognized as such. It's not my fault if I did that to her. Just think, she did as many as fifteen tricks a day. I wound up getting jealous, and I killed her, I know I did. But I'm not responsible for my actions. I was madly in love with her. I could not live without her.
>
> MADAME ROSA: You certainly couldn't live without her, Mr. Kadir, because Aïcha brought in a certain amount of cash per day. Then you killed her, so she couldn't bring in any more. Aside from that, Mr. Kadir, how have you been?
>
> KADIR: I'm all right, Madame Rosa. I'm dying, it's my heart.

MADAME ROSA: Mazeltov.

KADIR: Thanks. I'd like to see my son.

MADAME ROSA: You owe me for three years of boarding, and it's been eleven years since I've had any news from you.

KADIR: News from me, what do you mean?

MADAME ROSA: Money.

KADIR: How was I supposed to get it?

MADAME ROSA: I'd rather not discuss that.

KADIR: Madame, when we entrusted you with our son, I was in full command of my faculties. I had three women working for me in the central market, one of whom I loved dearly. I even had a certain social status: Youssef Kadir, well known to the police. That's right, Madame. Youssef Kadir, well known to the police. It was even printed in the newspapers.

MADAME ROSA: Mr. Kadir, no one has the right to abandon his child like a pile of garbage, for eleven years, without offering a penny.

KADIR: But it was materially impossible. I've got a medical certificate to prove it.

MADAME ROSA: Papers which prove things don't interest me.

KADIR: Madame, I can't bring Aïcha back to life, but I'd like to embrace my son, ask him to forgive me, and pray for me. Is that him [pointing at Momo]?

MADAME ROSA: Moïse [Moses, the Jewish child she is raising together with Momo]!

MOÏSE: Yes, Madame Rosa?

MADAME ROSA: Go say hello to your papa!

MOÏSE: Hello, Papa.

KADIR: Excuse me, did you say Moïse?

MADAME ROSA: Of course. I said Moïse, and so what!

KADIR: Moïse is a Jewish name! I entrusted you with a Muhammad, Madame, not a Moïse.

MADAME ROSA: Are you sure?

KADIR: Sure of what, Madame? Eleven years ago I entrusted you with a three-year-old Muslim boy, named Muhammad. I gave you an Arab boy in good and due form and that's what I want back. I've got nothing against Jews, Madame, God forgive them. . . .

233

MADAME ROSA: Are you sure you're not Jewish?

KADIR: You don't have to be Jewish to be persecuted, Madame. Jews aren't the only ones with a right to be persecuted. Under no circumstances do I want a Jewish son. I've got enough trouble as it is!

MADAME ROSA: Just calm down and don't get upset, because there might be some mistake. Let me check. . . . Momo, hand me those papers. . . . Ah! Here we are! Here we are! . . . On November 5th, 1966, give or take a bit . . .

KADIR: What do you mean?

MADAME ROSA: Just to round things off. I took in two boys. One was a Muslim [*"dans l'état musulman"* in the original French] and the other a Jew [*"dans l'état juif"*]. The same day . . . The . . . It's becoming all too clear! I made a mistake. I mixed up the religions.

KADIR: What?

MADAME ROSA: Yes, I raised Muhammad as Moïse and Moïse as Muhammad. Since they both arrived the same day, well . . . I got them mixed up. Which means that the little Moïse is now living in a very fine Muslim family in Marseille, and the little Muhammad, your son, who's right here, has been brought up as a Jew, with a bar mitzvah and a strict kosher diet—don't you worry. . . .

KADIR: What's that? My son is strictly kosher? He's bar mitzvahed? My Muhammad has been turned into a Jew?

MADAME ROSA: What can I say? I made a mistake. You must realize that a three-year-old boy doesn't have a striking identity. Even if he's circumcised. So I made a mistake. I brought up Muhammad as a good little Jew. You have to realize, that when you leave your child for eleven years, without seeing him, you shouldn't be surprised that he has become a Jew. . . .

KADIR: I was locked up in a clinic!

MADAME ROSA: Listen to me, he used to be an Arab and now he's a little Jew, that's all it is. He's still your son!

KADIR: It's not the same! He was baptized!

MADAME ROSA: Mr. Kadir, please! Baptized! God forbid! No, Moïse was brought up as a good little Jew. Isn't that right, Moïse?

MOÏSE: Yes, Madame Rosa.

KADIR: I want my son back in the same state I left him in! I want my son back in an Arab state! Not in a Jewish state!

MADAME ROSA: In my house, there's no such thing as an Arab state and a Jewish state. So, if you want to take back your son, you'll have to take him in his present state. Because first you go and kill the child's mother, then you have yourself declared a psychiatric case, and now you come and raise hell because the kid was brought up as a decent Jew. Moïse, go embrace your father, even if it kills him. He's still your father!

KADIR: That's not my son [he collapses and dies].

Momo does not mourn the father who dies in front of his eyes only moments after they meet for the first time since he was a toddler. With all his rhetoric of victimhood, his pride at being known by the police, his distorted sense of honor and identity, Kadir is a manifestation of the notion that while individuals may be the product of their circumstances, if they end up as pimps and murderers, and if they abandon their children, they have no right to appeal for compassion. They are responsible for their deeds and should pay the price, rather than being declared irresponsible thanks to a skewed concept of morality and accountability. Gary has as little patience with excusing the crimes of the "wretched of the earth" as he has with the sanctimonious arguments in their favor by the intelligentsia. But he is most outraged by the predilection to determine one's identity, traits, past, and future according to religion, race, and ethnicity, anchoring the individual's entire existence in something that has been arbitrarily imposed by others. Gary's own obscure origins as well as the tragedies of his generation evidently made him intolerant of such discourse of identity, just as they motivated and facilitated his own predilection for metamorphosis. One is what one makes of oneself, not what others assert or identify. Being a Jew, or an Arab, is a matter of choice, not fate, even if fate imposed Jewishness on individuals who never were and never would have chosen to be Jewish had the world not judged its inhabitants by categories entirely foreign to their own self-perception.

Madame Rosa, however, worries about the effect this bizarre encounter with his presumed biological father may have on Momo. Typically for Gary, the rejection of all social conventions, loyalty to identity, and biological determinants is predicated here on the seemingly absurd yet deeply truthful logic that pervades the entire narrative. For one thing, it turns out that Madame Rosa had concealed from Momo his real age so as to be able to keep him with her longer. Thanks to the encounter with Kadir, Momo discovers that he is not eleven but fourteen years old. For another, by lying to Kadir about his son, Madame Rosa saves Momo not only from a criminal father but also presumably from the father's hereditary mental disease (which of course never existed in the first place). Thus lies are presented as more moral than truth.

MADAME ROSA: Has all this upset you, Momo?

MOMO: No, Madame Rosa, I'm glad to be fourteen years old.

MADAME ROSA: Yes, it's better this way. And you know, having a father with psychiatric problems is the last thing you needed, especially since that sort of thing is sometimes hereditary.

MOMO: You're right, Madame Rosa. I was lucky.

MADAME ROSA: And Aïcha was very popular. Who knows who your real father was in all that mess.

Momo's own understanding of his situation, although it initially appears as distorted by ignorance and deprivation, is soon shown to be far superior to that of Ramon, the psychologist partner of the young filmmaker who wants to adopt and "civilize" the young Arab, viewing him as she does as a still-tamable urban savage in desperate need of a warm bourgeois home:

MOMO: When she was young and beautiful she peddled her ass, but it wasn't aesthetic any more after being in a German camp. So she opened a place for the kids of whores. They could be blackmailed at any time, and they've got to hide their kids, because some of the neighbors are mean and denounce you to Public Welfare. . . .

RAMON: You said that your father came yesterday.

MOMO: He just came out of the hospital. He boarded me before he killed my mother, then he was taken to the hospital as a psychiatric case. And then he came to get me back, but Madame Rosa wouldn't allow it, because it's not good for me to have a crazy father, it could be hereditary.

As Momo speaks, one has the distinct impression that his potential adoptive parents, who are educated, elegant, and well meaning, have no idea what he is talking about. To be sure, their desire to give him a better life is both sincere and in many respects laudable, and after the death of Madame Rosa they do rescue him from falling through the cracks into a life of crime and poverty. But they will help him without ever learning about the other side of their own society, without ever grasping that true selflessness, devotion, and love come from suffering, humiliation, and terror. Doctor Katz, who knows much more about this world as Madame Rosa's physician and friend, still cannot fathom the kind of ethics that Momo has forged for himself from the worldview of an aging prostitute survivor of Auschwitz and the reality of the underbelly of French society in the *banlieue*. Since Madame Rosa refuses to be taken to hospital but insists on dying in her own bed—she was taken once and will never agree to go again, whether to a concentration camp or to a city hospital—Momo hopes to help her die in peace:

> MOMO: Say, doctor, couldn't you kill her, just between Jews?
>
> KATZ: What? Kill her? What in the world are you talking about?
>
> MOMO: Yeah, kill her to put an end to her suffering.
>
> KATZ: That's impossible, Momo. Euthanasia is strictly forbidden, against the law. We're living in a civilized country. You don't know what you're saying.
>
> MOMO: I know what I'm saying. Besides, I'm Algerian. Over there people have the sacred right of self-determination. Does the sacred right of self-determination exist, or doesn't it?
>
> KATZ: Yes, of course it exists. . . . Of course. It's a noble and grand thing. But what does it have to do with Madame Rosa?
>
> MOMO: Madame Rosa has the sacred right of the people to self-determination. And if she wants to die, that's her right and you ought to help her. A Jewish doctor must do it so there's no antisemitism involved. Jews shouldn't torture each other. It's disgusting.
>
> KATZ: My poor child, you don't know what you're saying.
>
> MOMO: I'm not yours and I'm not even a child. I'm fourteen years old and my mother was a whore and my father killed her. . . . If you were a good Jew with a good heart, you'd perform an act of mercy and give her an injection and save her from life.
>
> KATZ: We don't have the right to shorten her suffering, Momo.

And thus Momo proves that while the "sacred right of self-determination" does not include one's right to die, the ethical code of civilization does not give us the right to shorten the suffering of those who want to be "saved from life." Unlike Wilhelm Meister in Johann Wolfgang von Goethe's foundational *Bildungsroman,* and much more in line with Franz Kafka's "A Report to an Academy" presented by a humanized Ape (Jew), the life ahead of Momo is one in which he will have to apply the morality of the gutter to the immorality of its civilized upper crust.[12] What is the moral of the story? It is the motto that Momo learned from his old Muslim teacher, before his teacher too became old, senile, and pathetic: *"On ne peut pas vivre sans quelqu'un à aimer"* (one cannot live without having someone to love). It is, ultimately, Momo's love for Madame Rosa that helps him survive her death, just as it is her love for him that makes her life bearable. By liberating Madame Rosa from life as he lights a menorah in her "Jewish hole" and wishes her a painless death (to which she responds by muttering "*inshallah*," or "may God grant it" in Arabic), Momo performs a rite of love that transcends the lies and conventions of their victimization and neglect. By dying and decomposing, Madame Rosa liberates Momo from abandonment and oppression and facilitates his entry into a new world where he may possibly thrive without ever forgetting the yawning abyss under his feet.

Madame Rosa is to my mind perhaps the best cinematic unraveling of the survivor/non-survivor, or Jew/non-Jew, dichotomy that haunts representations of the "Jew" in film. It shares many qualities with *The Pawnbroker,* but in some ways is more irreverent, less self-important, and ultimately more compassionate and humane. It is a socially conscious film about the atrocity of the Holocaust, but it is just as derisive of contemporary political correctness and self-righteousness as it is a bitter condemnation of the devastation wrought by Nazism and genocide. It does not glorify poverty, does not justify the crimes of the underclass, but it ridicules the rhetoric of sympathy without empathy and pity without action and exposes the injustices and blindness of the modern welfare state and amoral medical ethics. And, in contrast to so many other films on the topic, it dismantles the stereotypes on which much of the representation of the "Jew" has been constructed, using ruthless humor and relentless sarcasm.

FAITH AND BETRAYAL

Madame Rosa portrays the heroic anti-hero by inverting the meanings of conventionally despised occupations and personal traits. Rather than presenting Madame Rosa's goodness as a contradiction, the film shows how it is derived directly from her experience as a prostitute and her dedication to the children of whores. Similarly, her courage and determination do not stand in opposition to, but rather are firmly rooted in, her unending fear of Auschwitz. She is also the antithesis par excellence of the stereotypical Jew: nothing about her is Jewish, apart from the fact of her persecution by the Nazis and the circumstances of her death, choreographed for her by an Arab orphan. The creation of a character who is both a Jewish victim of Nazism and a prostitute—not because of Nazi coercion or as a consequence of persecution but as a profession chosen before the war and abandoned in its aftermath—hardly fits in with the conventional representation of Jews and survivors. If Nazerman in *The Pawnbroker* was a professor before the war and becomes a ruthless pawnbroker after the Holocaust, Madame Rosa, unable to "peddle her ass" after the camps, raises the children of women who have no choice but to continue selling their bodies. If Nazerman teaches Jesus Ortiz how to become "a usurer, a man with secret resources, a witch, a pawnbroker, a sheeny, a mockie, and a kike," Madame Rosa teaches Momo how to become a human being. Anything but a hero, she is also not a victim; she is neither active as a fighter against oppression nor does she passively accept fate. In the face of inhumanity and indifference she instills a spark of goodness into the soul of a child. That this child is himself a victim of other types of prejudice and oppression rather than the benefactor of past persecution signifies all the more that the lesson of atrocity is to fight its recurrence rather than to lament its past manifestations.

Another type of the "Jew" as anti-hero is at the polar opposite of the Jewish prostitute, namely, the rabbi. Traditionally, the relationship between the Jewish religious leadership and heroism was somewhat uneven. On the one hand, Jewish history has known many cases of stubborn resistance to conquest, occupation, or enforced conversion, including death or even mass suicide in the name of "sanctifying God's name" (*kiddush hashem*). On the other hand, Diaspora Jewry learned that the best way to survive as Jewish communities within an alien and often hostile Christian environment was to find some sort of accommodation with the powers in place. This survival strategy for communities in which the religious authorities had a great deal of influence did not make for much grandstanding or extravagant heroism. Actual physical resistance, let alone military resistance, was not the norm for a population that was usually denied—and just as often evaded—martial activity. Whatever role Jews played in European society until the era of emancipation, it was rarely that of soldiers.

As the Jews emerged from the ghettoes and as the nation-state instituted compulsory, universal military service, identifying patriotism with sacrifice on the "fields of honor," the situation changed dramatically.[13] Emancipation and assimilation fueled militant patriotism among increasingly secularized Jews. But traditional Jewish religious authorities both feared the rapid encroachment of modernity on the old way of life and were more influential among communities less affected by these trends. Nevertheless, while martial heroism was still seen by the traditional religious establishment as the reserve of the "goyim," the general trend was toward progressive secularization in an era of nationalism and conflict. The stated goal of Zionism was to "normalize" the existence of the Jews by bringing them to a national home. Hence the "typical" Diaspora Jew was associated—very much in line with antisemitic imagery—with cowardice and physical weakness. Instead, a new "muscular Jew" was required who would be equipped with the requisite prowess to (re)conquer the Promised

Land, often represented both as an empty space and as populated by uncivilized "natives" without any rights for the land.[14]

The Holocaust enhanced this dichotomy of views and radically transformed its parameters. Traditional European Jewry was almost entirely wiped out, Jewish religious leadership was seen as having led its flock like sheep to the slaughter, and only those secular young men and women, be they left-wing or right-wing Zionists, Bundists, nationalists, or communists, were seen as the heroes who, while unable to stop the catastrophe, at least saved Jewish national honor.[15] To be sure, within the orthodox Jewish community some voices suggested that the Shoah was, in fact, God's punishment for the rapid secularization of the Jewish masses prior to the rise of Nazism. But this was an internal argument that had little impact outside the boundaries of these self-enclosed groups.[16] Still, even during the Holocaust, and certainly in its wake, another view of the role of religion in Jewish survival existed side by side with the secular and often anti-religious perception of militant, fighting nationalism. This more positive appreciation of the religious leadership was reinforced by the decline of militarist sentiments, the realization of the scale of the Jewish catastrophe, and the struggle over the definition of Jewish identity both in newly established Israel and in other concentrations of Jewish populations, especially the United States. Other factors that must have played a role were allegations of collaboration with the Nazis by the Jewish councils; disillusionment with the rhetoric of heroism and sacrifice in Europe, the United States, and Israel; and the revelations of the Eichmann trial in Jerusalem. Particularly in Israel, attempts to link the Jewish resisters of the Holocaust with Israeli heroism against the Arabs somewhat misfired and were received with growing skepticism even among secular intellectuals. The view of resistance as physical and cultural survival rather than armed confrontation opened the road to accepting the stance of traditional Judaism.[17]

Thus between the martyrdom of armed resistance and the sacrifice of *kiddush hashem*, the new/old heroism of physical and spiritual survival found its place. This was also the site where the rabbi as the spiritual leader and moral compass of his community could reclaim a role as a voice of reason and kindness, wisdom and courage in the face of inhumanity and barbarism. The rabbi was neither a martyr nor a fighter. He represented the urge for continuity and renewal, not for a glorious death; and he had the interest of the living community and its future at heart, not an ill-defined posterity that would forge its identity from the mythical memory of hopeless and meaningless bloodshed. He represented the Jewish notion of history as opposed to its modern nationalist face: not *kiddush hashem* or *kiddush ha'umah* (sanctification of the nation) but *kiddush hakhayim,* the sanctification of life.[18]

But if the continuation of Jewish life after the Shoah depended both on the existence of *she'erit ha'pletah* (the surviving remnant) of the Jews and on an allegiance to Jewish identity as symbolized by religious practice—be it orthodox or liberal—there was still the need to contend with three major philosophical issues. First, there was the question that has haunted the Jews since biblical times, namely, how could God allow the destruction of his people without either proving thereby his nonexistence or his evil nature? Second, how could Jews rely on the wisdom of religious authorities when both as individuals and as a group they so often misled, and at times even betrayed, their communities during that time of horror and mass murder? Third, how could this not lead the Jews to abandon any religious practice and faith in God and, consequently, either merge into the nations in which they found themselves or join the Jewish State as secular nationalists? In other words, did the Holocaust prove that religion was the fortress of Jewish continuity or that it was its tomb?[19]

This is the core of Eli Cohen's *The Quarrel* (1991), which is more a filmed play than a film, based on Chaim Grade's short story "My Quarrel with Hersh Raseyner."[20] A chance encounter between two old friends in a Montreal park in 1948 on Rosh Hashanah, the Jewish New Year, evolves into a dispute over personal and collective faith, loyalty, and betrayal. Chaim Kovler (R. H. Thomson), a Yiddish poet and writer, and Hersh Raseyner (Saul Rubinek), a rabbi and head of a yeshiva for Holocaust orphans, have had this argument before, as students at a Białystok yeshiva before the war. Chaim, the more brilliant and tempestuous of the two, left his religious studies; Hersh, more solid and measured, completed them. But this is not only a resumption of the old quarrel, because in the meantime the Holocaust has destroyed their community, murdered their families, and created a vast existential void from which the two of them, each in his own way, are trying to trace a path back to faith—in God, in humanity, in life. Their heroism is rooted in their very insistence on continuing life after the destruction; but it is also ultimately based on their recognition of the fragility of religious faith and of individual human goodness in the face of evil. In other words, their heroism derives from coming to terms with their faults, lies, deceptions, and repressions. After the Holocaust, nothing is as it seemed: the hero, if there be such a thing, must by definition be an anti-hero if he is to exist at all.

The dispute between Chaim and Hersh centers on two related issues. One is faith: Does the Holocaust teach one to trust God or to rely on man?

The second is betrayal: the betrayal of God by man, the betrayal of man by God, and the betrayal of one's fellow human beings. Can one be forgiven for having betrayed one's family in the face of extinction? Can one even speak of betrayal under such extreme circumstances? Must one assume guilt or can one be absolved of it by reference to the true perpetrators of the deed? The film provides no answers, but is propelled forward by the relationship between these two men, who were the closest of friends, bitterly broke with each other when Chaim left the yeshiva, and now meet again as the last remnants of a destroyed world.

While they made different choices even before the catastrophe, both men carry within themselves the burden of betrayal—a burden that so many other survivors have also had to carry. Through their meeting and the ultimate renewal of their friendship far away from the ashes of its original social and human context, they finally unburden themselves of the guilt that has haunted them ever since. True friendship and understanding, the film suggests, can serve as a greater support than either faith or reason. As the film ends, a voiceover proclaims: "Rav [Rabbi] Yakov [Jacob] once taught that when Joseph lived in Egypt he was great and powerful. He saved the Kingdom and rose from slave to prince; only the mighty Pharaoh was above him. Joseph had friends, disciples, wealth, and slaves. He had everything. But until his brothers came, Joseph was alone."

To be sure, just as their chance meeting begins a process of (qualified) healing, so too they must part and go on their respective paths. Hersh will remain a rabbi, and Chaim will remain a writer. In their own way they will keep looking for that spark of humanity that was almost entirely extinguished during the Holocaust. It is a spark found not in the myth of heroism and perfection, but in the reality of fractured, fragile, tortured, physically imperfect, and morally compromised human beings.

Nevertheless, Chaim and Hersh offer two polarized views of the world, both informed by their own experiences yet still repressing the most painful aspect of their own personal trauma. In response to Chaim's insistence on reason as opposed to faith, Hersh argues:

> Reason is a tool. When a German did nothing while his Jewish neighbor was being shipped off to the camps, he was only doing what you and I would do if we were just following our reason. His life was in danger if he helped a Jew. Preserving his own life was a reasonable thing to do. And those few heroes who did help, it wasn't reason that commanded them. So how do we protect ourselves if reason fails us? By relying on something higher than reason. If a person does not have the almighty to turn to, if there's nothing in the universe that's higher than human beings, then what's morality? Morality is a matter of opinion: I like milk, you like meat.

Hitler likes to kill people, I like to save them. Who's to say which is better? Do you begin to see the horror of this? If there is no master of the universe, then who's to say that Hitler did anything wrong? If there's no God then the people that murdered your wife and children did nothing wrong. . . .

I have seen the real face of the world, and so have you. It's cruel, it's empty.

Chaim's reasoning is just as powerful, however, indicating that ultimately what matters is not whether one takes the path to God or to reason, but whether one's conclusion from the horror wreaked by humanity is to join in the killing or to try and rekindle the spark of humanness and compassion:

In Paris after the war I met an old Lithuanian woman. During the war she smuggled many Jews from the Vilna Ghetto and she also saved Jewish books. The Nazis caught her and sentenced her to death but by a miracle she came out alive. . . . She told me she is an atheist. So why did she risk her life to save Jews? Not because she believes in Hersh Raseyner's God but because she believes in human beings and loves them. . . . If you ask me what makes people moral, it is neither God nor reason. It is a faith, your faith, that God wants you to be good . . . that human beings must help each other.

But the moment of recognition, the moment in which the dispute ends and the two friends recognize each other's humanity in their failings, comes when they confess their own betrayals to each other. These are not grand theological betrayals, not abandonment of God or tradition, but small, human-scale betrayals, of a nature that remains deeply lodged in their souls and has shaken forever their belief in absolute truths. Initially, Hersh merely mentions that while he survived Auschwitz, his wife and both children were murdered. Chaim elaborates a little more: "I lost everyone. I was married, Hersh. Two boys. I was in Vilna. I fled to Russia with a close friend, running like scared dogs through the countryside. I left Sarah and the boys behind, I was told the Nazis, they only wanted men for the work there, only the men, who could have guessed, Hersh, I made the wrong choice. In Russia I stayed alive by believing I would see them again." Hersh responds: "There was no right choice. Chaim, it doesn't help to blame yourself." But, of course, Hersh blames both himself and his friend. At first he says: "All I know is that I am guilty, all Jews are bound to one another. I am guilty for not influencing other Jews, for not changing them." And Chaim immediately understands: "Not changing me?"

HERSH: Not changing you. . . .

CHAIM: You still see me as someone who betrayed you. You and God.

HERSH: No, we betrayed each other, and God punished us.

CHAIM: My leaving the yeshiva did not cause the Nazis. . . . I have no responsibility for what happened to your family. None, I'm sorry.

HERSH: Chaim, Chaim, we are all responsible.

CHAIM: There were no sins, Hersh, that could ever justify God sending Hitler. God abandoned us. No, he humiliated us. It was humiliation. Six million of his Chosen People. One million children. The children did not abandon God, Hersh. How could we ever forgive him for not saving the children?

HERSH: If I knew God, I'd be God.

CHAIM: If I knew God I would put him on trial.

But the real guilt lies elsewhere. It is not collective. It is entirely personal. Hersh tells Chaim about his father, who always criticized him for not being as smart as his friend. Nor did he approve of Hersh's marriage. "There were times," Hersh says, "God forgive me, I hated him." But then he apologized:

He came over once, it was a few weeks after the Germans invaded, he came over to talk. Yom Kippur is coming, he said, and I haven't asked you for forgiveness, . . . He said, bring Peshale here. I went to the kitchen to get Peshale. When we came out, he was crying. I never saw him cry before. And then he apologized for being a cruel father and a bad Jew. And he walked over to Peshale and said, your father is a very good man, forgive me for saying that he and his family were not good enough for me, and you Peshale, you showed me more about being a good Jew than I ever knew, please, if you can, both of you, forgive me. And then, he hugged me, Chaim.

But this is still only part of the story. Later that day the rest of it and the root of Hersh's guilt will be revealed. But before that Chaim encounters Shiah, one of Hersh's young disciples from his new yeshiva, and they speak of heroism:

SHIAH: You were going to start the yeshiva together. . . . Then you cut your roots and spread your poison everywhere. . . . Why did you leave the yeshiva? . . . All Jews are responsible for one another! . . . My rebbe smuggled the Torah into Częstochowa. He was ready to lose his life for that Torah. Would you have done the same for your books? . . . There were lots of people in the camps who wanted to help others, but they were frightened. Only people with the faith of my rebbe were able to overcome their fears, because my rebbe feared God more than he feared the Nazis.

CHAIM: I admire your love for your rebbe but there were other heroes in the camps and they were not all religious.

SHIAH: You're wrong, you're wrong. When I was sick the Nazis sent me to the death block and no one tried to rescue me, [not] my friends, [not] my brother. But my rebbe crawled under the barbed wire and carried me back on his shoulders. Would you have done what he did? Did you try and save anyone? What about your family?

CHAIM: My wife and sons were killed by the Nazis while I suffered in Siberia.

SHIAH: So why didn't you take them with you? . . .

CHAIM: And your brother, who didn't save you, did you go and save him? And your rebbe, did he save his family? . . . And suppose it was me, me, who carried you from the death block on my shoulders, would you now make me your rabbi? And if it was a Christian who saved you, would you now be a Christian?

Finally the truth comes out. As they sit on a bench in the sunshine, Hersh says, "the night that my father came . . ." Chaim interrupts him, "I still have the image of you two hugging, as long as I live I'll remember that story. . . ." But Hersh continues:

He leaned forward to kiss me and I turned my head away. He was asking me for forgiveness but I couldn't. He left my house, walked very slowly, he was bent over, and I could see finally that I could hurt him. And now I realize it felt good. I was sure that I was going to see him the next day. It was Yom Kippur. I would go to his house and I would kiss him. And that was the day that the Germans started the deportations. He spent the last night of his life rejected by me. He was shot before I could reach him. I sent him to his death alone. I am cruel. I am a cruel man. . . . You don't say anything, Chaim? Say something. I feel so alone.

Chaim finally replies: "Are you more cruel than I? I deserted my family." As the children play ball in the park, calling to each other happily in French, he continues:

It was Sarah who pushed me to go, to leave, she cried, she begged, she even, she pushed me through the door, we will be safe, she said over and over. I knew I shouldn't, I left. When we reached Riga I found out the truth. So, what should I do, should I save myself or should I go back to be with them? I agonized in the barn all night, where we were hiding. I woke up, I decided to go back. My friend, he grabbed me by my coat, he yelled, the only life you can save now is your own. Come on, the truck's going. I allowed myself to become convinced. I could have gone back to be with them. I didn't. And now, there is no grave where I can ask their forgiveness.

Then they dance a Hasidic dance, and when they are done, they find themselves surrounded by local people clapping hands, calling out bravo, bravo!

Hersh and Chaim lost their wives and children in the Holocaust. Chaim has passing affairs with women taken with his poetic powers; Hersh has none. Both have not yet been able to come to terms with their loss. They are lonely, lost, and friendless. Although they may never meet each other again, and will never reconcile their differences, they are each other's only true friends. Their memories are full of ghosts, but these are ghosts that both of them knew intimately: they can share each other's memories of a world that will be no more.

Yet most survivors married again and almost as quickly also had children. There was a veritable baby boom among the young and the not so young, an urgent need to fill the void, make up for the loss, give life one more chance. The displaced-persons camps soon swarmed with children.[21] Chaim and Hersh would also probably marry and raise families. But what would become of their children? How would they grow up surrounded by their parents' ghosts, the siblings they never knew, their parents' former spouses, the mothers and fathers of their dead half-brothers and half-sisters, the vanished grandparents and uncles and aunts? What sort of generation would grow up from families emptied of content and nights filled with screams and nightmares? How would the burden of guilt be transmitted to the second generation and beyond?

The children of soldiers could boast of their fathers' exploits, true or imagined. The children of survivors inherited shame, guilt, and fear. Names were occasionally whispered, memorial candles lit, strange-sounding locations mentioned. The dead were always present and always absent. The memory of the utter helplessness of the time fused with the complete inability to put together again what had been so irreparably shattered. What sort of role models could such parents provide? Where would their children find examples of heroism when their homes were populated by the broken remnants of the catastrophe? Could one find comfort in faith or in rebellion, in loyalty to the past or in the erection of a new world cleansed of both the victims and the perpetrators, the hopes and the disillusionments of a burnt-down, still-smoldering continent? Jeroen Krabbé's *Left Luggage* (1998) attempts to examine the reactions of survivors' children in two very different milieus, the completely secular and the deeply orthodox, in early 1970s Antwerp. Based on a novel by Carl Friedman, the film is about the betrayal and coercion of religion and its ability to heal and hold together what would otherwise fall apart.[22] Well-meaning and occasionally sensitive, *Left Luggage* is concerned once again with the heroism of the fallen, the courage that emerges from the layers of repression and pretense, and the truth that is concealed under self-deception and obsession.

It is also a kitschy and at times ignorant film, which only reinforces the sense that even as it addresses the attempt by individuals and communities to forge ahead as if the catastrophe had never happened and the world that was lost is still within reach, it simultaneously reflects the total eradication of the past and the inability of the present to reconstruct it faithfully, if only as a cinematic image. This is the story of Chaja Silberschmidt (Laura Fraser), a fun-loving but earnest twenty-year-old student of philosophy, anti-bourgeois rebel, and (somewhat disillusioned) proponent of free love, who becomes a nanny for the Kalmans, a Hasidic family, where she must confront both the antisemitism of gentile society and the rigidly conservative traditions of orthodox Judaism.

While there initially seems to be nothing in common between her secular parents and her new employers, it soon transpires that both are still obsessed with the trauma of the Holocaust. Chaja's father (Maximilian Schell) is compulsively searching for the two suitcases filled with personal belongings he had buried somewhere in Antwerp before being deported to the camps. Her mother (Marianne Sagebrecht), also a survivor of the camps, is just as compulsively preoccupied with baking and weaving. But as she escapes the oppressive atmosphere of her home to the radically different environment of an orthodox household, Chaja discovers that the Kalmans too live under the shadow of the catastrophe. Increasingly attached to their four-year-old son Simcha (Adam Monty), Chaja traces his inability to speak to his harsh treatment by his father (Jeroen Krabbé), who is overwhelmed by a deep sense of guilt for having helplessly watched his own father and brother being hanged in a concentration camp for refusing to curse the Torah. While Mr. Kalman cannot show his son any love, Simcha responds to Chaja's affection and joie de vivre and is well on the way to recovery when he accidentally drowns in the pond next to which he had learned to love, be loved, and thus to speak. The community accuses the outsider Chaja of having poisoned the boy's mind, but Mrs. Kalman (Isabella Rossellini), who has formed a deep bond with this liberated young woman, absolves her of guilt and pronounces her as having surpassed all the daughters of Israel. This in turn leads to a reconciliation of sorts between Chaja and her own father, as she joins him in his endless search for the lost memories buried somewhere under the city's postwar tenements.

Left Luggage thus highlights the fate of the second generation, whose members have, until recently, received little attention, and simultaneously dispels some of the misconceptions about post-Holocaust Jewish life. Rather than presenting assimilation as the best remedy to the trauma, the film depicts secular Jews as incapable of communicating with the rest of the world just as much as with their own children. Similarly, instead of portraying the orthodox as an anachronistic but nevertheless cohesive and warm community, the film insists on the inarticulate tensions, phobias, and manic obsessions that lurk just under the surface.

Both the secular and the religious families, both the survivors and their children, share the same quality of heroic anti-heroes. With the partial exception of the somewhat too angelic Chaja, they are all morally flawed, emotionally mutilated, spiritually vulnerable, and socially insecure. They share the condition of exile, never entirely belonging to any social or political framework beyond their own identity as Jews and survivors. The Kalmans and their community expect nothing else; the Silberschmidts live one life out of the home and another within it. Chaja, the liberated rebel, feminist, antiwar activist, and sexual revolutionary in tight miniskirts and flashy blouses, is ultimately sucked into the same apparently unavoidable predicament. Is this a predetermined or a self-imposed fate? Is it an imagined or an existential condition? The film does not quite grapple with these questions. Encountering antisemitism from her best friend and fellow rebel, and also from the degenerate concierge at the Kalmans' tenement, Chaja seems to be on the verge of reclaiming her Jewish identity and turning her back on the rhetoric and playacting of the 1968 student revolution. She accepts that both the parents she had loathed for their endless carping about a lost past, and the strange-looking orthodox Jews she despised for their oppression of women and children and rejection of modernity, are, in their respectively imperfect and often wrongheaded ways, trying to cope with the consequences of a disaster for which no sure cure has yet been invented. She ends up loving them for their faults as much as for their merits.

At the core of this film, however, is the sense of guilt shared by both fathers. One is guilty for being unable to remember where he hid his suitcases, which represent the memory of his family destroyed in the Holocaust; the other is guilty for not having died with his father and brother when they stood up to the Nazis and refused to relinquish their faith. This guilt obstructs and poisons their relationships with their children. Both fathers love their children excessively and do not know how to express their love; their fear of losing them, and of the unbearable pain such loss would entail, encrusts them in a protective shield that inevitably brings about that very consequence with the tragic irony of a self-fulfilling prophecy. Yet the only way to recover their lost children is to come to terms with what is unrecoverable, the losses of the past. They must tear down their heroic facades and admit their weakness and vulnerability, their need for compassion and understanding. In other words, they must complete the process of mourning that will ultimately consign the dead to oblivion. It is only when Mr. Kalman remembers himself as a child exposed to the horror of the camps that he can grasp what his own son is subjected to, being made to pay for another child's failure to die for his father's faith. In its own somewhat inarticulate way, then, *Left Luggage* touches a crucial point in the legacy of the "Jew" as anti-hero: that this anti-heroic stance is far more heroic than all the pyrotechnics of battle and sacrifice, for it compels its carriers to concede their feelings of guilt for having survived the inferno and to lay the ghosts of the past to rest. Only this can liberate their children from guilt for events that occurred before they were born and from the ghosts of people they never knew.

VICTIMS INTO SABRAS

In *Left Luggage* the Jews are victims of their pasts, their traumas, and their traditions, but also of contemporary prejudice and antisemitism. They are victims of others' ignorance of their own lives and fate, but also of their own ignorance of the rest of the world and of each other. Their ignorance is matched by that of the filmmaker. Thus Simcha is buried in a coffin by an orthodox Jewish community that would have only buried its dead wrapped in a shroud, and the Yiddish spoken by the Jews sounds more like *"mauscheln"*—the mutilated German that was derisively ascribed to the Jews—than like the living language that would have been spoken by this community.

Ignorance of Jewish life in the Diaspora—combined with prejudice as well as ideological barriers to empathy—is not reserved to European film-makers, however. An important genre of Israeli films has now investigated the Zionist image of the "Diaspora Jew," the paradigmatic anti-hero of national revival, who must be transformed into the "new Jew," the Hebrew pioneer and warrior, and later into the Israeli citizen and soldier, in order to enter the utopia of Jewish national existence. Such films as *Left Luggage* and *The Quarrel* juxtapose the "Jew" as a defeated, humiliated, and morally flawed anti-hero with this same character's heroic, Phoenix-like ability to rise again from the ashes and rebuild Jewish existence from the wreckage of genocide. In Israel, however, this reconciliation of images is far more difficult, since much of the discourse on identity is based on asserting this polarity. For the "Diaspora Jew" provides the crucial foil of the anti-hero against which the "new Jew," the heroic Israeli, can be measured. This polarity has been deeply ingrained in Zionist ideology since its very beginning. It also has obvious, albeit rarely acknowledged and often not even recognized links with the antisemitic discourse that was at the root of Zionism in the first place.

Zionism wanted to "take the Jew out of the Diaspora and to take the Diaspora out of the Jew." Physically moving from Europe to Palestine was not enough: One had to undergo also a mental transformation, whose accomplishment depended not least on "inverting the pyramid" of Jewish occupations and creating a "healthy" society, the majority of whose population would be farmers and workers.[23] But upon arrival in Palestine, the Zionists found that while they may have left their old enemies behind in Europe, and even if they shed their "Diaspora traits" in the new land, the land was not empty and its population was increasingly resentful of the growing numbers of colonizers arriving from overseas.

Thus the picture is further complicated by the fact that the "new Jew" had another anti-heroic foil, namely the Arab, depicted as cowardly, primitive, cunning, and vicious, that is, as combining the qualities of the "Diaspora Jew" as ascribed to him by antisemitism with the qualities of the native taken from colonial imagery. To be sure, both these anti-heroes were far more ambiguous. The "Diaspora Jew," while serving as the negative image of the heroic Hebrew, simultaneously provided the fundamental legitimization for Zionism, and as such was linked both historically and often intimately to the "new Jew." Indeed, at times the anti-hero and the hero were one and the same: the "Diaspora Jew" transforming himself into the "new Jew" in a heroic process of positive metamorphosis, an almost perfect inversion of Kafka's Gregor Samsa. Similarly, the Arab anti-hero also presented precisely those qualities that Zionism hoped to emulate. For here was a figure who was attached to the land (as opposed to the Jew's predilection for *Luftgeschäften*, or "wheeling and dealing")—a figure who was always ready to fight for honor and soil—unlike the "Diaspora Jew," who cared little for honor and had no soil to defend or call his own. Indeed, the imaginary Arab, a figure taken from Orientalist literature on the "noble savage" as much as from actual encounters, in many ways "reminded" the Zionist pioneers of the biblical supermen they wished to become through a giant leap across two thousand years of dispersion. Here indeed lies one of the paradoxes of Israeli self-representation: the "new Hebrew" fighter was modeled after his enemies, the Cossack horsemen left behind in Europe and the Bedouin warriors they met in Palestine.

In a certain sense, the most radical interpretation of the "Jew" as anti-hero belongs to Israeli cinema. This type has little to do with the endearing, if often endlessly frustrating New York Jew à la Woody Allen. For here is a concerted attempt to invert conventional views even at the price of redeploying old stereotypes. The opposition between the "new Jew" and the "Diaspora Jew" in Israeli representations goes beyond anything we find in European and American depictions of Jews, including such heroic sagas as *Exodus* or *Cast a Giant Shadow,* whose aim is to suggest a constructive link between the Diaspora and the Jewish State rather than to underline their irreconcilable differences. It is as if we observed Philip Roth's Portnoy from the perspective of the Israeli female soldier who emasculates him. Whether the Jewish anti-hero serves as a defining negative image for the emergence of the Israeli hero—especially, but not exclusively, in early Israeli representations—or subverts the myth of the "new Jew" and converts him into a refashioned and often disturbing version of the Israeli anti-hero—as is the case in many Israeli movies since the 1970s—it is clear that the trope of the "Jew" as anti-hero is a crucial component of Israeli self-perception.

Moreover, as we can find in Israeli movies of the last few decades, the stereotype of the Arab anti-hero, who initially served to facilitate the emergence of the "new Jew," has been turned on its head. Now it is the Israeli anti-hero, often in the shape of occupier and perpetrator of atrocities, who serves as the facilitator for the emergence of the Arab as hero—not because of any inherent interest in representing Arabs, but because of the logic of stereotypes, which tends to dictate symmetry. In other words, this cinematic Arab hero does not exist primarily for his own sake—few Israeli filmmakers are truly concerned with creating credible Arab-Palestinian characters—but for the sake of shedding what is seen as a searing light on the allegedly failed experiment of creating a "new Jew."

This failure—assessed in moral as well as political terms—is underlined with what some would see as a typical Israeli harshness and brutality (despite its origins in left-wing circles advocating compromise and peace) through the attribution of quasi-Nazi qualities to the newly emerging Israeli anti-hero, the Jewish Goliath intent on crushing the Palestinian David and inheriting his land. It is hard to miss the irony of such representations—although some Israeli filmmakers and their critics miss it nonetheless—since this can only be seen as a sort of closing of the circle: Nazi filmmakers presented the genocide of the Jews as the eradication of perpetrators; Zionist representations imagined the Arabs to be a new version of the Nazis; and post-Zionist Israeli filmmakers present the Palestinians as the "Jews" of the Middle East, persecuted by Nazi-like Israeli occupiers.

It is interesting to note the differences between the Israeli cinematic hero/anti-hero and his equivalent in such European films as *Europa, Europa, Samson,* or *Border Street.* In the latter, the Jewish anti-hero transcends

251

his un-heroic "Jewish qualities" in order to survive or at least to fight and die heroically. His moral essence remains intact or is even elevated, but he is transformed from a passive victim of history to an active participant. In the former, however, the Israeli hero, precisely because of his actions, is morally compromised and gradually transformed into an anti-hero/perpetrator, robbing himself of the justification of the fight and making his enemies into heroic victims. The Israeli hero/anti-hero lacks the protean qualities of such characters as Solly in *Europa, Europa,* but he also lacks the straightforward, uncomplicated "American" heroism of Rudi in *Holocaust.* He is what he is: but while he does not change, he becomes increasingly entangled in crimes and atrocities. It is his insistence on remaining what he is, rather than any external transformation, which changes him from hero to anti-hero, until he becomes a cinematic Jewish perpetrator whose figure combines images from antisemitic fantasy just as much as from Nazi self-presentation. And at least part of his tragedy is that the enemy is no longer the same, even if in the back of his mind he is still always fighting the Germans.

Representations of Israelis as perpetrators are, of course, not limited to Israeli fiction but are also manifested in propaganda, media, and political discourse. Anyone observing recent events in the Middle East must concede that the explosion of violence there provides fertile ground for polarized images and self-representations of victims and perpetrators. The Jewish State has been involved from its very inception in violence. It was born in war and has lived by the sword ever since. It is still a country of compulsory universal conscription, and its young men rarely manage to complete their years of regular or reserve service in the military without experiencing at least one war. Moreover, Israel's foreign wars are intimately connected with civilian interethnic, religious, and ideological strife. They are wars over land, water, historical continuity, memory, and existence. Hence there is potential for particularly extreme violence.

But Israel is also a country composed of survivors of genocide and their offspring, along with immigrants from lands in Africa and the Middle East who were made unwelcome in their ancestral homes even if they did not encounter mass killing.[24] Moreover, the country contains a large Arab minority, and it occupies densely populated territories, many of whose inhabitants trace their origins to homes that once existed in what has become the State of Israel. To this should be added millions of Palestinian refugees, who were expelled or fled in 1948 and their descendants, living in neighboring Arab countries or across the seas.[25] Conversely, many non-Israeli Jews feel a special link with Israel even if they do not intend to live there. Israel, therefore, is not only made of two peoples fighting over the same narrow sliver of territory; it is composed of people whose traumatic past has given them a uniquely personal view on victimhood and the perpetration of violence, and its concerns and conflicts involve masses of Jews and Arabs beyond its borders.

The making of the "surviving remnant" (*she'erit ha'pletah*) of the Holocaust into the "new Jew" in Palestine/Israel is closely and critically examined in several Israeli films, especially those of the late 1980s and 1990s. Various explanations have been offered for the manner in which Israelis and, more specifically, Israeli fiction and film have changed their attitudes toward the Holocaust, the relationship between the survivors and Israeli society, and the links between the event and the Arab-Israeli conflict.[26] In the highly politicized context of Israeli life, which encroaches liberally both on art and its criticism, interpretations have been as partisan as the subjects of their ire or admiration. By and large, however, it is probably possible to distinguish three (partially overlapping) approaches in representations of the triangular relationships among survivors, Sabras, and Arabs. The first approach, especially in the early decades of the Jewish State, was infused with political Zionism. It sought to make survivors into Israelis and to conceal the fact that many Sabras were recent arrivals themselves, and it drew a positive image of the Sabra as clean, optimistic, heroic, and constructive, while juxtaposing this type with the physically and mentally "unhealthy" survivor as well as with the obstructive, primitive, and conspiring Arab. The second approach, which can be seen as a reaction to the overexposure of society to politics, sought a much more intimate view of the protagonists and was critical of the ideological dogmas that tended to erase the individual in favor of the collective. It thus had more empathy for the victims of history, which in this context were the survivors and the Palestinians. The third approach, which more or less overlaps with the second approach and has gained momentum in the last couple of decades, has some similarities with the first in that it is also concerned with politics and ideology, but it is distinguished by what has come to be known as a post-Zionist attitude that is highly critical of contemporary Israeli policies, expressing a certain nostalgia for a simpler and more innocent past, and tending quite consciously to invert the traditional roles of Israeli representations by glorifying the downtrodden (viewed as survivors, Palestinians, and Mizrahim, or Oriental Jews from North Africa and the Middle East) and demonizing the Sabra as crass, corrupt, and violent, lacking both culture and moral fiber.

One of the most moving films of the mid-1990s, which can be generally related to the intimate approach though it is not lacking in political perspective, is Orna Ben-Dor Niv's *Newland* (1994).[27] Even the title of the film is highly ironic. The single most influential Zionist text ever written is, of course, Theodor Herzl's *Old New Land,* a utopian novel depicting the creation of a Jewish State in the Middle East, published in 1902. Herzl's statement at the end of the novel, "If you wish it, it is not a fable"—especially in its crisper Hebrew translation, "im tirtsu, ein zo agadah"—became a staple of the Zionist combination of dreaming the impossible and focusing on the practical.[28] The title also refers, however, to the story "New Land," published by Amos Kenan in May 1950 in the Canaanite journal *Alef,* which expressed great longing for a different and more exotic world apart from the claustrophobic reality of the new Jewish State. Thus, once the utopian new land dreamed up by Herzl became reality, the new utopia moved elsewhere. The Canaanite movement longed to return to the biblical myth of Hebraic splendor. The founders and descendants of "Gush Emmunim"—the "Block of the Faithful" that formed the post–1967 settler movement—looked forward to a Messianic future. Romantics and sentimentalists idealized the "old country" of Europe, rich in culture and memories of past Jewish civilization. Optimists and realists envisioned the United States as the new "Promised Land" of boundless spaces and opportunities, both of which were so scarce in Israel. For the domestic critics of the new Jewish State, this narrow strip of land is as far from the myth of the past as it is from the prophesies of the future, distinguished as it is mostly by economic hardship, cultural mediocrity, and all-too-frequent eruptions of violence and bloodshed.[29]

In a certain sense, *Newland* demonstrates that this allegedly coerced transformation of identity is itself largely a retrospective construction.[30] The original Zionist myth of what has been called the "mythological Sabra"—the native Israeli/Palestinian Jew—was most clearly represented in Moshe Shamir's classic novel from the period, *With His Own Hands* (*Be'moh yadav,* 1951), whose protagonist is born not from the womb of Jewish life in the Diaspora but, like Botticelli's Venus, "from the sea." Conversely, the newly arrived survivors of the Holocaust were not infrequently described as "human debris," polluted remnants of a destroyed world, who must be thoroughly recast in the mold of the Sabra. In fact, as powerfully depicted in *Newland,* the difference between the Sabras and the newcomers was often a matter of a few years and rapid—often quite superficial—assimilation.[31]

The story of two siblings, Jan (Michael Pelman) and Anna (Ania Bukstein) Stetner, who arrive in the newly established State of Israel shortly after the Holocaust, *Newland* sketches a sensitive portrait of the encounter between the new Jews of Israel and the remnants of the Diaspora who wash to the shore. The film could have been an indictment of the Israeli-Zionist attempt to rapidly transform the desperate and traumatized children who survived the horrors of war and genocide. And, indeed, Jan and Anna are given new names (Dan and Ilana) and are encouraged to change their habits, clothes, and language so as to integrate into their new land. But the film's goal is to undermine rather than confirm stereotypes—both those prevalent in the early years of the State of Israel and their inverse version, now commonly accepted by much of the public and especially the intelligentsia.

Thus, just as Jan, who is already a teenager, seeks to erase his old identity and find a place in a nearby kibbutz, it turns out that Uri (Amnon Fisher), the young instructor who served as Jan's model of an authentic Sabra, is himself a child survivor who had swiftly made himself into a "new Jew" and refuses to admit any link to his old Diaspora identity. Jan's transformation is initially accomplished by means of a few external changes recommended by Uri, who knows from his own experience how one goes about putting on this new mask of identity: rolling up one's shorts as was the fashion at the time among Israeli youths, wearing sandals, denying any connection with other recently arrived immigrants, and calling himself Dan. When Anna visits the kibbutz with some children from the camp, Jan/Dan passes by proudly driving a tractor and intentionally ignoring her so as not to be identified with that foreign-looking group. In fact, however, such a radical metamorphosis entails much more, demanding, as it does, new modes of thinking and conduct, and the suppression of memories and feelings related to one's previous existence. Anna, who is still a child, refuses to undergo this change. She will not give up her name lest their mother, whom they still hope to find, will no longer recognize her. She relentlessly clutches her soiled, smelly old teddy bear, which remains her only prop in a life of turmoil and confusion as Jan drifts away.

The film sets up stereotypes and destroys them one by one. The Sabra is a Diaspora Jew, while the Jewish survivor quickly becomes indistinguishable from all other Sabras. The Mizrahim, seen with a fair amount of derision in early Israeli representations and depicted more recently as the victims of the Ashkenazi, European-born elite, are shown in a more nuanced manner: while the Moroccan Bardugo (Rami Danon) runs the black market and a flourishing prostitution business in the camp, Malul (Shuli Rand), who is also Moroccan, is victimized by Bardugo, and constitutes the kind soul of the film, saving Anna when she falls ill. The transition camp is a kind of laboratory of the new society in the making. In this Babel of languages, new friendships are formed, new families are made, while

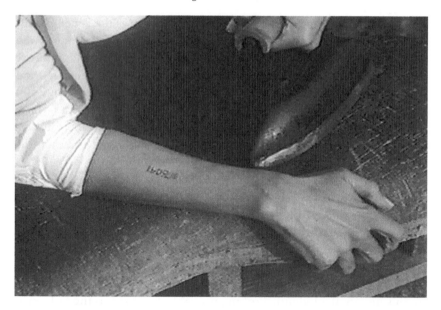

The Jew branded (*Newland*): After she overhears the Israeli doctor remarking that she must have saved herself from the Nazis through prostitution, Roza tries to erase her mark of shame—the concentration camp number tattooed on her arm—with a hot iron.

the old memories, resentments, and hatreds continue taking their toll. Roza (Eti Ankri) and Tzadiko (Asher Tzarfati), Greek Jews who lost their respective families in the Holocaust, are awaiting their first child; but when Roza overhears the Israeli doctor (Sinai Peter) who had just examined her remark that she must have survived the Nazis by prostituting herself, she burns the Auschwitz number tattooed on her arm with a hot iron to erase this apparent indicator of immorality. The process of transforming oneself from a Jewish victim to an ordinary human being thus entails a great deal of physical and psychological violence against oneself.

The sustained, fundamentally well-meaning, but also ignorant and intolerant effort to make Anna integrate into the new land is symbolized by the attempt to compel her to give up both her old name and her old teddy bear, her only two links to the world she left behind and her desperate hope to find her mother. This little fragment of the past she has labored so hard to preserve must now be consigned to oblivion so that she will be able to look forward and build a new life. As the film suggests, what distinguishes the "old Jew" from the "new Jew" is that the former had a past and the latter has a future. This is the Zionist motto; but the process of tearing oneself from the past and forging a new present calls for a great deal of force, even if the originator of this violence was the Nazi murder machine. Eventually, precisely because it was subjected to violence, the past comes back to haunt the future, and future struggles are interpreted through the lens of past events. When the kibbutz instructor throws the teddy bear into the garbage, her act symbolizes the Israeli treatment of the past, where the Diaspora and the Holocaust are seen as closely linked to each other: they should be assigned to the dustbin of history, along with memories of lost homes, parents, languages, and names, to make room for a brave new world. But in the case of Anna, or at least in her fantasies, this process never takes place, because she is unwilling or unable to perpetrate this kind of violence on herself and her memories. Stripped of them, and tucked into a neat, bare bed in the children's room at the kibbutz, she dreams of herself flying high to the sky with the only two souls she knows, her brother and the teddy bear.

Anna has become a victim of her rescue; she now seeks liberation from the freedom she perceives as imprisonment in a world without love or memory. But she also symbolizes the incomplete, perhaps impossible creation of the "new Jew," the survival of the multiple layers of identity that must resurface in memory, emotion, and representation. As the past is erased, it reawakens as dream and fantasy; the birth of the Israeli necessitates the assassination of the "Jew": yet under the surface of the "new Jew," his old identity lingers on as trauma and temptation. As the children are transformed, they even more than the adults, both expose the malleability of the Jew—as, for instance, also in the films *Au revoir les enfants, Europa, Europa, Ivan and Abraham,* and *Because of That War*—and, at the same time, they insist that the "old" identity, that hard core that forms the "Jew," remains unchanged under all the masks and costumes.

Newland plays on a number of motifs common in the Israeli discourses on Diaspora and Zionism, Holocaust survival and Israeli resurrection, cowardice and accommodation versus assertiveness and courage, the confrontation between the dark secrets and moral ambiguities associated with "over there," and the harsh light of puritanical and moral certainties of emerging Israeli society. If the conscience of *Madame Rosa* is an old Jewish prostitute, in *Newland,* the survivor who comes to Israel is made into a whore, so to speak, by a doctor's nonchalant comment, reflecting a not uncommon view at the time of young female survivors. Thus the film exposes without much fanfare the manner in which young Israelis saw themselves as superior to the survivors without wanting to know much, if anything, about their experiences in the hell of the Holocaust. But the film does not simply inverse the roles, depicting survivors as true heroes and Sabras as false ones. Indeed, it has empathy for both. Before his transformation into Dan, Jan always wears a heavy coat, in whose pockets he carries a variety of cigarettes, notes in different currencies, and other salable articles intended to save him and his sister from all emergencies. He is a sort of wandering Jew with no home, no language, no parents. When he visits the kibbutz for the first time with a friend from the camps, they are hunted down by one of the local teenagers, who, swinging a lasso, in a scene somewhat reminiscent of Abraham's whipping by horsemen in *Ivan and Abraham,* suggests the "antisemitism" of kibbutz youths vis-à-vis a "typical" Diaspora Jew, and the degree to which the kibbutz has made them into clones of Jew-hunting Cossacks—the stuff of traditional Jewish phobias. Yet Jan is also taken in and offered a new life he is truly seeking. In a certain sense, unlike Anna, he has found his future. What this future will look like and to what extent it will be stamped by the violence of the past and the suppression of memories that facilitated its emergence will become clearer with time. This is also the subject of several other important Israeli films of that period.

Two other films, made by Eli Cohen and based on the memoirs of actress and co-screenwriter Gila Almagor, can be seen as an almost direct chronological continuation of *Newland.*[32] *The Summer of Aviya* (1988) and *Under the Domim Tree* (1995) comprise a sort of cinematic *Bildungsroman* about the troubled childhood and coming of age of Aviya (Kaipo Cohen) and her relationship with her mother, Henia (Gila Almagor), in the early years of Israel. *The Summer of Aviya* opens with a play put on by the students at a kibbutz boarding school to celebrate the end of the school year. The school is a so-called educational institution (*mossad chinuchi*), established by kibbutzim in order to absorb orphans or children from broken families, mostly Holocaust survivors but including also some Sabra children, and later also children of Jewish immigrants from Arab lands.[33] The year is 1951, and Aviya (whose name means "her father" in Hebrew) is about to perform a key role in the play, dressed as an Arab so as to look like the ancient Hebrews who ruled the land before the Exile. Parents and guardians have gathered to watch the children. But as Aviya's mother arrives—her dress and makeup giving her a more "European" look than the rest of the adult audience in this parched landscape of stones and thorns—Aviya loses her voice. Henia takes her daughter home to the little town where they live, and in a fit of fury, claiming to have discovered lice, crops the girl's hair very close to the skull. Aviya's summer with her mother has begun.

The Diaspora Jew in Newland (*Newland*): Wrongly accused of theft in a kibbutz, Jan—renamed Dan after arriving in Israel as a child survivor—tries to buy off a member of the kibbutz by showing him the goods he regularly carries inside his trench coat, a symbol of his status as a wandering Diaspora Jew.

As it turns out, Henia has just been released from a mental institution. At the end of the summer she will have to be taken there again following another breakdown. The film suggests that she is a Holocaust survivor, who even fought with the partisans, and that Aviya's father was killed by the Nazis. Aviya, for her part, refuses to believe that her father died, and decides that a new immigrant from Europe who arrives with his wife in their town during that summer is her real father. In fact, as suggested by the story itself, by Almagor's autobiography, and by the sequel, *Under the Domim Tree*, whose screenplay was also co-authored by Almagor, Henia must have come to Palestine before the war, not least because Aviya was born in Palestine (presumably in 1939). Moreover, it turns out that her father was killed by Arabs in Palestine before she was born, rather than by the Nazis. Indeed, in *Under the Domim Tree*, Aviya visits her father's presumed grave (although there is no certainty that it is the right one). Almagor's own father, who came from Germany, was indeed killed by an Arab sniper in Palestine.[34]

This ambiguity and confusion—about whether Aviya is the child of a survivor and a victim of the Nazis, or the child of a mentally ill mother who invents a Holocaust past and whose husband was in fact the victim of Arab violence—is crucial to the narrative of both films. In *The Summer of Aviya*, the girl is searching for her identity, and her only source of information about the past is her mentally unbalanced mother. She wants to believe that her mother was a hero, a partisan, and that her father is still alive. But even in the wretched little development town in which they live, her mother is at the bottom of the social ladder, both because of her mental condition and because she works as a washerwoman. She sends Aviya—who now must cover her head with a kerchief, not to look like an "authentic" Israelite but to cover her cropped hair—to bring the folded washing to the customers. Aviya's status as the butt of the neighborhood children's derision and the adults' superior pity has nothing to do with her possible (albeit fabricated) link to the Holocaust. Indeed, many other immigrants in that town are from among *she'erit ha'pletah* (the surviving remnant). Rather, her status has more to do with poverty and the lack of a stable, protective parent.

The invention by Henia of having not only been a Holocaust survivor but also a heroic partisan thus serves the purpose of a double inversion. First, in this film Holocaust survivors in Israel are not the exception but the norm: In Aviya's town, most people came from Europe, either before or after the Holocaust, mostly as refugees fleeing the Nazis or as survivors of the camps. Second, Henia's presumed status as a partisan both commands respect and some understanding of her condition, presumably caused by her traumatic experiences. But third, it turns out that she is "simply" deranged. Being the daughter of a woman who has lived much longer in Palestine than most others, indeed, being herself a Sabra, diminishes rather than enhances Aviya's status in the neighborhood. The conventional Israeli view of the "Jew" as hero is as a fighter in Palestine/Israel, or as a Holocaust resister and partisan. But within the confines of Aviya's world, fighting Israelis are entirely irrelevant, while claims of having fought against the Nazis or even having been in the camps may have to do more with a desire for social acceptance, as well as with a sense of guilt, than with reality. From this perspective, the revelation that Aviya's father was killed by Arabs, which conventionally might have given him some heroic aura, is rather a letdown.

By the end of that summer of 1951, Aviya has had to mature. Her mother is taken to the psychiatric ward, and she returns to her school. She realizes that the father she had "adopted" was merely a product of her fantasy; she also realizes that the petit-bourgeois circle that develops in her neighborhood around an older teenager who plays the piano and teaches ballet will remain closed to her. It seems that Aviya's only home is the kibbutz. Yet the *mossad* (institution) is neither truly part of the collective life in the kibbutz—since it is for children whose parents, whether living or dead, are not members of the kibbutz—nor is it necessarily the "natural" environment for Aviya. The irony of *Under the Domim Tree* is that Aviya is an exception within a group of children who, vis-à-vis Israeli society in general, are themselves exceptional, even though hundreds of thousands of Holocaust survivors have arrived in Israel, and their numbers will soon eclipse those of the "old Yishuv," the pre-State Jewish population of Palestine. For even among Holocaust survivors, surviving orphaned children were an exception.

Under the Domim Tree thus complicates the simplistic narrative, according to which the main challenge and obstacle for Holocaust survivors was the need to adopt their new land and adapt to its ways. For in this educational institution, it is Aviya, the young Sabra, who strives to be accepted into a group of survivor children who have much more in common with each other than with her, and who are also certain that she would never be able to understand the kind of pain and suffering that they endured and still suffer from. To be sure, these are indeed deeply traumatized children: They long for the lands and languages they once knew and yet associate them with terror and sorrow; they hope against hope to find a parent, or for that matter anyone, willing to show them some love and affection, yet they are suspicious of signs of intimacy and afraid of another loss. They crave to belong, and since they are in Israel, they mostly do their best to shed their "Diaspora traits" and become Israelis like the rest. But now the year is 1953, and these teenagers are preparing themselves for life in a country that is still very poor, flooded to capacity with immigrants, still licking its own wounds from a costly war against the Arabs, and short on compassion, tolerance, and patience.

Thus *Under the Domim Tree* reverses all conventional views of Jewish heroism in Israeli cinematic representation. It takes an intimate look at relations between people rather than making grand ideological statements or striving to debunk them. Aviya's mother turns out to have been a hero only in her fantasy; her father turns out to have been shot by an Arab sniper without any claims for glory or heroism. Ariel (Juliano Mer), the instructor of the group, is a stereotypical Sabra, a burly, rough, good-hearted, and well-meaning young man. But Ariel is shown to be clueless in his interaction with the youngsters under his tutelage and incapable of understanding their traumas. Even physically he seems less hardy, suffering from blisters when they search the surrounding area for one of the children who ran away and committed suicide. Eventually, it is Ariel who learns a lesson in maturity and humanity from the children, rather than vice versa, whereas the institution's psychologist lacks even Ariel's empathy for the youths and causes so much harm that she is ultimately compelled to leave. Indeed, although the *mossad chinuchi* was intended to transform the Holocaust's child survivors into new, "healthy" Israelis, in this film it is the children who transform the *mossad*. The resulting synthesis is the new Israeli identity where the memory of the past must be reawakened rather than repressed, even as invented memories and fantasies must be regulated, corrected, and even put on trial in order to bring a modicum of justice to the children and their lost families.

The true heroes of the film are therefore the child survivors, those who were the traditional anti-heroes of Israeli representations, the "human dust" and "debris of humanity," the broken spirits of the destruction who had to be restored and remolded in the shape of the proud and strong Israeli. Yet here they appear as more humane, exhibiting more vitality, solidarity, and determination than their Israeli mentors. As they fend for themselves in the harsh light of the new land, they infuse their longing for the world and families they lost—along with their fears, traumas, and repressed violence—into the soul of the society they will eventually help build. Jurek (Ohad Knoller) and Zevik (Jenya Katsen), as one of the girls says, "lived together for two years in the forest. When they were found they were like animals; no, they *were* animals." When under stress, the two lads run out into the night howling like wolves (somewhat reminiscent of the boys escaping through the woods in *Diamonds of the Night,* or the children who become prey for child-devouring hunters as in *The Ogre*). Jurek and Zevik's survival under these conditions seals a bond between them that only death can break.

Jola (Orli Perl) receives the incredible news that her father was found alive in Warsaw and prepares to go and visit him, equipped with letters from all her comrades seeking news about their own parents. But at the last moment she is told that her father has just died. Not only is she heartbroken, but also the rest of the group is again deeply traumatized, realizing that the miracle they all secretly pray for will never happen. Mira (Riki Blich), as it turns out, escaped to the institute from an abusive adoptive couple, both Holocaust survivors claiming to be her parents. During a court hearing Mira finally succeeds, after years of traumatic repression, to recall her true parents, brother, family name, and address in Lublin. She cries out, "I want to be who I really am. I want my name back!" And Aviya finally finds her father's abandoned grave in a cemetery in Haifa, pushed into this quest by Mira's bitter assertion to Jola that she was lucky compared to the rest of them, because having lost her father only after the war, she at least has a grave to visit and weep on.

The only straightforward, adult hero in *Under the Domim Tree* is Vim Van Fliman (Tom Van Dee), a gentle, gentile Dutchman, former Resistance leader, and savior of Jewish children. In an inversion of the Zionist myth of the "new" Jew making the desert bloom, this non-Jewish hero is determined to grow tulips, despite the objections of more practical kibbutz members who dismiss him as an irrational dreamer. Vim plants the flowers on the slope leading to the *domim* tree (*domim* is the ungrammatical derivation of the Hebrew word *dom*, or "silence," making this into the "Tree of Silence"), to which the youths retire in solitude whenever they are overwhelmed by their traumas. Thus it is the gentile, blond, truly heroic Vim who accomplishes the Zionist vision and brings a measure of compassion, love, and beauty to the lives of these scarred, love-hungry orphans and abandoned youths. In this Vim is a kind of Israeli Janusz Korczak (a non-Jewish Israeli to match Korczak's non-Polish Pole). As the tulips blossom from under the stones leading up to the Tree of Silence, they represent the youth that can finally flourish from the rocky land of the kibbutz, replacing trauma with joy and hope.

The relationship that develops between Aviya and Jurek is revealing of the film's underlying message. During a vehement debate between the youths over the restitution agreement with Germany, Aviya refuses to voice an opinion because she "was not there." Jurek, who agrees with her position, is in fact attracted precisely to her Sabra identity: he even wants her to teach him to pronounce the guttural Hebrew "r" and plans to change his name to the very Israeli-sounding Yoram, or perhaps Uri. As he says to Aviya, he envies the decisive, "staccato" speech and no-nonsense mannerisms of the Sabras. Jurek initially believes that Aviya indeed comes from the imaginary ideal home she describes to him. But when he asserts that she cannot understand the suffering of the other youths, she takes him along with her to visit her mother in the psychiatric ward and reveals to him her own source of pain, even as he and her mother (who, like him, came from Poland) find a common language. Realizing Henia's delusion about having experienced the Holocaust, Jurek mutters: "Some people want to forget where they've been, some people want to remember where they've never been."

This last observation is, of course, part and parcel of the second-generation confrontation with the Holocaust, which is all about consciously imagining oneself into a reality one would have done everything possible to avoid: shedding the heroic posture and taking up that of the victim.[35] Those youngsters who transformed themselves from Diaspora Jews into Israeli Sabras also made the transition from the mode of victimhood to that of heroism. But another dynamic was at work as well. For this model for heroism was found in that very Diaspora from which they had escaped, with the proviso that it was associated with the perpetrators. This link, between victims turned heroic and heroism deemed murderous, created in due course an image of the "new Jew" as increasingly resembling the destroyers of Jewish civilization in Europe.

VICTIMS OF THE SABRAS

Ilan Moshenson's *The Wooden Gun* (1979) paints a troubling picture of Israeli children in Tel Aviv in 1950. The context is a neighborhood "war" between two gangs of children, some of whose parents are survivors of the Holocaust. As the children fight for control of the neighborhood, they are also reacting to the recent war of 1948 and to the newcomers streaming in from Jewish refugee camps in Europe. For the children, the Arabs are still an enemy who must be destroyed; the survivors are intruding foreigners who appear weak and contemptible. To these survivors, the young Israelis are reminiscent of Nazi hooligans. For the parents, the wretched economic conditions of a poor land struggling to absorb the immigrants and recover from a bloody war, combined with the violence and brutality of the young generation, is a cause for despair that leads some of them to leave the country.

Ashamed of their parents, baffled by the inability of the adults to tell them about the hell they recently escaped, and bombarded by their teachers with patriotic speeches and slogans, the children drift toward aggression against each other and humiliation of vulnerable adults. For them, the only heroes are those who fight and win, but their own social environment is a mixed bag of defeated and worn-out survivors, on the one hand, and militant former soldiers from the 1948 War of Independence, who groom their sons for a second round against the Arabs, on the other. *The Wooden Gun* is a film about Israel before the Eichmann trial, a land whose strong sun failed to shed light on the memories of horror locked in the souls of so many new citizens, even as the radio relentlessly broadcast appeals for lost family members, and whispered conversations about the fate of relatives were held behind closed doors. These were the background sounds of daily life in Israel shortly after its establishment, which are subtly woven into a cinematic narrative seen entirely from the perspective of the young protagonists.

The future heroes of a new nation in *The Wooden Gun* emerge from a childhood of unexplained absences and inarticulate bewilderment. Hence, their urge is to turn their backs on a past they cannot grasp and to avenge an enemy they cannot encounter by harassing the wretched survivors or turning their rage on local threats. The "new" heroic Jew is therefore hardly liberated from his past. Rather, he is a somewhat warped product of the Holocaust, compensating for the catastrophe of destruction by claims of ultimate triumph over the Arabs—perceived as the allies and successors of the German foe. These rough-and-ready young Israeli men—molded in stridently nationalist Israeli schools; subjected to the mixed messages of mourning, renewal, and militancy in their homes; and exposed to the rowdy, violent street-culture of a society in a constant state of flux—are very different from the ideal type of the Sabra, whose handsome Aryan appearance reflects calm confidence about the future and no troubled memories of a traumatic past.

The Wooden Gun succeeds in linking the creation of the "new" Israeli with the memory of Jewish victimhood and humiliation precisely by sketching a realistic, unsentimental picture of the Jewish State's early years. The young heroes of the nation are depicted as both the victims and the avengers of an atrocity whose reality is transmitted to them either through empty slogans or as unspoken, nightmarish images of horror. In depicting the hopes, frustrations, and delusions of this transformation of the "Jew," we can find some interesting parallels between European films, such as *Sunshine* and *Europa, Europa,* and Israeli productions, such as *Newland, Under the Domim Tree,* and *The Wooden Gun.* In the former, the "Jew" tries to become a gentile so as to fit in or simply in order to survive, but this transformation is never complete and is ultimately doomed to failure. In the latter, we see the next possible phase of this process. Some such survivors may end up as Nazerman in *The Pawnbroker* or as Herman in *Enemies, a Love Story.* But many of those who go to Palestine/Israel must now leave behind the fruits of a painful process of assimilation into European society—a process that culminated in disaster—and adapt to the rough, "Oriental" context of the Jewish State, to the unremitting heat and relentless prejudices and passions of its inhabitants. In such films as *Newland* and *Under the Domim Tree,* we follow the newly arrived children being forced through the sieve of cultural transformation: we do not yet know what the consequences of this remaking will be. In *The Wooden Gun,* the children have already been remade, and it is their parents who are puzzled at seeing their transformed and often estranged children.

Neither film, however, presents the "Jew" as actual perpetrator, even if the children of *The Wooden Gun* come close to killing the leader of the rival gang. Nevertheless, such associations are suggested both in *Newland* and in *The Wooden Gun*. In the former, the link between Jews as victims and as perpetrators refers directly to the Holocaust but is then reconstructed within the context of transforming the "old Jew" into an Israeli. When Anna falls ill, Jan reminds her of the time when their father begged their uncle, who became rich by collaborating with the Germans, to help him escape from Poland. But the uncle just rolled up the window of his car and drove off, leaving the father standing alone in the middle of the road. Later in the film, Anna reminds Jan how he drove past her on a tractor in the kibbutz without even acknowledging her presence. Just as the uncle did not want to be associated with a Jewish victim, so Jan did not want to be seen with his "foreign-looking" sister. (Survivors of the Holocaust who came to Israel were often derisively called "soap," a macabre reference to the apocryphal story that the Nazis made soap out of Jewish corpses.) "You were just like our uncle," remarks Anna to her brother, implying that Jan is collaborating with the Sabras just as the uncle had collaborated with the Nazis, erasing their names, identities, and memories from his mind, and thus abandoning the mother they had originally set out to find in Israel.[36]

In *The Wooden Gun* the association between the Jewish victim and the Israeli perpetrator is made in several interlinked ways. The child protagonist, Yoni Schreiber (Arik Rosen), is torn between his father and his mother, who represent the two opposite poles of post-Holocaust and post-independence Israeli-Jewish identity. Yoni's mother (Judith Soleh) lost her entire family in the Holocaust. He finds her one evening sifting through photographs from "there," and asks, "When will you tell me the whole story about the Holocaust?" But she will only say, "When you grow up." Conversely, Yoni's father was wounded in battle in 1948. His motto to his son is that the new state is "a tough land and needs tough men." He is impatient with his wife's insistence that he go to the port of Haifa to see whether any surviving relatives may disembark there. Haifa is not only the port of arrival, but also that of departure. Another family leaves the neighborhood under cover of darkness on their way "to Haifa," a code phrase for leaving the country at a time when this was seen as an act of treason and betrayal.

Attitudes to violence are molded by the children's understanding of recent events, which is distorted by the half-truths, propaganda slogans, and terrifying silences that conceal the scale of the tragedy from which so many adults have just emerged. Yoni's father (Michael Kafir)—who advocates toughness for grown-ups—tries to dissuade his son from fighting yet another "war" against the opposing gang, led by their classmate, Adi Kaufman.[37]

YONI: I can't stop it. Adi must not win. He's a tyrant, he's cruel.

FATHER: Do you try to understand him? A child who grew up without parents? No one knows what a terrible end they met in Europe.

YONI: We don't want to kill him. We'll just hurt him in a way that will make them not want to fight again. We'll break up his gang once and for all.

FATHER: You want to go on an attack that will hurt other children and that may hurt you. And which has few chances of succeeding.

YONI: And what happened in the War of Independence? And in Normandy, and in El Alamein?

FATHER: You can't use the wars of the grown-ups as an example for your wars.

YONI: It's exactly the same thing. We checked it.

FATHER: Your war is unnecessary and dangerous.

YONI: War is a children's game in every neighborhood.

FATHER: Not in our neighborhood.

YONI: But why?

FATHER: You'll understand when you grow up.

YONI: Because of the Holocaust?

FATHER: Because of nothing. Because we say so.

YONI: We know. It's because of the Holocaust. We can play like all other children. We just ask that you don't interfere.

At this point the father, who is hardly a man of peace, loses his patience with Yoni and whips him with his belt until the mother bursts in and stops the violence. Shortly thereafter Yoni escapes from home.

The children's attitudes toward Holocaust survivors are also a complex mix of aggression, empathy, and ignorance. On the one hand, they happily play cruel pranks on new arrivals and justify their actions by asserting: "Too many immigrants come to Israel . . . 200 thousand came this year alone. . . . Who needs them? They should stay in Europe." When they shoot a bird with their newly acquired wooden gun, one of the neighbors calls out, "You are just like the goyim!" In response they chant, "Go back to Europe. They should take you to Germany." On the other hand, all of them lost family members in the Holocaust, and they have relatives in Israel or Europe who barely survived it. This makes for a great deal of ambivalence, which, as the film shows, can at times trigger even greater violence. As they prepare for "battle," the children discuss an encounter with a woman who suggestively calls herself Palestina (Ophelia Strahl), a half-deranged survivor who lost her entire family in the Holocaust and lives in a shed on the beach of Tel Aviv.

DARZI: Palestina saw us stealing the boards, she got scared and ran away from us and hid behind some hut like I don't know what.

ZVIKA: She's crazy.

EINSCHWEIN: She saw how her children were shot in Europe.

SHMULIK: Her parents *and* her children. Almost everyone who was in Europe had uncles or grandparents killed there, right, Einschwein?

EINSCHWEIN: Whoever didn't escape was killed.

YONI: Our family managed to escape.

ZVIKA: So where are they now?

YONI: They're in Poland again. My mother says that now that the gates will be opened they will come to Israel soon. We are waiting for them.

EINSCHWEIN: My grandparents and all my cousins were also killed in the Holocaust.

ZVIKA: Damn the Germans.

EINSCHWEIN: You wait, one day our army will pay back all those who persecuted our people.

ZVIKA: They always killed our people. Now we'll kill theirs.

SHMULIK: Whose?

Connections between the children's violence and the violence perpetrated on their families are made in a variety of ways in the film. When the children train with their new wooden rifles, an elderly homeless man shouts, "*Schiessen! Schiessen!*" ("Shoot!" in German), laughing widely at the apparent madness of the situation. When Yoni threatens Adi with his rifle during the "battle," Adi retreats, his arms raised, muttering, "that's against the rules," and the entire scene is made to look precisely like the famous photograph of the Jewish child raising his hands in the Warsaw Ghetto. When Yoni finally shoots and Adi collapses, the neighbors shout, "It's their education, [they're] just like the goyim, Nazi! Nazi!"

The Jew as Perpetrator (*The Wooden Gun*): Yoni Schreiber threatening Adi Kaufman, leader of the opposing gang in his neighborhood, with a wooden gun, in a scene that is later conflated in his mind with the famous photograph of the Jewish child threatened by a German soldier in the Warsaw Ghetto.

The education referred to by the recent immigrants is depicted in an especially merciless light, as a mélange of Zionist, socialist, and Bolshevik rhetoric. After several acts of violence between the gangs, the school principal (Louis Rosenberg) calls the boys to his office and addresses them with all the enthusiasm of a labor-party election speech:

> We've heard about your violent and cruel actions. Children! You, who are being educated in a school of the [socialist] working class, you, who are called upon to follow the path of A. D. Gordon, Berel Katznelson, Haim Brenner [well-known Zionist leaders and writers], you, who have had the good fortune to be the first generation of the [national] revival [*ge'ulah*, lit., "salvation"], you are denying all that is sacred and dear to this people. The entire nation is looking to you, the eyes of persecuted brothers, the souls of millions of martyrs, frightened, imploring, expectant eyes [here the principal pulls the ears of one of the giggling boys and says in Polish, "you little devil!"]. What a formidable task has been put on your shoulders! What maturity history demands of you! What terrible tasks destiny has prepared for you! You are required to build and to create, to strengthen and to erect, to love and to respect! Think, think well of the wonderful role that history has foreseen for you! [At this point he smashes his fist

into a framed photograph of Theodor Herzl, the "visionary of the Jewish State," causing the frame to crash to the floor and the boys to burst out laughing.] You are corrupt children! A destructive element! We will spit out the criminals and the hooligans.

The irony here is, of course, that the young Sabras, the promise of the future, find this speech completely ridiculous, preferring violence to the high-flown rhetoric of their elders, despising the survivors for whom they are supposed to serve as a model, admiring only those who fought in 1948, and viewing the Arabs as the equivalent of the Nazis. Conversely, the principal switches swiftly—in the good-old Leninist tradition—from promising them the future to vowing to spit them out as "destructive elements." The violence of the children is shown to be implicit also in their educators' pedagogy and thus to be part and parcel of the Zionist undertaking as such, precisely because it entails the transformation of souls and territory, and the transplant of one people by the removal of another. The crass nationalism and simplistic messages of the principal's speech, also reflected in the sarcastic depiction of the school's celebration of Independence Day, fail to have any positive influence on the children. At the same time, however, the speech does distort their minds: The school is seen as the breeding ground of Israeli mentality in the 1960s and 1970s, the site at which the "new Jew" was made into a morally callous, brutal fighter, frustrated with his inability to reverse history or to find a lasting solution to contemporary dilemmas, dedicated to the use of force and reliance on an iron will, yet inwardly fragile because of the repression of past trauma and the suppression of a conquered population. Unlike the classical image of the Sabra as concealing his sweet and good nature under a thorny skin, this cinematic Sabra compensates for his bitter nature and inner turmoil by an aggressive and violent exterior.

Believing he has killed Adi, Yoni escapes to the beach. He stumbles down the sandy rocks and hurts his knee. Terrified, he watches as Palestina, all dressed in black, appear as if she is rising from the waves, in an ironic reference to that epitome of the Sabra, Elik, who was "born from the sea" without any hint of the Diaspora (and possibly again also as a reversal of Venus emerging from the seashell, this time as a siren of the Holocaust wrapped in a widow's shroud rather than as the goddess of beauty and innocence in a bride's dress). But Palestina kneels next to him, hugs him as neither his mother nor his father ever did, and leads him into her shed. Inside Yoni sees photographs hanging from the flimsy walls, and mutters, "Is that you? Are these your children? You had children. Where is this? Who are these? Were they shot? The Nazis shot them." And she replies:

"They will all come, they are all coming, mother, father, grandfather, grandmother, boy, girl, cat, they are all coming, Palestina is waiting, here, on the beach."

Now Yoni recognizes the photograph of the child in the Warsaw Ghetto, and as he recalls his gang-mates urging him to shoot Adi, the photograph on the wall momentarily comes to life: Is it he, Yoni, who is now pointing the gun at that child? For the first time in the film Yoni bursts out crying. Palestina hugs him and says, "Don't cry, child hero, boy soldier hero in Palestine don't cry." The other boys are standing now outside her shed and pelting it with stones as they sing patriotic Israeli songs. But when Yoni comes out they stop. They tell him that Adi did not die after all, and he calls to Palestina, "He's alive, you hear, he's alive!" Then he climbs up the rocks and looks out to the sea.

The association between the ghetto child and Yoni reverses the roles of the "Jew": For Adi, who raises his arms in *The Wooden Gun*, is after all supposed to represent an invincible young Israeli taught to fight back, while the gun being pointed at him is held not by an SS man but by Yoni, another young Israeli, now recast as a merciless avenging soldier. Yet this Israeli hero is ultimately tended by a woman survivor, a widow and an orphan, who heals his wound and comforts his soul not by suppressing the memory of past atrocity but by reminding him of the source of his pain and by giving him the love that his parents cannot provide. We should note, however, that the gun he holds is still a hybrid of a toy and a weapon. We do not know in which direction boys such as Adi and Yoni will evolve. But according to the trajectory sketched out in Israeli cinema, toys must eventually become deadly weapons and children will inevitably reenact their war games in battle: The "new Jew" is thus transformed into a perpetrator.

In Daniel Wachsmann's *Hamsin* (1982) and Uri Barabash's *Beyond the Walls* (1984) we meet the children of the 1940s and 1950s—those we saw in *Newland*, *The Summer of Aviya*, *Under the Domim Tree*, and *The Wooden Gun*—as the grown-ups of the 1980s. And yet, although these by now seemingly "pure" (cinematic) Israelis are often engaged in the struggle with the Arabs, they nevertheless still betray their links to a more complex and troubling past. This past may be experienced as a faint or disturbingly vivid memory; it may be direct or vicarious. But it is centered on the Holocaust and always associated with the figure of the Diaspora Jew, that perfect antithesis of the Israeli—a helpless victim on whose behalf the avenging "new Jew" was called into existence.

Both *Hamsin* and *Beyond the Walls* are allegories of the Arab-Israeli conflict and, whether intentionally or not, of the reversal of roles between perpetrator and victim and between the Diaspora Jew and the Israeli. The goal of these films is to expose the injustice of occupation; but while they deliver this message with uncommon power, they also reflect the contradictory Israeli predilection both to legitimize forceful action and to empathize with the weak and downtrodden. This is a complex exercise, because it is difficult to draw comfortable parallels between the "Jew" in Israel and the antisemite, let alone the Nazi, in Europe; also, the Palestinians do not quite fit the analogy with Diaspora Jewry. But the very notion that the link between the conflict in the Middle East and the Holocaust is not encapsulated only in the argument that Nazism proved the necessity of Zionism, but also that the Jews in Israel are reversing the roles they had internalized over millennia of exile, is so scandalous that it draws attention even when it is merely hinted. Indeed, as we will see in the discussion of Asher Tlalim's *Don't Touch My Holocaust* (1994) that concludes this book, a direct confrontation with the connections between genocide in Europe and conflict in Israel/Palestine only exposes the limits of analogy and uncovers the falsity of the increasingly common rhetoric of equivalence, even as it depicts the fateful cycle of demonization and violence whereby each outburst is justified as a response to its precursor.

Hamsin is a sensitive film that carefully weaves in, but entirely reverses the meaning of, several themes found in earlier representations of the "Jew" in cinema.[38] Gedalia (Shlomo Tarshish), a Jewish landowner in the Galilee, wants to purchase more land from the local Arabs in order to create a cattle ranch. He warns his Arab neighbors that their lands are about to be confiscated in any case by the Jewish State, and reminds them of their long-standing relationship with his recently deceased and highly respected father. The elders of the Arab village are persuaded by his arguments, but the younger generation views him as a mere tool of their removal. Conversely, the other Jews in the *moshava* (agricultural village) resent Gedalia's dealings with the Arabs and are scandalized by the close friendship between him and his Arab laborer, Khaled (Yassin Shoaf). Acts of agricultural sabotage turn the Jewish farmers unanimously against their Arab neighbors, while militant patrols by the Jews incite the Arabs. In the midst of this simmering conflict, Gedalia discovers that Khaled is sleeping with his sister, Hava (Hemda Levy). In a fit of rage, he murders Khaled by unleashing a bull that gores him to death.

This tragedy of Jewish-Palestinian relations contains various echoes of Jewish and antisemitic visions of the Diaspora. The Arab who tried to collaborate with the Jew ends up by defiling his sister and must therefore be killed. The Jew who believes that one can work with the Arabs is proven wrong by "his" own Arab helper's perceived betrayal. The prejudices of the other Jewish farmers thus appear to have been justified. The Jews cultivate the wasteland. Conversely, the Arabs hang out among the Jews, work in occasional jobs, or sell produce presumably grown by others. They drink coffee, smoke cigarettes, grumble, and plan acts of sabotage and vengeance. In stark opposition to Jewish creativity, the Arabs appear as disgruntled, shifty, and untrustworthy, in brief, a thoroughly destructive element. On the face of it, then, this is the story of Jew Süss as a Palestinian farmhand.

And yet, under this surface presentation, *Hamsin* in fact reverses these conventional Israeli views and proposes a far more subversive perspective on reality. Paradoxically, however, what seems to be a revolutionary assault on Israeli self-representation as both creative and enlightened constitutes simultaneously a return to the traditional anti-Jewish rhetoric of the Diaspora. From this vantage point, the Jews are newcomers to a land that belongs to others. They are set on changing all customs and rules to suit their own needs, yet they may also tire of the whole undertaking and move elsewhere, true to their "essence" as a wandering people. Even when they do own some older property, such as Gedalia's paternal house, they let it become dilapidated or turn it into a museum. Instead of respecting history and tradition, they destroy its reality and put its remnants on display as a commercial enterprise. Because the Jews enter the scene as a disruptive element that transforms the natural and social order, their very presence engenders resentment and violence.

Thus *Hamsin* does not provide one simple picture of the reality of Jewish-Arab relations but offers a complex set of contradictory models superimposed on each other. The Jews are big and strong farmers, more akin to the *goyim* in Eastern European Jewish folk tales than to the stereotype of the intellectual, urban Jew or the Hasidic shtetl-dweller. Indeed, Gedalia takes on the characteristics of the American cowboy, as he rides his horse in a cloud of dust swirling in the hot wind blowing from the desert, the *Hamsin*. The relentless heat represents the simmering political, ideological, and sexual tensions between Jews and Arabs and between farmers and herders in this seemingly eternal struggle over land. The ultimate release of this tension, first through sexual love and then through physical violence, is as inevitable as the gunfight at the end of *High Noon* (1952). Yet Gedalia's mother, we learn, came from a different, urban background, and wants to save her daughter Hava from the dreariness of village life. Hava, who left the *moshava* to study at the university, is in fact the only character who wants to merge into the traditional life of the village. By sleeping with

273

Khaled in the parental home they rebuilt together, she symbolizes a return to a mythical rural solidarity. Hava is attracted to Khaled—represented conventionally as a sexually potent "other," controlled by his female intellectual superior—and she seeks the raw and harsh life on the land. But Hava appears also as an outsider, a colonial tourist who will eventually end up in more elegant and sophisticated urban surroundings.

Similarly, *Hamsin* does not sentimentalize the Arabs, who take a somewhat protean role, both as an indigenous population deeply rooted in the land and as an unstable and dangerous element. In this sense, while the cinematic Jew shifts here from being a goy-like farmer to becoming a rootless wanderer, the Arab shifts from being a Jew-like victim of racial prejudice and domination to becoming a Jew-like parasite, betrayer, and race-polluter. The film never opts for the Palestinian perspective, even as it depicts the plight of the Palestinians in a much more empathic manner than is generally found in Israeli representations. Nor does it entirely take up the view that the Palestinians are "the Jews of the Middle East," with its implicit corollary that Israeli Jews are for the Palestinians what the antisemites—or the Nazis—were for European Jews. In part, Wachsmann avoids this symmetrical reversal of roles simply because the realities on the ground do not correspond to such a depiction. In part, however, this must also have to do with the fact that a total reversal would have made the Arab into the central figure in a tale that is ultimately about the transformation of the Jew.

A less subtle reversal of roles is the focus of *Beyond the Walls,* whose less optimistic Hebrew title, *Me'achorei ha'soragim* (Behind Bars), reflects its stark depiction of Israeli-Palestinian relations. Unlike many of the Israeli films discussed here, *Beyond the Walls* was a relative commercial success, becoming one of the bestselling Israeli films beyond the borders of the Jewish State. This achievement can probably be ascribed to the fact that the film spins a good tale with a seemingly uplifting moral angle. The prison setting—a convention of numerous action films—along with the violence, the emergence of heroic characters, and the clear-cut distinction between good and evil, are all obvious selling points in commercial theaters. But while catering to public taste in terms of character portrayal and setting, the film overturns some other dearly held conventions of Israeli cinema and society.

Taking place entirely within the confines of a high-security prison, *Beyond the Walls* begins with the struggle between Uri Mizrachi (Arnon Zadok), leader of the Jewish criminal inmates, and Issam Jabarin (Muhamad Bakri), head of the Arab political prisoners. While Uri is a tough, hardened criminal with little education and a great deal of experience and physical prowess,

Issam is contemplative, intellectually inclined, and politically suave. From this perspective, the film features a total reversal, associating the Jews with the underworld, sexual depravity, drug addiction, and unpredictable violence, and portraying the Palestinians as politically motivated victims of a just cause. All the stereotypes of Israeli society, according to which Arabs are intellectually and morally inferior to the Jews, are thus turned on their head.

Eventually, however, Uri and Issam unite in a mutual struggle against the prison authorities, who obviously represent the Israeli State. The warden is a brutal, corrupt official, who uses the weaknesses of both sides to his own material benefit while also turning them against each other so as to remain in control of the volatile prison population. His depravity and cynicism, and his ability to resort to overwhelming force by calling in regular Israeli troops during a hunger strike declared by all inmates, relativize the criminality of the Jewish prisoners and the danger posed by Palestinian activists. Thus the film not only turns the Jews into criminals and the Palestinian freedom-fighters into heroic victims, but it also unites criminals and political fighters against a source of oppression and injustice, the warden, and through him, the State.

In the course of the film, the Jewish criminals also undergo a moral transformation. Initially they humiliate and sexually abuse a new inmate jailed for contacts with the PLO, viewing this left-wing Israeli officer as a traitor as well as a representative of the privileged Ashkenazi elite to which they, as Sephardic Jews, have no access. But this internal Israeli rift is also resolved in the face of a tyrannical regime. Thus, by the end of the film, all sides are firmly united in their struggle against the greater criminality of their jailers. As the warden tries to break the hunger strike by proposing to Issam that he can meet his wife and child, whom he has never seen, Issam opts to stay with the rest and to maintain the solidarity with the prisoners. Similarly, Uri, whose daughter is his only source of tender emotion and remorse, commits himself to a political struggle that is certain to eliminate his chances of ever coming out of the prison's walls.

Well-acted, violent, and disturbing, *Beyond the Walls* may be seen as the culmination of the cinematic Jew's transformation from victim into hero into perpetrator, bringing with it as it does certain elements of representation that belong to the early years of cinematic antisemitism. To be sure, Barabash may have had none of this in mind. But structurally, *Beyond the Walls* presents a picture of the Israeli State as one in which Jewish criminals are incited against Arab freedom-fighters by a wicked, cruel, and corrupt regime that uses brute force and humiliation to perpetuate its rule. The film spends little time providing a context for the conflict. Emotions are strong, violence is rampant, but nuance is not always evident. As an allegory of conditions in Israel, the film delivers a powerful message; as a statement on the transformation of Jewish existence, it employs crude representational techniques and seems to be unaware of their pernicious potential.

If in *Europa, Europa* Solly joins the Hitler Youth as a budding Nazi in order to save his skin from extermination, in *Beyond the Walls* Uri joins the Palestinians when he grasps that their struggle against the prison authorities—and by extension, against the Jewish State—is just. The outcasts of Israeli society, Jewish criminals and Palestinian nationalists, join hands to bring a more just conclusion to a history of bitter animosity. In this sense, Issam does indeed become the Jew. This transformation is accomplished also through an intentionally ironic conversion of physical types. Traditional Zionist depictions of the "new Jew" liked to depict him as "Aryan"—tall, blond, light-skinned, and blue-eyed. Thus the Diaspora Jew was liberated from the antisemitic stereotype, not merely by moving from Europe to Zion, but by metamorphosing into a type akin to those collectively remembered as his persecutors. In *Beyond the Walls,* however, it is Issam who is light-skinned, fair-haired, and blue-eyed, whereas the dark, hairy, and burly Uri combines the European stereotype of the "Jew" with the Israeli stereotype of the "Arab." The hold of the Israeli—and, it must be said, by now also European—convention, that the Israeli Jew is more "Aryan," was reflected in yet another ironic twist. During the 1984 Venice Film Festival, Bakri was taken to be the Jewish actor and Zadok was thought to be the Palestinian.[39]

Beyond the physical aspect, the better-educated Issam is also the voice of righteous rebellion against oppression, a role often taken by Jews in the first half of the twentieth century. He offers not a naked power struggle, but compassion and understanding, solidarity for the oppressed—be they Jews or Arabs—and a future of greater humanism and solidarity. Thus Issam ends up enlightening the violent Jewish criminals and liberating them from the oppression of their own distorted psyches and deprived childhoods, just as he also leads them on a path of political justice. From this perspective, *Beyond the Walls* heralds the transformation of Israeli Jews into Palestinians even as it metamorphoses the Palestinians into the new Jews of the Middle East.[40]

SABRAS AS VICTIMS

Yet this is not where the circle neatly closes. The Sabra does not conveniently turn into the new perpetrator in what would be a final twist of fate, creating a nemesis resulting from an attempt by the "Jew" to break out of the original antisemitic stereotype, bringing him back precisely to the beginning—a fantasy of the murdering "Jew" who must be annihilated at all costs to save the rest of suffering humanity. To be sure, such images are proliferating once more as we enter the third millennium. Antisemitic fantasies seem to be on the rise in a variety of cultures, political ideologies, and religions; at times it is difficult to avoid a certain sense of déjà vu. But history is not cyclical, and historical events do not repeat themselves even as farce. If the new is built on the old, it is nevertheless different from it precisely by dint of its novelty, however close to the original it may appear at first sight. Still, the cinematic image of the "Jew" has by now taken into itself all its previous incarnations, and while it keeps mutating over time, these mutations are, so to speak, occurring within the same representational genetic pool.

In this last incarnation of the "Jew" as anti-hero we find the Sabra, who had transformed the Jewish victim into a hero and then found his own targets of victimization, finally succumbing to himself. For the Sabra as victim is, ultimately, the victim of his own incarnation, forced to face the enemies he created and the ghosts of a past he repressed, both of which are the inevitable outcome of his own making. Here the "Jew" is not simply transformed back into the old image of the perpetrator; if there is some circularity in these revolving images, what emerges is anything but a perfect circle, however vicious it may be. For ultimately, it is the Sabra who recognizes that rather than shedding his Diasporic, protean rootlessness and metamorphosing into an unchanging, territorially rooted "new Jew," he is the hybrid product of two irreconcilable yet inseparable aspects: that of the victim of past persecutions who cannot free himself of collective and personal trauma, and that of the avenger who must obsessively return to the scene of the crime. In this sense, the Sabra becomes the victim of his own transformation, repeatedly torturing himself even as he inflicts upon others the pains and delusions of a past that will not go away.

The child protagonists of such films as *The Wooden Gun, The Summer of Aviya, Under the Domim Tree,* and *Newland* were the regular and reserve soldiers who fought in the Yom Kippur War of 1973. Born in the 1940s and 1950s, some of them were children during the Holocaust or had just missed it; others saw the last years of the triangular Arab-Jewish-British conflict in Mandate Palestine or came into the world shortly after the birth of Israel. In 1973 they experienced the end of Israeli innocence in a war that pushed their country over the threshold, into an era of ever-increasing violence, cynicism, hopelessness, and fanaticism in which Israeli society finds itself today. This war was the end of the grand illusion, drenched in blood and writhing in confusion, a bewildering mélange of eerie silence in vast empty spaces with mind-numbing noise and sudden, mass destruction of bodies, lives, and matériel. I also experienced some of it.[41]

Amos Gitai's *Kippur* (2000) is probably the best cinematic evocation of that war made to date, portraying the initial shock, the confusion mixed with bravado and arrogance, and the grim realization that this was no blitzkrieg, like in 1967, but a meat-grinder of a war where people died before they discovered where the enemy was or which way the front had moved. Nor did it bring about any clear resolution. The war ended in an equivocal victory followed by endless recriminations and guilt, both immediate and deeply rooted. It plunged Israeli politics into a quagmire from which it has yet to emerge, and it severely shook people's confidence in the leadership and their faith in a better future. Avoidable through prior compromise, this war was inevitable because the inability to anticipate it made compromise unthinkable. And because it happened, all the wars that followed it were both avoidable and inevitable for the same reason. Which is why despair, frustration, rage, and cynicism run so deep in the region.

Kippur provides a superb example of how one makes an antiwar war movie. There is no heroism in it whatsoever, even as the helicopter rescue crew on which it focuses repeatedly lands in the battlefield trying to save wounded pilots and tankmen, until it too is shot down by a Syrian missile. We never see the enemy, or observe any exhilarating infantry charges or close combat. Most of the time there is silence, occasionally interrupted by shellfire or distant machine guns. What we see is the immediate aftermath of battle: the gore of severed limbs and tortured bodies, the endless fear and horror on the men's faces, and the quiet determination to continue extracting the human debris of war and patch it up somehow in the gleaming white hospitals in the rear.

The 1973 War was a traumatic event for Israeli society. Its aftermath had mixed results. It eventually brought about the peace treaty between Israel and Egypt, following the Israeli evacuation of the Sinai Peninsula. It also gravely weakened the Labor Party, which had dominated Israeli politics since the establishment of the State, and brought to power, four years later, Menachem Begin's right-wing revisionist party. In some ways, the war accelerated trends that had existed long before: the erosion of socialist values, the corruption of the ruling elite, the rise into political consciousness of the Sephardic community—whose loyalties increasingly shifted toward the right—and the intensification of messianic and fundamentalist tendencies, especially among the new type of settlers in the West Bank represented by Gush Emmunim (Block of the Faithful) and its various extremist offshoots.[42]

But the trauma of the war had other long-lasting effects on the individual and collective psyches of Israelis as well as on their universe of representation and self-perception. It is curious to note that Diaspora Jewry experienced the two weeks of tension that preceded the Six Day War of 1967 as a pre-Holocaust event, with profound repercussions on these communities' sense of dependence on Israeli existence. Conversely, however much anxiety was felt by Israelis before 1967, its effects were all but wiped out by the astounding victory and the conquest of vast territories (relative to the size of the Jewish State between 1948 and 1967). Indeed, there were many—even among those on the left, who on principle saw an opportunity to sue for peace in exchange for territories—who perceived the victory of 1967 as the "coming of the Third Temple," the final liberation of Israel from fear of imminent destruction and the reoccupation of the historical lands of the Israelites as outlined in the Bible.

Rather, it was 1973 that came as a severe shock and trauma. The six happy years between 1967 and 1973 were spent in an atmosphere of invincibility—even though Israel sustained numerous losses during the War of Attrition, especially along the Suez Canal. But in 1973 the image of the indomitable Israeli macho was shattered, just as its counterimage of the cowardly Arab soldier was shown to have been a mere propaganda ploy based on prejudice that did little to protect Israeli troops from well-trained, well-equipped, and highly motivated Egyptian and Syrian units. The shock of the initial attack, coming as it did on the holiest day of the Jewish calendar—militarily somewhat of a miscalculation, since rounding up the reservists directly from the synagogues was relatively easy, but psychologically devastating—evoked memories of other historical traumas in the Jewish past. As I already noted, Moshe Dayan, then minister of defense, spoke on October 7, the second day of the war, about the possible destruction of the Third Temple, implying that Israel might actually be overrun by the enemy in the north and the south.[43] But when people spoke of the end of the Temple, they had also a much closer trauma in mind, one which was always at the core of Israeli identity and that surfaced now at the moment of perceived imminent destruction (a view that was more a reflection of deep-seated existential anxiety than of military reality).

Dori Laub, founder of the Fortunoff Archive of videotaped Holocaust testimonies at Yale University and a psychoanalyst who himself survived the Shoah as a child, has commented that confrontation with the repressed memories of the event often comes when one experiences another trauma as a "second Holocaust." Indeed, Laub became interested in this phenomenon when he worked with Israeli soldiers who suffered from battle fatigue

syndrome during and after the Yom Kippur War (a psychological phenomenon that was only recognized by the Israeli military at that time due to its
massive incidence). As it turned out, large numbers of troops suffering
from battle fatigue relived the trauma of experiencing the Holocaust as
children, growing up with parent survivors, or being exposed to images
and visions of the Holocaust throughout their childhood.[44]

Kippur succeeds in touching on this issue with a great deal of subtlety.
Here is the moment in which the tough "new Jew," the Israeli combat
soldier, is reduced to what had made him what he is and yet what he had
always desperately sought to repress, forget, and avoid. What both legiti-
mizes his existence and threatens to undermine it—his past as a "Jew," a
persecuted, helpless victim—is a stereotype that Israeli identity must by
definition negate. Both the frantic fragility of Israeli identity and its immense strength are at the core of this link: I cannot become again what I
was, but what I am is the precise consequence of that past existence. There
is something fanatic and maniacal about this identity, but it is at the same
time chillingly sober and reconciled with the omnipresence of horror and
destruction. There is an element of paranoia in it, but even more so of
realism—it is ultimately based on a sense of loss that cannot be compensated,
and on a recognition that, just beyond one's vision, lurks a threat that must
be thwarted without distracting one from the road stretching ahead. It is
a state of traumatized readiness, where present mayhem can only evoke
the past yet compels one to concentrate strictly on the present.

Two brief scenes in *Kippur* capture this conundrum with almost perfect
understatement. As the main protagonist Weintraub (Liron Levo) and
Klauzner (Uri Ran Klauzner), the team's doctor, are resting between missions, they begin a casual conversation that rapidly changes into something quite different:

> WEINTRAUB: Don't you miss home?
>
> KLAUZNER [rolling a cigarette for Weintraub]: You know, I had a Belgian
> grandfather, who could roll cigarettes in the dark with one hand.
>
> WEINTRAUB: Your grandfather was Belgian? Mine was a banker in Milan.
>
> KLAUZNER: In Milan?
>
> WEINTRAUB: Yes. I thought you were Polish.
>
> KLAUZNER: I'm half-Belgian and half-Polish. When my mother fled with
> me from the Nazis in Poland when I was two years old we escaped to
> Belgium, to Brussels. There they caught her. Before they caught her and
> sent her to the camps she managed to send me to some adoptive family

and I was raised there. I didn't even know that I was Jewish. Poor thing, when she came back from the camps she began looking for me. And when she arrived I didn't even recognize her, I didn't know this was my mother. I didn't want to go with her. So I stayed there and that was it, I grew up in Belgium.

WEINTRAUB: So what happened to your mother?

KLAUZNER: She passed away, after about half a year, probably of a broken heart, or something.

WEINTRAUB: Just imagine. I thought of telling you about missing my girlfriend and got from you a story about your mom and the Nazis.

KLAUZNER: At least it's good to be able to miss something that exists.

After the helicopter is shot down and the rescue team is itself rescued and taken to a hospital, Klauzner calmly briefs the hospital doctor about the condition of his comrades. When the doctor asks him, "Are you wounded?" he responds: "I want to be with my mother," and then seems to lapse into a coma (as happened with the doctor who was actually with Gitai's rescue team in 1973).[45]

Born in 1950, Gitai, whose original family name was Weintraub, was a reserve soldier in 1973 and participated in helicopter rescue missions along the Syrian front until his chopper was shot down and he was severely wounded. Gitai's father was a Bauhaus architect, and his mother was born in Palestine when it was still under Ottoman rule. Similarly, his protagonists have been gathered from all corners of the earth, remnants of events they know little about and finding themselves in a war which is yet another maelstrom of destruction and bewilderment. And all the while they are trying to discover who and what they are. It is hardly surprising that in the early 1990s, Gitai directed three films focused on the legend of the Golem.[46]

The trauma of 1973 also saw the "return" of Israelis to the Holocaust, and through it–however crooked that path might have been—to Jewish identity in the Diaspora, not only as trauma but also as an object of empathy, knowledge, and fantasy. This "return" entailed dialogue with survivors and visits to the killing sites; but it also meant visits to the sites of present and former Jewish life, study of the past, and, not least, it provided a new focus for the creative imagination. The hubris of (imagined) Israeli prowess culminated not merely in near-defeat for the military but also in the nemesis of recurring (irrational) Holocaust anxiety. Yet this recognition of shared fates and historical trajectory could either moderate or radicalize the two polar perceptions of the Israeli: either as a righteous hero avenging his murdered people, or as a perpetrator polluted by the murderers.

Repeated trauma may breed fanaticism, irrationalism, and messianism, just as it can call forth tolerance and restraint, often in the very same society, or even in a single psyche. Thus the Sinai Peninsula was evacuated and a peace treaty was signed with Egypt. But the occupied West Bank was transformed by its settlers' fantasy into the biblical land of Judea and Samaria, whose "reconquest" was a matter of historical and divine justice. Some are still dreaming of bringing back the Messiah by pitching tents on hilltops and stealing Palestinian land; others are beset with memories of a past catastrophe and struggle increasingly in vain to prevent what they see as its approaching recurrence.

THE "RETURN" TO THE HOLOCAUST

Interestingly, Asher Tlalim's film *Missing Picture* (1989) also explored the traumatic impact of the Yom Kippur War on the lives of its victims. Only then did he turn to what he termed "the ultimate trauma which overshadows all the static memories of our daily life: the Holocaust."[47] This resulted in Tlalim's remarkable *Don't Touch My Holocaust* (1994). The film is about the "return" to the Holocaust by an Israeli generation that had previously rejected its hegemonic hold on public discourse; its "discovery" by the Oriental Jews, or Mizrahim, who had hitherto seen it as an instrument of Ashkenazi moral and political dominance; and its emergence in the consciousness of Israeli Arabs, who have mostly viewed it as a legitimizing tool for the State's policies of segregation, dispossession, and repression. Based on David (Dudi) Maayan's play *Arbeit macht frei vom Toitland Europa* (Work frees from the deathland of Europe), performed in Israel and Germany between 1993–1996, the film also investigates the making of the play and its effects on the actors and the participating audience.[48]

Don't Touch My Holocaust is the Israeli equivalent of Claude Lanzmann's *Shoah*. It is far less reverential and far more outrageous, politically incorrect, and artistically experimental. But it is an exploration of memory and its loss, and in a certain sense it is more respectful of the witnesses, and more overwhelmed and mystified by the trauma, than *Shoah*. Lanzmann's obsessive preoccupation with the minutiae of the event makes him strip, cut open, and then discard the individuals whose witnessing makes up the backbone of his film. But *Shoah* is an attempt to comprehend the Holocaust by one who had not experienced it, whereas *Don't Touch My Holocaust* is an exploration of the Shoah's impact on the second generation of those living in its shadow: Israeli Jews, Israeli Arabs, and Germans. Made by members of the second generation and conceiving this group as its target audience, the film is dedicated to the lingering memory of the victims while providing a record for posterity, not of what actually happened but of the event's curious predilection to be simultaneously remembered and forgotten even by those who had the greatest obligation always to remember and never to forget. I, too, belong to that generation, which is still struggling with and against the memory of catastrophe.

Don't Touch My Holocaust operates on three levels in two locations. Its main characters represent several types of relationships that exist between contemporary identity and past atrocity. The central figure, linking the survivors and the second generation, is Smadar (Madi) Yaaron-Maayan, who plays both a fictional survivor, Zelma Grinwald, and herself, a young Israeli woman obsessed with the memory of her deceased father, a Holocaust survivor who symbolizes her own link to Europe and the Shoah.

Three figures represent the complex links between the Holocaust and Israeli identity among the Mizrahim: Dudi Maayan (director of the play), Asher Tlalim (director of the film), and the actor Muni Yosef. Maayan and Tlalim are of Moroccan origin, while Yosef is of Iraqi background. In the film, Muni also doubles as Zelma's disturbed son, Muni, whose survivor mother is paranoically overprotective and yet compulsively reenacts her Holocaust experience to the point of transforming the boy into an imaginary participant in the horror.

Finally, the perverse relationship of Israeli Arabs with the Holocaust is represented by the actor Khaled Abu-Ali. Khaled plays himself, an Israeli Arab torn between his realization of the enormity of the Holocaust and his loyalty to his own family, community, and national identity. He also plays Zelma's Arab housecleaner, whom she subjects to a torrent of patronizing abuse. Here the film exposes the manner in which the Holocaust polluted the minds even of those who were its victims, and it strives to undermine our comforting tendency to perceive the survivors as morally elevated by their encounter with inhumanity.

These three levels of interaction with the Holocaust are explored in two polar geographical locations. First, we join the troupe on a journey of memory exploration in Israel. Here all the conventions of Holocaust discourse in the Jewish State are challenged and confronted: the views, rationalizations, and prejudices of the political left and the right; the Jews and the Arabs; the Ashkenazim and the Mizrahim; and the survivors and the second generation. The film refuses to yield to any single perspective and interpretation, whether its source is strident, nationalist Zionism, self-righteous political correctness, self-interested Arab-Palestinian diminution and instrumentalization of the Jewish catastrophe, or self-legitimizing Ashkenazi monopolization of the event. It must be said that only an Israeli film can undertake such an unsparing examination of identity with any measure of success. No European or American filmmaker would have the sensibilities needed for this task, nor the courage and moral authority to step on so many toes and to unravel so many opposing myths. For that matter, even when compared to several other important Israeli films on this topic, *Don't Touch My Holocaust* stands out as a unique work, distinguished by its combination of energy and subtlety, ruthlessness and self-criticism, mockery of deeply entrenched platitudes, and empathy for the true victims of inhumanity.[49]

The second geographical location in which this complex of split memories and identities is explored is Germany. This, by and large, is a less successful part of the film, essentially because the filmmaker and his team are far less familiar with the complexities of German memories and confrontations with the past. Hence we encounter a fair amount of clichés about and by Germans—as self-flagellating, former members of the 1968 student revolution; beer-guzzling burghers; guilt-ridden children of Nazis; or racist neo-Nazis—that tell us much more about Israeli (and Arab) prejudices vis-à-vis the Germans than about the Germans themselves. Nevertheless, what makes the transition to Germany crucial is its effect on the various Israeli perspectives and self-perceptions.

The name of the film refers to many of these perspectives. On one level, it has to do with the domestic Jewish-Israeli debate over ownership of the Shoah. Thus the film confronts and ultimately rejects the argument that the Holocaust is exclusively the affair of European Jewry and has no relevance for the Mizrahim. It also refers to the Jewish-Arab competition over atrocity: the Jews claim a uniqueness of suffering that may justify otherwise unacceptable actions, while the Palestinians claim that Israeli Jews are enacting upon them what the Germans did to their forefathers. This argument too is rejected by the film, without thereby diminishing in any way its criticism of Israeli occupation policies and the use of the Holocaust as a tool for legitimizing repression. Tlalim's title may also be an ironic reference to Claude Lanzmann's assertion of cinematic monopoly over the event, according to which the only film that could be made on the Holocaust was his own *Shoah*.[50] Finally, the title refers to the history of the film's own making. Seeking funding for the production, Tlalim turned to the German television network ZDF. But instead of supporting him, ZDF, along with the European network ARTE, sent German film director Andres Veiel to make his own film of the play. Veiel's film, *Balagan* (1993), which was much more generously funded, was actually screened before Tlalim's, winning several awards. Clearly, Tlalim resented the fact that his idea had been ripped off by none other than a German corporation and a German filmmaker.

Indeed, if *Don't Touch My Holocaust* is weakest where it concerns the German scene, *Balagan* serves as a useful demonstration for the persistence in Europe of precisely those stereotypes that Tlalim and Maayan have tried so hard to dismantle. Without going into a detailed analysis of Veil's film, suffice it to note that—as some of its more astute critics have pointed out—*Balagan* misinterprets the preoccupation of the play, *Arbeit macht frei*, with the conundrum of post-Holocaust Israeli identity, by presenting it as Jewish-Israeli self-recrimination. A German film about an Israeli play, which criticizes the Israeli obsession with the Holocaust and Israeli policies vis-à-vis the Palestinians, obviously has different meanings from an Israeli film on the same topic. This would be the case even for a much subtler film than Veil's. The assumption here seems to be that if Israelis can say that the Holocaust has been exploited by the Jews for their own ends, then there is no reason for Germans to keep quiet about this issue. But, of course, when Germans such as the author Martin Walser speak about the instrumentalization of the Holocaust, they have no interest whatsoever in the burden of the event on Jewish identity but rather wish to remove what they perceive as an obstacle on the path to a normalization of German identity. In other words, they want "finally" to "liberate" Germany from the stranglehold of the Holocaust.[51]

Apart from providing a simplistic political view of the Holocaust's impact on Israeli politics especially vis-à-vis the Palestinians, *Balagan* is also much more preoccupied with the scenes of nudity and violence in the play. Indeed, rather than seeing them as criticism of the predilection by postwar filmmakers to exploit the Holocaust as a setting for particularly titillating plots, not to mention the porn industry's attraction to the camps, Veil falls directly into the trap set for him by Maayan. European critics of *Balagan,* which was generally very well received, were complicit in sanctioning and further disseminating this distorted, voyeuristic perception of the Holocaust. Thus, for instance, the German paper *Die Tageszeitung* described Madi as playing the role of an "anorectic ghetto whore." Nothing could better expose the persistence of images in the mind of this writer, and probably of many of his readers, of starved Jews as suffering from their own diseases and of women victims as willing sexual objects. A French film journal, for its part, saw *Balagan* as providing a "restrained" version of the play, and went on to describe *Arbeit macht frei* as nothing but a "sexualization of the Shoah."[52]

In the present context it is ironic that two films about a play intended to break down barriers and conventions betray such an inability to understand the other side. While *Don't Touch My Holocaust* presents Germans through the prism of its makers' prejudices, *Balagan* provides a reassuringly stereotypical portrayal of the Holocaust, Israeli Jews, and Arabs. In yet another ironic twist, *Don't Touch My Holocaust* uses clips from the Polish film *Ambulance* (1962), made by Wajda's former assistant Janusz Morgenstern. This fifteen-minute film, which lacks any dialogue and evokes in an indirect manner the fate of Janusz Korczak and his children, was considered to be one of the classics of Holocaust cinema of its time, although it lacks any direct reference to Jews. Tlalim, for his part, makes no reference to the origins of this film-within-a-film. Because it is a stark, black-and-white depiction of a single scene, *Ambulance* can at first be mistaken by the audience for a documentary. But as the film is shown, Zelma steps in front of the screen and points out the makeup on the actor's face.[53]

Tlalim, who adopts Lanzmann's position and rejects all documentary footage in favor of contemporary reflections, memory, or overt acting, thus exposes the thin line separating documentation and fiction. Using a film as a documentary and then "exposing" it as fiction is a comment on the limitations of both fiction and documentation in representing the Holocaust. It may also be a more direct criticism of a specific film that was certainly not about "my Holocaust" in that, like so many movies produced at the time, it evaded the fact that the event was first and foremost about killing Jews. Conversely, while Tlalim's film avoids Nazi footage, it presents itself as entirely truthful. As Maayan says, he and his team interviewed hundreds of witnesses in order to come as close as possible to the "living material." Consequently, he argues, "everything said in the play was said before by someone," that is, by a witness. This, says Maayan, was part of the creation of "the lexicon of the language of the play."

Hence *Don't Touch My Holocaust* is both an intensely personal film and a uniquely powerful statement on the fate of the "new Jew" (and, to a lesser extent, of the non-Jewish Israeli citizen) at the turn of the century. A mélange of intimate confessions, testimonies, insightful observations, farce, comedy, and collective humiliation and degradation, the film pokes a finger deep into the Israeli psyche and reveals that half a century after the Holocaust and the establishment of the Jewish State, the "new Jew" of Zionist aspirations is perhaps more than ever the victim of the circumstances of his own creation.

The first part of the film, entitled "Through the Mirror," is an exercise in introspection by second-generation Israelis, which concludes with their realization of being traumatized by an event that they did not experience. The subjects' inability to find any direct access to the Holocaust is a function not only of the fact that it occurred before they were born but also because it was perpetrated against Jews whose very existence was allegedly in total contradiction to that of their own "new" Israeli identity. They ask, "Where did it all begin?" For Madi, "it all began with the great despair. . . . It began with the great expulsion." But what is it that began? Ultimately, they are seeking the roots of the Holocaust, because those roots have been attributed directly to the need to fabricate a "new Jew." But this also means that they are seeking their own beginning, tracing it back to the inferno in which the old identity was incinerated. They know that, unlike the mythological Sabra, they were not born "from the sea," but from the despair of the great destruction. For Dudi Maayan "it began at a very clear point in the present," when he and his troupe "began to go on creative journeys forward and backward" in time. Thus "the real beginning . . . is the moment I arrived at Acre," in other words, when they began working on *Arbeit macht frei*. And crucial to the making of the play, just as much as to its intended message, was the recovery of the troupe's links to the Holocaust and thus the roots of their own identities.

Initially, they know very little. When Maayan asks his colleagues in 1989 what is the meaning of the term "Arbeit macht frei," neither Muni nor Khaled have any idea. Only Madi, who is already consciously obsessed with the subject, provides what sounds almost like a textbook definition: "Work liberates. That's the sign that was at the entrance to the concentration camps, labor camps, and extermination camps, during World War II, by the Nazis." For Maayan, the inability of Israelis to remember key terms in their own recent history is a measure of trauma and anxiety rather than ignorance. He argues that "this phenomenon," whereby "you erase entire units of memory," is the consequence of this memory being "made up of millions of traumatic events. Wherever I go and point a finger—something has happened, something has happened . . . But because it is a burden, such a heavy burden, you don't want to remember it, you forget it."

It is in order to plug this memory hole as well as to understand its causes that the group sets out to interview hundreds of people: Not only survivors, but also members of the second generation like themselves, so many of whom live in families of, or in close proximity to, survivors. And soon they discover that the main conundrum of post-Holocaust Jewish identity is that telling the event to the children was just as damaging to them as not telling it. In other words, neither silence nor speech could normalize the atrocity or diminish the effects of the trauma and its capacity to infect subsequent generations. Thus one young woman remembers her grandfather telling her that

> he came from Ukraine and had there a very large family with ten siblings. He always told them that they had to flee and go to Israel and they told him that he understood nothing, and [she remembers him saying] that he was smart and left before [the Holocaust] and they all stayed and perished. He says the Germans are a bad people and we shouldn't go back, that our place is here, that's it. He used to say it many times, he kept repeating it. That's a very strong memory since no one else would tell, even though there are lots of survivors and victims on both sides [of her family].

This woman also remembers "teachers in school with numbers on their arms. I always . . . thought, where had they been and what happened to them and what happened to their families? It always preoccupied me a great deal." And then there were movies, which seem to have implanted images in her mind that the stories could not provide. Hence she remembers, "many of my dreams . . . had elements of the Holocaust, that I'm in conflict with the Nazis or I'm running away or I'm dead, they shoot me, a lot of things that apparently entered into me in a very obsessive manner."

This is a young woman raised in Israel whose parents, even grandparents, were not directly exposed to the Holocaust. She both heard a great deal about it and at the same time was told nothing. There were moral lessons, such as that "this is our place" and that "the Germans are a bad people," and there were coded clues, such as the numbers tattooed on the teachers' arms. But there were no specific details, only cinematic images, mostly of course Nazi newsreels that were shown over and over again, especially on Holocaust Memorial Day on Israeli television. Another woman recalls this same relationship between the omnipresence of the Holocaust in her childhood in Israel and the absence of any explanation. She remembers "a mad woman in the neighborhood who would shout things from the balcony and was dressed in the kind of dresses such women wear, like my mother." This was apparently a survivor, and in her mind she associates this woman with her mother, who also came from "there" but evidently was not a Holocaust survivor. And she remembers another man who was "always with a transistor radio attached to his ear and in pajamas and was said to be a survivor and to have lots of rags and newspapers at home. He had a facial twitch and his head would turn up with an open mouth like a scream." For this witness, the incongruence between such inarticulate suffering and the mobilization of the event for nationalist propaganda became increasingly unbearable, not least because neither provided the actual story of the event:

> The Holocaust Memorial Day is rather hateful [to me]. It's interesting, because I think it contrasted with the actual memories that really moved me. All those [official] things at school did not touch my heart at all. . . . It wasn't truthful, it was a ceremonial event, it . . . created resistance in me, it doesn't seem right. I think that the pain is so enormous, and the ceremony is so much a ceremony, that it makes me mad that they do it at all. . . . Nowadays I try to avoid Holocaust Memorial Day.

This young woman switches from past to present tense because her distaste for the public commemoration of the Holocaust has grown over the years. Ironically, she is being interviewed by the Israeli Arab Khaled. Not having known about the Holocaust until his late twenties, Khaled was spared this potent mélange of inarticulate suffering and factual ignorance, and he is therefore less sensitive to the empty rhetoric of public ceremonies. Now he interrupts her monologue with his own story:

> You know, last year, when the siren [that signals the beginning of commemoration and prompts most Jews to stand still for a moment's silence] went off, it caught me in the middle of the street, and I stopped and a couple of Arabs made fun of me, they pushed me and said, why did you stop, why are you stopping for the Jews, what do you care? They really laughed at me. But I stop every year. What do you do?

When he starts speaking, the woman looks at him with interest, but as he reaches the point of his conflict with other Arabs, her gaze drifts away, not so much in disapproval as in disinterest. That, she seems to be thinking, is his business. "Sometimes I stand," she replies. "I think that this year I ignored it. This year something has changed."

But the Holocaust *is* Khaled's business, not only because he has now learned about it, or because he is a key member of a troupe staging a play about its memory, or because he works as a guide for Jewish and Arab visitors to a Holocaust museum in Kibbutz Lohamei Hagetaot (Ghetto Fighters). It is also his business because as an Arab growing up in the Jewish State, he cannot be dissociated from the Jewish-Israeli compulsive preoccupation with the event. Even if the Holocaust is precisely what separates the Arab and Jewish citizens of Israel, the very presence of this mental wall—much harder to remove than any physical barrier that may yet be erected—makes it into a crucial if often unacknowledged component also of Israeli-Arab identity.

The play *Arbeit macht frei* included an obligatory visit to the kibbutz's Holocaust museum; in its German version, there was a visit to the museum in the Wannsee Villa in Berlin, where the Final Solution was coordinated on January 20, 1942. Madi, in her role as Zelma, guides the group through the museum and in the process both suggests links between the past and the present and points out the limits of analogy and understanding. In the process, she also exposes the extent to which the ignorance and conventional imagination of her audience constrain their capacity to sketch a mental picture of the Holocaust, even though it presumably constitutes an important part of their identity. Thus, for instance, she quotes almost verbatim from the opening speech of Attorney General Gideon Hausner at the Eichmann trial, but her audience does not recognize the source, displaying thereby that propaganda is most effective when its recipients are ignorant of its tools:

> If I am standing here on my own two feet then I will dedicate every moment to shock you and not to give you a moment's rest because I am not alone here there are six million with me whose voice was muffled and whose ashes were buried. Mr. Richter [the judge], today for the first time I present the charge for the murder of an entire people. Does this quote ring a bell for any of you? . . . Anyway, what is very important to me is that we try . . . to understand how it could be that an entire nation followed one leader and turned the world into a bloodbath. And [that we] ask ourselves can this happen again? Do we know what is happening around us?

Madi wants the audience to think of past atrocity in terms of their own reality and yet, along with the rest of the troupe, rejects any facile analogies between the Holocaust and the Intifada (the Palestinian uprising), European Jewry and the Palestinians, the Nazis and the Israelis. For this is the second conundrum of the play/film: How can one criticize Israel without excusing the Nazis? Madi says to the audience: "When we reach the complex of ghettos and expulsions, I would actually like to hear from [you] some example of a ghetto, but a ghetto that is now in the world if there is one in your mind?" The members of the group hesitate. One of them suggests the Gaza Strip. Another proposes the ultra-orthodox neighborhood of Meah Shearim in Jerusalem. Thus they reveal their own political positions and biases. Zelma responds: "You know, I once had a boy here in the group, he said to me, I have a ghetto inside myself."

Zelma thus tries to jar her audience from conventional and ultimately comforting analogies—comforting in the sense that by the very act of making them one perceives oneself to be already on the side of the righteous. But beyond this warning, Zelma strives to impress upon the audience that they cannot possibly grasp the reality of the very thing they are observing in the museum. As she relentlessly taunts and provokes the visitors in the garbled non-language of the perpetually uprooted, Zelma leads them to a cast figure of a dying camp inmate:

If you watch this musselman, a person who weighs as much as my bones and whose brain is sclerotic, this living dead, can you imagine where— you can see how the stomach sticks to the back, quite literally—where he or she can hide a piece of food in his body, even if she cannot eat it? The creativity of these people, who had no artistic pretension, of course, who only wanted to live, I think this is one of the climaxes of that era.

The musselman takes up a central role in the film. First, this figure represents the incomprehensible existence of the Jewish victim in the camps; he is the only authentic yet permanently voiceless witness, the one that haunted Primo Levi and came to symbolize the very heart of an incommunicable atrocity.[54] And second, the term "musselman" has a double meaning within the context of Israeli identity. For "musselman" apparently comes from the German word for Muslim and the custom of this religion's adherents to physically prostrate themselves in prayer (the Arabic word *islam*, which means submission, is derived from *aslama*, to resign oneself). The Jewish musselman prostrated himself not before Allah but before the Aryan gods of Nazism, a half-dead, starving skeleton, crawling on the ground under the boots of the SS. But the repeated use of the term in the film cannot but bring to mind the Israeli-Arab relationship, whereby the Arab Muslim is perceived as both subservient and pernicious, prostrating himself before his Jewish masters at one moment and stabbing them in the back (or blowing himself up) in the next. And because the musselman remains the epitome of Jewish victimhood, this association with the Palestinian Arab is jarring and disturbing enough to evoke both empathy and rage.

In her role as herself, Madi realizes that she will never truly grasp the condition of a musselman: "I can try to get very close to it or walk around it. But to understand it?" She develops such intimacy with "this entity of the camp" that it seems to her almost "like my own family." Finally, she shows a video clip taken in 1988 of herself in a terribly emaciated condition, trying to transform herself into a musselman, and she reports: "I wanted to be very thin and I just lost weight . . . I almost didn't eat, and I fell in love with it, little by little, and then I became anorexic and it had to be stopped because it could have actually damaged . . . the inner organs." And what is the purpose of this attempt to become a Holocaust victim? "It's this impulse to break through the wall of the myth, the myth that these were not people, they were saints with a halo. . . ."

But Madi's personal link to the catastrophe is accomplished by merging, and at times confusing, the act of mourning for her father and her grief about the Holocaust, both of which she attempts to internalize by inflicting pain and hunger on herself. Thus she also tattoos her arm with the date of her father's death, as a combined homage to him and to all other Holocaust victims. She associates directly between his fate and her obsession with the Holocaust:

> Prague was my home and Czechoslovakia was my homeland. Because I lived there for three critical years, between the ages of seven and ten. . . . And also because my father is by origin Czech and I know that this was his homeland, his true home, from which he was torn away, because of the spirit of the time, the circumstances, all sorts of silly Zionist ideas, and I see myself in large part as a displaced Central European. I mean I came here but I also belong very much there.

This sense of belonging to two worlds and yet to neither, of feeling at home in lands and cultures to which in truth one has at best a tenuous connection, of fitting in but remaining an outsider, is, to some extent, both the effect and the temptation of this generation's preoccupation with the Holocaust. It is a preoccupation that both greatly expands one's horizons beyond the narrow confines of Israel and yet alienates one from everything that is here and now, either here or there:

> I think that all my work is in fact variations or different aspects of mourning my father and my childhood. . . . I miss it so much, it hurts, and it's that constant digging . . . an open wound. . . . And my father is at the forefront of it all. My father didn't live like a human being and didn't die like one. . . . He was victim of the times into which he was born . . . not only the war. . . . The way he was born . . . since he was an unwanted baby . . . his mother, my grandmother, would wrap bandages on her belly, trying to hide her pregnancy. . . . Already then they tried to cover him, to hide him, to push him back in. And when he came out he was such a beautiful baby, Aryan, you know, blond, blue-eyed, handsome, with a beautiful soul. . . . When he was twelve his parents went to a death camp and he continued to writhe through this life and suffer blows until the day of his death . . . he later ended up in Israel, but he suffered terribly here . . . he didn't belong here at all.

And so Madi's ultimate identification with the Holocaust is through her father's fate, and vice versa, her entire identity is wrapped around her father's tragic childhood that determined the course of what she perceives as a failed life.

But aside from this deeply personal, empathic, somewhat nostalgic, and obviously self-centered link with the Holocaust—Madi's Holocaust—there are other types of identification that she vehemently and angrily rejects, an officially sponsored representation that tends to be translated into a pornographic attraction to extreme violence:

What I received is really a mythology. If there is a Greek mythology of the gods, then there is a mythology of the Holocaust, of the other planet, of the people there who were gods, saints, devils, and angels. Both the victim and the victimizer were greater than life. The intensities of their destruction, of their suffering, were not of this world, so to speak. Their ability to become an opposite expression, a negation of good, was extraordinary. Look at the pornographic literature of the Holocaust: it's fantastic, very arousing. Why are there so many pornographic films inspired by the concentration camps, the German officer and Helga marching in her boots and the whores, the *Feldhuren,* and the cannibalism, the stories of slaughtering a prisoner and cooking his flesh and eating it and all those possible things that are there and all you need to do is pick them from the shelf . . . ?[55]

In yet another extraordinary scene, Madi/Zelma sits at her piano and performs an exercise in musical stream-of-consciousness, running the entire gamut of Nazi-German and Zionist-nationalist songs on heroism, devotion, and sacrifice. She begins by poking fun at the Zionist claim of ancestral roots in the land of Israel. In a parody of a popular song that represented Israel at the Eurovision Song Contest, she comments that while "the gentiles" sing of "love and such things which are nonsense," in Israel "music . . . expresses my connection to my homeland." She then sings the lines, "This is the song that grandpa used to sing to daddy and now it's me. . . . Here I was born, here my children ["blond with blue eyes may they live to 120," Zelma interjects] were born, here is my home, and you are with me and another thousand friends." As Zelma comments ironically: "Oh, what luck I have, after 2,000 years, my wanderings have finally come to an end."

Getting into her stride, Zelma goes on to compare the Nazi Party anthem and the Israeli song canon celebrating fallen heroes:

"Die Fahne hoch!" [Hold up the flag.] That's the Horst Wessel anthem. He was a soldier with the damn Germans. And the communists killed him. So his friends made him a memorial song. . . . [She switches to Israeli songs] "He had a curly lock of hair." Yes, I found all those elements in this music that express the brotherhood of soldiers. "His eyes were full of laughter. . . . Love sanctified by blood, you will bloom here once again." Blood is a fundamental word I found in this music. "We'll remember everyone," *die Ganzen:* "Those with the beautiful locks of hair and good looks." They generally have that hair, those who are gone. . . . And the girls are always surrounding them, the handsome and the good and the tall and those who are head and shoulders above, who are the first to go, and they laugh to high heaven, they were always having a good time. "We are both from the same village, same height, same lock of hair." But when they were little, when Horst Wessel was a little boy, I can see him standing in those damn German shorts with his suspenders, singing. What was he singing? I don't know. But I can see him, blond and blue-eyed, and a big lock of hair and he is singing.

As opposed to Madi/Zelma, whose link to the Holocaust is the most intense and intimate, Khaled is the most distant from the event. From his perspective, growing up in the Arabic village of Sakhnin in the Galilee, the genocide of the Jews was historically and geographically too far removed to have any impact on him. But of course Khaled discovers that the Holocaust is in fact part and parcel of his own identity as an Arab citizen of the Jewish State. As he says,

> People didn't talk about it in the neighborhood. I didn't know anything about it until I was twenty-seven years old and went to Yad Vashem [the Shoah memorial and museum in Jerusalem] . . . and then to the Ghetto Fighters' [museum] and then I started to think that the Holocaust belongs to the Jews.

Subsequently Khaled becomes a guide at the kibbutz museum. But the ambiguity of his relationship to the event only intensifies. On the one hand, he is deeply moved by it—as, for instance, when he tells the story of Avraham Bomba (actually his friend) cutting his own wife's hair before she was sent to the gas chamber—and he is angered by manifestations of ignorance and indifference by the visitors. On the other hand, elements of the present conflict constantly intervene. When he tells Arab teenagers that Jewish resisters threw Molotov cocktails at the Germans, he adds as an afterthought, "You can see this in the West Bank." But while Khaled insists on the distinction between the Holocaust and the Intifada, many of the Arab visitors see things differently. Thus one of the students asserts: "You can say that what they did to the Jews in Poland they're doing now here with the Palestinians, same thing, they are going in the same direction."

Asher Tlalim, who is standing behind the camera, is so startled by this statement, made next to a model of Treblinka, that he asks: "Do you think that what's happening in the Intifada and what happened in World War II is the same thing?" Undeterred, the student responds, "It's the same thing, yes." Tlalim persists, pointing out the difference between systematic genocide and brutal occupation: "Do you think there's the same system here?" But the student, in a line that could have been taken directly from Ernst Nolte, confidently retorts: "The difference is that they [the Jews] died by gas, in Palestine it's not by gas."[56] Two young women join in: "Yes, yes, it's similar. They're killing the little children and the old people and the women." Tlalim asks them: "And the Jewish soldier is as cruel as the Nazi?" The response is an unequivocal "Yes." On this point another Arab lad adds his opinion:

They're killing the little children and the old people

The Jew as Nazi (*Don't Touch My Holocaust*): Two Arab-Israeli teenagers at the Holocaust museum in Kibbutz Lohamei Hagetaot (Ghetto Fighters), their back to a model of Treblinka, insist that the genocide of the Jews and Israeli policies vis-à-vis the Palestinians are similar, and that the Jewish soldier is as cruel as the Nazi.

> In Germany there's a dead man and in Israel there's now a dead man. . . . It doesn't matter how they kill him. He [the Israeli soldier] kills him, it's the same thing; he's a pig just like the Nazi soldier.

Finally, an older Arab comes up to the camera and sums up the discussion:

> I say that I wish they killed them in the West Bank the way they killed them in Treblinka. Because in Treblinka they killed them in one day and that was it, no more pain, but in the West Bank they kill and torture them day after day, and it's harder, it's harder because they suffer.

As in its other two perspectives on the relationship between Israeli identity and the Holocaust, the film provides an unsparing and unsentimental look at Arab perceptions of Jewish and Palestinian victimhood. Blatantly resistant to all forms of political correctness, self-righteousness, and complacent convention, the film demonstrates that in the eyes of those under Israeli occupation, the "Jew" has become the Nazi. As we know now, this view, combined with the old antisemitic canards which were at the root of Nazism in the first place, has become increasingly widespread in recent years, whether among adherents of the Islamist movement and much of the Arab and Muslim world, or among sectors of the European and to a significantly lesser extent also the American political left and extreme right.[57] This image plays a double role, for it both denies the Jews their assertion of victimhood and also depicts them as the equivalent of those who perpetrated their genocide. Described as Nazis, the Jews become anathema; as such, they deserve neither pity nor compassion.

Yet *Don't Touch My Holocaust* does not leave matters there. It sympathizes with the plight of those teenagers taken to a museum about the genocide of their oppressors—even as the film, in the person of the director himself, expresses astonishment at this reversal of roles. And it shows the ambiguity of Khaled's figure, who is able to empathize with the victims of the Holocaust through his preoccupation with studying, teaching, and "playing" it, and through his association with Jewish Israelis, but who sympathizes deeply with the plights of his own people. Khaled thus becomes a metaphorical Jew, drifting between the world of his traditional village (or shtetl) and the modern urban (or "gentile") surroundings in which he works with his Jewish colleagues. Akin to the characters in I. L. Peretz's writings, he has one foot in the old world and one in the new, and is thus neither here nor there but always torn between the two.

Khaled tries to rationalize the Arab teenagers' reactions to the museum:

> While I'm explaining [what the Holocaust was about], the Arab person is thinking: How can a people that went through something as sad as this, how can a person, a Jew, grab a gun and murder a man, how? He can't understand it. I say, those who murder, they weren't there, in the Holocaust. Those who hold guns in the [occupied] territories, they weren't in the Holocaust.

To be sure, neither the question nor the answer is necessarily relevant to these Arab teenagers. It is primarily the Jews, not the Arabs or, for that matter, the Christians, who wonder how a Jew can commit injustice after the Holocaust. On the face of it, there is no reason to expect a higher morality from those who suffered from injustice (it is not uncommon to explain or even excuse terrorism, which is the killing of innocents, as a reaction to injustice). Why, then, would Jewish occupiers be any less brutal than gentile occupiers? In fact, it is the Israelis who expect themselves to behave differently, and because of this notion of inherent moral superiority fool themselves into believing that they can conduct what was called in the early years after 1967 an "enlightened occupation." Refusing to admit that just like all other occupations in history, this one too has brutalized both the military and civilian society, Israelis simply cover their eyes and ears and maintain that they are better than others (which depends on the object of comparison) and that the suffering of previous generations somehow makes them immune to both moral condemnation and ethical transgressions.

Thus Khaled is posing a Jewish question that betrays his own split loyalties or sympathies rather than accurately describing what goes on in "the mind of an Arab person." His answer to the question, namely, that only those who were not "there" are capable of cruelty and oppression, is similarly a reflection of his exposure to Israeli rhetoric. To be sure, we would all like to believe that at least those who were directly exposed to inhumanity were humanized rather than brutalized by their suffering. But the overwhelming evidence points in the other direction. *Don't Touch My Holocaust* attacks this comforting convention from an especially sensitive angle, by exposing the vulnerability of men such as Khaled to the oppression of those with whom they empathize, and by showing that intolerance and prejudice can also infect the survivors of racial genocide. In the early postwar years, there were those who suspected survivors of having been polluted by their victimizers. More recently, there has been a tendency to view survivors as morally superior to the rest of humanity. The film rejects both positions: There is no equivalence between victims and perpetrators, nor does suffering elevate. The only thing one may say with any certainty is that the survivors of genocide are so deeply scarred that they may pass on their trauma to younger generations, who were spared the actual experience of degradation, humiliation, torture, and mass murder.

When not guiding tours at the kibbutz's Holocaust museum or working with his troupe, Khaled can be found marching at a Palestinian funeral of a protester killed by Israeli security forces, the crowd chanting, "In blood, in spirit, we will redeem you, martyr!" Back with the troupe, he is transformed into Zelma's faithful housecleaner. Zelma does not recognize him as an individual but merely as a representative of something foreign, exotic, and potentially dangerous. She calls him Mihmid, a generic Arabic name, rather than by his given name, and speaks of him in the plural; and she wonders why an Arab would have such "Aryan" looks. She attributes to him the typical qualities of the colonized: laziness, filth, subservience, and treachery:

> ZELMA: Mihmid, come here a minute, one two, one two, about face, up down. . . . Here is my Arab! About face! [to the audience] Look at this Arab: Blond with blue eyes. . . . How are you?
>
> KHALED: Khaled [is my name]. Fine, ta'aban.
>
> ZELMA [to the audience]: You know what ta'aban means? Ta'aban means that he, that they are tired, they work a little bit and automatically they get tired, it's something genetic that runs in their veins. But he is so nice

and he is really trying. . . . [to Khaled] Well, give us some example of what I taught you. . . . [to the audience] It cost me so much work to get him [to do it], look at him, what Aryan looks he has.

KHALED [singing the Palestinian national song in Arabic]: Biladi, biladi [My land, my land] . . .

ZELMA: Mihmid, not this Palestinian shit! In Yiddish, what I taught you.

KHALED: Ah, Yiddish [he speaks broken Yiddish].

ZELMA: You give them a finger they want the whole hand.

This bizarre scene, in which the Jewish survivor of racial persecution is humiliating an Arab for his ethnicity and culture, yet at the same time marvels at his Aryan looks and strives to make him into a subservient, Yiddish-speaking Diaspora Jew (that is, into herself), is precisely the moment of inversion. Here the "Jew" is liberated from his stereotypical straight-jacket by transforming the rest of the world into the object of phobia and abuse, an exercise of such universal proportions that it ends up encompassing everyone, including the director of the play (and Madi's husband), and ultimately Zelma herself. A veritable tour de force of self-hatred:

They [the Arabs] are so sly, it's something inside them, pardon me . . . they can at any moment, I always say to Muni [her son], never turn your back to them, they can run you with a knife; but the Russians [Jewish immigrants], they are so nice, flooding the country, taking all the work places, but they stink a bit, it's because they eat herring. . . . But the Ethiopians [Jewish immigrants], they are so nice, they are like little monkeys that just came down from the trees, it'll take us years to civilize them. . . . [pointing at Dudi Maayan] You think it's Maayan? It's Abekasis, you know. They [Jewish immigrants from Morocco] change their names because they suffer from an inferiority complex, because they were not burned by the damn Germans, but you [the Moroccan Jews] were also part of their plans, yes Sir, it was a matter of time . . . but they stink a bit . . . maybe it's something in their pigmentation, and they throw away food, I have seen them, they don't know what real hunger is like that burns like fire in my bones. . . . Ignoramuses, Communists, Negroes, dirty Jews![58]

Thus everyone is infected. Zelma's fear and hatred is ultimately directed at herself, and through her it is transmitted to her offspring. Indeed, if Khaled is "humanized" in his relations with Jews, as compared with those Arabs who do not want to know about the Holocaust as anything more than the cause and the model of their own misfortune, he too is polluted by that knowledge. When the troupe visits Germany, the Jewish actors feel to some extent liberated. They perform what can only be described as part juvenile prank and part victory rite. "It was the climax of our visit," says

Maayan. "We sat on top of Hitler's bunker and sang [nationalist] settlers' songs and urinated on the bunker. It was a cynical reaction, but it touched some very dark places." Muni makes a speech that both mimics Israeli political rhetoric and is straight from the heart: "Guys . . . this is a historical moment! I would like to say that as an Israeli, as a Jew, by being here on top of the grave of that son of a bitch who determined our lives . . . [we show that] we are back here and we're stepping on his fucking bunker." Maayan echoes the sentiment: "There's a part in me that wants to dance on the killer's grave . . . as if to say, we got back at them. No, they . . . didn't finish the job because here we are as Israelis." It is only after this ritualized victory dance over Hitler's grave, he claims, that "I could talk to them [the Germans] on the same level."

But things do not work out that way for Khaled. For him the visit to Germany is not liberating but terrifying. All at once he realizes that he hates Germany because he feels that the Nazis are after him, that everywhere he turns he might be attacked by some neo-Nazi racists, even though, as he says about himself, he is "an Arab Jew." This transference of fear from the Jew to the Arab is part of the film's logic. Khaled's Holocaust is his fear of Germans. Once implicated in the Jewish-Israeli preoccupation with the event, it has become part of his identity. He can imagine himself as a persecuted Jew in Germany and refuses to leave his hotel room for fear of being chased down by racists.

By the time Dudi Maayan and Muni Yosef arrive in Germany, they have already made the Holocaust into their own affair. But they too have had to undergo a process of recognition and release of repressed memory before seeing themselves as Jewish victims of the Nazis (and seeking liberation from this newly acquired self-perception in the land of the perpetrators). For, as the film asks in a blatant, tongue-in-cheek manner: What does a Moroccan have to do with the Holocaust? As the Mizrahim in Israel have argued, the European Jews hijacked suffering from them and treated them as second-class (Jewish) citizens by asserting a monopolized "ownership" of the Shoah. And yet the Mizrahim have also been uprooted from their lands and culture and transplanted into a new and often hostile, or at least patronizing, society, which sought to change them into its own (European) image. Thus Maayan envies Madi's deeper "roots," even though she is the daughter of a survivor whose entire family was murdered in Europe. These imagined roots are, of course, part of the Zionist fantasy that was much more powerful among immigrants from Europe than among those who were evicted from their homes in North Africa and the Middle East. As Zelma sarcastically comments when she recollects her imaginary childhood in Israel, such fantasies consisted of a farmer, a white house, trees, and flowers. In other words, the Zionist ideal of life in the newly settled, ancient Promised Land, dreamt up in Europe:

> I truly believed that the farmer, all by himself, would really grow [bread] and we would see those teeny weenie stalks with little breads on top that [were there] for us to eat and be big and strong and healthy and beautiful and good and sturdy and just and live forever! And that small white house of mine was the world, nothing else existed.

And so, even as Zelma is the embodiment of the European-Jewish survivor, and Madi insists on tracing herself back to Europe, this little fantasy conjured up by European Zionists distinguishes between them and the Mizrahim. Hence Maayan's feeling that Madi has grown up in the kind of home he never had:

> Throughout my life I haven't known the ability to go back to the place where I was born. The fact that I can enter Madi's room and she tells me: I was born here, or I grew up here, and it's possible today to return to places that were there in the past, this is a pattern I am unfamiliar with because I always left places and could never return to them.

This is the crux of the irony. Maayan, who cannot claim direct links with the Holocaust, finds himself less part of Israeli society both because his past is strewn with less destruction and because he feels less rooted in Israel than the remnants of the Shoah, who came there only a few years before or concurrently with his own family. The Holocaust as a root of stability, as a home, is a strange notion indeed. Speaking in Casablanca, the town from which his parents came to Israel shortly before his birth, passing by a poster of Humphrey Bogart's eponymous film with all its romantic connotations to the war years, Maayan comments:

> My father told me that the Germans had already arrived and that they were in North Africa and it was only a matter of time [until they would come to get the Jews]. My parents lived in Casablanca in surroundings very similar to the Old City [of Acre]. . . . In a certain sense, there is a connection between my life in Acre and my family's life in Casablanca.

This is the beginning of the link. After all, the Nazis certainly did target North African Jewry as well. In Eichmann's figures of Jewish populations in Europe presented at the Wannsee Conference as future subjects of the "Final Solution," the large number of Jews allotted to France clearly included its North African possessions. But there is another, "positive" connection: The Jews in Casablanca lived in similar conditions to those of urban Arab populations in Palestine. In this sense, the Mizrahim were more of the region, they belonged more to what was to become Israel, than those who survived Hitler's genocide. Hence, implies Maayan, they have an equal claim both on the Holocaust and on Israeli society,

As the film's director, Tlalim, notes, "I went to look for Dudi's house and I found my own. The house where I was born, in Tangier." For Tlalim also has to "prove" that he has some connection with the Holocaust despite the fact that he was born in Morocco. But he does so largely through Maayan and Muni. Indeed, Maayan makes a strong argument for his privileged status as an observer of and commentator on the impact of the Holocaust on Israel. "The fact that I am not directly hurt and was not the son of [a survivor] gives me easier access to all kinds of places, which is an advantage . . . in my work." However, he asserts,

> beyond that, I see myself as a Holocaust survivor and was damaged in the same manner [as children of survivors]. . . . Most of my friends are graduates of the "survivors' academy." . . . As a child in this country I had to go through all those ceremonies year after year, to recite absolutely meaningless texts, to open up my innermost soul. . . . I was supposed to feel guilty, to be responsible for something that had nothing to do with me. So on a very basic level I was equally damaged. . . . We are all in the same boat, in the same traumatic pot.

Finally, however, Maayan claims a very specific connection to Acre that he had denied for many years, and which makes it into his home after all, a home to which he returns without being aware of it and only recognizing it as such in retrospect.

> My connection with Acre begins with the fact that I was born here. My parents came here in 1948 to a *ma'abara* [transition camp] . . . and after a few years my family left and began wandering in the country. . . . Years later, when we founded the Acre Theater Center, and came here, it took me a while to realize that I'm returning to the place where I was born.

It is only in this rediscovered and acknowledged birthplace that he can finally make his play on Israelis and the Holocaust.

Muni, for his part, discovers that his own link to the Holocaust goes back to his childhood village, Moshav Mazor (a moshav is a semi-collective agricultural community):

> We sat at the table and started searching for connections, what's our link to the Holocaust. I said, I have none, my parents came from Iraq, what connection have I got with the Holocaust? . . . And suddenly I said, hey, of course I have a link, I was born in a moshav of Hungarians who were all survivors of the Holocaust.

301

Here we find the same "discovery" of a link that is real and deep and decisive, and yet has been repressed for many years. Muni, the Iraqi, grew up surrounded by Holocaust traumas. And yet, when asked, he initially could not remember. This is not a "constructed" identity or an "imagined" community: It is located at the deepest, most crucial level of consciousness. It is, ultimately, what makes these people dream, imagine, feel, and act. This "typical" Israeli Jew, this Sabra, is the product of an impossible balance between repression and acknowledgment of growing up with inexpressible, unbearable trauma:

> In the moshav, there wasn't a Holocaust atmosphere on the surface, but there was something below the surface, you always felt it. . . . There were always some secrets that you didn't talk about, of many people who lost a family there and made a new family, all kinds of dark secrets.

Yet these "dark secrets" were not mute. As an elderly woman in the moshav tells Muni, "whoever was there and went through what I went through, some of it had to remain, in me, the children, the grandchildren." And she tells him the story that she told her daughter ever since she was a child, over and over again:

> To this day I see [Dr. Josef] Mengele before my eyes with his boots all shiny like a mirror and his uniform, standing on a ramp and people passing by him and going on two paths . . . pointing with his finger, either there or there. . . . When I got there he said: "Give the child to the woman behind you. . . ." There was an old woman behind me. I said: "No, I don't want to." . . . "What do you mean you don't want to? I gave an order!" At that moment two men took the child away from me, gave it to her, I was kicked and beaten and I walked away and I began crying and screaming and he yelled after me: "You are still young, you'll be back, until then you can still work!" I fainted. . . . And the child remained with the old lady who was selected to the gas chambers.

Her daughter, who has been standing there all along in silence, now speaks:

> When I was a child I had all kinds of fears. I would dream of people on bunks, of corpses, and everything my mother told me, and I always asked, how can a person go through this and remain mentally [sane], how can one go on living, surviving . . . what with everything we had here, in Israel, which was also not an easy life, and my parents had to start all over again.

Yet beneath this deep empathy and admiration for her parents, there lurks something else. Muni says: "I ask myself how, for a child who heard these stories in childhood, how does it affect him?" (Now we remember that Muni also doubles as Zelma's disturbed son, a role he is learning to play from this very encounter.) Both women respond in unison: "Badly." But initially they are reluctant to divulge in what way. The mother says: "There were all kinds of problems after the children were born. Mental problems. And fears." Prompted again, she adds: "We went several times to the doctor and she was given tranquilizers, and it's all over. The doctor said then that it must be because of that." And the daughter clarifies: "Probably from all the stories that mom told me in my childhood."

Finally the truth comes out. First the mother tells the story but misses the crucial part:

> It was when her daughter was born and . . . had a heart condition that she [the mother of the baby] went into a state of shock. . . . A normal girl might have been affected for a month or two. But with her it took longer, much longer, because then she remembered all those things.

But this does not make the connection with the mother's specific trauma. Then the daughter provides the missing link:

> There were problems with the girl. She was born with a heart condition and perhaps the shock would not have been so great but they didn't bring her to me for nursing, and I had to leave the hospital that day and I just went to the maternity ward, to the nursery, where the mothers feed the babies, and I couldn't find her, and I was sure that that was it, I started to cry terribly, everything turned black, I saw there was no baby, it's dead, and I asked myself how could mom stand it and I don't have the mental strength to take it, I simply collapsed.

As if to confirm her daughter's weakness as opposed to her own strength, the mother adds: "I spent some two months with her after that and she . . . didn't want to see the baby, or her husband, she was in terrible shock, [she] even [didn't want to see] me. . . ."

These were the stories and the people of Muni's childhood. When he says, "Even I, although my parents are from Iraq, even I was influenced by the moshav . . . ," the mother responds, "I know," as if nothing could have been more normal. "That's because you grew up here."

Ostensibly, then, the question is not whether one is a direct offspring of Holocaust survivors, or of European origin, or, to a certain extent, even if one is a Jew. The issue is that within Israeli society everyone has been affected. The tremendous effort that was devoted to creating a "new Jew" divorced from the Diaspora and all its phobias and traumas was negated by the Holocaust, whose repression, or distorted transmission through maniacal retelling, ideologically oriented rhetoric, or empty ceremonies, only deepened the rift between the external prowess and confidence and the internal chaos and confusion of the emerging Sabra. One had to return to the scene of the crime and tell the story all over again in order to repair the damage. But that was, of course, impossible. As Maayan notes:

> Except for . . . actually being there, we did everything, and that's the tragedy of our generation, that we weren't there . . . a great spiritual tragedy. . . . From the historical perspective, there's the Creation, then the Flood; let's say ten great events. . . . What actually happens to the individual in such times is incredible, you can't grasp [it]. . . . Occurrences like the Holocaust are illuminated events. Imagine spending twenty-four hours in Satan's court. When a man was in a camp and saw corpses being burnt what he saw was something else. It's like the simple man who saw the Prophet Elijah and described his going up to heaven in flames. Hear Oh Israel, the Lord is our God the Lord is One. This is what people inside the crematoriums said. What did they see when they recited that sentence?

The only other perspective is its opposite. Hence in the second part of the film, entitled *Spiegelweg*, the protagonists go through the looking glass and arrive in Germany. The director notes: "Only when we got to Germany we realized that there is an Israeli side and a German side." But this is hardly a novel idea, nor do the Israeli protagonists discover much either about Germany or about themselves. One is also skeptical about the effects of the play on the German audience, which goes through the now somewhat tired conventions of bearing itself and blaming or defending its parents in front of the camera. Similarly, one can find here a conventional Israeli view of Germany, tinged with a fair amount of wishful thinking that has little to do with contemporary reality. Maayan asserts:

> There is an atmosphere of deep sadness here. I look at them and I can totally and lovingly accept it when they say that they suffer every day and every night because of the Holocaust. It sounds the same as when an Israeli says it, and in that sense we are very similar, we and they. They've been screwed in one way, and we've been screwed in another way. But we are human beings, and it is very difficult to avoid a feeling of satisfaction, no, not satisfaction, but a sort of pleasure, to see them at their lowest.

Thus contempt and hatred become intermingled with a powerful longing for similarity and equivalence, not least, perhaps, because there is such longing among some intellectual circles in Germany as well. But there is no such similarity: it is rooted in the nightmare of the eternally protean Jew. It is a fantasy. And *Don't Touch My Holocaust* ultimately acknowledges this fact. The "Jew," even as anti-hero, is not the "German." The latter is the subject of another obsession. Neither the first, nor the second or third generation, even if compulsively engaged with the same event, can share the same perspective. Growing up in the homes of silent perpetrators has little in common with growing up in the homes of silent victims, except for the fact that the perpetrators and victims were protagonists in the same event. Hence, when Maayan speaks to his German audience (through an interpreter), he speaks to them about the Israeli Jew, not the German.

> We had to come to terms with our history. Our history going back from the founding of the state was untouchable and we just had to open it up to see how we understand that history now. It took us a very long time to sink back, to go all the way back to Auschwitz itself, to go back and to see how wretched our lives are. We are not special in this regard. Any Israeli, if you push his secret button, will pour it out. There is a collective anguish here, and it's clear that we had to use history, to go back, in order to reach the present. We live in this present, and history is between us and the present, and we want to push it back now, so that we will be able to move forward, and be like all other human beings.

To be sure, there is such a wish also in Germany: to be treated like everyone else, to be finally excused from the status of perpetrators, to emerge from the shadow of Auschwitz. But this is where the similarity ends. Because in reaching back, which is what we must indeed do, we end up in very different worlds.

It is that hellish world of sadism and cannibalism, torture and pain, this carnival of death and mutilation projecting into the present and refusing to let go, which brings the film to a close. Shooting this scene in Berlin justifies the entire trip to Germany. For the combination of Jewish-Israeli attitudes toward Germany and the responses of the Germans transform these infernal closing moments of the film into a liberating catharsis, even as they simultaneously implicate the audience in violence, voyeurism, and hysteria. Here we have the Israeli coming to Germany as a "new Jew," no longer dependent on the gaze of the gentile to define his identity. Simultaneously, this very same "new Jew" strips off the facade of nonchalant heroism to expose the elements of which he is made: not because he is created through the gaze of the Germans, but because he insists on acting out his identity in their face. He is no longer the morally pure, innocent hero emerging from the ashes, but is sullied by wars and violence, traumas and repressed memories, nightmares and fantasies. Now he can look them in the eye and rebuild himself. But he has no need to become an imaginary Nazi, to transform himself in the image of his opposite in order to liberate himself from the chains of a past that could not be faced, and could not be forgotten.

Thus, when Madi pulls a piece of bread out of her vagina as a musselman hiding her last morsel of food, she is transformed into the Jewish whore only in the imagination of the German (re)viewer. This transformation is

Second-generation musselman (*Don't Touch My Holocaust*): Madi Maayan pulling a piece of bread out of her vagina as a musselman hiding her last morsel of food, in a scene depicted by a German reviewer as representing an "anorectic ghetto whore."

about the Germans, not the Jews. But her action symbolizes the attempt to reach as deeply as possible into the anus mundi of the camps so as to be able to finally emerge from them. Those who see this as a sexual fantasy are merely observing the mirror of their own minds. But can we also say that in these scenes of horror we find false identification and encounter the limits of truthfully representing horror? Is the "new Jew" caught here helplessly in the iron grip of the past: the cinematic "Jew" nailed onto a chronicle of victimhood and antisemitic imagery, doomed to relive all the horrors of the past in deed or fantasy? We watch this with our mind's eye; hence, we share responsibility for what we see.

In the last stunning and wrenching scene of the film, Khaled dances madly on a table surrounded by beer bottles, transforming himself into an object of self-inflicted pain and humiliation, in a frantic attempt to internalize the horror of the Holocaust and to expose the brutality of voyeuristic humanity. Can one find identity in other people's disasters? As he flagellates his naked body with a cudgel, the Germans surrounding him reach for the bottle opener hanging by a string from his neck, happily downing their beers while they peer at him in fascination. A young woman

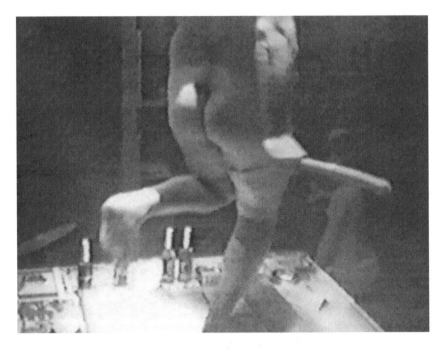

Palestinian as Jewish victim (*Don't Touch My Holocaust*): Palestinian actor Khaled Abu-Ali dancing and beating himself on a table stacked with beer bottles, which members of the audience try to open by grabbing the bottle-opener dangling by a string from his neck.

joins Khaled on the table and begins beating his naked body, dancing with him in some sort of sadomasochistic fantasy.

The audience, who a few hours earlier sought understanding and reconciliation and expressed total incomprehension of their fathers' violence, are now part of the scene. They participate in an act of humiliation and sadism, reenacting a past they wish to repress or exorcise, yet they are hardly aware of doing so.[59] Their target is the "Jew" in this reenactment of Auschwitz, but the body is Palestinian, the body that in the minds and fantasies of so many Europeans has now replaced that of the Jew and has become the Jew's victim. Yet this is a Palestinian who teaches the Holocaust, who acts in a play about the Holocaust, and who is terrified in Germany. The Shoah here becomes at once entirely universal and intensely personal: it is a site of murder, and all who touch it are implicated and polluted. And yet it is also, in its reenactment as play, a site of liberation, from which one might, absent the cudgel, begin the long path back to humanity.

Pietà and reconciliation (*Don't Touch My Holocaust*): The Israeli Arab Khaled, exhausted after his flagellation, is comforted by the Israeli Jew and daughter of Holocaust survivor Madi, in her role as musselman, while the German audience files past them to the exit.

In the end Khaled collapses into the arms of Madi, his flagellated, naked body clasped by her musselman's skeletal frame. A pietà from hell and a kind of reconciliation: the Israeli Arab hugged by the survivor's daughter as the Germans who beat him pass meekly by.[60] Perhaps only this kind of insane topsy-turvy world of stereotypes turned on their head can set off a process of liberation from the stranglehold of the cinematic "Jew." But surveying the political scene today, one might conclude that the image of the pernicious "Jew" can still look forward to a long and prosperous future.[61]

Don't Touch My Holocaust is about the question of ownership: Whom does the Holocaust belong to and what are the implications of owning it? Tlalim himself has argued that his film

> is about looking at ourselves in the mirror . . . without putting the blame on the Germans and without adopting a victim's perspective. . . . What is behind this film . . . is the belief that we are ill, we all suffer from dark dreams . . . from some childhood trauma and the only way to face it is to examine it. . . . I tried in this film to observe Israeli society mercilessly yet affectionately in an effort to understand what we are made of.[62]

There is no doubt that certain audiences perceived *Don't Touch My Holocaust* as offensive. Clearly it is relentless in exposing both the destructive effects of the memory of atrocity on the present and the distortion of contemporary identity and consciousness caused by a cynical ignorance of the past. Its attempt to grapple with the explosive triangle—of Israeli-Palestinian, Sephardic-Ashkenazi, and Jewish-German relations—is too ambitious to be entirely successful. But ultimately, despite its harsh criticism of the manipulation of the Shoah in Israeli politics and education, *Don't Touch My Holocaust* depicts Israelis (and to some extent also Palestinians) as victims of a past they cannot undo and of which they are often only dimly aware.

Indeed, *Don't Touch My Holocaust* goes a step beyond more political and simplistic Israeli films as, for instance, *Beyond the Walls,* precisely by facilitating a greater degree of empathy with the tragedy of the "Jew" in the modern world, and most specifically in Israel. It is about the fate of cutting oneself off from the Jewish past, only to be stranded in a land that is a morass of history and memory and myth, where the only legitimization for existence is a return to a powerfully repressed and never reworked history, and where the conundrum of representation is such that the rejection of one stereotype almost inevitably opens the door to another.

* * *

From the Golem of Prague, the savior of the Jews who metamorphosed into a symbol of their demonic essence, to *Don't Touch My Holocaust,* the return to the greatest site of Jewish victimhood through the prism of second-generation Israelis, the route of the cinematic "Jew" has closely followed the fortunes and misfortunes of the past eighty years. In the course of this journey, Jewish self-representation was converted into antisemitic cinematic discourse; the representation of Jewish victimhood borrowed in turn from antisemitic imagery; Jewish heroism remained haunted by fantasies of perpetrators; and the victimization of Arabs was represented through echoes of Jewish suffering. To be sure, among the thousands of films featuring the "Jew," endless variations on these themes have been tried more or less successfully. But by and large, I would suggest that these were the parameters through which the image of the "Jew" was represented in cinema, reflecting but also molding the popular imagination. Certainly, despite the manner in which I have ordered these changing images, there is no clear chronology here and a great deal of overlap, even if overtly antisemitic films are no longer in vogue while the new Israeli cinema would not have been conceivable thirty or forty years ago.

Is there anything we can learn from the transformation of the "Jew" in cinema? First, I believe it reflects the changing place of Jews in society from the turn of the previous century—through the Holocaust, the creation of the State of Israel, the immense demographic and geographical shifts in Jewish populations, and the changing public attitudes toward Jews. Second, this process teaches us about the manner in which powerful images remain deeply embedded in the creative imagination, even as the circumstances that originally gave them birth undergo profound changes. Whatever one can say today about the "Jew," either as an individual or as a cinematic creation, that "Jew" is also the product of all the images and fantasies that give this word sense and meaning. In this, cinema has played a profound role in the last eighty years, and can be expected to keep doing so in the future, combined now increasingly, of course, with other forms of popular media. Whether the basic paradigms of such representations will remain as I have outlined them here, or will be entirely transformed, remains to be seen. But that such representational paradigms keep determining much of what we believe is our self-understanding and perception of others seems to be beyond doubt.

Since I began writing this book, antisemitism has experienced a significant rise. This has meant that the popular mental picture of the "Jew" has been stamped by images that have little to do with reality and everything to do with fantasy, phobia, and forms of representation. The recent report by the Center for Research on Antisemitism at the Technische Universität in Berlin, submitted to the European Monitoring Center on Racism and Xenophobia, and posted on the Internet only after a great deal of public pressure, noted that

> Jews in the European Union Member States are well integrated socially, economically and culturally, and as such the typical motives of xenophobia (fear of competition for jobs, housing and social welfare, linguistic and cultural otherness of migrants, external appearance) are hardly of consequence. Instead, the Jews are basically imagined to be a nationally and internationally influential group, allegedly controlling politics and the economy. Hence, anti-Semitism has other motives and a different structure from racism.[63]

This is an important observation. It indicates that certain images of the "Jew" have become so deeply entrenched in the minds of Europeans that they are no longer affected by reality and are prone to gain greater influence on the collective psyche at times of anxiety and instability. These images have traveled from Europe to the United States, but most especially to the Islamic world. They obviously have many sources, but just as in the premodern era, when the image of the "Jew" was created more through pictorial representation in churches and other public buildings, now it is disseminated through the print and electronic media, through the Internet, and, not least, through the powerfully suggestive medium of film. Conceived from its very beginning as a space of fantasy, film is precisely the site where reality drifts away and the imaginary takes over. It is for this reason that the cinematic "Jew" is of such crucial importance to the public *imaginaire* of this stereotype. Having been screened now for close to a century, this "Jew" has wandered from country to country, changing shape and character, language and nationality. But some "essential" elements of this image keep resurfacing no matter the aesthetic or political stance of its makers. For a notoriously protean type, the "Jew" has remained remarkably stable. When one reads the hateful texts about the "Jew" and examines the Nazi-like pornographic illustrations of this character, one is tempted to escape from this sordid reality into the happier fantasy world of the cinema. But it is precisely there that one encounters the formation of stereotypes and the impregnation of viewers' minds by those stereotypes. In other words, see you in the movies.

Introduction

1. Omer Bartov, "He Meant What He Said: Did Hitlerism Die with Hitler?" *TNR* (February 2, 2004): 25–33.

2. In 1963 Pope John XXIII convened the second Vatican Council, which resulted in the declaration *Nostra Aetate* ("In Our Time"). The key statement in the declaration reads: "True, authorities of the Jews and those who followed their lead pressed for the death of Christ . . . still, what happened in His passion cannot be blamed upon all the Jews then living, without distinction, nor against the Jews of today." The Pope also removed the words *perfidis judaeis* ("perfidious Jews") from the Good Friday liturgy. James Carroll, *Constantine's Sword: The Church and the Jews* (Houghton Mifflin: Boston, 2001), 38–39.

1. The "Jew" as Perpetrator

1. Gershom Scholem, *Kabbalah* (New York: Dorset Press, 1974), 351–55; Moshe Idel, *Golem: Jewish Magical and Mystical Traditions on the Artificial Anthropoid* (Albany: State University of New York Press, 1990); Gustav Meyrink, *The Golem*, trans. Mike Mitchell (Riverside, Calif.: Dedalus/Ariadne Press, 1995). Robert Irwin, "Gustav Meyrink and His Golem," in Meyrink, *The Golem*, 20, notes that Meyrink's novel was serialized in *Die Weissen Blätter* in 1912–1914, and that once published in book form in 1915 it was received with acclaim and rapidly sold 200,000 copies.

Irwin also makes the interesting point that the original title of the novel was *The Eternal Jew.*

2. An earlier lost version was co-directed by Wegener in 1914 and was very popular in Germany. Wegener also made a sequel, *The Golem and the Dancing Girl,* in 1917. A French version was made in Czechoslovakia in 1936, a Polish comic variation was screened in 1951, and many other movies have subsequently exploited the theme. But the 1920 film, whose subtitle, "How He Came into the World," indicates that it was in fact a prequel to the 1914 film, is the best known and most influential. Lotte H. Eisner, *The Haunted Screen: Expressionism in the German Cinema and the Influence of Max Reinhardt,* trans. Roger Greaves (Berkeley: University of California Press, 1990), 56–63; Ephraim Katz, *The Film Encyclopedia,* 2d ed. (New York: Harper Perennial, 1994), 1439–40; John Walker, ed., *Halliwell's Film Guide,* rev. ed. (New York: Harper Perennial, 1995), 439; http://members. fortunecity.com/roogulator/horror/golem20.htm (accessed April 5, 2004). Interestingly, the supervising director of the 1920 version was Ernst Lubitsch, who debuted as an actor in German cinema during World War I, specializing in lovable schlemiel (bumbler) characters such as Sally Pinkus and Moritz, and being charged by some with exploiting and disseminating antisemitic stereotypes. Scott Eyman, *Ernst Lubitsch: Laughter in Paradise* (Baltimore: Johns Hopkins University Press, 2000), 41–57. Films on Jewish themes, both fiction and documentaries, were made by American and European companies as early as the late nineteenth century. The first movies on Jewish subjects that featured Jewish actors were made in pre–World War I Warsaw. Of the 2,016 fictional films made in prerevolutionary Russia, 69 dealt with Jewish subjects, and about half were adaptations of Yiddish plays or novels and were performed in Yiddish. Lucjan Dobroszycki and Barbara Kirshenblatt-Gimblett, *Image Before My Eyes: A Photographic History of Jewish Life in Poland Before the Holocaust* (New York: Schocken Books, 1977), 243–44.

3. John Whiteclay Chambers II, "*All Quiet on the Western Front* (U.S., 1930): The Antiwar Film and the Image of Modern War," in *World War II, Film, and History,* ed. John Whiteclay Chambers II and David Culbert (New York: Oxford University Press, 1996), 13–30.

4. Katz, *The Film Encyclopedia,* 1439.

5. For background, see Galit Hasan-Rokem and Alan Dundes, eds., *The Wandering Jew: Essays in the Interpretation of a Christian Legend* (Bloomington: Indiana University Press, 1986).

6. Jacob Katz, *Out of the Ghetto: The Social Background of Jewish Emancipation, 1770–1870* (Cambridge, Mass.: Harvard University Press, 1973).

7. Robert S. Wistrich, *Antisemitism: The Longest Hatred* (New York: Pantheon Books, 1991); Albert S. Lindemann, *Esau's Tears: Modern Anti-Semitism and the Rise of the Jews* (Cambridge: Cambridge University Press, 1997); James Carroll, *Constantine's Sword: The Church and the Jews* (Boston: Houghton Mifflin, 2001).

8. Wegener's earlier film, *The Student of Prague* (1913), was in fact shot in the old town in Prague. Eisner, *The Haunted Screen,* 41–42.

9. One wonders about the relationship between this scene and the terrifying speech Adolf Hitler delivered to the Reichstag on January 30, 1939: "During the time of my struggle for power it was in the first instance only the Jewish race that received my prophecies with laughter when I said that I would one day take over

the leadership of the State, and with that of the whole nation, and that I would then among other things settle the Jewish problem. Their laughter was uproarious, but I think that for some time now they have been laughing on the other side of their face. Today I will once more be a prophet: if the international Jewish financiers in and outside Europe should succeed in plunging the nations once more into a world war, then the result will not be the Bolshevizing of the earth, and thus the victory of Jewry, but the annihilation of the Jewish race in Europe!" But of course a strange inversion of roles was always at the heart of antisemitic discourse. *Nazism 1919–1945: A Documentary Reader,* vol. 3, *Foreign Policy, War and Racial Extermination,* ed. J. Noakes and G. Pridham (Exeter, U.K.: Exeter University Publications, 1988), 1049.

10. Sander L. Gilman and Steven Katz, eds., *Anti-Semitism in Times of Crisis* (New York: New York University Press, 1991), esp. chaps. 2, 3, 5. See also Sander L. Gilman, *The Jew's Body* (New York: Routledge, 1991); and Gilman, *Jewish Self-Hatred: Anti-Semitism and the Hidden Language of the Jews* (Baltimore: Johns Hopkins University Press, 1986). Lyda Salmanova, who plays Miriam, was in fact married to Wegener.

11. David Stewart Hull, *Film in the Third Reich: A Study of the German Cinema* (Berkeley: University of California Press, 1969); Hilmar Hoffmann, *The Triumph of Propaganda: Film and National Socialism, 1933–1945,* trans. John A. Broadwin and V. R. Berghahn (Providence, R.I.: Berghahn Books, 1996); Eric Rentschler, *The Ministry of Illusion: Nazi Cinema and Its Afterlife* (Cambridge, Mass.: Harvard University Press, 1996); Sabine Hake, *Popular Cinema of the Third Reich* (Austin: University of Texas Press, 2001), esp. chap. 2. Throughout the period of the Third Reich 1,094 feature films were made, of which 48 percent were comedies, 27 percent melodramas, 11 percent action films, and only 14 percent propaganda films. The latter were made mainly just after the "seizure of power" and in the early years of the war. *Nazism 1919–1945: A Documentary Reader,* vol. 4, *The German Home Front in World War II,* ed. J. Noakes (Exeter, U.K.: University of Exeter Press, 1998), 505–506.

12. Rentschler, *The Ministry of Illusion,* 154. Marcel Ophuls's film *The Sorrow and the Pity* (1969) includes excerpts from the synchronized French version. See also David Welch, *Propaganda and the German Cinema, 1933–1945* (Oxford: Clarendon Press, 1983), 284–304.

13. Lion Feuchtwanger, *Jew Süss,* trans. Willa and Edwin Muir (New York: Viking Press, 1926).

14. In 1827 Wilhelm Hauff published a successful novel titled *Jew Süss* that supported segregation between Jews and gentiles but doubted the justice of Oppenheimer's execution. Reclam, the Leipzig publisher that published the book in 1868, reissued it in the 1940s. See also Baruch Gitlis, *Film and Propaganda: The Nazi Anti-Semitic Film* (in Hebrew) (Givatayim: Revivim, 1984), 142–46; Na'ama Sheffi, "Jud Suess: A Jewish Mirror of German History," unpublished paper, presented at the German Studies Association Meeting, 2001. The most important examination of the film to date has just been published, including the historical background, the making of the film, its dissemination (especially in France), its reception, and its postwar history. See Claude Singer, *Le Juif Süss et la Propagande Nazie: L'histoire confisquée* (Paris: Les Belles Lettres, 2003). On Feuchtwanger's association with Rathenau and the latter's impact on the writing of the novel, see ibid., 53–55. The book also contains many remarkable photographs.

15. Despite its rabid antisemitic content, *The Eternal Jew* can be easily purchased through a variety of Internet sites. The scenes discussed here were shot in the Warsaw and Lodz Ghettoes. They were also subsequently used in postwar films, such as Andrzej Wajda's *Korczak* (1990). See Welch, *Propaganda and the German Cinema*, 294. Dr. Meir Mark Dworzecki testified at the Eichmann trial in Jerusalem that in the Jewish Ghetto in Vilna, there was "a Hebrew theatre, which produced the *Eternal Jew* by David Pinski [1872–1959] . . . out of a desire to call upon the youth, by means of the theatre, to revolt. The Eternal Jew goes out into the Diaspora, to live in the outside world, until he can return to his fatherland. We introduced into it words that were not in the text of [the Moscow-based Hebrew language repertory company] 'Habimah.' And this Jew was changed into one calling for a revolt, a revolt against the Romans. We knew that the 'Romans' of the ghetto were the Germans." *The Trial of Adolf Eichmann*, Session 27, May 4, 1961. The complete transcript of the trial is at http://www.nizkor.org/hweb/people/e/eichmann-adolf/transcripts/ (accessed April 5, 2004). And see David Pinski, *Der eybiger Id: Tragedye in fier obteylungen* (New York: M. Gurevitsh, 1914).

16. Patricia Szobar, "Telling Sexual Stories in the Nazi Courts of Law: Race Defilement in Germany, 1933 to 1945," *Journal of the History of Sexuality* 11, nos. 1–2 (January/April 2002): 131–63. Dorothea is played by the actress Kristina Söderbaum, who was also Harlan's wife, and one of three highly popular Swedish actresses who played Aryan women in Nazi films. The other two were Zarah Leander and Kirsten Heiberg. Welch, *Propaganda and the German Cinema*, 219, n. 75; 225, n. 92.

17. Rentschler, *The Ministry of Illusion*, 154.

18. Ibid., 162.

19. Omer Bartov, *Mirrors of Destruction: War, Genocide, and Modern Identity* (New York: Oxford University Press, 2000), chap. 3.

20. This dialogue passage has been transcribed directly from the film. A full text (translated into Hebrew) is also to be found in Gitlis, *Film and Propaganda*, 205–51.

21. On the notion of "white" and "red" women in the fascist imagination, see Klaus Theweleit, *Male Fantasies,* trans. Stephen Conway, 2 vols. (Minneapolis: University of Minnesota Press, 1987–1989).

22. Ruth Ellen Gruber, *Virtually Jewish: Reinventing Jewish Culture in Europe* (Berkeley: University of California Press, 2002).

23. Stephen Eric Bronner, *A Rumor about the Jews: Reflections on Antisemitism and the Protocols of the Elders of Zion* (New York: St. Martin's Press, 2000); Norman Cohn, *Warrant for Genocide: The Myth of the Jewish World Conspiracy and the Protocols of the Elders of Zion,* new ed. (London: Serif, 1996); Binjamin W. Segel, *A Lie and a Libel: The History of the Protocols of the Elders of Zion,* trans. and ed. Richard S. Levy (Lincoln: University of Nebraska Press, 1995). The Egyptian television series is called "A Horseman Without a Horse." See Robert Fisk, "Protests Rage as Egyptian TV Shows Series Based on Infamous Anti-Semitic Text," *TI,* November 9, 2002; "'Elders of Zion' Airs on Egyptian TV," *World Net Daily,* November 7, 2002.

24. Dennis E. Showalter, *Little Man, What Now: Der Stürmer in the Weimar Republic* (Hamden, Conn.: Archon Books, 1982).

25. On *I Accuse*, see Michael Burleigh, *Death and Deliverance: "Euthanasia" in Germany c. 1900–1945* (Cambridge: Cambridge University Press, 1994), 210–19,

which also provides evidence of the film's popularity. On the Catholic bishops' opposition to euthanasia and silence on the Holocaust, see Beth A. Griech-Polelle, *Bishop von Galen: German Catholicism and National Socialism* (New Haven, Conn.: Yale University Press, 2002).

26. Harlan actually visited the Lublin Ghetto and brought back 120 Jews for parts in the film, although mention of this in the press was forbidden. In an interview with *Der Film* published in January 1940 Harlan also noted that the reason for which Süss was executed, having relations with a Christian woman, makes for "an interesting parallel with the Nuremberg Laws." Welch, *Propaganda and the German Cinema,* 285–86.

27. Boaz Neumann, *The Nazi World View: Space, Body, Language* (in Hebrew) (Haifa and Tel Aviv: Haifa University Press and Maariv Press, 2002).

28. Primo Levi, *The Drowned and the Saved,* trans. Raymond Rosenthal (New York: Summit Books, 1988).

29. For images from Terezín, excerpts from *Der Führer schenkt den Juden eine Stadt,* information on its history and victims, and examples of the art and music produced there, see *Terezín* (1991), a film made by Studio ONDRA KF with the Terezín Memorial. See also *The Führer Gives a City to the Jews,* a copy of which can be found at the National Center for Jewish Film of Brandeis University and at the Mason Library of Keene State College. I thank the latter for lending me their copy.

30. Anne D. Dutlinger, ed., *Art, Music, and Education as Strategies for Survival: Theresienstadt, 1941–45* (New York: Herodias, 2001); Rudolf M. Wlaschek, ed., *Kunst und Kultur in Theresienstadt: Eine Dokumentation in Bildern* (Gerlingen: Bleicher, 2001); Elena Makarova, Sergei Makarov, and Victor Kuperman, *University over the Abyss: The Story behind 489 Lecturers and 2,309 Lectures in KZ Theresienstadt 1942–1944* (Jerusalem: Verba Publishers, 2000); Cara De Silva, ed., *In Memory's Kitchen: A Legacy from the Women of Terezín,* trans. Bianca Steiner Brown (Northvale, N.J.: J. Aronson, 1996); Hana Volavková, ed., *I Never Saw Another Butterfly: Children's Drawings and Poems from Terezín Concentration Camp, 1942–1944,* 2d ed. (New York: Schocken Books, 1993).

31. Jean Renoir, *My Life and My Films,* trans. Norman Denny (New York: Da Capo Press, 1991); André Bazin, *Jean Renoir,* ed. François Truffaut, trans. W. W. Halsey II and William H. Simon (New York: Da Capo Press, 1992); Jonathan Buchsbaum, *Cinema Engagé: Film in the Popular Front* (Urbana: University of Illinois Press, 1988); Alexander Sesonske, *Jean Renoir: The French Films, 1924–1939* (Cambridge, Mass.: Harvard University Press, 1980).

32. Pierre Birnbaum, *The Anti-Semitic Moment: A Tour of France in 1898,* trans. Jane Marie Todd (New York: Hill and Wang, 2002); Birnbaum, *Anti-Semitism in France: A Political History from Leon Blum to the Present,* trans. Miriam Kochan (Cambridge, U.K.: B. Blackwell, 1992); Eugen Weber, *Action Française: Royalism and Reaction in Twentieth-Century France* (Stanford, Calif.: Stanford University Press, 1962); Weber, *The Hollow Years: France in the 1930s* (New York: Norton, 1994); Vicki Caron, *Uneasy Asylum: France and the Jewish Refugee Crisis, 1933–1942* (Stanford, Calif.: Stanford University Press, 1999); Robert Soucy, *French Fascism: The Second Wave, 1933–1939* (New Haven, Conn.: Yale University Press, 1995); David Caroll, *French Literary Fascism: Nationalism, Anti-Semitism, and the Ideology of Culture* (Princeton, N.J.: Princeton University Press, 1995); Pierre Marie Dioudonnat,

Je suis partout, 1930–1944: Les Maurrassiens devant la tentation fasciste (Paris: La Table Ronde, 1973); Pierre-André Taguieff, ed., *L'antisémitisme de plume, 1940–1944: Études et documents* (Paris: Berg, 1999); Bartov, *Mirrors of Destruction,* chaps. 2–3.

33. Text taken from published script and compared to the film. Jean Renoir, *La Grande Illusion: Découpage integral* (Paris: Seuil/Avant-Scène, 1971), 48–51 (my translation). See also Jean Renoir, *La règle du jeu: Lecture accompagnée par Domenica Brassel et Joël Magny* (Paris: Gallimard, 1998).

34. Born Israel Moshe Blauschild in 1900 in Paris to Romanian-Jewish immigrants, Dalio fled France with his wife in 1940 just ahead of the German invasion after his picture appeared on posters depicting "the typical Jew." He found refuge in the United States, where he played, *inter alia,* a supporting part in *Casablanca.* Dalio resumed his career in France after the war. Katz, *The Film Encyclopedia,* 320–21.

35. Annette Becker, *War and Faith: The Religious Imagination in France, 1914–1930,* trans. Helen McPhail (New York: Berg, 1998). For the most recent survey of antisemitism in the German military in World War I and in the Weimar Republic's veterans associations, see Brian Crim, "From *Frontgemeinschaft* to *Volksgemeinschaft*: The Role of Antisemitism within the German Military and Veteran Community, 1916–1938," Ph.D. diss., Rutgers University, 2002.

36. Text from Renoir, *La Grande Illusion,* 132–35, and transcribed from the film (my translation).

37. Ibid. (my translation). Thanks also to Judy and Gérard Vichniac for helping with some of the more difficult passages in the review cited here.

38. Ibid.

39. Ibid.

40. This passage has been transcribed directly from the film. See also Gitlis, *Film and Propaganda,* 227–28.

41. Stuart Liebman, "The First Film Documentary of the Liberation of the Camps: The Case of Majdanek," unpublished paper, 2002; Liebman, "Les premières constellations du discours sur l'Holocauste dans le cinéma polonais," in *De l'histoire au cinéma,* ed. Antoine de Baecque and Christian Delage (Paris: Editions Complexe, 1998), 193–216.

42. For background see Bolesław Michałek and Frank Turaj, *The Modern Cinema of Poland* (Bloomington: Indiana University Press, 1988), 1–79, 129–72.

43. There were 5,811 Jews in Suwałki in 1931, about a third of the total population. The approximately 6,000 Jews living there at the outbreak of World War II were deported at the end of November 1939. The community was not reconstituted after the war. *Simon Wiesenthal Center: Multimedia Learning Center:* http://motlc.wiesenthal.com/text/x31/xm3158.html (accessed April 5, 2004), citing the *Encyclopedia Judaica* (Jerusalem: Kesher Publishing House, 1972). See Dr. Kasriel Eilender, *A Brief History of the Jews in Suwalki,* for somewhat higher figures and a more detailed historical sketch: www.shtetlinks.jewishgen.org/suwalki/history.htm (accessed April 5, 2004). And also Yehudah Alro'i and Yosef Khrust, eds., *Jewish Community Book: Suwalk and Vicinity* (in English and Hebrew) (Tel Aviv: Ya'ir, 1989).

44. Władysław Stanisław Reymont, *Ziemia Obiecana,* 2 vols. (Warsaw: Gebethner i Wolff, 1899); translated as *The Promised Land,* trans. M. H. Dziewicki, 2 vols. (New York: A. A. Knopf, 1927).

45. Gruber, *Virtually Jewish;* Michael C. Steinlauf, *Bondage to the Dead: Poland and the Memory of the Holocaust* (Syracuse, N.Y.: Syracuse University Press, 1997).

2. The "Jew" as Victim

1. Elected *hetman* (leader) of the Zaporozhian Cossacks in 1648, Bohdan Khmel'nyts'kyi (c. 1595–1657) led their rebellion against Polish rule, during which his Cossacks and the Ukrainian peasantry murdered anywhere between tens of thousands to hundreds of thousands of Jews and destroyed numerous communities. The Pereiaslav agreement of 1654 resulted in the union of the Cossack-controlled territory of Ukraine under Khmel'nyts'kyi with Muscovy, but in 1667 Ukraine was divided between Muscovy and Poland. A national hero for the Ukrainians, Khmel'nyts'kyi is remembered as the scourge of Israel by the Jews. Paul Robert Magocsi, *A History of Ukraine* (Seattle: University of Washington Press, 1996), 195–227.

2. Much of the information in this and the next few paragraphs is drawn from David G. Roskies's introduction to S. Ansky, *The Dybbuk and Other Writings,* ed. David G. Roskies, trans. Golda Werman (New York: Schocken Books, 1992), xi–xxxvi; and Ruth R. Wisse's introduction to *The I. L. Peretz Reader,* ed. Ruth R. Wisse, multiple translators (New Haven, Conn.: Yale University Press, 2002), xiii–xxx. According to the First All-Russia Census of 1897, almost 35,000 Jews were living at the time in Vitebsk, making just over 52 percent of the total population. The vast majority spoke Yiddish. See: http://www.physics.brocku.ca/~edik/Vitebsk/ (accessed April 5, 2004); Baruch Karu, *Vitebsk* (in Hebrew) (Tel Aviv: The Organization of Immigrants from Vitebsk and Its Environs in Israel, 1957); Grigori Aronson, Jacob Lestschinsky, and Avram Kihn, eds., *Vitebsk Amol: Geshikhte, Zikhroynes, Hurbn* (New York: n.p., 1956).

3. Claude Singer, *Le Juif Süss et la Propagande Nazie: L'histoire confisquée* (Paris: Les Belles Lettres, 2003), 20, notes that Veit Harlan used the same technique employed by Charlie Chaplin, but in reverse. Chaplin watched such films as Leni Riefenstahl's *Triumph of the Will* (1935) when he prepared for the role of Hitler-Hynkel in *The Great Dictator,* so as to learn the Führer's manners of speaking and body language. Harlan, for his part, repeatedly watched such films as Lothar Mendes's *Jew Süss* (1934), and most notably Waszynski's *The Dybbuk.* Though not mentioned by Singer, the distinct similarity between Ferdinand Marian's gestures and manners of speech as Süss and those of Solomon Mikhoels in his role as Menachem Mendel in the classic film *Jewish Luck* (1925) would suggest that this silent production was also on his list.

4. Lucjan Dobroszycki and Barbara Kirshenblatt-Gimblett, *Image Before My Eyes: A Photographic History of Jewish Life in Poland Before the Holocaust* (New York: Schocken Books, 1977), 240–42. Habimah ("The Stage") went abroad on a tour in 1926 and split up in the United States the following year, with some of its members staying there, while others settled in Palestine. In 1958 it became the National Theater of Israel: http://www.wzo.org.il/home/dev/habima.htm (accessed April 5, 2004).

5. Roskies, "Introduction," in Ansky, *The Dybbuk,* xxvi and note 10, cites "Mishpat Ha-dybbuk" (The Trial of *The Dybbuk*), a transcript of a public tribunal that took place in Tel Aviv in 1926. Witnesses for the prosecution included the celebrated

poet Avraham Shlonsky, while Zalman Rubashov (later president of Israel under the name Shazar) was on the defense. The prosecution won a "conviction" by accusing the play of mixing "legendary, realistic and symbolist" elements. It conceded, however, that *The Dybbuk* had a powerful effect on the audience and expressed the hope that "the new life in Eretz Israel and our cultural awakening" would have a similar effect.

6. On the origins of the dybbuk myth and its sexual connotations, see Jeffrey H. Chajes, "Spirit Possession and the Construction of Early Modern Jewish Religiosity," Ph.D. diss., Yale University, 1999; Chajes, "Judgments Sweetened: Possession and Exorcism in Early Modern Jewish Culture," *JEMH* 1, no. 2 (1997): 124–69.

7. Sander L. Gilman, *Jewish Self-Hatred: Anti-Semitism and the Hidden Language of the Jews* (Baltimore: Johns Hopkins University Press, 1986); Peter G. J. Pulzer, *The Rise of Political Anti-Semitism in Germany and Austria,* rev. ed. (Cambridge, Mass.: Harvard University Press, 1988).

8. Jacques Kornberg, *Theodor Herzl: From Assimilation to Zionism* (Bloomington: Indiana University Press, 1993); Abraham B. Yehoshua, *The Wall and the Mountain: The Unliterary Reality of the Writer in Israel* (in Hebrew) (Tel Aviv: Zemorah-Bitan, 1989).

9. On the Bund, an Eastern European Jewish socialist workers' party that advocated the integration rather than assimilation of the working-class, Yiddish-speaking Jewish masses, and its relationship to other Jewish movements and political parties, see Daniel Blatman, *Notre liberté et la vôtre: Le mouvement ouvrier juif Bund en Pologne, 1939–1949* (Paris: Cerf, 2002); Zvi Gitelman, ed., *The Emergence of Modern Jewish Politics: Bundism and Zionism in Eastern Europe* (Pittsburgh, Pa.: University of Pittsburgh Press, 2003).

10. There were 165,0000 Jews (over 35 percent of the total population) in Odessa on the eve of World War I, and 180,000 (close to 30 percent of the total) in 1939. Most were murdered by the Romanian and German occupying forces. *Museum of Tolerance Online: Multimedia Learning Center,* http://motlc.wiesenthal. com/pages/t056/t05682.html (accessed April 5, 2004), citing *Encyclopedia Judaica* (in Hebrew) (Jerusalem: Keter, 1972); *The Complete Works of Isaac Babel,* ed. Nathalie Babel, trans. Peter Constantine (New York: Norton, 2002), 27–28; see "Preface" by Nathalie Babel, 227–29 ("Gedali"). Further in Patricia Herlihy, *Odessa: A History, 1794–1914* (Cambridge, Mass.: Harvard University Press, 1986); Steven J. Zipperstein, *The Jews of Odessa: A Cultural History, 1794–1881* (Stanford, Calif.: Stanford University Press, 1985).

11. Vasilii Semenovich Grossman, *Zhizn': Rasskazy* (Moscow: Pravda, 1947), which also contains the story "V gorode Berdicheve."

12. John Garrard and Carol Garrard, *The Bones of Berdichev: The Life and Fate of Vasily Grossman* (New York: Free Press, 1996), 1–67. Grossman's disenchantment with Stalinism determined his postwar fortunes. The account of Nazi atrocities he helped to put together and his monumental novel on the war were never published in the Soviet Union. See now *The Complete Black Book of Russian Jewry,* compiled by Ilya Ehrenburg and Vasily Grossman, ed. and trans. David Patterson (New Brunswick, N.J.: Transaction Publishers, 2002), which contains a detailed contribution by Grossman on the murder of the Jews of Berdichev, recently further enhanced by the opening of the files of the Extraordinary State Commission of the

USSR, including the documents of the Berdichev Town Commission recorded in April 1944, shortly after Grossman himself interviewed eyewitnesses; Grossman, *Life and Fate: A Novel,* trans. Robert Chandler (New York: Harper and Row, 1985); Grossman, *The Years of War (1941–1945),* trans. Elizabeth Donnelly and Rose Prokofiev (Moscow: Foreign Languages Publishing House, 1946); Garrard and Garrard, *The Bones of Berdichev,* xxii. The Jews constituted more than half the population of Berdichev in the 1920s and about a third of its more than 65,000 residents just prior to the German invasion in 1941. *Museum of Tolerance Online: Multimedia Learning Center,* http://motlc.wiesenthal.com/text/x03/xm0321.html (accessed April 5, 2004), citing *Encyclopedia of the Holocaust* (New York: Macmillan, 1990).

13. *The Patriot* was described as "harmful . . . Zionist . . . and demonstrating hatred of the revolution and what it stands for." Like *The Black Book,* it was criticized by the Soviet authorities for singling out the victimhood of the Jews at the expense of all other Soviet nationalities. Askoldov was told to "remake the film, get rid of the Jews, set it in the thirteenth century, and use the Mongols as your minority." Not only was *The Patriot* banned, but the hallucinatory Nazi concentration camp scene was cut out and ordered destroyed, and Askoldov was prevented from making any more films. According to Askoldov, when shooting this sequence in Kamenetz-Podelsky, southeast of Kiev, the local people cried out upon realizing that the arcaded space into which they were being herded as extras playing the Jews was precisely where the Nazis had executed the Jewish population of the town. David Howard, "Son of Glasnost: Alexandr Askoldov," *The World and I* 8 (1988): http://cgis.jrep.com/Arts/Article-16.html (accessed April 7, 2004).

14. As Howard notes in "Son of Glasnost," while the subtitles contain the word "Jew," in the Russian original soundtrack the word used is "people."

15. In view of the recent complaints about a surfeit of memory and excessive preoccupation with the Holocaust, allegedly at the expense of other people's suffering and victimhood, Yefim's words (both in 1934 and in 1967) are especially telling.

16. Translation of this passage is based on the subtitles, with some modifications. Compare with Gedali's words in the story "Gedali": "'The International, we know what the International is. And I want the International of good people, I want every soul to be accounted for and given first-class rations. Here, soul, eat, go ahead, go and find happiness in your life. The International, *Pan* Comrade, you have no idea how to swallow it!' 'With gunpowder,' I tell the old man, 'and seasoned with the best blood.' . . . The Sabbath begins. Gedali, the founder of an unattainable International, went to the synagogue to pray." *The Complete Works of Isaac Babel,* 229.

17. Askoldov is an Orthodox Christian who professed hope in the return of "spirituality and high religiosity" to Soviet society upon Gorbachev's ascendancy. His father, a decorated Red Army hero of the civil war, was executed in 1937. According to his own account, Askoldov was hidden by a Jewish family in Kiev when the Soviet secret police arrived to arrest his father. The family was apparently later murdered in Babi Yar. Howard, "Son of Glasnost"; Derek Malcolm, "Fighter for Love," *The Guardian* (May 6, 1989), Weekend Arts.

18. Gulie Ne'eman Arad, *America, Its Jews, and the Rise of Nazism* (Bloomington: Indiana University Press, 2000); Peter Novick, *The Holocaust in American Life* (Boston:

Houghton Mifflin, 1999); Jeffrey Shandler, *While America Watches: Televising the Holocaust* (New York: Oxford University Press, 1999); Arthur D. Morse, *While Six Million Died: A Chronicle of American Apathy* (New York: Random House, 1968); David S. Wyman, *The Abandonment of the Jews: America and the Holocaust, 1941–1945* (New York: Pantheon Books, 1984).

19. Steven Alan Carr, *Hollywood and Anti-Semitism: A Cultural History Up to World War II* (Cambridge: Cambridge University Press, 2001).

20. It has been suggested that Rains had some Jewish ancestry, and the actor himself is said to have wondered about his origins. But no evidence of this seems to have ever been produced. See John T. Soister with JoAnna Wioskowski, *Claude Rains: A Comprehensive Illustrated Reference to His Work in Film, Stage, Radio, Television and Recordings* (Jefferson, N.C.: McFarland, 1999). See also: http://www.network54. com/Hide/Forum/message?forumid=103538&messageid=990376881 (accessed April 6, 2004).

21. Ephraim Katz, *The Film Encyclopedia,* 2d ed. (New York: Harper Perennial, 1994), 507–508. Garfield was blacklisted under McCarthyism and died of a heart attack in 1952, at the age of 39. He was named by none other than Elia Kazan (b. 1909), who was not forgiven by many of his colleagues for having "named names" in his testimony to the House Un-American Activities Committee (HUAC). Ibid., 728–29. Between 1945 and 1957 Kazan directed ten critically acclaimed films. He won Academy Awards as best director for *Gentleman's Agreement* and *On the Waterfront* (1954), and was nominated best director for *A Streetcar Named Desire* (1951) and *East of Eden* (1955). His direction of the Broadway dramas *A Streetcar Named Desire* (1947) by Tennessee Williams and *The Death of a Salesman* (1948) by Arthur Miller were extremely influential. Miller broke with Kazan after his second testimony to the HUAC. In 1999, the decision to give Kazan, then 89, the Lifetime Achievement Award from the Academy of Motion Picture Arts and Sciences reawakened the memories of that time. Michael Mills, "Elia Kazan: Postage Paid," http://www.moderntimes.com/palace/kazan/ (accessed April 6, 2004); David Walsh, "Filmmaker and Informer," World Socialist Web Site, http://wsws.org/ articles/1999/feb1999/kaz1-f20.shtml (accessed April 6, 2004); Richard Bernstein, "Kazan and Miller: Long Bitter Debate from the '50s: Views of Kazan and His Critics," *NYT,* May 3, 1988, in: http://www.english.upenn.edu/~afilreis/50s/kazan-miller.html (accessed April 6, 2004).

22. Jean-Paul Sartre, *Anti-Semite and Jew,* trans. George J. Becker (New York: Schocken Books, 1948).

23. This dialogue passage has been transcribed directly from the film.

24. This passage has been transcribed directly from the film.

25. This passage has been transcribed directly from the film.

26. This passage has been transcribed directly from the film.

27. For Kathy, antisemitism is simply an obstacle on the path to happiness. She would rather it went away, at least from her private life. But her resentment quite typically is also against the objects of prejudice. As she says angrily: "Oh, I hate it I hate it I hate everything about this horrible thing. They always make trouble for everybody, even their friends, they force people to take sides against them." Her final reconciliation with Phil is accomplished by allowing Dave and his family to stay at her summer house. But since Dave is married to a Jew and will be there only temporarily, this constitutes a much lesser threat than that of Kathy marrying a Jew.

28. This passage has been transcribed directly from the film.

29. This passage has been transcribed directly from the film.

30. Richard Brooks, *The Brick Foxhole* (New York: Harper and Brothers, 1945). The same year he made *Crossfire,* Edward Dmytryk (1908–1999) was found guilty of communist affiliations by the House Un-American Activities Committee (HUAC), was sentenced to a year in jail, and then went into self-imposed exile in Britain. Returning to the United States in 1951, he gave incriminating testimony to HUAC on several Hollywood personalities and was taken off the blacklist. Like Kazan, his work seems to have declined in subsequent years.

31. This and subsequent passages have been transcribed directly from the film.

32. Arthur Miller, *Focus* (New York: Reynal and Hitchcock, 1945).

33. Lawrence Douglas, *The Memory of Judgment: Making Law and History in the Trials of the Holocaust* (New Haven, Conn.: Yale University Press, 2001), 11–37, 97–113. The film was also screened at the trial of Holocaust denier Ernst Zundel in Canada in 1985. For the debate over the screening of the film at the Eichmann trial, see *The Trial of Adolf Eichmann,* Session 70, June 8, 1961. The complete transcript of the trial is available at: http://www.nizkor.org/hweb/people/e/eichmann-adolf/transcripts/ (accessed April 6, 2004).

34. Joanne Reilly, *Belsen: The Liberation of a Concentration Camp* (London: Routledge, 1998); Jon Bridgman, *The End of the Holocaust: The Liberation of the Camps* (London: Batsford, 1990); Robert H. Abzug, *Inside the Vicious Heart: Americans and the Liberation of Nazi Concentration Camps* (New York: Oxford University Press, 1985). On the death marches, see Daniel Blatman, "Die Todesmärsche—Entscheidungsträger, Mörder und Opfer" and Andzej Strzelecki, "Der Todesmarsch der Häftlinge aus dem KL Auschwitz," both in *Die nationalsozialistischen Konzentrationslager: Entwicklung und Struktur,* ed. Ulrich Herbert, Karin Orth, and Christoph Dieckmann (Göttingen: Wallstein, 1998), 1063–92, 1093–112, respectively.

35. Claude Lanzmann, *Shoah: An Oral History of the Holocaust. The Complete Text of the Film,* transcription of English subtitles (New York: Pantheon Books, 1985), 11. I have compared the text in the book with the film itself and made corrections or added the original language where I felt it was necessary. A similar account was given by this witness, also originally in Yiddish, under the slightly different name Michael Podchlewnik: "When the truck arrived . . . We had to wait two or three minutes. Fumes came out of the truck, from the people that were inside. . . . Then five or six men came up and opened the doors and laid the bodies on the ground. . . . And a Ukrainian and a German . . . extracted the gold teeth and removed the gold rings. If they could not remove them, they cut off the whole finger. . . . The bodies . . . we [then] had to throw down into the pit . . . I had already been working for a few days, when people from my town whom I knew arrived. . . . Among them were my wife and my two children . . . I lay down by my wife and the two children and wanted them to shoot me. Then an SS man came up to me and said: 'You still have strength enough, you can yet work.' He hit me twice with his stick and dragged me away to continue working . . . I came back at night and wanted to hang myself. But my companions wouldn't let me. They said: 'As long as one is alive, there is still some hope; maybe you will yet have some hope to save yourself.'" *The Trial of Adolf Eichmann,* Session 65, June 5, 1961.

36. Lanzmann, *Shoah,* 12.

37. Ibid., 13.

38. Ibid., 53–55.

39. Ibid., 55, 62.

40. Ibid., 83.

41. Ibid., 88–92.

42. Ibid., 99–100.

43. Ibid., 100.

44. Ibid.

45. Kalman Teigman testified that when he was deported from Warsaw to Treblinka in August 1943, "I was standing near the window, and I noticed that Polish men, railway workers, were making signs to us that we were traveling to our deaths. They drew their hands across their throats, as a sign for being slaughtered. At all events, no one wanted to believe it. 'How could it be that they could take young, fit people and send them straight to their deaths?' We did not want to believe this." *The Trial of Adolf Eichmann*, Session 66, June 6, 1961.

46. Ibid., 117.

47. Ibid., 125–26. Another story was circulating in Auschwitz and subsequently came to be known in various versions. Dr. Aharon Beilin, who was deported from Białystok to Auschwitz in February 1943, recounted that the doctor attached to his Sonderkommando in Birkenau "brought us information that Schillinger [an especially sadistic SS man] had been killed by a woman from one of the transports which, according to accounts, was a transport of foreign nationals who had been gathered together in Warsaw, in the Polonia Hotel, and ultimately they came to Auschwitz. . . . [These were] Jews possessing foreign citizenship. And this Schillinger told the women to undress, and one woman said she did not undress in front of men. In consequence he raised his whip, his cane—he always walked around with a cane—and he wanted to strike her. At this point, she drew a revolver and killed him with one shot." *The Trial of Adolf Eichmann*, Session 69, June 7, 1961.

48. Lanzmann, *Shoah*, 163–65.

49. Hanoch Bartov, *Dado: Forty-Eight Years and Twenty Days*, 2d ed. (in Hebrew) (Dvir: Or Yehudah, 2002) 2:420–23.

50. This passage has been transcribed directly from the film.

51. See more in Omer Bartov, *Mirrors of Destruction: War, Genocide, and Modern Identity* (New York: Oxford University Press, 2000), 185–212.

52. Roman Polanski's *The Pianist* (2002) also recreates the German crew filming in the ghetto. This may be more a citation of his mentor Wajda's film *Korczak* than a direct reference to *The Eternal Jew*. But unlike Wajda and Gouri, Polanski does not show the original Nazi footage. Polanski's movie is based on Władysław Szpilman, *The Pianist: The Extraordinary True Story of One Man's Survival in Warsaw, 1939–1945*, trans. Anthea Bell (New York: Picador, 2003).

53. Thomas Keneally, *Schindler's List* (New York: Simon and Schuster, 1982).

54. Transcribed and translated by me from the Hebrew original in the film. The witness was Dr. Martin Foeldi, a lawyer from the city of Uzhgorod in Carpatho-Russia. This part of Czechoslovakia was occupied by Hungary in November 1938. Foeldi was an officer in the Czech army and a former officer in the Austro-Hungarian army. He was deported with his family to Auschwitz in May or June 1944, where the selection he describes took place. *The Trial of Adolf Eichmann*, Session 53, May 25, 1961.

55. Michal Govrin, *The Name,* trans. Barbara Harshav (New York: Riverhead, 1998).

56. Transcribed and translated by me from the Hebrew original in the film. The English text in the official transcript translation is a little different. Indicatively, before citing Mala's words to the SS man, the witness says: "Again, this may be a legend." See *The Trial of Adolf Eichmann,* Session 70, June 8, 1961, testimony by Raya Kagan, who was deported from France to Auschwitz, arriving there on June 24, 1942. Mala Zimetbaum had escaped from Auschwitz with a Polish inmate in summer 1944, carrying incriminating documents about the camp. Both were caught and tortured before their execution.

57. Translated by me from the Hebrew original in the film. Testimony by Yisrael Gutman, who participated in the Warsaw Ghetto uprising and was subsequently transferred to Majdanek and then to Auschwitz. Roza (or Rozja) Robota had smuggled explosives to the members of the Sonderkommando who then blew up the crematorium in Birkenau during their revolt on November 6, 1944. She was tortured before her execution. The English translation in the trial transcript is slightly different. See *The Trial of Adolf Eichmann,* Session 63, June 2, 1961.

58. Transcribed and translated by me from the Hebrew original in the film. Testimony by Yehuda Bakon, who lived in Moravska Ostrava, Czechoslovakia, before the war. He came to Auschwitz from Theresienstadt in December 1943, at age fourteen. The English translation in the trial transcript is slightly different. See *The Trial of Adolf Eichmann,* Session 68, June 7, 1961.

59. Transcribed and translated by me from the Hebrew original in the film. Testimony by Nachum Hoch, from the village of Borsa in Transylvania, Romania, who was deported to Auschwitz in 1944, at age sixteen. The event described took place in October 1944. The text in the film abbreviates the original statement. See slightly different English translation in *The Trial of Adolf Eichmann,* Session 71, June 8, 1961.

60. Transcribed and translated by me from the Hebrew original in the film. Testimony by Yitzhak (Antek) Cukerman (Zuckerman), among the leaders of the Warsaw Ghetto uprising. Text in the film combines several statements made by Cukerman in his lengthy testimony. See slightly different English translation in *The Trial of Adolf Eichmann,* Session 25, May 3, 1961.

61. Transcribed and translated by me from the Hebrew original in the film. For the full text in English, see *The Trial of Adolf Eichmann,* Session 25, May 3, 1961. Dr. Moshe Beisky, later judge on the Israeli supreme court, having testified about the double hanging of a boy in the Płaszów concentration camp near Cracow in mid-1943, was pointedly asked by Attorney General Hausner: "15,000 people stood there—and opposite them hundreds of guards. Why didn't you attack them, why didn't you revolt?" Beisky replied: "To this there is no single reply. What I can talk of is the general situation. And perhaps from this it can be deduced. . . . This was already in the third year of the war. . . . The whole of Jewry was already in a state of depression owing to what they had endured. . . . [Then there was] terror-inspiring fear. People stand facing machine guns, and the mere fact of gazing upon the hanging of a boy and his cries—and then, in fact, no ability remains to react. Something else: The belief in the fact that nevertheless the war would somehow come to an end, that we should not, because of that, endanger 15,000 people. One

could ask . . . If we did [rebel], where could we go? . . . And let us not forget . . . in 1943 we did not yet know what was the fate of our families and what had happened to all those who had been taken away in the deportations. . . . Therefore, there was also the hope that by carrying on with the work . . . it was impossible to imperil the lives of 15,000 people." Ibid., Session 21, May 1, 1961. The poet Abba Kovner, among the leaders of the Jewish resistance in Eastern Europe, had issued a manifesto to the Jewish youth in Vilna as early as January 1, 1942: "Let us not go like sheep to the slaughter, Jewish Youth! . . . In front of our eyes our parents, our brothers and sisters are being torn away from us. . . . It is true that we are weak, lacking protection, but the only reply to a murderer is resistance. Brothers, it is better to die as fighters than to live at the mercy of killers. Resist, resist, to our last breath." Yet he went on to testify: "Your Honors, a question is hanging over us here in this courtroom: how was it that they did not revolt? . . . I, as a fighting Jew, would rise in protest with all my strength at this question, if it contains a vestige of accusation. . . . In order to fight . . . one first of all requires organization . . . by virtue of the order of a national authority, or by virtue of an internal movement. For the Jews of Europe the order of a national authority did not apply . . . [and] an internal movement [had to operate under] conditions of terror, separation and paralysis. . . . An organization of this nature can be created only with people determined in their resolve . . . [who] are not usually to be found amongst those beyond despair, subjugated, and those tortured to the extreme. . . . Because of this despair . . . because of the fact that they had been deprived of their human image, it was not an easy matter for this manifesto to be accepted. It is not accidental and it is not to be wondered at. On the contrary, it is astonishing that there existed a minority who believed in this manifesto and did what they did in the course of two years. The surprising thing, in my opinion, is that a fighting force existed at all, that there was armed reaction, that there was a revolt. That is what was not rational." Characteristically, the presiding judge reacted with impatience to this speech, commenting: "Mr. Kovner, we have to make progress," and after Kovner completed his testimony, he chided the prosecutor: "Mr. Hausner, we have heard shocking things here, in the language of a poet, but I maintain that in many parts of this evidence we have strayed far from the subject of this trial. There is no possibility at all of interrupting evidence such as this, while it is being rendered, out of respect for the witness and out of respect for the matters he is relating. It is your task to prepare the witness, to explain matters to him, and to eliminate everything that is not relevant to the trial, so as not to place the Court once again—and this is not the first time—in such a situation. I regret that I have to make these remarks, after the conclusion of evidence such as this." Ibid., Session 27, May 4, 1961.

62. I have largely relied here on the English transcript of the trial, comparing it to the Hebrew original in the film. The citation is longer than the mutilated recording in the film. As is well known, Ka-Tzetnik collapsed after a few minutes of testimony and was ushered to a hospital suffering from a complete nervous breakdown. *The Trial of Adolf Eichmann*, Session 68, June 7, 1961.

63. Throughout this book I speak of the "Jew" as male. This has to do primarily with the fact that within the antisemitic imagination the threatening "Jew" is masculine, even though the lecherous "Jewess" is also a common figure. I also use

this form because it implies a stereotype that lacks any individuality, including that of gender. It must be stressed, however, that gender played an extremely important role in the Holocaust, as indicated here and in other places in this book. In reality the experiences and fates of women differed substantially from those of men. Women were also often misrepresented in retrospect, in accounts of resistance, sacrifice, and victimhood. But while this is suggested throughout this book, I have chosen to keep the male identity of the "Jew" so as to underline its stereotypical nature, that is, the contradiction between the term and the reality it purports to reflect.

64. Curt Bois (1901–1991), a renowned German actor and comedian, began his career as a child prodigy in 1908, worked for a while with Ernst Lubitsch in early 1920s Berlin, and spent seventeen years as an exile from the Nazis in Hollywood (1933–1950), during which time he also played a minor part in *Casablanca*. His last role was in Wim Wenders's *Wings of Desire* (1988).

65. Bartov, *Mirrors of Destruction,* 185–212.

66. Saul Friedländer, ed., *Probing the Limits of Representation: Nazism and the Final Solution* (Cambridge, Mass.: Harvard University Press, 1992).

67. Gerhard Schreiber, "Die italienische Militärinternierten—politische, humane und rassenideologische Gesichtspunkte einer besonderen Kriegsgefangenschaft," in *Die Wehrmacht: Mythos und Realität,* ed. Rolf-Dieter Müller and Hans-Erich Volkmann (Munich: R. Oldenbourg, 1999), 803–14.

68. Erika Milvy, interview with Roberto Benigni: "I Wanted to Make A Beautiful Movie," Salon.com, October 10, 1998: http://archive.salon.com/ent/movies/int/1998/10/30int.html (accessed April 6, 2004); Ruth Ben-Ghiat, review of *Life Is Beautiful,* in *AHR* 104 (1999): 298. Annette Insdorf, *Indelible Shadows: Film and the Holocaust,* 3d ed. (Cambridge: Cambridge University Press, 2003), 289, reports that Benigni told her at Cannes that "his (non-Jewish) father was 'in Albania when Italy stopped fighting. So when the Germans found Italian soldiers, they brought them to Intervelebogen, a camp that had no gas chambers or crematoria.' (He added that his father used to tell him and his sisters stories at night of the camp: 'We laughed, to avoid the trauma,' he recalled)."

69. Arnost Lustig, *Diamonds of the Night,* trans. Jeanne Němcová (Washington, D.C.: Inscape, 1978).

70. Stuart Liebman and Leonard Quart, "Czech Films of the Holocaust," *Cineaste* 22, no. 1 (April 1996): 49–51.

71. Peter Hames, *The Czechoslovak New Wave* (Berkeley: University of California Press, 1985), 188.

72. Erica Fischer, *Aimée & Jaguar: A Love Story, Berlin 1943,* trans. Edna McCown (New York: HarperCollins, 1995).

73. Saul Friedländer, *Reflections of Nazism: An Essay on Kitsch and Death,* trans. Thomas Weyr (Bloomington: Indiana University Press, 1993).

74. Cited in: http://www.zeitgeistfilms.com/films/aimeeandjaguar/presskit.pdf (accessed August 11, 2004).

75. Ibid.

76. The "official site" cited above provides the following "historical background" for the film, taken from the chapter "The Battle of Berlin," in Wolfgang Ribbe, ed., *Geschichte Berlins* (Munich: C. H. Beck, 1987): "The actual 'Battle of Berlin' began

in the night of the 18–19 November 1943, with extensive raids by 440 bombers, of which 402 hit their targets. The main targets were government headquarters, the administrative centers in the inner city, the most populated residential areas, and those industrial centers deemed important to the war effort by economics experts. At the end of November and the beginning of December 1943, further heavy air raids followed, during which more than 8,000 people were killed, 68,226 buildings completely destroyed, 5,837 heavily damaged, and 6,533 suffering medium damage. 250,000 Berliners were now homeless. . . . In January, February and March 1944, the intensive bombardment continued. Residential areas all over the city sank into ash and rubble. . . . The Fortress and Liberator bombers, known as 'flying fortresses,' then concentrated on bombing the industrial targets and transport facilities. . . . The dreadful consequences: During the battle of Berlin, 16 large-scale offensives took place. They cost the Royal Air Force 537 of its best bomber aircraft and almost 4000 personnel, 5.4% of the bombers sent out and 6.2% of those which reached their targets. On the German side, the attacks took 6166 civilian lives, and 18,431 people were seriously injured. 1.5 million people were made homeless and 9.5 sq km of the city were destroyed." See also now W. G. Sebald, *On the Natural History of Destruction,* trans. Anthea Bell (New York: Random House, 2003); Jörg Friedrich, *Der Brand: Deutschland im Bombenkrieg 1940–1945* (Berlin: Propyläen, 2002); Günter Grass, *Crabwalk,* trans. Krishna Winston (Orlando, Fla.: Harcourt, 2002).

77. William Styron, *Sophie's Choice* (New York: Random House, 1979).

78. Isaac Bashevis Singer, *Enemies, a Love Story* (New York: Farrar, Straus and Giroux, 1972); first published in Yiddish in the Jewish daily newspaper *Forward* in 1966, under the title "Sonim, di Geshikhte fun a Liebe."

79. Rafael Moses, ed., *Persistent Shadows of the Holocaust: The Meaning to Those Not Directly Affected* (Madison, Conn.: International Universities Press, 1993); Novick, *The Holocaust in American Life;* Tom Segev, *The Seventh Million: The Israelis and the Holocaust,* trans. by Haim Watzman (New York: Hill and Wang, 1993); Moshe Zimmerman, *Leave My Holocaust Alone: The Impact of the Holocaust on Israeli Cinema and Society* (in Hebrew) (Haifa and Tel Aviv: University of Haifa Press and Zemora-Bitan, 2002).

80. In the last film discussed in this book, *Don't Touch My Holocaust* (1994), Muni Yosef, an Iraqi-born Israeli Jew raised as an immigrant child in a communal village established by Holocaust survivors, is told by one of the founders of the village how, fifty years earlier, Dr. Josef Mengele, in a well-pressed uniform, ordered her to hand over her baby to the old woman who stood behind her, so that she would carry it with her to the gas chamber, while the mother was selected for slave labor. See also Zimmerman, *Leave My Holocaust Alone,* 297. Several testimonies at the Eichmann trial tell similar or even more harrowing stories. Dr. Aharon Peretz testified about the "children action" in the Kovno (Kaunas) Ghetto in late March 1944: "I saw a mother whose three children had been taken, she approached the truck and shouted to the German: 'Give me my children.' And he asked: 'How many children do you have?' She answered: 'Three.' And he said: 'You can take one.' She climbed on the truck—three children turned their heads towards her and, needless to say each child wanted to go with the mother. The mother was unable to choose, and she climbed down from the truck alone—went away from

the truck." *The Trial of Adolf Eichmann,* Session 28, May 4, 1961. Dr. Leon Weliczker Wells described a mass shooting of 2,000 in the Janowska concentration camp next to Lvov in Eastern Galicia, on October 25, 1943: "In certain cases, when we used to bring women and children, very often the women would throw in the children and jump in after them, into the fire [in the pit with the bodies of those previously shot]—even before it was time to shoot. . . . Once a mother came with her child, and when she undressed she spat in the face of the SD guard—they took the child by the legs, knocked its head against a tree and put it in the fire, and hanged her by the feet . . . with the head down." Ibid., Session 23, May 2, 1961. Dr. Josef Buzminsky described a scene in the Przemyśl Ghetto in August 1942: "This Keidash [SS man] caught a woman who had been hiding with a baby about a year and a half old. She held the child in her arms. She began to beg for mercy from Keidash, who shot her, leaving the baby alive. On the other side of the fence stood Poles who raised their hands with the intention of catching the child. She wanted to give the child to them. He snatched the baby from her, fired two shots into her stomach, and then took the child in his hands and tore him apart the way you tear up a rag. The baby yelled. He threw the child away and laughed. The mother drenched in blood crawled towards the baby and in this way they died together." Ibid., Session 24, May 2, 1961. Noach Zabludowicz testified about an event that occurred in Ciechanow, western Poland, on November 5, 1942: "When we were lined up in rows on the day of the deportation [to Auschwitz], there was a woman who held a few months' old baby girl in her arms. The baby began to cry, to wail. One of the SS men turned to her and said: 'Please give me the child.' Naturally she resisted, but he said this in a very kindly way and she, despite herself, handed over the child—in fear. He took the baby in his hands and threw her down with her fore-head hitting the road, and the baby died. The mother was not even able to cry out." Ibid., Session 21, May 1, 1961. Rivka Yoselevska described the mass killing of the Jews of Powost-Zagorodski in the Pinsk region of Byelorussia. In August 1942 she was led to the killing site with her little daughter: "We stood there facing the ditch. I turned my head. He [the SS man] asked, 'Whom do I shoot first?' I didn't answer. He tore the child away from me. I heard her last cry and he shot her. Then he got ready to shoot me, grabbed my hair and turned my head about. I remained stand-ing and heard a shot but didn't move. He turned me around, loaded his pistol, so that I could see what he was doing. Then he again turned me around and shot me. I fell down." Ibid., Session 30, May 8, 1961. Esther Goldstein was deported with her family from Katzow in Carpatho-Russia (Hungarian territory at the time) to Ausch-witz in 1944. As they exited the freight car, her sister was holding her baby daugh-ter and five-year-old son. An SS man came up to them: "My mother was standing near us. He asked her whether she was our mother, and she said yes. Then he said to her: 'Give the children to your mother.' She said: 'No, they are mine, I will not hand them over.' There was an argument. Afterwards, he called to a prisoner in prisoner's garb to translate to her, possibly in Yiddish, perhaps she would under-stand better. Then he said to her: 'If you want to live, give your children to your mother.' She said: 'No, they are mine, I will not hand them over.' Then the SS man came up to her, took the little girl and gave her to my mother, and he took the boy also by force." Ibid., Session 70, June 8, 1961. More testimonies to this effect can be found, inter alia, in the Fortunoff Video Archive for Holocaust Testimonies at

Yale University and the Survivors of the Shoah Visual History Foundation established in 1994 in Los Angeles by Steven Spielberg. Such novels/memoirs as Ka-Tzetnik's *House of Dolls*, trans. Moshe M. Kohn (New York: Simon and Schuster, 1955), and films such as Sidney Lumet's *The Pawnbroker* (1965) and Liliana Cavani's *The Night Porter* (1974), explore or to some people's minds exploit the territory of sexual slavery under the Nazis. A hint of sexual abuse, a matter often shunned even in the most brutally candid testimonies, appears in Dr. Wells's account of the mass killings in the Janowska camp: "When, for example, arrived 24 of the girls from the concentration camp—on 26 August 1943—after the night that they spent with the SS people—they were picked from the concentration camp. When they were offered to stay with the SS people—some of the girls started to run away and were taken this time right away to the fires. This time they were standing on the trucks; the trucks backed up to the fires and they were standing at the edge of the truck. Every one of them got a shot in the neck and was then kicked so that she fell straight into the fire." Ibid., Session 23, May 2, 1961. For an explicit account of female camp inmates trying to survive by becoming the sexual partners of male inmate functionaries, see Ilona Karmel, *An Estate of Memory* (New York: Feminist Press, 1986), originally published in 1969.

81. Amir Weiner, *Making Sense of War: The Second World War and the Fate of the Bolshevik Revolution* (Princeton, N.J.: Princeton University Press, 2001); Michael C. Steinlauf, *Bondage to the Dead: Poland and the Memory of the Holocaust* (Syracuse, N.Y.: Syracuse University Press, 1997); Robert G. Moeller, *War Stories: The Search for a Usable Past in the Federal Republic of Germany* (Berkeley: University of California Press, 2001); Annette Wieviorka, *Déportation et génocide: Entre la mémoire et l'oubli* (Paris: Plon, 1992); Ido de Haan, *Na de ondergang: De herinnering aan de Jodenvervolging in Nederland 1945–1995* (The Hague: Sdu Uitgevers, 1997).

82. Text transcribed directly from the film.

83. Bartov, *Mirrors of Destruction*, 198–202.

84. Hanna Yablonka, *The State of Israel vs. Adolf Eichmann*, trans. Ora Cummings and David Herman (New York: Schocken Books, 2004); Hannah Arendt, *Eichmann in Jerusalem: A Report on the Banality of Evil* (New York: Viking Press, 1963).

85. On the Yekkes, see Segev, *The Seventh Million*, pt. 1. All three judges were born in Germany: Moshe Landau (1912) completed his legal studies in London; Yitzhak Raveh (1906) received a doctorate of law from Berlin and Halle Universities and served as magistrate in Berlin; Benjamin Halevi (1910) received his doctorate of law—magna cum laude—from the University of Berlin. They all immigrated to Palestine in 1933. Yablonka, *The State of Israel vs. Adolf Eichmann*, 134; http://www.remember.org/eichmann/trial.htm (accessed April 6, 2004). Conversely, Gideon Hausner (1915) was born in Lvov, Poland, emigrated to Palestine in 1927, and studied law at the Hebrew University. See http://www.knesset.gov.il/mk/eng/mk_eng.asp?mk_individual_id_t=373 (accessed March 29, 2004); http://motlc.wiesenthal.com/text/x09/xm0988.html (accessed March 29, 2004).

86. This text and later citations are transcribed directly from the film, compared with and amended according to the transcript of the trial; translation from Hebrew and German occasionally revised. Compare to *The Trial of Adolf Eichmann*, Session No. 106, July 21, 1961. See also Mark Roseman, *The Wannsee Conference and the Final Solution: A Reconsideration* (New York: Metropolitan Books, 2002).

87. This passage has been transcribed directly from the film. Compare to *The Trial of Adolf Eichmann*, Session No. 107, July 24, 1961.

88. This passage has been transcribed directly from the film. Eichmann made a similar statement during the testimony to the defense attorney, Dr. Servatius, in ibid., Session 79, June 26, 1961. Responding to the assertion that he had been as satisfied with the results of the Wannsee Conference as were Heydrich and Müller, he said: "Yes, indeed; but my satisfaction was . . . relative to my personal self-examination. . . . I had to render an account to myself, to determine to what extent I was personally connected with the result of the Wannsee Conference. I was reassured by the thought that . . . I had striven to be on the lookout for possible solutions—possible peaceful solutions—which would be acceptable to both parties, but would not require such a violent and drastic solution of bloodshed. . . . Having thus made clear to some extent my own wishes, when it came to the outcome of the Wannsee Conference, I felt something of the satisfaction of Pilate, because I felt entirely innocent of any guilt. The leading figures of the Reich at the time had spoken at the Wannsee Conference, the 'Popes' had given their orders; it was up to me to obey, and that is what I bore in mind over the future years."

89. Lanzmann, *Shoah*, 99–100.

90. This text refers to *The Trial of Adolf Eichmann*, Session No. 106, July 21, 1961.

91. Douglas, *The Memory of Judgment*, 154–56; Segev, *The Seventh Million*, pt. 5. Yehuda Bauer, *Jews for Sale? Nazi-Jewish Negotiations, 1933–1945* (New Haven, Conn.: Yale University Press, 1994), chaps. 9–12.

92. This text refers to *The Trial of Adolf Eichmann*, Session No. 106, July 21, 1961. The dialogue with Judge Halevi, however, did not take place as it appears in the film, since the order of the lines has been changed and digitally pasted in a manner that entirely obscures this operation. For instance, Eichmann uttered the last sentence in this exchange at least thirty minutes *before* Halevi's question to which, in the film, it appears to be the answer. In fact Eichmann's response was: "In what form, may I ask? To shoot oneself, in the last resort?" Nevertheless, the digital rearrangement of the recording does not alter the general drift of this extraordinary exchange. Thus, see also Eichmann's response to Dr. Servatius's question about his attitude to the issue of guilt, in Session 88, July 7, 1961: "As for the deeds of which I am accused, they concern taking part in the deportations. Since this was a political directive, I believe that only the person who bears or bore the responsibility for this political decision can have a guilt feeling in the legal sense, since in the absence of responsibility, there can in the end be no guilt. . . . Where the state leadership is good, the subordinate is lucky; where it is bad, he is unlucky. I was unlucky, because the head of state at that time issued the order to exterminate the Jews. My participation in the deportations resulted from the fact that the highest authority for SS police jurisdiction, Himmler, gave the orders for the deportations to the Chief of the Security Police and the Security Service, who had judicial authority over me. . . . The criminal code of the SS and police jurisdiction specifies that the penalty for disobedience is death. . . . I had to obey. I was in uniform. It was wartime."

93. Ibid., Session 88, July 7, 1961.

94. Ibid., Session 96, July 13, 1961.

95. Ibid., Session 95, July 13, 1961.

96. Ibid.

97. Ibid., Session 106, July 21, 1961.

98. Ibid.

99. Giorgio Agamben, *Homo Sacer: Sovereign Power and Bare Life,* trans. Daniel Heller-Roazen (Stanford, Calif.: Stanford University Press, 1998), 49–58, referring to the parable, "Before the Law," in Franz Kafka, *The Metamorphosis, In the Penal Colony and Other Stories,* trans. Joachim Neugroschel (New York: Simon and Schuster, 1995).

100. Ján Kadár's *The Shop on Main Street* (1965) was eventually also accused of Zionist inspiration. While it concerns the fate of the Jews in a small town, Czechoslovak audiences saw it as an accurate portrayal of life in Slovakia under the occupation and of degrees of collaboration and complicity. Other Czech films on Jewish themes, which came under antisemitic or anti-Zionist attacks, include Alfred Radok's *Distant Journey* (1949), Jiří Weiss's *Romeo, Juliet, and Darkness* (1960), and Jurai Herz's *The Cremator* (1968). Hames, *The Czechoslovak New Wave,* 30, 49–51.

101. "It has all been swept away by catastrophe, and the passage of time. What my father and mother felt at that moment disappeared with them; what I felt has been lost forever, and of this heartbreak there remains only a vignette in my memory, the image of a child walking back down the rue de la Garde, in the opposite direction from the one taken shortly before, in a peaceful autumn light, between two nuns dressed in black." Saul Friedländer, *When Memory Comes,* 2d ed., trans. Helen R. Lane (New York: Farrar, Straus, Giroux, 1991), 87–88.

102. Lumet's film is based on Edward Lewis Wallant, *The Pawnbroker* (New York: Harcourt, Brace and World, 1961). For a recent analysis of the film and its particular American genealogy, going back to a film made by Sigmund Lublin in 1897, D. W. Griffith's *Old Isaacs* and *The Pawnbroker* (both 1908), and especially Charlie Chaplin's *The Pawnshop* (1914), see Alan Rosen, "'Teach Me Gold': Pedagogy and Memory in *The Pawnbroker,*" *Prooftexts* 22, no. 1–2 (winter/spring 2002): 77–117. He also notes that while Nazerman is a latter-day manifestation of Shylock, their roles are reversed: Shylock claims the essential physical identity of all humans; Nazerman insists on (and both laments and mocks) the uniqueness of the Jewish way of life. See further in Patricia Erens, *The Jew in American Cinema* (Bloomington: Indiana University Press, 1984); Lester D. Friedman, *The Jewish Image in American Film* (Secaucus, N.J.: Citadel Press, 1987); Miriam Hansen, *Babel and Babylon: Spectatorship in American Silent Film* (Cambridge, Mass.: Harvard University Press, 1991).

103. Rosen, "'Teach Me Gold,'" 85–86.

104. Dr. Josef Buzminsky testified at the Eichmann trial that during the deportations to Bełżec from the Przemyśl Ghetto in 1942 "I saw how they brought a certain well-known doctor, an old man, Dr. Grebstein, who had once been a colonel in the Austrian army. He showed them photographs and his diploma certifying that he was a colonel; he thought that this would save him. The SS men—I saw this with my own eyes—laughed, beat him to death and tore the diploma to pieces." *The Trial of Adolf Eichmann,* Session 24, May 2, 1961. Dr. David Wdowinski, one of the commanders of the Warsaw Ghetto uprising who was later transferred to the Budzyn labor camp, near Lublin, testified that in summer 1943, "when the Jewish prisoners returned from work, it appeared that one had escaped. At the head of

this group, there was a man named Bauchwitz, who was from Stettin, in Germany. His family, as we got to know, had converted to Christianity when he was a boy of six or seven.... [Bauchwitz] took it upon himself... [when] the matter... became known later on, at a roll call. And then the commandant decided to hang him.... And he then said: 'I have only one request.' The commandant asked: 'What is your request?' And he said: 'I was a German officer in the First World War, and I fought at Verdun. Of my entire battalion only a few survived. And I was awarded the Iron Cross, first class. For this reason, because this is what I am, I ask that I should be shot and not hanged.' To this, the Wachtmeister replied: 'Whether you have the Iron Cross, first class, or not, whether you were an officer or not, in my eyes you are a stinking Jew, and you will be hanged.' He then mounted the gallows and asked for permission to address a few words to the assembled Jews in the camp. He was given permission, and then he said: 'I was born a Jew, and all that I remember of my Judaism is one prayer—in fact, only the opening words of that prayer, and they are: "God of Abraham, Isaac and Jacob," and that is all I remember. But I want to, and I am going to die as a Jew—and I ask you Jews to say Kaddish [the Jewish prayer for the dead] for me.' And we did." Ibid., Session 67, June 6, 1961.

105. Among the most powerful evocations of this sentiment of failed or impossible liberation, see Charlotte Delbo, *None of Us Will Return,* trans. John Githens (New York: Grove Press, 1968); Jean Améry, *At the Mind's Limits: Contemplations by a Survivor on Auschwitz and Its Realities,* trans. Sidney Rosenfeld and Stella P. Rosenfeld (Bloomington: Indiana University Press, 1980); Primo Levi, *The Reawakening: A Liberated Prisoner's Long March Home through East Europe,* trans. Stuart Woolf (Boston: Little, Brown, 1965).

106. Rosen, "'Teach Me Gold,'" 89.

107. Lumet's father had a minor role in the film. Katz, *The Film Encyclopedia,* 853; Robert H. Abzug, "Facing Survivors in Fiction and Film," Museum of Tolerance Online, Multimedia Learning Center, *SWCA* 5 (1997) http://motlc. wiesenthal.com/resources/books/annual5/chap13.html (accessed April 6, 2004). Rosen, "'Teach Me Gold,'" notes that in the original novel the local Mafioso is Sicilian, that is, a foreigner like Nazerman, whereas Ortiz is black, and rightly points out that the film both accepts the argument by Hannah Arendt (made just as the film was being produced) of the Jews' complicity in their persecution and universalizes it to include America's ethnic minorities. Rosen also argues convincingly that while the film's critics spoke about its debt to French cinema and European culture, the film (and novel)—through Nazerman's prism of a European professor turned wretched pawnbroker—presents Europe primarily as a "teacher" of inhumanity.

108. Somewhat reminiscent of *The Commissar,* the Polish-Catholic Jadwiga becomes Jewish by having a child from a Jew, just as the communist commissar Vavilova is humanized by giving birth in the home of a Jewish family.

109. Atina Grossmann, "Trauma, Memory, and Motherhood: Germans and Jewish Displaced Persons in Post-Nazi Germany, 1945–1949," *ASG* 38 (1998): 215–39.

110. There are, however, indications of a rise in antisemitism especially in Europe but also in the United States, and its legitimization most notably by sectors of the left-liberal persuasion (since right-wing antisemitism is still perceived as pernicious). Similarly, we are experiencing today the emergence of a new type of

Western-inspired Muslim antisemitism, whose reach goes far beyond that of Islamic fundamentalists. See, e.g., Murray Gordon, *The "New Anti-Semitism" in Western Europe* (New York: American Jewish Committee, 2002); Robert S. Wistrich, *Muslim Anti-Semitism: A Clear and Present Danger* (New York: American Jewish Committee, 2002); Raphaël Draï, *Sous le signe de Sion: L'antisémitisme nouveau est arrivé* (Paris: Michalon, 2001); Jean-Pierre Allali, *Les habits neufs de l'antisémitisme: Anatomie d'une angoisse* (Paris: Desclée de Brouwer, 2002); Pierre-André Taguieff, *La nouvelle judéophobie* (Paris: Mille et une nuit, 2002). And on the related new wave of anti-Americanism, see Dan Diner, *"Feindbild Amerika": Über die Beständigkeit eines Ressentiments* (Munich: Propyläen Verlag, 2002); Philippe Roger, *L'Ennemi américain: Généalogie de l'antiaméricanisme français* (Paris: Le Seuil, 2002); Jean-François Revel, *L'Obsession antiaméricaine* (Paris: Plon, 2002).

111. Sartre, *Anti-Semite and Jew;* Omer Bartov, *Germany's War and the Holocaust: Disputed Histories* (Ithaca, N.Y.: Cornell University Press, 2003), chap. 8. Bartov, *Murder in Our Midst: The Holocaust, Industrial Killing, and Representation* (New York: Oxford University Press, 1996), chap. 6. Victor Klemperer, *I Will Bear Witness: A Diary of the Nazi Years,* trans. Martin Chalmers, 2 vols. (New York: Random House, 1998–1999), 1:68–69, 118, 199, 289, 292, 319, 340, 450–51; 2:30, 47, 51, 85–88, 90, 106, repeatedly refers to Zionism as the Jewish equivalent of Nazism, expressing the rage of an assimilated and converted Jew both against Jewish nationalism and against the Nazis who remade him into a "Jew." See also Bartov, *Germany's War and the Holocaust,* chap. 7.

112. For the larger context, see Frank Stern, *The Whitewashing of the Yellow Badge: Antisemitism and Philosemitism in Postwar Germany,* trans. William Templer (Oxford: Pergamon Press, 1992); Hermann Kurthen, Werner Bergmann, and Rainer Erb, eds., *Antisemitism and Xenophobia in Germany after Unification* (New York: Oxford University Press, 1997).

113. Thomas Strittmatter, *Erste Stücke: Viehjud Levi, Polenweiher, Der Kaiserwalzer, Brach* (Munich: Schneekluth, 1985).

114. Thomas Mann, *Mario and the Magician,* trans. H. T. Lowe-Porter (New York: A. A. Knopf, 1931).

115. Cornelia Essner, *Die "Nürnberger Gesetze" oder die Verwaltung des Rassenwahns, 1933–1945* (Paderborn: Ferdinand Schöningh, 2002); Saul Friedländer, *Nazi Germany and the Jews,* vol. 1: *The Years of Persecution, 1933–1939* (New York: HarperCollins, 1997).

116. Gerhart Waegner, "Von Heimat und Ausgrenzung," *NZZ* (November 5, 1999): 68.

117. Ibid.

118. Omer Bartov, "Spielberg's Oskar: Hollywood Tries Evil," in *Spielberg's Holocaust: Critical Perspectives on Schindler's List,* ed. Yosefa Loshitzky (Bloomington: Indiana University Press, 1997), 41–60.

119. Rainer Werner Fassbinder, *Der Müll, die Stadt und der Tod* (Frankfurt am Main: Verlag der Autoren, 1981).

120. Lale Andersen, *Der Himmel hat viele Farben: Leben mit einem Lied* (Stuttgart: Deutsche Verlags-Anstalt, 1972). Further in Gertrud Koch, *Die Einstellung ist die Einstellung: Visuelle Konstruktionen des Judentums* (Frankfurt am Main: Suhrkamp, 1992).

121. On Kluge's film *The Patriot* (1979), see Bartov, *Murder in Our Midst,* chap. 7. I am also thinking here, for instance, of Schlöndorff's *Le Coup de Grace* (1979) and Wenders's *Wings of Desire* (1988).

122. On the "discovery" of klezmer music in contemporary Europe, see Ruth Ellen Gruber, *Virtually Jewish: Reinventing Jewish Culture in Europe* (Berkeley: University of California Press, 2002), pt. 4.

123. Bartov, *Germany's War and the Holocaust,* chap. 8.

124. Feidman is a fourth-generation klezmer player who was among the first to introduce this music to postwar youths. According to Gruber, "Feidman eventually developed an almost mystical vision of klezmer as a universal language that could unite people and has been one of the most important influences in popularizing klezmer in Europe, particularly in Germany." Some musicians have criticized him for just this reason. Alan Bern, the musical director of the American neoklezmer group Brave New World, argues that "there are obvious reasons why" Feidman's universalization of klezmer music "has tremendous appeal" in Germany, where "people's feelings of guilt and need for forgiveness and desire for dialogue . . . are getting loaded on to a sort of contentless idea," while "the entire [Jewish] culture is being made to disappear along with that. It's as if Jews didn't have anything to do with klezmer music. To approach it that way, it's like a second destruction of our culture." Quoted in Gruber, *Virtually Jewish,* 189–90, 210–13. This is of course precisely what happens in *Beyond Silence.*

125. My own translation of the German in the film; the English subtitles are somewhat inaccurate or abbreviated.

126. In a similar vein, in October 2002, at a meeting of scholars, artists, filmmakers, and intellectuals at Strasbourg, France, as part of the "European Union Initiative" to teach the Holocaust in the continent, Madame Simone Veil, survivor of the Holocaust, the first president of the European Parliament, and a major political figure in France seen by many as the first lady of Europe, argued that such a meeting in the contested city of Strasbourg should serve as the opportunity for final reconciliation between the Germans and the French. Thus a meeting about the genocide of the Jews became a site of reconciliation between European states. Similarly, the research institute next to Birkenau in Poland serves as a meeting place between Polish and German youths. Again, the site where about a million Jews from all over Europe were murdered is used to bring understanding between the nation that perpetrated the Holocaust and the nation on whose land—and with whose often-willing collaboration—the genocide was implemented.

127. Just like Ansky and Chagall, the prolific and highly respected Gerdt (1916–1996) was also born in the Vitebsk province.

128. For background, see Timothy Snyder, *The Reconstruction of Nations: Poland, Ukraine, Lithuania, Belarus, 1569–1999* (New Haven, Conn.: Yale University Press, 2003); Zvi Gitelman et al., eds., *Cultures and Nations of Central and Eastern Europe: Essays in Honor of Roman Szporluk* (Cambridge, Mass.: Harvard University Press, 2000); Ezra Mendelsohn, *The Jews of East Central Europe between the World Wars* (Bloomington: Indiana University Press, 1983); Mendelsohn, ed., *Jews and Other Ethnic Groups in a Multi-Ethnic World* (New York: Oxford University Press, 1987); Deborah Dash Moore, ed., *East European Jews in Two Worlds: Studies from the Yivo Annual* (Evanston, Ill.: Northwestern University Press, 1990).

129. Sholem Aleichem, *Tevye the Dairyman and the Railroad Stories,* trans. Hillel Halkin (New York: Schocken Books, 1987).

130. Jan T. Gross, *Neighbors: The Destruction of the Jewish Community in Jedwabne, Poland* (Princeton, N.J.: Princeton University Press, 2001).

131. Friedländer, *When Memory Comes;* Louis Begley, *Wartime Lies* (New York: Knopf, 1991); Binjamin Wilkomirski, *Fragments: Memories of a Wartime Childhood,* trans. Carol Brown Janeway (New York: Schocken Books, 1996). See also Bartov, *Mirrors of Destruction,* 80–89, 216–30.

132. Michel Tournier, *The Ogre,* trans. Barbara Bray (Garden City, N.Y.: Doubleday, 1972), orig. pub. as *Le roi des Aulnes* (Paris: Gallimard, 1970), and published in Britain as *The Erl-King* (London: Collins, 1972).

133. "Who rides by night in the wind so wild? / It is the father, with his child. / The boy is safe in his father's arm, / He holds him tight, he keeps him warm. // My son, what is it, why cover your face? / Father, you see him, there in that place, / The elfin king with his cloak and crown? / It is only the mist rising up, my son. // 'Dear little child, will you come with me? / Beautiful games I'll play with thee; / Bright are the flowers we'll find on the shore, / My mother has golden robes fullscore.' // Father, O father, and did you not hear / What the elfin king breathed into my ear? / Lie quiet, my child, now never you mind: / Dry leaves it was that click in the wind. // . . . 'I love you, beguiled by your beauty I am, / If you are unwilling I'll force you to come!' / Father, his fingers grip me, O / The elfin king has hurt me so! // Now struck with horror the father rides fast, / His gasping child in his arm to the last, / Home through thick and thin he sped: / Locked in his arm, the child was dead." Johann Wolfgang von Goethe (1782), in *Goethe: Selected Poems,* ed. Christopher Middleton, trans. Michael Hamburger, David Luke, Christopher Middleton, John Frederick Nims, and Vernon Watkins (Princeton, N.J.: Princeton University Press, 1994), 87.

134. One of Schlöndorff's best films, *Le Coup de Grace* (*Der Fangschuss*) (1976), is in fact more powerful than the novel by Marguerite Yourcenar, *Coup de Grâce,* trans. Grace Frick (New York: Farrar, Straus and Cudahy, 1957), on which it is based.

135. See now the recent essay by Elisa New, "Good-bye, Children; Good-bye, Mary, Mother of Sorrows: The Church and the Holocaust in the Art of Louis Malle," *Prooftexts* 22, nos. 1–2 (winter/spring 2002): 118–40.

136. Simonetta Falasca-Zamponi, *Fascist Spectacle: The Aesthetics of Power in Mussolini's Italy* (Berkeley: University of California Press, 1997); George L. Mosse, *Masses and Man: Nationalist and Fascist Perceptions of Reality* (Detroit: Wayne State University Press, 1987).

137. Günter Grass, *The Tin Drum,* trans. Ralph Manheim (London: Secker and Warburg, 1959).

138. To be sure, one can also evoke here the Talmudic saying "He who saves one soul, it is as if he saved the entire world." From this perspective, Abel's rescue of Ephraim signifies the sparks of humanity that the Kabbalah asserts will lead to the final redemption, or "repair" (*tikkun*), of the universe. One can also think here of the child survivors running through the night in *Under the Domim Tree* (a film I will discuss below), one riding the other's shoulders as they howl "like animals" in obsessive reenactment of their life in the forests of Nazi-occupied Poland.

139. See http://www.kirjasto.sci.fi/tournier.htm (accessed April 6, 2004); Michel Tournier: Biographie, http://www.academie-goncourt.fr/m_tournier.htm (accessed April 6, 2004); Volker Schlöndorff—Dirk Jasper Filmlexikon (Internet) http://www.djfl.de/entertainment/stars/v/volker_schloendorff.html (accessed April 6, 2004).

140. Jaroslav Hašek, *The Good Soldier Schweik,* trans. Paul Selver (Garden City, N.Y.: Doubleday, Doran and Company, 1930); Katz, *The Film Encyclopedia,* 473–74, 930; Milan Kundera, *The Joke,* trans. David Hamblyn and Oliver Stallybrass (New York: Coward-McCann, 1969); Kundera, *The Book of Laughter and Forgetting,* trans. Michael Henry Heim (New York: Knopf, 1980).

141. Tzvetan Todorov, *The Fragility of Goodness: Why Bulgaria's Jews Survived the Holocaust* (Princeton, N.J.: Princeton University Press, 2001); Omer Bartov, "The Anti-Hero as Hero," *TNR* (August 13, 2001): 33–38.

3. The "Jew" as Hero

1. Lester D. Friedman, *The Jewish Image in American Film* (Secaucus, N.J.: Citadel Press, 1987), 9–52, 96–146.

2. Jurek Becker, *Jacob the Liar,* trans. Leila Vennewitz (1969; reprint, New York: Arcade, 1996).

3. The remake of this film, *Jakob the Liar* (1999), directed by Peter Kassovitz and starring Robin Williams as Jakob Heym, can only serve to illustrate that an extraordinary novel can also be made into a bad film, even though in most basic details Kassovitz remains quite close both to the novel and to the original 1974 film (which was the only East German film ever to be nominated for Best Foreign Language Film at the Academy Awards). The main reasons for the weakness of this film are, to my mind, the poor and exaggerated acting, which tries to expose every emotion and leaves nothing to the imagination, thereby transforming the subtle, melancholy humor of the original into an embarrassing farce; and the unfortunate Hollywood insistence both on depicting gruesome violence and on providing a happy ending. Jakob is beaten into a pulp toward the end of the film. Lina imagines their transport to the death camp as an encounter with an American jazz band, complete with black musicians and fur-clad white singers performing on a Soviet tank; this is hardly a scene that the girl, who grew up in a ghetto and could not even recognize an oil lamp, would have been able to imagine. For a much more believable fantasy of survival, see the end of Wajda's *Korczak,* discussed below. This holds true also for the fantastic ending of *Life Is Beautiful* and the entire plot of *Train of Life* (see below), both of which are incredible yet remain within the bounds of the possible contemporary imagination.

4. As Mel Brooks said in relation to his own comedy, *The Producers* (1968): "Look at Jewish history. Unrelieved lamenting would be intolerable. So, for every ten Jews beating their breasts, God designated one to be crazy and amuse the breast-beaters. By the time I was five I knew that one. . . . You want to know where my comedy comes from? . . . It comes from the feeling that, as a Jew and as a person, you don't fit into the mainstream of American society. It comes from the realization that even though you're better and smarter, you'll never belong." Friedman, *The Jewish Image in American Film,* 171–72. The role of entertainment in ghettos and camps—as

long as conditions somehow allowed such activities—is well known. See, e.g., Rebecca Rovit and Alvin Goldfarb, eds., *Theatrical Performance during the Holocaust: Texts, Documents, Memoirs* (Baltimore: Johns Hopkins University Press, 1999). On the links between representations of World War I and the Holocaust, see Omer Bartov, *Murder in Our Midst: The Holocaust, Industrial Killing, and Representation* (New York: Oxford University Press, 1996), chap. 2. On the debate surrounding *Life Is Beautiful* and more generally on humor in Holocaust representations, see Annette Insdorf, *Indelible Shadows: Film and the Holocaust,* 3d ed. (Cambridge: Cambridge University Press, 2003), 286–92.

5. One should also remember in this context that the entire Nazi system was based on Hitler's and Goebbels's idea of the Big Lie, that is, that while people may be able to decipher conventional lies, a systematic falsification of reality sponsored by a modern totalitarian state's propaganda machinery creates a truth that most human beings cannot perceive as a lie. This was, to be sure, the insight of George Orwell, *Nineteen Eighty-Four* (New York: Harcourt, Brace, 1949), but it can already be found in Hitler's *Mein Kampf* (Munich: Verlag Franz Eher Nachfolger, 1925).

6. Chaplin is said to have commented later that had he known the extent of Hitler's atrocities he would never have made the film. Talia Bloch, "Laughing in the Face of a Tyrant," *Aufbau* (September 19, 2002): http://www.aufbauonline. com/2002/issue19/15.html.

7. See more in Michael B. Oren, *Six Days of War: June 1967 and the Making of the Modern Middle East* (New York: Oxford University Press, 2002), 18.

8. Yitzhak Arad, Yisrael Gutman, and Abraham Margaliot, eds., *Documents on the Holocaust: Selected Sources on the Destruction of the Jews of Germany and Austria, Poland, and the Soviet Union* (Yad Vashem: Jerusalem, 1981), 433–34, including an English translation as well as a copy of the original handwritten Yiddish-language manifesto; see also *The Trial of Adolf Eichmann,* Session 27, May 4, 1961.

9. Avraham Shapira, ed., *The Seventh Day: Soldiers' Talk about the Six-Day War,* recorded and edited by a group of young kibbutz members, trans. and ed. Henry Near (London: Deutsch, 1970).

10. See also Jan Wiener, *Immer gegen den Strom: Ein jüdisches Überlebensschicksal aus Prag, 1939–1950,* ed. Erhard Roy Wiehn (Constanz: Hartung-Gorr, 1992).

11. Heda Margolius Kovály, *Under a Cruel Star: A Life in Prague, 1941–1968,* trans. Francis Epstein and Helen Epstein with the author (New York: Holmes and Meier, 1997); W. G. Sebald, *Austerlitz,* trans. Anthea Bell (New York: Random House, 2001).

12. Michael Stanislawski, *Zionism and the Fin-de-Siècle: Cosmopolitanism and Nationalism from Nordau to Jabotinsky* (Berkeley: University of California Press, 2001); Délphine Bechtel et al., eds., *Max Nordau (1849–1923): Critique de la dégénérescence, médiateur franco-allemand, père fondateur du sionisme* (Paris: Cerf, 1996); Max Nordau, *Degeneration* (Lincoln: University of Nebraska Press, 1993).

13. Tzvetan Todorov, *Facing the Extreme: Moral Life in the Concentration Camps,* trans. Arthur Denner and Abigail Pollak (New York: Metropolitan Books, 1996), chap. 1. The 28-year-old writer-director of *Fighter,* Amir Bar-Lev, was attracted to the fact that "Jan really believes he was the agent of his own fate . . . [and] never considered himself a victim per se." Born in Los Angeles to an Israeli father, Bar-Lev says that his background gave him a different sense of identity from that of

other American Jews: "Often when you talk to people our age, young Jews, [and ask them] what it means to be Jewish, Hitler comes up in the first couple of sentences; that bothers me, because I don't want Hitler in my psyche. I don't think he belongs there. I don't think the perpetuity of Judaism in the face of adversity is the paramount goal of [being Jewish]." Similarly, *Fighter*'s co-producer Alex Mamlet says that "in a lot of ways Wiener's story helped shape my definition of what it was like to grow up Jewish in America. He personified a lot of things that I never really saw [before] as an example of a kind of Jewish strength and resiliency." See Shlomo Schwartzberg, "When Friends Collide," *JR:* http://cgis.jrep.com/Arts/Article-16.html (accessed April 7, 2004).

14. Ephraim Katz, *The Film Encyclopedia,* 2d ed. (New York: Harper Perennial, 1994), 240–42.

15. Insdorf, *Indelible Shadows,* 59–64; Stephen M. Weissman, "What Made Charlie Run? From Destitution to Global Acclaim: A Look at Chaplin on the 100th Anniversary of his Birth," *LAT,* April 16, 1989: http://www.american.edu/academic.depts/soc/run.html (accessed April 7, 2004); Aaron Hale, "Chaplin," http://www.csse.monash.edu.au/~pringle/silent/chaplin/aaronhale.html (accessed April 7, 2004); Joseph Heller, *Catch-22* (New York: Simon and Schuster, 1961).

16. Chaplin recalled complimenting Jews as geniuses to a young girl he met on a ship in 1921 when he learned she was Jewish. He said that he recollected saying, "'No, I am not Jewish,' as she was about to put that question, 'but I am sure there must be some somewhere in me. I hope so.'" David Robinson, *Chaplin, the Mirror of Opinion* (Bloomington: Indiana University Press, 1984), 290.

17. "Chaplin Discusses His 'Dictator' Film," *NYT* (October 14, 1940), 27; Charles Chaplin, "Mr. Chaplin Answers His Critics," *NYT* (October 27, 1940), 133.

18. *Nazism 1919–1945: A Documentary Reader,* vol. 3, *Foreign Policy, War and Racial Extermination,* ed. J. Noakes and G. Pridham (Exeter: Exeter University Publications, 1988), 1049.

19. This is especially the case with Joachim C. Fest, *Hitler,* trans. Richard and Clara Winston (New York: Vintage Books, 1974), who also made a popular film on the Führer with similar suggestions of Hitler's qualities as hero and genius: *Hitler, eine Karriere* (1977). See the photographic volume based on the documentary, Joachim C. Fest and Christian Herrendoerfer, eds., *Hitler, eine Karriere* (Frankfurt/M.: Ullstein, 1977).

20. See also Hans-Jürgen Syberberg, *Hitler, a Film from Germany,* trans. Joachim Neugroschel (New York: Farrar Straus and Giroux, 1982); Susan Sontag, "Fascinating Fascism," in Sontag, *Under the Sign of Saturn* (New York: Anchor Books, 1980); Saul Friedländer, *Reflections of Nazism: An Essay on Kitsch and Death,* trans. Thomas Weyr (Bloomington: Indiana University Press, 1993).

21. Insdorf, *Indelible Shadows,* 64–70.

22. Ibid., 67.

23. "To be, or not to be: that is the question: / Whether 'tis nobler in the mind to suffer / The slings and arrows of outrageous fortune, / Or to take arms against a sea of troubles, / And by opposing end them? To die ... / ... But that the dread of something after death / The undiscovered country from whose bourn / No traveller returns, puzzles the will / And makes us rather bear those ills we have / Than fly to others that we know not of? / Thus conscience does make cowards of

us all; / And thus the native hue of resolution / Is sicklied o'er with the pale cast of thought, / And enterprises of great pith and moment / With this regard their currents turn awry, / And lose the name of action. . . ." (*Hamlet,* Act III, Scene 1).

24. ". . . I am a Jew. Hath not a Jew eyes? Hath not a Jew hands, organs, dimensions, senses, affections, passions; fed with the same food, hurt with the same weapons, subject to the same diseases, healed by the same means, warmed and cooled by the same winter and summer, as a Christian is? If you prick us, do we not bleed? If you tickle us, do we not laugh? If you poison us, shall we not die?" These are the lines most often quoted. Less often quoted is the final part of the soliloquy: "And if you wrong us, shall we not revenge? If we are like you in the rest, we will resemble you in that. If a Jew wrong a Christian, what is his humility? Revenge. If a Christian wrong a Jew, what should his sufferance be by Christian example? Why, revenge. The villainy you teach me, I will execute, and it shall go hard but I will better the instruction" (*The Merchant of Venice,* Act III, Scene 1).

25. Insdorf, *Indelible Shadows,* 285–86.

26. See http://www.paramountclassics.com/train/cas.html (accessed April 7, 2004).

27. Primo Levi, *The Drowned and the Saved,* trans. Raymond Rosenthal (New York: Summit Books, 1988).

28. Saul Friedländer, *When Memory Comes,* trans. Helen R. Lane (New York: Farrar, Straus, Giroux, 1979); Shlomo Breznitz, *Memory Fields* (New York: Knopf, 1993); Louis Begley, *Wartime Lies* (New York: Knopf, 1991); *Au revoir les enfants: A Screenplay by Louis Malle,* trans. Anselm Hollo (New York: Grove Press, 1988). Friedländer was hidden under circumstances strikingly similar to those depicted in *Au revoir les enfants,* but unlike the film's Jewish protagonist, Jean Bonnet (Kippelstein)—who is eventually betrayed and handed over to the Gestapo—Friedländer survived the war. Interestingly, in his *Reflections of Nazism,* 74, 77, 100–101, Friedländer includes Malle's film *Lacombe Lucien* (1974) in his list of cinematic representations of Nazism as kitsch. The gap between experience and observation, as well as between memory and fiction, is not easily bridged, especially when dealing with traumatic events.

29. Solomon Perel, *Europa, Europa,* trans. from the German by Margot Bettauer Dembo (New York: Wiley, in association with the U.S. Holocaust Museum, 1997), but originally published in Hebrew as *My Name Is Shlomo Perel* (Tel Aviv: Yedi'ot Aharonot / Sifre Hemed, 1991).

30. Solomon Perel's tale can now also be related to the tragic story of the *Wall Street Journal* correspondent, Daniel Pearl, who was murdered in Pakistan by Islamic extremists in late January or early February 2002. Pearl, who went to Pakistan as an American investigative reporter, was butchered in the most heinous manner as a Jew with alleged links to Israel. To my mind, this is an interesting and troubling reversal of roles: Solly was persecuted as a Jew and glorified as a Nazi; Pearl was working as an American and murdered as a Jew. Would Daniel Pearl have been murdered if he were not a Jew? Possibly, but his last moments, in which he was forced to say that he *was* a Jew, as if that were some admission of guilt, before his throat was slit, evoke memories that stretch back centuries (and remind one of the most terrifying scene in the film *Sunshine,* which I will discuss below). Indeed, these are echoes from Christian Europe that have been exported to a Muslim

world subjected to the impact of a new and savage fundamentalism, which bears little resemblance to traditional Islam and is deeply imbued with antisemitic prejudice.

31. See note 12, above.

32. Holland was born in 1948 in Poland to a Jewish father and a Catholic mother. Her father was arrested by the KGB and died under interrogation when she was thirteen. She studied and worked in Prague, returned to Poland in 1971, but moved to Paris following the imposition of martial law in Poland in 1981. See Dan Lybarger, "The Miracle Worker: An Interview with Agnieszka Holland on *The Third Miracle*," March 23, 2000, http://www.tipjar.com/dan/thethirdmiracle. htm (accessed April 7, 2004), which originally appeared in the March 23–March 29, 2000, issue of *Pitch Weekly;* and http://www.heinemann.com/shared/authors/ 186.asp (accessed April 7, 2004).

33. Solly's circumcision is exposed when he is surprised by a Wehrmacht soldier while taking a bath. The soldier, however, is a homosexual—which means, under the circumstances, that he is by definition an anti-Nazi. Subsequently the two befriend each other. In one scene, the German soldier—who was an actor— plays Shylock, pulling his nose out of a blanket and saying: "Could I play a Jew?" This juxtaposition between homosexuals and Jews as persecuted groups reminds one of the history behind the making of *Crossfire*. Conversely, Solly's notion of undoing his circumcision comes to him from seeing the object of his desire, his Aryan girlfriend, wearing a turtleneck sweater. But it is precisely her "normality" that compels him to try and undo his "abnormality," whereas none of this was required with the "abnormal" German soldier. While the soldier becomes a friend, the girl simply causes Solly an infection. The circumcised penis as a focus of identity, danger, and fascination also features in *Ivan and Abraham*, when the two boys compare penises.

34. See, for instance, Inge Deutschkron, *Outcast: A Jewish Girl in Wartime Berlin*, trans. Jean Steinberg (New York: Fromm International Pub. Corp., 1989).

35. Katz, *The Film Encyclopedia*, 1087–88; Roman Polanski, *Roman* (New York: Morrow, 1984), 396–425.

36. Władysław Szpilman, *The Pianist: The Extraordinary True Story of One Man's Survival in Warsaw, 1939–1945*, trans. Anthea Bell (New York: Picador, 2003).

37. Andrzej Szpilman, "Foreword," ibid., 8.

38. Polanski also wrote about his life during the Holocaust in his 1984 memoir. He devotes 26 pages out of a total of 451 to a typically dry and detached, if perceptive, account of the entire German occupation of Poland. Polanski, *Roman*, 21–47.

39. Wolf Biermann, "Epilogue: A Bridge Between Władysław Szpilman and Wilm Hosenfeld," in Szpilman, *The Pianist*, 211.

40. Hosenfeld had already found out about the gassing of the Jews in July 1942. The following month he wrote: "What cowards we are, thinking ourselves above this, but letting it happen. We shall be punished for it too. And so will our innocent children, for we are colluding when we allow these crimes to be committed." On September 6, 1942, he mentioned Treblinka for the first time as a gassing installation. He also revealed his own previous ambivalence toward—or perhaps even support for—the Nazis, when he wrote on February 14, 1943: "When the terrible

mass murders of Jews were committed last summer, so many women and children slaughtered, I knew quite certainly that we would lose the war. There was no point in a war that might once have been justified as a search for free subsistence and living space—it had degenerated into vast, inhuman mass slaughter, negating all cultural values. . . ." On June 16, 1943, he wrote: "We have brought shame upon ourselves that cannot be wiped out; it's a curse that can't be lifted. We deserve no mercy; we are all guilty." On July 6, 1943, he elaborated: "When the Nazis came to power we did nothing to stop them; we betrayed our own ideals. . . . The workers went along with the Nazis, the Church stood by and watched, the middle classes were too cowardly to do anything, and so were the leading intellectuals . . . and now we must all take the consequences." "Extracts from the Diary of Captain Wilm Hosenfeld," in Szpilman, *The Pianist,* 193–208. In other words, he rightly saw himself as complicit—a German officer in occupied Warsaw. While Biermann is right to say that he should be celebrated as a righteous gentile, that is not the same as putting his fate on a par with that of the Jewish victims, which is precisely what Polanski's film seems to end up doing.

41. See the chapter "The Gray Zone," in Primo Levi, *The Drowned and the Saved,* trans. Raymond Rosenthal (New York: Summit Books, 1988).

42. Miklós Nyiszli, *Auschwitz, a Doctor's Eyewitness Account,* trans. Tibère Kremer and Richard Seaver (New York: Fell, 1960). For the most recent study, see Eric Friedler, Barbara Siebert, and Andreas Kilian, *Zeugen aus der Todeszone: Das jüdische Sonderkommando in Auschwitz* (Lüneburg: Klampen, 2002). Further in Yisrael Gutman and Michael Berenbaum, eds., *Anatomy of the Auschwitz Death Camp* (Washington, D.C., and Bloomington: Indiana University Press and United States Holocaust Memorial Museum, 1994), esp. the chapter by Henryk Świebocki; Rebecca Camhi Fromer, *The Holocaust Odyssey of Daniel Bennahmias, Sonderkommando* (Tuscaloosa: University of Alabama Press, 1993); Serge Klarsfeld, ed., *David Olère, 1902–1985: Un peintre au Sonderkommando à Auschwitz. Catalogue* (New York: Beate Klarsfeld Foundation, 1989); Filip Müller, *Eyewitness Auschwitz: Three Years in the Gas Chambers,* ed. and trans. Susanne Flatauer (Chicago: Ivan R. Dee, 1999); Jadwiga Bezwińska and Danuta Czech, eds., *Amidst a Nightmare of Crime: Manuscripts of Members of Sonderkommando,* trans. Krystyna Michalik ([Oświęcim] State Museum, 1973); Gideon Greif, *"We Cried Without Tears": Testimonies of the Jewish Sonderkommandos in Auschwitz* (in Hebrew) (Jerusalem and Tel Aviv: Yad Vashem/Yediot Aharonot/Sifre Hemed, 1999).

43. Claude Lanzmann's *Sobibor, October 14, 1943, 4 p.m.* (2001), is to my mind a cinematic failure precisely because it lingers with undisguised pleasure on the details of how the Jewish inmates killed SS men, yet entirely ignores the main moral issue of an uprising by the same men who facilitated mass murder. See further in note 145, below.

44. The uprising took place on October 7, 1944. During eight weeks, between May 15 and July 9, 1944, approximately 437,400 Jews were deported from Hungary—the vast majority of them to Birkenau. Hence the rebellion occurred too late to hamper this unprecedented swift destruction of about half of Hungarian Jewry. The postponement of the uprising was due largely to pressures of the Polish underground in Birkenau. The Poles wanted to wait for the Red Army to come

closer: they had a chance of survival. The Jewish Sonderkommando knew that they were about to be exterminated. Hence the differences between the existential conditions of these groups dictated their schedule. When speaking of Jewish "passivity" in the Holocaust, one should stress that neither the Soviet POWs nor the Polish political prisoners in Birkenau ever rebelled, although, unlike the Jews, the Polish resistance was well equipped for a revolt (and apparently lent little or no help to the Jews). See further in Gideon Greif, "Die moralische Problematik der 'Sonderkommando'-Häflinge," and the different interpretation in Henryk Świebocki, "Spontane und organisierte Formen des Widerstandes in Konzentrationslagern am Beispiel des KL Auschwitz," both in *Die nationalsozialistischen Konzentrationslager: Entwicklung und Struktur,* ed. Ulrich Herbert, Karin Orth, and Christoph Dieckmann (Göttingen: Wallstein, 1998), 959–82, 1023–45, respectively.

45. Kazimierz Brandys (1916–2000) became known both for his early espousal of communism and socialist realism in his postwar writing and for his subsequent disenchantment with the party and its literary dogmas. See his *Samson* (Warsaw: Czytelnik, 1949). The book came out also in Yiddish and Italian: *Shimshn,* trans. M. Volanski (Buenos Aires: Heymland, 1958); *Sansone,* trans. Franciszka Frova and Giovanna Tomassucci (Rome: Edizione e/o, 1987).

46. Nachman Ben-Yehuda, *The Massada Myth: Collective Memory and Mythmaking in Israel* (Madison: University of Wisconsin Press, 1995); Yael Zerubavel, *Recovered Roots: Collective Memory and the Making of Israeli National Tradition* (Chicago: University of Chicago Press, 1995), chap. 5.

47. Ruth Ben-Ghiat, *Fascist Modernities: Italy, 1922–1945* (Berkeley: University of California Press, 2001).

48. For an interesting analysis, see Ewa Mazierska, "Non-Jewish Jews, Good Poles and Historical Truth in the Films of Andrzej Wajda," *HJFRT* (June 2000): 213–26.

49. Tadeusz Sobolewski, *Kino* 10, no. 95: http://www.wajda.pl/en/filmy/film32.html (accessed April 7, 2004).

50. Yisrael Gutman, *The Jews of Warsaw, 1939–1943: Ghetto, Underground, Revolt,* trans. Ina Friedman (Bloomington: Indiana University Press, 1989), part 3. On popular attitudes, see Joanna Beata Michlic, *Poles and Jews, 1880–2000* (forthcoming), esp. chap. 4, the section titled: "Witnessing the Warsaw Ghetto Uprising."

51. In a certain sense, the destruction of the ghetto facilitates Jakub's heroism: Now that the Jews are gone, he can join the Polish resistance fighters and communists in their fight against the Germans. Now finally a new and better world can be built on the ruins of the old, a world, it seems, that will be *judenfrei.*

52. Wajda was obviously relying in large part on Korczak's own diary. See Janusz Korczak, *Ghetto Diary,* trans. Jerzy Bachrach and Barbara Krzywicka (Vedder) (New Haven, Conn.: Yale University Press, 2003). The extensive introduction by Betty Jean Lifton provides the background for his life, the context in which he wrote the diary, and the circumstances of his death. Ibid., vii–xxx. The very last entry in the diary is quite accurately reenacted in the film: "I am watering the flowers. My bald head in the window. What a splendid target. He has a rifle. Why is he standing and looking on calmly? He has no orders to shoot. And perhaps he was a village teacher in civilian life, or a notary, a street sweeper in Leipzig, a waiter in Cologne? What would he do if I nodded to him? Waved my hand in a friendly gesture? Perhaps he

doesn't even know that things are—as they are? He may have arrived only yester-day, from far away. . . ." Ibid., 115. That day, August 5 or 6, 1942, Korczak and his children went to their deaths.

53. The Official Website of Andrzej Wajda: http://www.wajda.pl/en/filmy/film29.html (accessed April 7, 2004).

54. Ibid.

55. Ibid.

56. Ibid. And see Betty Jean Lifton, *The King of Children: The Life and Death of Janusz Korczak* (New York: St. Martin's Griffin, 1997).

57. The Official Website of Andrzej Wajda.

58. Mazierska, "Non-Jewish Jews"; Korczak, *Ghetto Diary*, xxii–xxiii, 94–95, 112.

59. As Lifton writes, "the Poles claim Korczak as a martyr, who would have been canonized if he had converted." One might say that precisely because he was a proud Pole, Korczak would not have converted at a time when Jews were perse-cuted for their religion and "race." This was the argument made by the great historian Marc Bloch in his testament. See his *Strange Defeat: A Statement of Evidence Written in 1940,* trans. Gerard Hopkins (New York: Norton, 1968).

60. Mazierska, "Non-Jewish Jews." Korczak, *Ghetto Diary*, vii.

61. Ibid. Indeed, in Wajda's *Land of Promise* (1974) Moryc Welt (played by the same Wojciech Pszoniak who plays Korczak) does cut a "typical" Jewish figure, and many of the other male and female Jewish characters speak in a heavily Jewish-accented Polish (or *żydlaczy,* which is the Polish equivalent of the derogatory German term *mauscheln* for "Jewish-speak"), thus "causing injury" to the Polish language. This was in conformity with a certain view of the era in which the film takes place and even more so with W. Reymont's antisemitic novel on which it is based. The use of żydlaczy is one reason why especially some Jewish viewers were offended by *Land of Promise.* Thanks to Joanna Michlic for pointing this out to me. Conversely, Polanski's *The Pianist* resolves the issue by using English, which ironi-cally may have ensured its identity as a Polish movie. In another curious twist, in the German-dubbed version of Polanski's controversial *The Fearless Vampire Killers; or, Pardon Me, but Your Teeth Are in My Neck* (1967), the Jewish characters (who include a Jewish vampire) speak in a mixture of *mauscheln* and Yiddish.

62. Writing in the Warsaw Ghetto when he was over sixty years old, Korczak related the following ruminations he had as a five-year-old child upon the death of his canary: "Its death had brought about the mysterious question of religion. I had wanted to put a cross on top of the grave. The housemaid said no, because it was only a bird, something much, much lower than man. Even to cry over it was a sin. So much for the housemaid. What was worse, the janitor's son decided that the canary was Jewish. And so was I. I too was a Jew, and he—a Pole, a Catholic. It was certain paradise for him, but as for me, if I did not use dirty words and never failed dutifully to steal sugar for him from the house—I would end up, when I died, in a place which, though not hell, was nevertheless dark. And I was scared of a dark room. Death—Jew—hell. A black Jewish paradise. Certainly plenty to think about." Korczak, *Ghetto Diary,* 11. For other comments on Jewish-Polish relations in the diary, see ibid., 15–17, 28–29, 37, 100–101, 105, 108–10. It should be mentioned also that the Polish monument commemorating Korczak is placed in the vast Jewish cemetery in Warsaw. Korczak also had Hebrew taught at his ghetto orphan-

age, had been to Palestine in 1934 and 1936, and though not a Zionist, was attacked as such by the Polish right wing and consequently lost his popular radio show. The film contains a scene in which Korczak is notified that his show will not be aired any longer, but his response is rather pacifying to postwar Polish ears: "War brings its suffering and tragedy but it erases the past which, I believe, will not repeat itself. I believe that never again will a Pole persecute his brother because he is a Jew. And I am glad to be able to live this moment." As Wajda clearly knew, the history of postwar Polish antisemitism hardly confirmed Korczak's prediction. Moreover, rather than hoping to rebuild a postwar Poland, he wrote in his diary about his desire to build an orphanage in the Galilee. Ibid., xviii–xix, 19–21, 78. But in the film Korczak says to one of the children: "When the war is over I will take care of German orphans."

63. Other significant scenes suggestive of pietás in films discussed in this book include the last scene in *The Golem*, when the ogre holds the child in his arms just before that child pulls out the star from his chest and thereby kills him; the girl in *Newland* holding her teddy bear; and the very last shot in *Don't Touch My Holocaust*, where the Israeli woman who played a musselman holds the naked Palestinian actor who had just flagellated himself on a table packed with beer bottles. One might mention here that the most important pietá in contemporary Germany is the greatly enlarged copy of a sculpture by Käthe Kollwitz, which was placed in the building of the Neue Wache in Berlin by former chancellor Helmut Kohl.

64. Here is Korczak's description of the scene: "An injection of caffeine for a hysterical new inmate following a collapse. His mother, wasting away of ulcerated intestines, was unwilling to die until the child had been placed in the Home. The boy was unwilling to go until the mother had died. He finally yielded. The mother died propitiously, now the child has pangs of conscience. In his illness, he mimics his mother: he moans (screams), complains of pain, then gasps, then feels hot, finally is dying of thirst. 'Water!' I pace the dormitory to and fro. Will there be an outbreak of mass hysteria? Might be! But the children's confidence in the leadership prevailed. They believed that as long as the doctor was calm there was no danger. Actually I was not calm. But the fact that I shouted at the troublesome patient and threatened to throw him out onto the staircase was evidence that the man at the helm had everything under control. The decisive factor: he shouts, he knows." Korczak, *Ghetto Diary*, 94.

65. Even the last scene, in which Korczak and his orphans march to the Umschlagplatz carrying the Star of David flag (as was indeed the case according to eyewitness accounts), strangely makes him into a heroic Polish character, charging toward certain death behind the national flag, as did the Polish cavalry in 1939. This is also reminiscent of the penultimate scene in the film *Border Street*, which I discuss below, where the "Jew"—this time a member of the working class—is transformed into a Polish hero, fighting the Germans under the Polish flag.

66. Anthony Kauffman, "István Szabó's Century of 'Sunshine,'" IndieWIRE: http://www.indiewire.com/people/int_Szabo_Istvan_000612.html (accessed April 7, 2004).

67. George L. Mosse, "Jewish Emancipation: Between *Bildung* and Respectability," in *The Jewish Response to German Culture: From the Enlightenment to the Second World War*, ed. Jehuda Reinharz and Walter Schatzberg (Hanover, N.H.: University

Press of New England, 1985), 1–16; István Deák, *Essays on Hitler's Europe* (Lincoln: University of Nebraska Press, 2001), 137–62.

68. For the best historical and cinematic analyses of *Sunshine,* see István Deák, "Strangers at Home," *NYRB* (July 20, 2000): http://www.nybooks.com/articles/8 (accessed April 7, 2004); Susan Rubin Suleiman, "Jewish Assimilation in Hungary, the Holocaust, and Epic Film: Reflections on István Sabó's *Sunshine,*" *YJC* 14, no. 1 (2001): 233–52.

69. On the debate in Hungary concerning Ivan's decision to revert to his grandfather's name, see Suleiman, "Jewish Assimilation in Hungary."

70. Kauffman, "István Szabó's Century of 'Sunshine.'"

71. Though much more terrifying than their Disney renditions, the Brothers Grimm's tales were quite tame and optimistic compared to the Nazi hell: "Early in the morning, Gretel had to go out and hang up the cauldron with the water, and light the fire. 'We will bake first,' said the old woman, 'I have already heated the oven, and kneaded the dough.' She pushed poor Gretel out to the oven, from which flames of fire were already darting. 'Creep in,' said the witch, 'and see if it is properly heated, so that we can put the bread in.' And once Gretel was inside, she intended to shut the oven and let her bake in it, and then she would eat her, too. But Gretel saw what she had in mind, and said: 'I do not know how I am to do it; how do I get in?' 'Silly goose,' said the old woman. 'The door is big enough; just look, I can get in myself!' and she crept up and thrust her head into the oven. Then Gretel gave her a push that drove her far into it, and shut the iron door, and fastened the bolt. Oh then she began to howl quite horribly, but Gretel ran away, and the godless witch was miserably burnt to death." J. Grimm and W. Grimm, *The Complete Grimm's Fairy Tales,* trans. Margaret Hunt, rev. James Stern (New York: Pantheon Books, 1976), 92–93.

72. When Moreau saves Stella, who has dark hair and eyes, by pulling her out of the line about to embark on an earlier transport, she is immediately re-placed by another, even younger "stand-by" child, rosy-cheeked and blond. This is the "choice," made with little fanfare in this film: saving one person often meant sacrificing another.

73. See, e.g., David Mills, "The Last Butterfly," *WP,* January 21, 1994: http://www.rottentomatoes.com/click/movie-1053669/reviews.php?critic=all&sortby=default&page=1&rid=35885 (accessed April 7, 2004), who writes that Moreau "is a more clearly heroic figure than . . . Schindler." The cover of the video cites New York City's WOR Radio as saying that *The Last Butterfly* is "a more person-alized and beautiful version of *Schindler's List.*"

74. Kachyna also offers a fantasy of safe return, in a last scene showing the murdered children returning to their mothers, including one who had tried to fly away from Terezín and crashed on the railroad track. This is the same fantasy as that of Wajda's *Korczak;* it is not about forgetting the reality of murder, but about remembering the fragile hopes of the children and insisting on our own refusal to accept that their lives could have been so arbitrarily extinguished.

75. For a more extended discussion of *Schindler's List,* see Omer Bartov, "Spiel-berg's Oskar: Hollywood Tries Evil," in *Spielberg's Holocaust: Critical Perspectives on Schindler's List,* ed. Y. Loshitzky (Bloomington: Indiana University Press, 1997), 41–60.

76. Schindler is the classical vicarious hero, acting heroically on behalf of the Jews who are incapable of such acts on their own. This kind of vicarious cinematic heroism is similarly manifested—though on a much more modest scale—in *Jew-boy Levi* (1999), where the Jew merely facilitates farmer Horger's daughter Lisbeth's display of heroism by becoming the target of antisemitic harassment (see further in chap. 2, "Redemptive Nostalgia"). German and Polish cinema in particular makes use of Jewish victims as providing the occasion for good gentiles to stand out.

77. The theme and title of the film is obviously derived from the collection *I Never Saw Another Butterfly: Children's Drawings and Poems from Terezín Concentration Camp, 1942–1944,* ed. Hana Volavková, 2d ed. (New York: Schocken Books, 1993). Another version is *I Have Not Seen a Butterfly Around Here: Children's Drawings and Poems from Terezín* (Prague: Jewish Museum, 1993). To be sure, the film depicts the Holocaust through a lens that facilitates identification by non-Jewish European audiences: we see here Jews as carriers of Central and Western European culture rather than as exotic *Ostjuden.* The Jews are normal people–and yet, even here they need the mediating influence of a gentile to be completely normalized as human victims. As part of the Eastern European film tradition, the Nazis are depicted as uncivilized brutes. Against this caricature of the Germans, a powerful scene in the movie shows women pouring human ashes of victims cremated in Terezín into the river, symbolizing the Holocaust as both a site of annihilation of people and of the annihilation of its own traces—precisely what Terezín has come to embody.

78. In a recent interview with Barbara Bogaev on National Public Radio's program "Fresh Air" (November 11, 2002), Lustig revealed that he was in fact one of these young men, although in reality the woman who liberated them of their virginity before the journey to Auschwitz was a prostitute. Lustig may have been the only member of these ten or eleven youths (the youngest was fourteen years old) who survived the Holocaust.

79. For a remarkable account of life under both dictatorships, see Heda Margolius Kovály, *Under a Cruel Star: A Life in Prague, 1941–1968,* trans. Francis Epstein and Helen Epstein with the author (New York: Holmes and Meier, 1997).

80. Generally on Polish-Jewish relations, see Michael Steinlauf, *Bondage to the Dead: Poland and the Memory of the Holocaust* (Syracuse, N.Y.: Syracuse University Press, 1997); Daniel Blatman, "Polish Jewry, the Six-Day War, and the Crisis of 1968," in *The Six-Day War and World Jewry,* ed. Eli Lederhendler (Bethesda: University Press of Maryland, 2000), 291–310; Michlic, *Poles and Jews.*

81. Stuart Liebman, "Les premières constellations du discours sur l'Holocauste dans le cinéma polonais," in *De l'histoire au cinema,* ed. Antoine de Baecque and Christian Delage (Paris: Editions Complexe, 1998), 196.

82. As in all subsequent citations from *The Last Stage,* the text has been transcribed directly from the film, but English subtitles provided have been somewhat amended.

83. For one of the most powerful texts on the experience of female political inmates in Auschwitz, see Charlotte Delbo, *Auschwitz and After,* trans. Rosette C. Lamont (New Haven, Conn.: Yale University Press, 1995). For a detailed analysis of the number of victims in Auschwitz, see Franciszek Piper, "The Number of Victims," in *Anatomy of the Auschwitz Death Camp,* ed. Yisrael Gutman and Michael Berenbaum (Bloomington: Indiana University Press, 1994), 61–80. Also derived

from Piper's research, a lower count of 1.1 million victims, of whom 890,000 were Jews, is offered in Robert Jan van Pelt, *The Case for Auschwitz: Evidence from the Irving Trial* (Bloomington: Indiana University Press, 2002), 106–16. For an analysis of how Auschwitz was represented in postwar Poland, including the debate on the identity and number of the victims, see Jonathan Huener, *Auschwitz, Poland, and the Politics of Commemoration, 1945–1979* (Athens: Ohio University Press, 2003).

84. For a more general analysis of the film, see Liebman, "Les premières constellations," 195–209.

85. While the International Red Cross Committee was planning to visit the family camp in Birkenau following its visit to Terezín on June 23, 1944, the rosy report on the latter by its delegate, Dr. Maurice Rossel, led to the cancellation of the trip to Auschwitz. Hence no such visit ever took place. Miroslav Karny, "The Vrba and Wetzler Report," in *Anatomy of the Auschwitz Death Camp,* 559. On smuggling information from Auschwitz to the outside world, see Martin Gilbert, "What Was Known and When," in *Anatomy of the Auschwitz Death Camp,* 539–52.

86. When Marta and Tadek meet outside the camp, they embrace under a cross, symbolizing the unity of (at least "Aryan-looking") Jews and Poles, resisters and communists, heroism, faith, and love.

87. According to Liebman, "Les premières constellations," 208, Jakubowska insisted that she used documentary footage of American aircraft, but the Hungarian cinematographer Béla Balázs argued that these were definitely Soviet planes. See also Stuart Liebman, interview with Wanda Jakubowska, in *SEEP* 17, no. 3 (fall 1997); "Béla Balázs on Wanda Jakubowska's *The Last Stop:* Three Texts," *SEEP* 16, no. 3 (fall 1996): 56–63, trans. Stuart Liebman.

88. See further in chap. 2, 60–61, and note 56. See also testimony by Raya Kagan, *The Trial of Adolf Eichmann,* Session 70, June 8, 1961. A dry, factual account of the escape on June 24, 1944, of Mala Zimmetbaum and Edward (Edek) Galinski, which eschews any details on Mala's heroism at their execution on September 15, 1944, can be found in Henryk Świebocki, "Prisoner Escapes," in *Anatomy of the Auschwitz Death Camp,* 509. In Michal Govrin's recent novel, *The Name,* trans. Barbara Harshav (New York: Riverhead Books, 1998), 331–32, she appears as Mala Auerbach, while her Polish lover is called Stashek (which should be "Staszek" in the Polish spelling). On Govrin's "invention" of this name, see her essay, "The Journey to Poland," in *In God's Name: Genocide and Religion in the Twentieth Century,* ed. Omer Bartov and Phyllis Mack (New York: Berghahn Books, 2001), 371, n. 3. Liebman cites several other texts and films that mention this story: Fania Fenelon, *Playing for Time* (New York: Athenaeum, 1997), 157–68, and its 1980 cinematic adaptation by Arthur Miller and Daniel Mann; Wieslaw Kielar, *Anus Mundi* (New York: Times Books, 1980), 215–55; Olga Lengyel, *Five Chimneys* (Chicago: Ziff-Davis Publishing, 1947), 124–25; Sara Nomberg-Przytyk, *Auschwitz: True Tales from a Grotesque Land* (Chapel Hill: University of North Carolina Press, 1985), 100–104; Sewerina Szmaglewska, *Smoke Over Birkenau* (New York: Henry Holt, 1947), 296. See Liebman, "Les premières constellations," 202, n. 21.

89. See more detail on the personnel, organization, and inmates of the women's camp in Birkenau, in Irena Strzekecka, "Women," in *Anatomy of the Auschwitz Death Camp,* 393–411.

90. Such proclamations were in fact made by the Western Allies rather than by the Soviets. See more in Gilbert, "What Was Known and When," 549.

91. These grossly inflated figures, unknown to have ever been anticipated as potential inmates of Auschwitz, are obviously cited in order to eliminate the distinction between the Jews who were actually the main victims of the camp and other European populations that were not.

92. See further in Hermann Langbein, "The Auschwitz Underground," in *Anatomy of the Auschwitz Death Camp,* 485–502; note 44, above.

93. Liebman, "Les premières constellations," 207, cites Czesław Miłosz's well-known statement that the communist depiction of the camps was predicated on the following elements: (1) prisoners must be seen as members of clandestine organizations; (2) the communists must appear as leaders of these organization; (3) all Russian prisoners must be distinguished by their moral force and heroism; and (4) prisoner conduct should be primarily dictated by their political stance.

94. Munk's other films include *The Man of the Blue Cross* (1955), *Man on the Tracks* (1956), *Eroica* (1958), *A Visit to the Old City* (1958), and *Bad Luck* (1960). *Last Pictures* (2001) is a reconstruction of events during the shooting of *The Passenger,* made by Munk's assistant at the time, Andrzej Brzozowski.

95. For some analyses of Andrzej Munk's films, and especially of *The Passenger,* see Stuart Klawans, "Life is Beautiful," FCM: http://www.filmlinc.com/fcm/ 1-2-2002/munk.htm (accessed April 7, 2004); http://www.polishculture-nyc.org/ munk.htm (accessed April 7, 2004); "Wry Smiles, Suspicious Glances: The Films of Andrzej Munk," in http://filmlinc.com/archive/programs/1-2002/munk/munk. htm (accessed April 7, 2004).

96. This and the subsequent citation have been transcribed directly from the film's English-language voiceover.

97. For the best analysis, see Stuart Liebman, "The First Film Documentary of the Liberation of the Camps: The Case of Majdanek," unpublished paper, Queens College and CUNY Graduate Center, 2002.

98. See further in Liebman, "Les premières constellations," 209–15, also citing, in reference to Stalin's reaction, Gene Moskowitz, "The Uneasy Past: Aleksander Ford and the Polish Cinema," *S&S* 27, no. 3 (winter 1957): 137.

99. On the memorial, see James Young, *The Texture of Memory: Holocaust Memorials and Meaning* (New Haven, Conn.: Yale University Press, 1993), 155–84.

100. All citations have been transcribed directly from the film. I have made some corrections to the English subtitles.

101. The film both presents and refutes the Polish antisemitic view of the Jews as cowards in an early scene: Natan refuses to give up his seat at the barbershop to a uniformed Mr. Wojtan, who is rushing to join the army following the German attack. Mr. Kuśmirak, who is also in line, says: "Such is their patriotism. A Polish officer is going to war and the Jews are in a hurry." But when Natan takes off his apron, we see that he too is in uniform.

102. This scene was of course repeated in Wajda's *Samson,* where Jakub emerges from the ruins of the ghetto as a Polish-communist freedom fighter.

103. One may also add here that while another element in Władek's transformation from antisemite to ally of the Jews is his love for Jadzia, the realization of this

love is facilitated by Jadzia's ambivalent status: It is her final decision to remain on the "Aryan" side, i.e., to be on the side of the Poles rather than that of the Jews, that cements their relationship. That she appears physically "Polish" rather than "Jewish" must have made this match all the more acceptable to contemporary viewers as well. There are obvious echoes here of the relationship between Phil and Kathy in *Gentleman's Agreement* (see chap. 2, "One of Us").

104. The first acknowledgment by Hollywood of the "Jew" as a heroic fighter in Palestine is George Sherman's *Sword in the Desert* (1949). On the shift from what he calls the "fashionable forties" and "frightened fifties" to the "self-conscious sixties," see Friedman, *The Jewish Image in American Film,* 41–71.

105. Judith E. Doneson, *The Holocaust in American Film* (Philadelphia: Jewish Publication Society, 1987); Jeffrey Shandler, *While America Watches: Televising the Holocaust* (New York: Oxford University Press, 1999).

106. Peter Novick, *The Holocaust in American Life* (Boston: Houghton Mifflin, 1999). Norman G. Finkelstein, *The Holocaust Industry: Reflections on the Exploitation of Jewish Suffering* (London: Verso, 2000), which claims to uncover the roots of this phenomenon, is in many ways one of its most pernicious manifestations.

107. Chapter 4 is largely devoted to this issue. See also Nurith Gertz, *Motion Fiction: Israeli Fiction in Film* (in Hebrew) (Tel Aviv: Open University of Israel, 1993); Yosefa Loshitzky, *Identity Politics on the Israeli Screen* (Austin: University of Texas Press, 2001); Miri Talmon, *Israeli Graffiti: Nostalgia, Groups, and Collective Identity in Israeli Cinema* (in Hebrew) (Tel Aviv: Open University of Israel, 2001); Moshe Zimmerman, *Leave My Holocaust Alone: The Impact of the Holocaust on Israeli Cinema and Society* (in Hebrew) (Jerusalem: Keter, 2002).

108. Although MGM had originally commissioned Leon Uris to write this epic, and financed his research for what became his greatest bestseller, the rights were subsequently bought by Preminger, who swiftly replaced Uris as scriptwriter with the blacklisted Dalton Trumbo. Patricia Erens, *The Jew in American Cinema* (Bloomington: Indiana University Press, 1984), 217–18; Friedman, *The Jewish Image in American Film,* 161–65. For a recent discussion of the film, see Loshitzky, *Identity Politics,* chap. 1.

109. The *Exodus* was boarded by Royal Marines off the coast of Gaza, and in the fighting that ensued three Jews died and twenty-eight were seriously wounded. The ship was then towed to the port of Haifa, its passengers were brutally removed from the ship, and they were loaded onto prison ships that took them first to France (which refused to cooperate) and then to Hamburg. The Zionist leadership in Palestine made effective use of this event to propagate the cause of an independent Jewish State. As the Yugoslav member of the United Nations Special Committee on Palestine, who had observed the scenes in Haifa, aptly put it, the *Exodus* saga was "the best evidence we have" for allowing the Jews into Palestine. See Martin Gilbert, *Israel: A History* (London: Doubleday, 1998), 145–46; Benny Morris, *Righteous Victims: A History of the Zionist-Arab Conflict, 1881–1999* (New York: Alfred A. Knopf, 1999), 183. See also Nissan Degani, *Exodus Calling* (in Hebrew) (Tel Aviv: Ministry of Defence, 1994).

110. Ari's sister Jordana (Alexandra Stewart) is also a sexy blond packed into tight khaki shorts and a khaki blouse, who hardly appears to be related to her dark-

haired, heavy-set mother. She thus similarly represents the transformation of the Diaspora Jewish female into a Wagnerian Brunhilde.

111. Newman's father was Jewish, but he was raised as a member of the Christian Science community. Sander L. Gilman, "'Die Rasse ist nicht schön'—'Nein, wir Juden sind keine hübsche Rasse!'" in *"Der schejne Jid": Das Bild des "jüdischen Körpers" in Mythos und Ritual,* ed. Sander L. Gilman, Robert Jütte, and Gabriele Kohlbauer-Fritz (Vienna: Picus Verlag, 1998), 70.

112. This and all subsequent dialogue passages have been transcribed directly from the film. Preminger himself was well aware of the irony of identity and appearance. Although he was Jewish, Preminger "looked" so Prussian that he played the role of a Nazi both on Broadway (in *Margin for Error*) and in Hollywood (in *The Pied Piper*). Katz, *The Film Encyclopedia,* 1098.

113. Ari's sweetheart Dafna, after whom his kibbutz is named, was tortured, mutilated, and killed by Arabs. But this event serves mainly to explain Ari's availability to Kitty, as well as providing a model of heroism to Karen and an illustration of Arab barbarism that eventually also claims Karen's life.

114. For the most updated research on Auschwitz, see Van Pelt, *The Case for Auschwitz.*

115. For literature on male and female prostitution in the camps and for its uses and abuses after the war, see Omer Bartov, *Mirrors of Destruction: War, Genocide, and Modern Identity* (New York: Oxford University Press, 2000), 185–212.

116. One is tempted to ask whether President Bill Clinton had this scene in mind when he bid farewell to the assassinated Israeli prime minister Yitzhak Rabin with the words *"shalom chaver"* (goodbye, friend).

117. As I will show in chapter 4, this distorted image is turned on its head once more in Israeli films of the last couple of decades, where the Israeli takes the form of the Nazi and the Arab becomes the persecuted Jew.

118. Ted Berkman, *Cast a Giant Shadow: The Story of Mickey Marcus Who Died to Save Jerusalem* (Garden City, N.Y.: Doubleday, 1962).

119. Friedman, *The Jewish Image in American Film,* 165; Erens, *The Jew in American Cinema,* 292. The first chief of staff of the Israeli Defense Forces (IDF) was Yacov Dori (1948–1949), who was succeeded by Yigael Yadin (1949–1952). The IDF does not have a military commander in chief, a post held by the minister of defense under the authority of the prime minister, who has consequently often retained this portfolio as well.

120. A curious event links the stories of the *Exodus* and Marcus. When it was flown back for burial in the United States, Marcus's body was escorted by Joseph Hamburger, the former captain of the *Exodus*. Gilbert, *Israel,* 205–209.

121. Katz, *The Film Encyclopedia,* 384.

122. In confrontations between Marcus and the general, John Wayne towers over Kirk Douglas, and the latter seems somewhat defensive even when attacking his commanding officer. Conversely, when shown with the Israeli officer Ram Oren (Stathis Giallelis), the blond and muscular Douglas towers over the dark, skinny, hunched, chain-smoking Oren.

123. Shavelson argued that his film "counters the myth that Jews walked to the gas chambers because they didn't know how to fight." In fact, the film shows that

they needed an American-trained soldier to teach them. Erens, *The Jew in American Cinema*, 292. See also Shavelson's own account on making the film: Melville Shavelson, *How to Make a Jewish Movie* (Englewood Cliffs, N.J.: Prentice-Hall, 1971).

124. Conversing with Marcus in the toy department of Macy's in New York City on Christmas Day, 1947, Safir also somewhat incongruously tries to illustrate the desperate situation in Palestine by saying, "Our children don't believe in Santa Claus, not anymore," implying that under normal conditions Jewish (American) children believe in Santa Claus just like everyone else. This and all subsequent citations have been transcribed directly from the film.

125. Marcus also predicts that the exotic Magda would not look as enticing if she were to end up "plucking chicken in Brooklyn," to which Magda responds with unfeigned surprise, considering that we cannot imagine Emma ever plucking chickens or, for that matter, living in Brooklyn. In a sense, the Jewish Magda will supposedly become an urban American Jew, whereas the non-Jewish Emma can be assured of a more appropriate suburban existence.

126. Brodkin had already produced *Judgment at Nuremberg* (1959), and Green had previously authored *The Artists of Terezin* (1969), whose influence can be seen in *Holocaust*. Doneson, *The Holocaust in American Film*, 149.

127. Ulrich Herbert, *Best: Biographische Studien über Radikalismus, Weltanschauung und Vernunft, 1903–1989* (Bonn: J.H.W. Dietz, 1996); Lutz Hachmeister, *Der Gegnerforscher: Die Karriere des SS-Führers Franz Alfred Six* (Munich: Beck, 1998); Yaacov Lozowick, *Hitler's Bureaucrats: The Nazi Security Police and the Banality of Evil,* trans. Haim Watzman (London: Continuum, 2002); Michael Wildt, *Generation des Unbedingten: Das Führungskorps des Reichssicherheitshauptamtes* (Hamburg: Hamburger Edition, 2002). See also Daniel Jonah Goldhagen, "The 'Humanist' as Mass Murderer: The Mind and Deeds of SS General Otto Ohlendorf," B.A. thesis, Harvard University, 1982; Gitta Sereny, *Into That Darkness: From Mercy Killing to Mass Murder* (New York: McGraw-Hill, 1974); Hannah Arendt, *Eichmann in Jerusalem: A Report on the Banality of Evil* (New York: Viking Press, 1963).

128. One of the most jarring distortions is the reenactment of the Wannsee Conference. In order to give Dorf more prominence, Eichmann's figure is shoved aside. Dorf is brought into the private celebration between "Gestapo" Müller, Eichmann, and Heydrich following the conference. Heydrich, who rarely used alcohol, appears as quite drunk. And, for no apparent reason, Hans Frank is shown as taking part at a meeting he never attended. Even the location of the meeting, hardly unknown in 1978, is moved from the infamous villa on the lake to a neoclassical building with a splendid staircase. For more accurate though hardly unproblematic cinematic reconstructions of this crucial event, see Heinz Schirk's *The Wannsee Conference* (1987) and Frank Pierson's *Conspiracy* (2002). These two docudramas try to reconcile the bureaucracy of genocide—as reflected in the protocol of the meeting taken down by Eichmann after the event—with the rough and brutal talk by the participants, which according to Eichmann's testimony at his trial was heard at the meeting but deleted from the protocol. They thus grapple with the problem of using a document that reflects one aspect of reality and reconstructing another known but unrecorded aspect of that same reality. In trying to make the killers into real-life characters, neither entirely banal nor obvi-

ously monstrous, the two films—but especially *Conspiracy*—show that the representation of evil all too often becomes a mere caricature of reality.

129. Cited in Eric L. Santner, *Stranded Objects: Mourning, Memory, and Film in Postwar Germany* (Ithaca, N.Y.: Cornell University Press, 1990), 75.

130. Ibid., 80.

131. Ibid., 104; see Doneson, *The Holocaust in American Film*, 144–96, for a wide-ranging analysis of responses; Anton Kaes, *From Hitler to Heimat: The Return of History as Film* (Cambridge: Harvard University Press, 1989), 30–35 (on responses to *Holocaust*), 161–92 (on *Heimat*).

132. Doneson, *The Holocaust in American Film*, 192–93. In France, *Holocaust* was similarly rejected at first as an aesthetically lamentable Hollywood soap opera, as an attempt by the Americans to give a lesson to the French, and as politically inopportune, even though the series says nothing directly about French collaboration and is far more critical of American and British policies. Once screened, however, it proved to be very successful with viewers. Ibid., 193–94. See also Friedrich Knilli and Siegfried Zielinski, eds., *Holocaust zur Unterhaltung. Anatomie eines internationalen Bestsellers: Fakten, Fotos, Forschungsreportagen* (Berlin: Verlag für Ausbildung und Studium, 1982).

133. Such an argument has also been made—to my mind with more justification—about another, more recent and controversial work on the Holocaust: Daniel Jonah Goldhagen's *Hitler's Willing Executioners: Ordinary Germans and the Holocaust* (New York: Alfred A. Knopf, 1996). See Omer Bartov, *Germany's War and the Holocaust: Disputed Histories* (Ithaca, N.Y.: Cornell University Press, 2003), chap. 6. One measure of the success of the miniseries is the fact that it brought the word "Holocaust" into general use in Germany, where hitherto such Nazi terms as *Judenvernichtung* (extermination of the Jews), *Judenverfolgung* (persecution of the Jews), or *Endlösung* (final solution) were normally used.

134. The earliest influential American film with a Holocaust-related theme was *The Diary of Anne Frank* (1959), directed by George Stevens and adapted by Frances Goodrich and Albert Hackett from their 1956 Pulitzer Prize–winning play. But while its characters are Jews, it is hardly an attempt to represent the realities of mass murder. Conversely, Stanley Kramer's *Judgment at Nuremberg* (1961), while it discusses German crimes, does not include a single Jewish character. Doneson, *The Holocaust in American Film*, 60–107; Insdorf, *Indelible Shadows*, 6–9.

135. Cited in Kaes, *From Hitler to Heimat*, 220, n. 53, from Cecil Smith, "Docudrama: Fact or Forum," *LAT* (April 17, 1978). On the roots of *Holocaust* in the film saga *Roots* (1977), see Doneson, *The Holocaust in American Film*, 145.

136. *Holocaust* was viewed by approximately half of the American population at the time, some 120 million people. It was shown in some fifty countries around the world to an estimated total of 220 million viewers. Ibid., 189, 196.

137. One should remember in this context the recent controversy over the roaming exhibition crimes of the Wehrmacht, whose underlying assertion was that there were no heroic German soldiers. This, more than anything else, still caused a wave of anger and resentment not merely among surviving veterans but also among second- and some third-generation Germans who felt that the "honor" of the Wehrmacht had been besmirched. See Omer Bartov, Atina Grossmann, and

Mary Nolan, eds., *Crimes of War: Guilt and Denial in the Twentieth Century* (New York: New Press, 2002), introduction and chap. 5. In response to my assertion in a newspaper article in Germany that the Wehrmacht, which had participated in war crimes on a massive scale, had no honor to lose, several hair-raising letters were sent to the editor who kindly shared them with me. See Omer Bartov, "Eine Frage der Ehre: Über konservative Attacken gegen die Wehrmachts-Ausstellung," *Die Woche* (November 5, 1999): 39.

138. The renewed preoccupation with German victimhood in recent years is reflected in several publications. See, e.g., W. G. Sebald, *On the Natural History of Destruction,* trans. Anthea Bell (New York: Random House, 2003); Jörg Friedrich, *Der Brand: Deutschland im Bombenkrieg 1940–1945* (Berlin: Propyläen, 2002); Günter Grass, *Crabwalk,* trans. Krishna Winston (Orlando, Fla.: Harcourt, 2002).

139. All quotes have been transcribed directly from the videocassette recording of the miniseries.

140. Ulrich Herbert, "Den Gegner vernichten, ohne ihn zu hassen: Loathing the Jews in the World View of the Intellectual Leadership of the SS in the 1920s and 1930s," unpublished paper, presented at the conference "Rethinking German Anti-Semitism, 1870–1933," Jerusalem, November 26–28, 1996.

141. Raul Hilberg, *The Destruction of the European Jews,* 3 vols., rev. ed. (New York: Holmes and Meier, 1985), 5–28. This was of course very much the view expressed in Lucy S. Dawidowicz, *The War Against the Jews, 1933–1945* (New York: Holt, Rinehart and Winston, 1975), a book that seems to have greatly influenced script-writer Green. See also James Carroll, *Constantine's Sword: The Church and the Jews* (Boston: Houghton Mifflin, 2001).

142. Noakes and Pridham, *Nazism 1919–1945,* 3:1199.

143. Czerniaków served as chairman of the Jewish Council until his suicide on July 23, 1942, soon after he was ordered by Höfle to facilitate mass deportations. Hilberg, *The Destruction of the European Jews,* 2:502.

144. This is of course taken from the manifesto to the Jewish youth in Vilna, issued by Kovner on January 1, 1942. See note 8, above.

145. *The Grey Zone* on the Sonderkommando revolt in Birkenau is the best film on this issue. Conversely, one of the worst Holocaust movies ever made is Jack Gold's *Escape from Sobibor* (1987), based on Richard Rashke's book of the same name (Boston: Houghton Mifflin, 1982). Aleksander "Sasha" Pechersky, the Jewish Red Army officer and inmate who organized the uprising, is played by the tall, blond, blue-eyed Dutch actor Rutger Hauer, a better candidate for the SS than any of the "real" members of Himmler's Black Corps in the film. The reconstruction of his love affair with the young Dutch-Jewish woman Luka, played by the beautiful and perfectly Aryan-looking Polish actress Joanna Pacula, catapults the film further into the zone of kitsch, as the lovers stroll on the death camp's grounds contemplating their mutual feelings. Even Alan Arkin, who plays the historical Leon Feldhendler, cannot save this cinematic catastrophe. For photos of the real Pechersky, see Yitzhak Arad, *Belzec, Sobibor, Treblinka: The Operation Reinhard Death Camps* (Bloomington: Indiana University Press, 1987), 323, 341, who also provides the most reliable account of the uprising: ibid., 322–33. See also Alexander Pechersky (Pechorskii), *Der Ofshtand in Sobibor* (Moscow: Emes, 1946); Dov Freiberg (Fraiberg), *To Survive Sobibor* (in Hebrew) (Ramlah: Hotsa'at Ha'mehaber, 1988);

Thomas Toivi Blatt, *From the Ashes of Sobibor: A Story of Survival* (Evanston, Ill.: Northwestern University Press, 1997). Another failed attempt to deal with this event is Claude Lanzmann's *Sobibor, October 14, 1943, 4 pm* (2001), which centers on an interview with Yehuda Lerner, one of the survivors of the revolt. Lanzmann made the interview while preparing *Shoah* (1985), but discarded it at the time and reworked it into this film only recently. Lanzmann's intention is clearly to create the kind of fighting Jewish hero absent from *Shoah*. In an interview to *The Guardian*, he said: "There is a strong parentage between Yehuda Lerner's story and *Tsahal* [the film he made about the Israeli Defense Forces]. I wanted to show how this man, who is profoundly non-violent, moves into violence. It is mythological, this film. It is David and Goliath. You remember how he compares the guard he kills to King Kong?" Thus Lanzmann strips the story of Sobibor of all its complexity and recreates it as myth; more authentic, but ultimately no less misleading, than Gold's fiasco. See Peter Lennon, "Ghosts of Sobibor," *The Guardian* (July 27, 2001): http://film.guardian.co.uk/interview/interviewpages/0,6737,527708,00.html (accessed April 7, 2004).

146. David I. Kertzer, *The Popes Against the Jews: The Vatican's Role in the Rise of Anti-Semitism* (New York: Alfred A. Knopf, 2001); John Cornwell, *Hitler's Pope: The Secret History of Pius XII* (New York: Viking, 1999); Guenter Lewy, *The Catholic Church and Nazi Germany*, 2d ed. (New York: Da Capo Press, 2000); Michael Phayer, *The Catholic Church and the Holocaust, 1930–1965* (Bloomington: Indiana University Press, 2000); W. D. Halls, *Politics, Society and Christianity in Vichy France* (Oxford, UK: Berg, 1995).

147. There were also numerous priests, pastors, monks, and nuns who rescued Jews. On this issue, and more generally on the complex relationship between religion and genocide, see Bartov and Mack, *In God's Name*.

148. Beth A. Griech-Polelle, *Bishop von Galen: German Catholicism and National Socialism* (New Haven, Conn.: Yale University Press, 2002).

149. Nathan Stoltzfus, *Resistance of the Heart: Intermarriage and the Rosenstrasse Protest in Nazi Germany* (New York: Norton, 1996). For a more skeptical view of the women's role in saving their husbands, see Wolf Gruner, "The Factory Action and the Events at the Rosenstrasse in Berlin: Facts and Fictions about 27 February 1943—Sixty Years Later," *CEH* 36, no. 2 (2003): 179–208. A film based on this story has recently been released: *Rosenstrasse*, d. Margarethe von Trotta (2003).

150. Scott Spector, "Edith Stein's Passing Gestures: Intimate Histories, Empathic Portraits," *New German Critique* 75 (fall 1998): 28–56.

4. The "Jew" as Anti-Hero

1. Both Chaplin and Allen were most probably inspired by such models as Ernst Lubitsch's early films, Menachem Mendel (Solomon Mikhoels) in *Jewish Luck,* and the entire cast of Joseph Green and Jan Nowina-Przybylski's *Yiddle with His Fiddle* (1936).

2. Further in Judith E. Doneson, *The Holocaust in American Film* (Philadelphia: Jewish Publication Society, 1987), 120.

3. Patricia Erens, *The Jew in American Cinema* (Bloomington: Indiana University Press, 1984), 329, citing Philip Roth, "Imagining Jews," *NYRB* (October 3,

1974): 22–28. Compare with a very different view in Alain Finkielkraut, *The Imaginary Jew*, trans. David Suchoff (Lincoln: University of Nebraska Press, 1994).

4. See more in Omer Bartov, *Mirrors of Destruction: War, Genocide, and Modern Identity* (New York: Oxford University Press, 2000), 185–212.

5. Émile Ajar (Romain Gary), *La vie devant soi* (Paris: Mercure de France, 1975), translated as *The Life before Us*, trans. Ralph Manheim (New York: New Directions, 1986); Romain Gary, *Vie et mort d'Émile Ajar* (Paris: Gallimard, 1981).

6. Romain Gary, "La vie devant soi," http://perso.club-internet.fr/delpiano/Gary.htm (accessed April 2, 2004).

7. Ibid.

8. Romain Gary, *Les racines du ciel* (Paris: Gallimard, 1956), translated as *The Roots of Heaven*, trans. Jonathan Griffin (New York: Simon and Schuster, 1958).

9. See more in http://www.kirjasto.sci.fi/rgary.htm (accessed April 7, 2004); http://www.alalettre.com/gary-intro.htm (accessed April 7, 2004); Jean-Marie Catonné, *Romain Gary/Émile Ajar* (Paris: P. Belfond, 1990); Dominique Bona, *Romain Gary* (Paris: Mercure de France, 1987).

10. Ephraim Katz, *The Film Encyclopedia*, 2d ed. (New York: Harper Perennial, 1994), 955, 1250–51.

11. Boris Schreiber, *La descente au berceau* (Paris: Luneau Ascot, 1984); Émile Ajar (Romain Gary), *L'Angoisse du roi Salomon* (Paris: Mercure de France, 1979), translated as *King Solomon*, trans. Barbara Wright (New York: Harper and Row, 1983).

12. Johann Wolfgang von Goethe, *Wilhelm Meister's Apprenticeship,* ed. and trans. Eric A. Blackall and Victor Lange (Princeton, N.J.: Princeton University Press, 1995); Franz Kafka, "A Report to an Academy," in Kafka, *The Penal Colony: Stories and Short Pieces,* trans. Willa and Edwin Muir (New York: Schocken Books, 1976), 173–84.

13. Jacob Katz, *Out of the Ghetto: The Social Background of Jewish Emancipation, 1770–1870* (Syracuse, N.Y.: Syracuse University Press, 1998).

14. Yael Zerubavel, *Recovered Roots: Collective Memory and the Making of Israeli National Tradition* (Chicago: University of Chicago Press, 1995).

15. Roni Stauber, *Lesson for This Generation: Holocaust and Heroism in Israeli Public Discourse in the 1950s* (in Hebrew) (Jerusalem: Yad Ben-Zvi Press/Ben Gurion University of the Negev Press, 2000).

16. Gershon Greenberg, "Orthodox Jewish Thought in the Wake of the Holocaust: *Tamim Pa'alo* of 1947," in *In God's Name: Genocide and Religion in the Twentieth Century,* ed. Omer Bartov and Phyllis Mack (New York: Berghahn Books, 2001), 316–41.

17. Israel Gutman, ed., *Major Changes within the Jewish people in the Wake of the Holocaust* (in Hebrew) (Jerusalem: Yad Vashem, 1996).

18. Yosef Hayim Yerushalmi, *Zakhor: Jewish History and Jewish Memory* (Seattle: University of Washington Press, 1996); Nachman Ben-Yehuda, *The Massada Myth: Collective Memory and Mythmaking in Israel* (Madison: University of Wisconsin Press, 1995).

19. See, e.g., Zachary Braiterman, *(God) after Auschwitz: Tradition and Change in Post-Holocaust Jewish Thought* (Princeton, N.J.: Princeton University Press, 1998); Richard L. Rubenstein, *After Auschwitz: History, Theology, and Contemporary Judaism,* 2d ed. (Baltimore: Johns Hopkins University Press, 1992).

20. Chaim Grade, *Musernikes: Poeme; Mayn Krig mit Hersh Raseyner: Esey* (Jerusalem: Hebrew University, 1969); the story is reprinted from *Idisher Kemfer* 32, no. 923 (1951). The film was adapted from a play by Joseph Telushkin with a screenplay by David Brandes.

21. Atina Grossmann, "Trauma, Memory, and Motherhood: Germans and Jewish Displaced Persons in Post-Nazi Germany, 1945–1949," *ASG* 38 (1998): 215–39; Zeev Mankowitz, *Life between Memory and Hope: The Survivors of the Holocaust in Occupied Germany* (Cambridge: Cambridge University Press, 2002).

22. Carl Friedman, *Twee koffers vol* (Amsterdam: Van Oorschot, 1993), translated as *The Shovel and the Loom,* trans. Jeannette K. Ringold (New York: Persea Books, 1996).

23. See, e.g., Walter Laqueur, *A History of Zionism,* 2d ed. (New York: Schocken Books, 1989); Jacques Kornberg, *Theodor Herzl: From Assimilation to Zionism* (Bloomington: Indiana University Press, 1993); Michael Stanislawski, *Zionism and the Fin de Siècle: Cosmopolitanism and Nationalism from Nordau to Jabotinsky* (Berkeley: University of California Press, 2001).

24. Hanna Yablonka, *Survivors of the Holocaust: Israel after the War,* trans. Ora Cummings (New York: New York University Press, 1999); Hanan Haver, Yehudah Shenhav, and Peninah Motsafi-Haler, eds., *Mizrahim in Israel: A Critical Observation into Israel's Ethnicity* (in Hebrew) (Tel Aviv: Hakibbutz Hameuchad, 2002); Yechiam Weitz, ed., *From Vision to Revision: A Hundred Years of Historiography of Zionism* (in Hebrew) (Jerusalem: Zalman Shazar Center, 1997).

25. Benny Morris, *The Birth of the Palestinian Refugee Problem, 1947–1949* (Cambridge: Cambridge University Press, 1987); Baruch Kimmerling and Joel S. Migdal, *The Palestinian People: A History* (Cambridge, Mass.: Harvard University Press, 2003).

26. Nurith Gertz, *Motion Fiction: Israeli Fiction in Film* (in Hebrew) (Tel Aviv: Open University of Israel, 1993); Nurith Gertz, *Myths in Israeli Culture: Captives of a Dream* (London: Vallentine Mitchell, 2000); Yosefa Loshitzky, *Identity Politics on the Israeli Screen* (Austin: University of Texas Press, 2001); Miri Talmon, *Israeli Graffiti: Nostalgia, Groups, and Collective Identity in Israeli Cinema* (in Hebrew) (Tel Aviv: Open University of Israel, 2001); Moshe Zimmerman, *Leave My Holocaust Alone: The Impact of the Holocaust on Israeli Cinema and Society* (in Hebrew) (Jerusalem: Keter, 2002); Tom Segev, *The Seventh Million: The Israelis and the Holocaust,* trans. Haim Watzman (New York: Hill and Wang, 1993); *Cinémateque* (in Hebrew) (May–June, 1994); Gershon Shaked, *No Other Place* (in Hebrew) (Tel Aviv: Hakibbutz Hameuchad, 1983); Michael Taub, ed., *Israeli Holocaust Drama* (Syracuse, N.Y.: Syracuse University Press, 1996); Moshe Zuckermann, *Shoah in the Sealed Room: The "Holocaust" in the Israeli Press during the Gulf War* (in Hebrew) (Tel Aviv: Hotsa'at H a'mehaber, 1993); Stauber, *Lesson for This Generation.*

27. Orna Ben-Dor Niv also made the influential film *Because of That War* (1988), which examines the relationship between two of Israel's top rock musicians and their parents, who are Holocaust survivors. This was the first time that Israeli popular culture, made by the second generation and consumed by the third, was linked so closely to the fate of the Jews in the Shoah.

28. Theodor Herzl, *Old New Land* (originally published as *Altneuland*), trans. Lotta Levensohn, introduction by Jacques Kornberg (Princeton, N.J.: Markus Wiener Publishers, 1987).

29. Talmon, *Israeli Graffiti,* 121, citing also Nurith Gertz, *The Canaanite Group: Literature and Ideology* (in Hebrew) (Tel Aviv: Open University of Israel, 1986); Amnon Rubinstein, "The Rise and Fall of the Mythological Sabra," in Rubinstein, *To Be a Free People* (in Hebrew) (Tel Aviv: Schocken, 1977), 111–16, where he writes about "Abroad, Abroad—The Enchanted Land." It is also interesting to note that Kobi Niv, the screenwriter for *Newland,* also wrote a scathing critique of *Life Is Beautiful,* in which he accused Benigni not only of providing support for the denial of the Holocaust but also of manufacturing a thinly veiled Christian theological parable that justifies the extermination of the Jews as punishment for the crucifixion of Jesus. Giosué (Jesus) is denounced this time by a German waiter and his father Guido (Judas) "corrects" his previous betrayal by paying with his own life to save the boy. As Giosué says in retrospect: "This was my father's sacrifice. This is the gift he gave me." While ingenious, this interpretation misconstrues the film even as it rightly identifies its Christian motifs. Kobi Niv, *Life Is Beautiful, But Not for Jews: Another View of the Film by Benigni* (in Hebrew) (Tel Aviv: N. B. Books, 2000), esp. 120–29.

30. One of the most vehement attacks on the "Zionist narrative" of bringing the survivors to Palestine/Israel is Idith Zertal, *From Catastrophe to Power: Holocaust Survivors and the Emergence of Israel* (Berkeley: University of California Press, 1998). Even harsher is Yosef Grodzinsky, *Good Human Material: Jews Facing Zionists, 1945–1951* (in Hebrew) (Jerusalem: Har Artsi, 1998). More balanced are Dina Porat, *The Blue and the Yellow Stars of David: The Zionist Leadership in Palestine and the Holocaust, 1939–1945,* trans. David Ben-Nahum (Cambridge, Mass.: Harvard University Press, 1990); Yablonka, *Survivors of the Holocaust.* See also Irit Keynan, *Holocaust Survivors and the Emissaries from Eretz-Israel: Germany, 1945–1948* (in Hebrew) (Tel Aviv: Am Oved, 1996); Anita Shapira, ed., *Haapala: Studies in the History of Illegal Immigration into Palestine, 1934–1948* (in Hebrew) (Tel Aviv: Am Oved, 1990).

31. Moshe Shamir, *With His Own Hands,* trans. Joseph Shachter (1951; reprint, Jerusalem: Institute for the Translation of Hebrew Literature, 1970). Of course, as pointed out by Loshitzky, *Identity Politics on the Israeli Screen,* 1, Ari Ben Canaan (Paul Newman) in *Exodus* is also "born from the sea," since he first appears emerging from the waves, just as his name, "son of Canaan," relates him to the ancient Hebrews rather than to any Diaspora existence, in precisely the same manner aspired to by Amos Kenan and his Canaanite movement. For differing views on the Sabra, see Oz Almog, *The Sabra: The Creation of the New Jew,* trans. Haim Watzman (Berkeley: University of California Press, 2000); Amnon Rubinstein, "The Rise and Fall of the Mythological Sabra"; Hanoch Bartov, *I Am Not the Mythological Sabra* (in Hebrew) (Tel-Aviv: Am Oved, 1995); Baruch Kimmerling, *The Invention and Decline of Israeliness: State, Society, and the Military* (Berkeley: University of California Press, 2001).

32. Gila Almagor, *Under the Domim Tree,* trans. Hillel Schenker (New York: Simon and Schuster, 1995); Almagor, *The Summer of Aviya: Girl with a Strange Name* (in Hebrew) (Tel Aviv: Am Oved, 1985).

33. The film opens with the following note: "'Youth Aliya' was established in 1933 in order to save youngsters from the threat of extermination by the Nazis. During the war and thereafter emissaries of 'Youth Aliya' continued to assemble children from their hiding places and bring them to the Land of Israel, where they

established their home. Dozens of youth villages were established for this purpose and absorbed 300,000 youngsters. The film 'Under the Domim Tree' is dedicated to this exceptional and glorious venture." For more, see Yablonka, *Survivors of the Holocaust*, 199–207, who notes that almost 80 percent of children accepted by Youth Aliya (*Aliyat Hano'ar*) between 1945 and 1949 were Holocaust survivors, of whom some 60 percent were integrated into kibbutzim. Some 11,500 children and youths came into kibbutzim in this period, of whom over 9,000 were Holocaust survivors. About 63 percent of the children integrated through Youth Aliya in 1946–1947, mostly Holocaust survivors, had lost both parents.

34. Nurith Gertz, "Space and Gender in the New Israeli and Palestinian Cinema," *Prooftexts* 22, no. 1–2 (winter/spring 2002): 183, n. 9, writes that "there is no evidence in that film that Henya [*sic*] is anything other than an authentic Holocaust survivor." Yet this would mean that Aviya was born just before the Holocaust in Europe and came to Palestine only after the war, whereas the film quite clearly portrays her as a Sabra (which Almagor is as well). See also Miriam Geldmacher, "Autorenportrait: Gila Almagor," http://www.lesenswert.de/almagor.html (accessed April 7, 2004). In *Under the Domim Tree*, Aviya says to her mother while visiting her in the closed psychiatric ward: "Mama, you were not there, you came to Israel before the war!" and tries to erase the numbers Henia had written on her arms in imitation of Auschwitz tattoos. Some reviewers give Aviya's age in *The Summer of Aviya* as ten. But in the sequel, when Aviya finds her father's grave in a Haifa cemetery, the date of his death is given there as 1939. Since she was born just after his death, this would make Aviya twelve years old in the first film, and fourteen years old in the second, which seems more reasonable considering her obvious budding maturity and interest in Jurek in *Under the Domim Tree*.

35. For a discussion of Bernhard Schlink and Binjamin Wilkomirski, who exemplify two rather warped ways of transferring oneself into past horrors, see Bartov, *Mirrors of Destruction*, 213–30.

36. Further on this in Bartov, *Mirrors of Destruction*, 185–212.

37. The film credits, and all other available information on *The Wooden Gun*, only provide a list of names for the boy actors—with the exception of Arik Rosen. The list includes: Nadav Brenner, Nissim Eliaz, Nir Barzel, Anatol Kotkes, Uri Darzi, Moshe Eisenberg, Yariv Rubinstein, Amnon Fisher, Amir Eden, Galit Zaksh, Shir Vardi, and Amir Birenboim.

38. See also analysis in Loshitzky, *Identity Politics on the Israeli Screen*, 116–27.

39. Ibid., 211, n. 13.

40. Mention should also be made of Raffi Bukai's *Avanti Popolo* (1986), in which two Egyptian soldiers, one of whom is a Shakespearean actor, are captured by Israeli reservists at the end of the Six Day War. Maltreated by his captors, the actor, who had always dreamed of playing Shylock, recites the famous soliloquy as he begs for a more humane treatment by the Israelis.

41. As a regular soldier in 1973, I missed the "action" of the Yom Kippur War while serving on the Jordanian front, where there was no fighting. Subsequently I was transferred to the "Syrian enclave"—the territory taken by the Israeli army following its counterattack in the latter part of the war—where a war of attrition continued for months after the official cease-fire. The silence and majesty of the landscape, on the slopes of the snow-covered Hermon Mount, was awe-inspiring.

But the heavy lava soil quickly turned into treacherous mud in the rain, and the daily shelling of our lines destroyed our positions and plowed the land. Every night we had to rebuild the line, only to see it smashed the following day. We had relatively few casualties. The reserve company that replaced us was less lucky; the bunker collapsed on it after sustaining a direct hit. Even as a twenty-year-old soldier I recall thinking that the scene was reminiscent of World War I. Gitai's film captures the reality of this war, especially on the northern front, better than anything else I have seen, including innumerable documentaries.

42. It is interesting to note that the integration of the immigrants of the 1940s and 1950s from North Africa and the Middle East into Israeli society focused on two features. First, there was their increasing engagement in the myth of the Israeli hero by way of progressively entering the ranks of combat units of the IDF, formerly reserved for the old elites, especially the kibbutzim. David ben Gurion said once that real integration of Sephardim and Ashkenazim would be accomplished when Israel had a Yemenite chief of staff. In fact, Yitzhak Mordechai, who was Israel's minister of defense in 1996–1999, is of Kurdish-Iraqi origin, and the current holder of this portfolio, Shaul Mofaz, who was also chief of staff in 1998–2002, is of Iranian origin. But one of the first indications of this shift was the book published by the ministry of defense after 1973 providing all the names of the fallen, many of which were distinctly Sephardi. The second way of integration is by acknowledging the Holocaust as a tragedy of the entire Jewish people and not only of European Jewry. This issue of the "ownership" of the Holocaust is, in part, what the film *Don't Touch My Holocaust* is about.

43. Hanoch Bartov, *Daddo: 48 Years and 20 More Days,* 2d ed. (in Hebrew) (Dvir: Or Yehuda, 2002), 2:420–23, and note 27.

44. Dori Laub and Nanette C. Auerhahn, "Knowing and Not Knowing Massive Psychic Trauma: Forms of Traumatic Memory," *IJPA* 74, no. 2 (1993): 287–303; Dori Laub, "The Empty Circle: Children of Survivors and the Limits of Reconstruction," *JAPA* 46, no. 2 (1998): 507–29; Dori Laub and Nannette C. Auerhahn, "Failed Empathy—A Central Theme in the Survivor's Holocaust Experience," *PP* 6, no. 4 (1989): 377–400.

45. Laub analyzes the tantalizingly similar case of Colonel Dr. Menachem S., who was reunited with his mother after she returned from the camps but could no longer relate to her as his mother: "The mother who comes back not only fails to make the world safe for the little boy as she promised, but she comes back different, disfigured, and not identical to herself. She no longer looks like the mother in the picture [which he carried throughout the war]. There is no healing reunion with those who are, and continue to be, missing, no recapture or restoration of what had been lost, no resumption of an abruptly interrupted innocent childhood." Colonel S. became a highly decorated officer in the Israeli army but did not consider his acts a manifestation of bravery since he "was convinced [that] he could walk in a hail of bullets and not be hit." Laub explains this as "part of a psychological construction which centered his life on the denial of the child victim within himself," making him "instead an untouchable and self-sufficient hero." Hence the epitome of the Israeli hero is the child Holocaust survivor whose heroism is motivated by his denial of a past existence and loss. Shoshana Felman

and Dori Laub, *Testimony: Crises of Witnessing in Literature, Psychoanalysis, and History* (New York: Routledge, 1992), 86–91.

46. *Birth of a Golem* (1991); *Golem, the Spirit of Exile* (1992); *Golem: The Petrified Garden* (1993).

47. Loshitzky, *Identity Politics on the Israeli Screen*, 39.

48. The best discussions of this film and some of its wider contexts are ibid., 36–46; Zimmerman, *Leave My Holocaust Alone*, 276–304; Régine-Mihal Friedman, "The Double Legacy of *Arbeit Macht Frei*," *Prooftexts* 22, no. 1–2 (winter/spring 2002): 200–20.

49. The most detailed analysis of Israeli cinema on the Holocaust is Zimmerman, *Leave My Holocaust Alone*.

50. Ibid., 306–307; Friedman, "The Double Legacy of *Arbeit Macht Frei*," 211.

51. This statement was made by Martin Walser in his acceptance speech upon receiving the German publishers' Peace Prize in October 1998. For the full text, see http://www.dickinson.edu/departments/germn/glossen/heft11/walser.html (accessed April 4, 2004). For discussion and references to the debate, see Bartov, *Mirrors of Destruction*, 214–16. Ironically, at the Berlin Film Festival of 1995, *Balagan* was also awarded the Peace Film Prize. See also Terri Ginsberg, "*Balagan* and the Problematics of Israeli/Palestinian 'Identity,'" http://www.gradnet.de/papers/pomo2.archives/pomo98.papers/tiginsbe98.htm (accessed April 4, 2004).

52. All citations taken from ibid., 214–15. See also Loshitzky, *Identity Politics on the Israeli Screen*, 187, n. 5. It should also be pointed out that critics of *Balagan* refer to the title of the film as the Hebrew word for chaos. In fact "balagan" came into Hebrew from Russian, in which it originally meant "booth," and from Polish, in which it means "mess," and is derived from the Persian word "balanchane," or balcony. See Avraham Even-Shoshan, *The New Dictionary* (in Hebrew) (Kiryat-Sefer: Jerusalem, 1983), 1:120. Indeed, a Soviet film named *Balagan* was made by Andrei Benkendorf in 1990.

53. Friedman, "The Double Legacy of *Arbeit Macht Frei*," 207; Insdorf, *Indelible Shadows*, 50.

54. Primo Levi, *The Drowned and the Saved*, trans. Raymond Rosenthal (New York: Summit Books, 1988), 83–84. See also Emil L. Fackenheim, *Jewish Philosophers and Jewish Philosophy*, ed. Michael L. Morgan (Bloomington: Indiana University Press, 1996), 124; and the ultimately disappointing discussion in Giorgio Agamben, *Remnants of Auschwitz: The Witness and the Archive*, trans. Daniel Heller-Roazen (New York: Zone Books, 1999).

55. On Auschwitz as the "other planet" as formulated by the writer Ka-Tzetnik, and on the pornography of the Holocaust, see Bartov, *Mirrors of Destruction*, 185–212. See also Dagmar Herzog, "'Pleasure, Sex, and Politics Belong Together': Post-Holocaust Memory and the Sexual Revolution in West Germany," *CI* 24 (winter 1998): 393–444.

56. "All the deeds—with the sole exception of the technical process of gassing—that the National Socialists later committed had already been described in the voluminous literature of the 1920s" about Soviet rule in Russia (often and indeed again very recently attributed to the Jews). Ernst Nolte, "The Past That Will Not Pass: A Speech That Could Be Written but Not Delivered," in *Forever in the Shadow*

of Hitler? Original Documents of the Historikerstreit, the Controversy Concerning the Singularity of the Holocaust, trans. James Knowlton and Truett Cates (Atlantic Highland, N.J.: Humanities Press, 1993), 21–22; and the speech by the Christian Democratic member of the German Bundestag Martin Hohmann, made on October 3, 2003: http://www.tagesschau.de/aktuell/meldungen/0,1185,OID2535644_TYP4,00.html (accessed April 7, 2004).

57. Matthias Küntzel, *Djihad und Judenhass: Über den neuen antijüdischen Krieg* (Freiburg: Ça ira, 2002); Werner Bergmann and Juliane Wetzel, Center for Research on Antisemitism at the Technische Universität in Berlin, "Manifestations of Anti-Semitism in the European Union: First Semester 2002," Synthesis Report on Behalf of the European Monitoring Center on Racism and Xenophobia (EMC). The report was submitted to the EMC in Vienna in March 2003 but was not published due to criticism that seems to have been motivated primarily by worries about the potential impact of its emphasis on antisemitic activities among Islamic communities in Europe. It is, however, widely available on the Internet: http://www.winsomegifts.com/win/win_EU_antisemitism.htm (accessed April 7, 2004). See also Omer Bartov, "He Meant What He Said," *TNR* (February 2, 2004): 25–33; Bartov, "The Holocaust as Leitmotif of the Twentieth Century," in *Lessons and Legacies,* vol. 6, ed. Dagmar Herzog (Evanston, Ill.: Northwestern University Press, forthcoming).

58. While she blames Maayan for changing his name, Madi's own double family name, Yaaron-Maayan, is made up of her husband's Hebraized Arab name and her father's Hebraized German name, Grinwald (whose approximate Hebrew translation is "Yaaron"). Her character, Zelma Grinwald, is thus yet another evocation of her father. Similarly, Asher Tlalim has meanwhile moved to London and reverted to his family's original Arab name, de Bentolila, of which Tlalim is the Hebraized version. But he, too, is married to an Israeli woman who traces her origins to Europe. Indeed, *Don't Touch My Holocaust* opens with the following dedication: "In memory of 7 year old Anna who perished in Auschwitz in 1942. Her father was my children's grandfather." This sort of dedication to a half-sibling who died before the filmmaker or author was born (in this case, the filmmaker's wife), with all the attendant sense of guilt and belated bereavement, can be found of course also, inter alia, in Art Spiegelman, *Maus* (New York: Pantheon Books, 1986). The question of mixed origins, Israeli identity, and life in exile, is now explored in Asher de Bentolila Tlalim's new film, *Galoot* (2003), which means exile or Diaspora in Hebrew. In this film the family, now in London, visits both his home in Morocco and his wife Ronit Yoeli Tlalim's home in Poland. See also Loshitzky, *Identity Politics on the Israeli Screen,* 186, n. 60; Friedman, "The Double Legacy of *Arbeit Macht Frei,*" 212.

59. Such scenes took place both in Acre and in Berlin. Days after the play, members of the audience expressed shock at their own behavior and asked for Khaled's forgiveness. Khaled accuses them of having become Nazis. They respond that he gave them a club and asked to be beaten. He answers: "And if I gave you a knife?" Of course, because he is an Arab, being beaten up by an Israeli has an entirely different meaning in Israel than being beaten up as a "Jew" in Germany. But the play insists on the link. The film, however, only shows the German scene. Loshitzky, *Identity Politics on the Israeli Screen,* 45; Zimmerman, *Leave My Holocaust Alone,* 288–89.

60. One thinks here of scenes "composed" by General Dwight Eisenhower, who ordered German citizens in towns next to liberated concentration camps to file by the piles of corpses.

61. See note 57, above. See also Pierre-André Taguieff, *La nouvelle judéophobie* (Paris: Mille et une nuits, 2002); Jean-François Revel, *Anti-Americanism,* trans. Diarmid Cammell (San Francisco: Encounter Books, 2003); Phyllis Chesler, *The New Antisemitism: The Current Crisis and What We Must Do About It* (San Francisco: Jossey-Bass, 2003); Gabriel Schoenfeld, *The Return of Anti-Semitism* (San Francisco: Encounter Books, 2004); Bernard Lewis, *What Went Wrong? Western Impact and Middle Eastern Response* (New York: Oxford University Press, 2002); Bernard Lewis, *The Crisis of Islam: Holy War and Unholy Terror* (New York: The Modern Library, 2003).

62. Loshitzky, *Identity Politics on the Israeli Screen,* 39–40.

63. Bergmann and Wetzel, "Manifestations of Anti-Semitism in the European Union," 9.

OMER BARTOV

is the John P. Birkelund Distinguished Professor of European History at Brown University. Born in Israel, he received his D.Phil. from Oxford University and is a recipient of fellowships from the Guggenheim Foundation, the National Endowment for the Humanities, and the Alexander von Humboldt Foundation, as well as Harvard and Princeton Universities. His many books include *Hitler's Army, Murder in Our Midst, Mirrors of Destruction,* and *Germany's War and the Holocaust.*

CPSIA information can be obtained at www.ICGtesting.com
Printed in the USA
LVOW01s1424140915

454093LV00023BA/675/P